STRUCTURAL ANALYSIS SYSTEMS

Software — Hardware
Capability — Compatibility — Applications

Volume 3

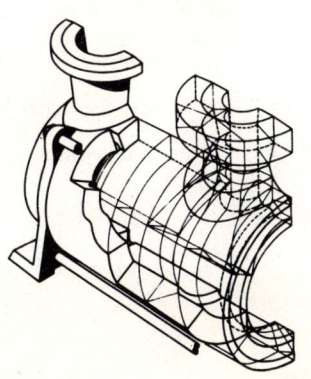

An international series of practical guidebooks
on structural analysis systems and their applications

Other Pergamon Titles of Interest

BATHE	Nonlinear Finite Element Analysis and ADINA 1983
COHN & MAIER	Engineering Plasticity by Mathematical Programming
COWAN	Predictive Methods for the Energy Conserving Design of Buildings
CROUCH	Matrix Methods Applied to Engineering Rigid Body Mechanics
GIBSON	Thin Shells
HARRISON	Structural Analysis and Design
HEARN	Mechanics of Materials, 2nd Edition
HOLLAND	Microcomputers and Their Interfacing
HORNE	Plastic Theory of Structures
JAMSHIDI & MALEK-ZAVAREI	Linear Control Systems
LEININGER	Computer Aided Design of Multivariable Technological Systems
LIVESLEY	Matrix Methods of Structural Analysis, 2nd Edition
NOOR & HOUSNER	Advances and Trends in Structural and Solid Mechanics
NOOR & McCOMB	Computational Methods in Nonlinear Structural and Solid Mechanics
PARKES	Braced Frameworks, 2nd Edition
ROZVANY	Optimal Design of Flexural Systems
SPILLERS	Automated Structural Analysis
WARBURTON	Dynamical Behaviour of Structures, 2nd Edition

Pergamon Related Journals *(Free Sample Copy Gladly Sent on Request)*

BUILDING AND ENVIRONMENT

CEMENT AND CONTRETE RESEARCH

CIVIL ENGINEERING FOR PRACTICING AND DESIGN ENGINEERS

COMPUTERS AND GRAPHICS

COMPUTERS AND INDUSTRIAL ENGINEERING

COMPUTERS AND STRUCTURES

FATIGUE AND FRACTURE OF ENGINEERING MATERIALS AND STRUCTURES

INTERNATIONAL JOURNAL OF APPLIED ENGINEERING EDUCATION

INTERNATIONAL JOURNAL OF SOLIDS AND STRUCTURES

JOURNAL OF ENGINEERING AND APPLIED SCIENCES

MATHEMATICAL MODELLING

STRUCTURAL ANALYSIS SYSTEMS

Software — Hardware
Capability — Compatibility — Applications

A. NIKU-LARI
Director, Institute for Industrial Technology Transfer
24 Rue des Mimosas, Gournay s/Marne
F93460 France

Volume 3

PERGAMON PRESS
OXFORD · NEW YORK · TORONTO · SYDNEY · FRANKFURT

U.K.	Pergamon Press Ltd., Headington Hill Hall, Oxford OX3 0BW, England
U.S.A.	Pergamon Press Inc., Maxwell House, Fairview Park, Elmsford, New York 10523, U.S.A.
CANADA	Pergamon Press Canada Ltd., Suite 104, 150 Consumers Road, Willowdale, Ontario M2J 1P9, Canada
AUSTRALIA	Pergamon Press (Aust.) Pty. Ltd., P.O. Box 544, Potts Point, N.S.W. 2011, Australia
FEDERAL REPUBLIC OF GERMANY	Pergamon Press GmbH, Hammerweg 6, D-6242 Kronberg, Federal Republic of Germany
JAPAN	Pergamon Press Ltd., 8th Floor, Matsuoka Central Building, 1-7-1 Nishishinjuku, Shinjuku-ku, Tokyo 160, Japan
BRAZIL	Pergamon Editora Ltda., Rua Eça de Queiros, 346, CEP 04011, São Paulo, Brazil
PEOPLE'S REPUBLIC OF CHINA	Pergamon Press, Qianmen Hotel, Beijing, People's Republic of China

Copyright © 1986 Pergamon Press Ltd.

All Rights Reserved. No part of this publication may be reproduced, stored in a retrieval system or transmitted in any form or by any means: electronic, electrostatic, magnetic tape, mechanical, photocopying, recording or otherwise, without permission in writing from the publishers.

First edition 1986

Library of Congress Cataloging in Publication Data
Structural analysis systems.
Includes indexes.
1. Structures, Theory of—Data processing—
Addresses, essays, lectures. I. Niku-Lari, A.
TA647.S77   1985   624   1'7'0285   85-9419

British Library Cataloguing in Publication Data
Niku-Lari, A.
Structural analysis systems: software, hardware, capability, compatibility, applications.
Vol. 3.
1. Structures, Theory of—Data processing
I. Title
624.1'71'02854   TA647
ISBN 0-08-032582-3

Cover drawing: Centrifugal pump casing.
Manufacturer: C.C.M.-Sulzer, France.
Software used: CA.ST.OR

Printed in Great Britain by A. Wheaton & Co. Ltd., Exeter

INTERNATIONAL EDITORIAL ADVISORY COMMITTEE

Dr. T. Andersson, *Sweden*
Prof. J. H. Argyris, *Federal Republic of Germany*
Prof. K. J. Bathe, *USA*
Prof. T. Belytschko, *USA*
Dr. M. Bernadou, *France*
Prof. B. A. Bilby, *UK*
Dr. A. Chaudouet, *France*
Prof. R. D. Cook, *USA*
Dr. T. Futagami, *Japan*
Prof. Guo Youzhong, *People's Republic of China*
Dr. L. Imre, *Hungary*
Prof. H. Liebowitz, *USA*
Mr. J. Mackerle, *Sweden*
Mr. W. M. Mair, *UK*
Dr. G. A. Milian, *Mexico*
Dr. D. Nardini, *Yugoslavia*
Dr. I. Paczelt, *Hungary*
Prof. G. Sander, *Belgium*
Prof. R. P. Shaw, *USA*
Prof. M. Tanaka, *Japan*
Prof. W. N. Wendland, *Federal Republic of Germany*

PREFACE

Recent years have seen a rapid increase in the number of structural analysis software existing in the world market.

Most of the current software journals are based on theoretical background. They provide academics and software developers with a very useful tool. People from industry however, who are non-specialists in finite or boundary element methods, have often difficulty in finding industry-oriented documents to help them select the software and hardware most suited to their needs.

This guidebook series aims to provide the engineer with up-to-date information about structural analysis systems existing around the world.

Each paper gives detailed information about a specific software, its capability, its limitations and several practical examples from industry with computer and user cost. It also gives to the user the necessary information about postprocessor capabilities, computer-aided design connection and software compatibility with the most common computers.

Most papers published in this volume follow the same logical structure to allow interactive comparison.

Our concern is to promote international co-operation on this important subject and to contribute to a better understanding between research and industry.

I would like to thank the distinguished members of the editorial committee for their scientific and technical help which made the publication of the present volume possible.

A Niku-Lari
Editor

EDITORIAL

Structural analysis aims to construct numerical models which represent the best behaviour of the actual engineering material and component. These models are used in research for better understanding of experimental results. In industry the structural analysis models allow both the optimization of design and the prediction of failure.

The structural analysis (SA) is therefore a multidisciplinary problem which demands knowledge of several scientific and industrial disciplines such as, engineering sciences, mechanical or civil engineering, informatics, applied mathematics, computer sciences, etc.

International competition gives to industry the necessary impulse to optimise the design of parts and structures.

The engineer should save material and energy and use new and lighter materials such as composites. No longer is one allowed to over-design parts for "security reasons", and new international criteria have to be considered.

Industry needs to design sophisticated parts working in very special environments, in space, in the human body, in the sea, etc.

The compatibility of the structural analysis systems with modern micro-computers allow small and medium size companies to make use of these new technologies. New super computers help to find rapid solutions to complex industrial design problems.

The evolution of interactive graphics allow the full integration of structural analysis programs in a computer aided design and manufacturing environment. Expert systems, application of artificial intelligence and computer-aided decision making bring new developments in this field.

Structural analysis systems existing in the world market are powerful bridges between research and industry. They bring theory in direct physical contact with the industrial application.

The SA technology is in a rapid evolution. More and more new computers and powerful software appear in the market and the industry faces a new problem - that of selecting the optimum structural analysis system.

The choice of a structural analysis software is an important decision which can often exercise a significant influence over the successful development of a research, manufacture, or design project. Depending on the engineering problem and hardware available, a good choice of the computer program can be both cost and time effective. This new international guidebooks series aims to provide the engineer with the most up-to-date information about structural analysis systems currently available in the world market, and their capabilities.

Editorial

Published under the guidance of a distinguished scientific committee whose members are internationally recognised specialists of finite or boundary element methods, the series should be considered as an essential practical reference tool for the modern engineer involved in such areas as structural, mechanical, civil, nuclear, aeronautical and design engineering, computer science and software development.

Each volume gives detailed information about a wide range of selected software packages describing their purpose, capabilities and limitations and provides several practical examples of industrial applications, often supported by case studies. It also gives to the user the necessary information about postprocessor capabilities, computer-aided design integration and software compatibility with the most commonly used computers.

The guidebooks are industry-oriented and should prove indispensible in helping potential users to select the soft and hardware most suited to their needs. Each volume commences with a program description in tabular form, rapidly directing readers to the program most likely to solve their industrial problems, and concludes with a case-study index.

Main areas covered in the series:

- Finite and boundary element programs
- Finite difference and other methods
- Computer graphics
- Artificial intelligence and expert systems
- Computer-aided decision making in engineering
- Computer-aided design and manufacturing (CAD/CAM)
- Integration of structural analysis and expert systems in engineering CAD/CAM environment
- Hard and software selection
- Micro-computer applications in engineering
- New development in structural analysis software and interactive graphics
- Industrial case study
  . Mechanical engineering
  . Aeronautics and nuclear
  . Biomechanics
  . New materials (composites, plastics, etc)
  . Civil engineering (offshore, seismic, earthquake, etc).

Authors wishing to submit a paper under one of the above headings for possible publication in future volumes are invited to submit their manuscript for editorial consideration of the international scientific committee to the address below.

Dr A Niku-Lari, Director
Institute for Industrial Technology Transfer
I.I.T.T.-international
24 Rue des Mimosas
93460 Gournay-sur-Marne
FRANCE
TEL: (1) 43.05.17.19

CONTENTS

Program Description Tables	xiii
ALSA: A Hybrid Stress Finite Element Program H. Alaylioglu	1
BEFE: Coupled Boundary Element-Finite Element Program G. Beer	11
BEWAVE: Pressure Wave Propagation by the Boundary Element Program P. H. L. Groenenboom, J. J. de Jong and C. A. Brebbia	23
CASTEM: Finite Element System A. Combescure, A. Hoffmann and P. Pasquet	35
ELASTODYNAMICS (2D): Applications of a Boundary Element Program M. Kitahara and K. Nakagawa	51
FEMFAM: Finite Element Analysis on Desktop Computers using the FEMFAM Package J. F. Stelzer	65
FEMPAC: An Integrated Finite Element System D. Sundström	89
FENRIS: Finite Element Nonlinear Integrated System A. Arnesen	101
FIESTA: The p-version Approach in Finite Element Analysis P. Angeloni, R. Boccelato, E. Bonacina, A. Pasini and A. Peano	113
FLEXAN: Static and Dynamic Analysis of Underwater Cables and Flexible Pipes Systems P. A. Schoentgen	137

LASSAQ: A Computer Program for Laminated Anisotropic Stiffened Shell
Analysis using Quadrilateral Shell Finite Elements   143
        A. Venkatesh and K. P. Rao

MODULEF: A Library of Computer Procedures for Finite Element Analysis   155
        M. Bernadou, P. L. George, P. Laug and M. Vidrascu

MSRC-RB: 3-D Elastoplastic Finite Element Program   175
        Gua Youzhong and Lu Jiayou

OSTIN: A Computer Program to Perform the Seismic Analysis of Rigid
Strip Footing on 2-D Zoned Viscoelastic Soils on Frequency Domain   179
        R. Abascal

RAPS: A Plot Program for Testing of the Model and for Plotting of the
Results of Finite Element Calculations   191
        D. Koschmieder and J. Altes

ROBOT: Program for Linear Analysis of Axisymmetric Structures   203
        I. Páczelt

SAMKE: Finite Element System   215
        S. Maksimović

STDYNL: A Code for Structural Systems   225
        B. A. Ovunc

SURFOPT: Shape Optimal Design for Minimum Stress Concentration by
Finite Elements with the Program System "SURFOPT"   239
        U. Spörl

ZERO-4: A Computer Program for Fluid-Structure Interaction Problems   251
        E. Bon, L. Brusa, A. Cella, R. Giacci and A. Greco

Case Study Index   263

PROGRAM DESCRIPTION TABLES

Program Description Tables

	METHOD				ELEMENT LIBRARY								GEOMETRY			SEE VOL
	Finite element	Boundary element	Finite difference	Other	Truss/beams	2D membranes	Plates	Shells	Axisymmetric	3D solids	Boundary elements	Special elements	2D analysis	3D analysis	Axisymmetric	
ADINA	x				x	x	x	x	x	x			x	x	x	1
AFAG	x			x	x									x		2
AIT	x				x	x	x	x	x				x	x	x	1
ALSA	x				x	x	x	x					x	x		3
ANSYS	x				x	x	x	x	x	x	x	x	x	x	x	1
AQUADYN		x		x							x			x		2
ASE	x				x	x	x	x	x	x	x	x	x	x	x	2
AXISYMMETRIC	x							x	x			x			x	1
BEASY		x									x		x	x	x	1
BEFE	x	x			x	x	x	x		x	x	x	x	x		3
BEMFFT		x		x							x		x			2
BEWAVE		x									x	x	x	x		3
BOSOR4	x		x				x	x					x		x	2
BOSOR5	x		x				x	x					x		x	3
CASTEM	x				x	x	x	x	x			x	x	x	x	3
CASTOR	x	x			x	x	x	x	x	x	x	x	x	x	x	1
DAPST	x				x	x	x	x	x				x		x	1
DEFOR	x				x									x		1
ELASTODYNAMICS (2D)		x									x	x	x			2
ESA	x				x	x	x	x				x	x	x	x	2
FEMFAM	x				x	x	x	x	x	x		x	x	x	x	3
FEMPAC	x				x	x	x	x	x				x	x	x	3
FENRIS	x				x	x	x	x	x	x		x	x	x	x	3
FIESTA	x								x					x		3
FLASH	x				x		x	x	x			x		x	x	1
FLEXAN	x											x		x		3
HYBRID	x					x						x	x			2
IBA	x				x	x	x	x	x				x	x	x	1
INFESA	x					x							x			2

TABLE 1. Modelization and Type of Discretization.

Program Description Tables

	METHOD				ELEMENT LIBRARY								GEOMETRY			SEE VOL
	Finite element	Boundary element	Finite difference	Other	Truss/beams	2D membranes	Plates	Shells	Axisymmetric	3D solids	Boundary elements	Special elements	2D analysis	3D analysis	Axisymmetric	
KYOKAI	x	x				x			x	x	x	x	x	x	x	1
LASSAQ	x				x		x	x					x			3
MEF/MOSAIC	x				x	x	x	x	x	x		x	x	x	x	2
MICRO STRESS	x				x								x	x		1
MODULEF	x				x	x	x	x	x	x		x	x	x	x	3
MSRC-RB	x									x				x		3
NE XX	x				x						x			x		1
OSTIN		x									x		x		x	3
PAFEC	x	x			x	x	x	x	x	x	x	x	x	x	x	1
PAID	x				x							x		x		1
PANDA			x										x			1
PDA/PATRAN	x			x	x	x	x	x	x	x			x	x	x	2
RAPS	x				x	x	x	x	x	x		x	x	x	x	3
RCAFAG	x			x	x								x			2
REST	x				x	x	x	x	x	x			x	x	x	2
ROBOT	x						x	x	x				x		x	3
S AND CM	x				x	x		x				x	x	x		1
SAMKE	x				x	x	x	x	x	x		x	x	x	x	3
SESAM '80	x				x	x	x	x	x	x		x	x	x	x	1
SIMP	x		x	x	x	x	x	x					x	x		2
STAR 2	x				x						x	x		x		2
STDYNL	x	x			x	x	x	x			x		x			3
STRUGEN			x		x	x	x	x		x			x	x		2
SURFOPT	x					x			x				x		x	3
THERMAL	x				x	x							x	x		1
TITUS	x				x	x	x	x	x	x		x	x	x	x	1
UCIN GEAR	x				x								x			1
Y12M																2
ZERO-4	x					x		x	x	x	x		x	x	x	3

TABLE 1. Modelization and Type of Discretization (continued).

Program Description Tables

| | \multicolumn{8}{c|}{MATERIAL} | \multicolumn{7}{c|}{CAPABILITIES} | SEE VOL |

	Linear elastic isotropic	Linear elastic anisotropic	Elasto-plastic	Nonlinear elastic	Viscoelastic/creep	Composites	Soil	Concrete	Static analysis	Dynamic analysis	Geometric nonlinear	Buckling/postbuckling	Heat transfer	Fracture mechanics	Fluid/structure inter	SEE VOL
ADINA	x	x	x	x	x	x	x	x	x	x	x	x	x	x	x	1
AFAG	x								x							2
AIT	x								x		x				x	1
ALSA	x	x							x	x						3
ANSYS	x	x	x	x	x	x		x	x	x	x	x	x	x	x	1
AQUADYN										x					x	2
ASE		x							x	x						2
AXISYMMETRIC	x								x	x	x	x			x	1
BEASY	x		x						x				x	x		1
BEFE	x		x			x			x							3
BEMFFT	x								x							2
BEWAVE				x						x				x		3
BOSOR4	x	x			x				x	x	x	x				2
BOSOR5	x	x	x		x	x			x		x	x				3
CASTEM	x	x	x	x	x	x	x	x	x	x	x	x	x	x	x	3
CASTOR	x	x		x					x	x		x	x	x	x	1
DAPST	x	x			x				x	x						1
DEFOR	x	x							x		x					1
ELASTODYNAMICS (2D)	x									x						2
ESA	x	x		x					x	x			x			2
FEMFAM	x	x							x	x	x	x	x		x	3
FEMPAC	x	x							x	x			x			3
FENRIS	x		x	x					x	x	x	x			x	3
FIESTA	x	x							x				x	x		3
FLASH	x	x							x			x				1
FLEXAN		x							x	x					x	3
HYBRID	x								x							2
IBA	x	x				x	x		x	x			x			1
INFESA	x					x			x							2

TABLE 2. Materials and Analysis Capabilities.

Program Description Tables

	Material								Capabilities							See Vol
	Linear elastic isotropic	Linear elastic anisotropic	Elasto-plastic	Nonlinear elastic	Viscoelastic/creep	Composites	Soil	Concrete	Static analysis	Dynamic analysis	Geometric nonlinear	Buckling/postbuckling	Heat transfer	Fracture mechanics	Fluid/structure inter	
KYOKAI	x	x			x	x			x				x			1
LASSAQ		x			x				x							3
MEF/MOSAIC	x	x		x		x			x	x	x	x	x	x		2
MICRO STRESS	x								x							1
MODULEF	x	x	x	x		x			x	x	x		x			3
MSRC-RB		x	x						x							3
NE XX	x								x							1
OSTIN				x		x			x							3
PAFEC	x	x	x	x	x	x	x		x	x	x	x	x	x	x	1
PAID	x								x	x			x		x	1
PANDA	x	x	x			x			x		x					1
PDA/PATRAN	x	x							x							2
RAPS									x	x			x	x		3
RCAFAG	x			x	x	x			x							2
REST	x									x						2
ROBOT	x	x							x							3
S AND CM	x								x	x			x			1
SAMKE	x	x			x				x		x		x			3
SESAM '80	x	x	x				x		x	x				x	x	1
SIMP	x								x	x						2
STAR 2			x		x		x		x							2
STDYNL	x		x			x			x	x	x					3
STRUGEN																2
SURFOPT	x								x							3
THERMAL	x								x							1
TITUS	x	x	x	x	x		x		x	x	x	x	x	x	x	1
UCIN GEAR	x								x							1
Y1 2M																2
ZERO-4	x								x	x					x	3

TABLE 2. Materials and Analysis Capabilities (continued).

Program Description Tables

| | \multicolumn{8}{c}{LOADING} | \multicolumn{7}{c}{PRE/POSTPROCESSING} | SEE VOL |

Program	Nodal/line	Pressure	Selfweight	Centrifugal	Thermal	Heat flux	Prescribed displacement	Other	Free format input	Mesh generation	Plot routines	Automatic node number	Combinations of load cs	Interactive graph	CAD interfaces	SEE VOL
ADINA	x	x	x	x	x	x	x	x	x	x	x	x	x	x	x	1
AFAG	x	x	x		x		x	x	x	x	x	x	x	x		2
AIT	x	x	x		x		x		x							1
ALSA	x	x	x				x	x	x	x	x	x	x			3
ANSYS	x	x	x	x	x	x	x	x	x	x	x	x	x	x	x	1
AQUADYN								x	x	x	x	x		x		2
ASE	x	x	x		x		x		x	x	x	x	x			2
AXISYMMETRIC	x	x						x					x			1
BEASY	x	x	x	x	x	x	x	x	x	x	x	x	x	x	x	1
BEFE	x	x	x	x	x		x	x		x	x		x	x		3
BEMFFT							x				x					2
BEWAVE		x												x	x	3
BOSOR4	x	x		x	x		x	x	x	x	x	x				2
BOSOR5		x			x		x	x	x	x	x	x				3
CASTEM	x	x	x	x	x	x	x	x	x	x	x	x	x	x		3
CASTOR	x	x	x	x	x	x	x	x	x	x	x	x	x	x	x	1
DAPST	x	x	x				x		x		x	x				1
DEFOR	x		x		x		x	x		x			x	x		1
ELASTODYNAMICS (2D)	x						x	x		x						2
ESA	x	x	x	x	x	x	x	x	x	x	x	x	x	x	x	2
FEMFAM	x	x	x	x	x	x	x	x	x	x	x	x	x	x		3
FEMPAC	x	x	x	x	x	x	x	x	x	x	x	x	x	x	x	3
FENRIS	x	x	x		x		x	x	x	x	x	x	x	x		3
FIESTA	x	x	x	x	x	x	x	x	x	x	x	x	x			3
FLASH	x	x	x	x	x		x	x	x	x	x	x	x	x	x	1
FLEXAN	x		x		x		x	x	x	x	x		x			3
HYBRID	x						x		x	x	x	x				2
IBA	x	x	x		x		x	x	x	x	x	x	x	x		1
INFESA	x	x					x		x	x	x	x		x		2

TABLE 3. Loadings and User Comfort.

Program Description Tables

	Nodal/line	Pressure	Selfweight	Centrifugal	Thermal	Heat flux	Prescribed displacement	Other	Free format input	Mesh generation	Plot routines	Automatic node number	Combinations of load cs	Interactive graph	CAD interfaces	SEE VOL
KYOKAI	x	x			x	x	x	x	x	x	x	x		x		1
LASSAQ	x															3
MEF/MOSAIC		x	x	x	x	x	x	x	x	x	x	x		x		2
MICRO STRESS	x	x	x		x		x		x		x					1
MODULEF	x	x	x	x	x	x	x	x	x	x	x	x		x		3
MSRC-RB	x	x	x			x	x	x				x				3
NE XX	x		x			x	x	x		x	x	x				1
OSTIN								x		x		x				3
PAFEC	x	x	x	x	x	x	x	x	x	x	x	x	x	x	x	1
PAID	x	x	x		x	x	x	x			x		x	x		1
PANDA							x	x	x			x				1
PDA/PATRAN	x	x	x		x		x	x	x	x	x	x	x	x	x	2
RAPS									x		x		x	x		3
RCAFAG	x	x	x		x		x	x	x	x	x	x		x		2
REST								x		x						2
ROBOT	x	x	x	x	x		x	x				x	x			3
S AND CM	x	x										x	x			1
SAMKE	x	x	x		x		x	x	x	x	x	x	x	x	x	3
SESAM '80	x	x	x	x	x		x	x	x	x	x	x	x	x	x	1
SIMP	x			x	x		x	x	x	x	x	x	x	x	x	2
STAR 2	x	x	x		x		x	x	x	x	x	x	x			2
STDYNL	x	x	x		x		x	x	x	x		x	x			3
STRUGEN									x	x	x	x		x		2
SURFOPT	x						x		x	x	x	x	x			3
THERMAL	x	x			x							x	x			1
TITUS	x	x	x	x	x	x	x	x	x	x	x	x	x	x	x	1
UCIN GEAR		x							x	x	x	x				1
Y1 2M																2
ZERO-4	x	x	x		x		x			x	x	x		x		3

TABLE 3. Loadings and User Comfort (continued).

Program Description Tables

	HARDWARE														SEE VOL
	CDC	IBM	Univac	Cray	Amdahl	Honeywell	Data General	Prime	VAX, DEC	HP	Apollo	Microcomputers	Other mainframes	Other minicomputers	
ADINA	x	x	x	x		x	x	x	x			x	x	x	1
AFAG										x					2
AIT	x	x								x					1
ALSA		x			x								x		3
ANSYS	x	x	x	x	x		x	x	x	x			x	x	1
AQUADYN				x					x						2
ASE	x	x								x					2
AXISYMMETRIC										x					1
BEASY	x	x	x	x				x		x			x	x	1
BEFE		x						x	x						3
BEMFFT								x							2
BEWAVE	x							x						x	3
BOSOR4	x	x	x					x							2
BOSOR5	x	x	x					x							3
CASTEM	x	x	x	x				x	x					x	3
CASTOR	x	x	x	x					x						1
DAPST	x									x					1
DEFOR		x							x	x				x	1
ELASTODYNAMICS (2D)		x											x		2
ESA										x				x	2
FEMFAM										x					3
FEMPAC	x	x	x		x	x	x	x	x	x	x	x	x	x	3
FENRIS		x		x					x		x			x	3
FIESTA	x								x						3
FLASH	x	x	x				x	x	x		x		x	x	1
FLEXAN	x	x		x					x						3
HYBRID													x		2
IBA		x							x	x				x	1
INFESA									x					x	2

TABLE 4. Hardware Compatibilities.

Program Description Tables

	CDC	IBM	Univac	Cray	Amdahl	Honeywell	Data General	Prime	VAX, DEC	HP	Apollo	Microcomputers	Other mainframes	Other minicomputers	SEE VOL
KYOKAI								x	x						1
LASSAQ									x						3
MEF/MOSAIC	x	x	x			x	x	x	x						2
MICRO STRESS												x			1
MODULEF	x	x	x	x		x			x		x		x		3
MSRC-RB													x		3
NE XX										x					1
OSTIN									x	x					3
PAFEC	x	x	x	x	x	x	x	x	x	x	x		x	x	1
PAID	x							x							1
PANDA	x	x							x						1
PDA/PATRAN	x			x			x	x	x		x		x	x	2
RAPS		x							x	x		x			3
RCAFAG										x					2
REST	x														2
ROBOT	x												x		3
S AND CM												x			1
SAMKE	x	x	x						x						3
SESAM '80	x	x						x	x					x	1
SIMP	x		x		x			x							2
STAR 2	x	x										x			2
STDYNL	x	x												x	3
STRUGEN	x	x							x				x		2
SURFOPT			x												3
THERMAL												x			1
TITUS	x	x	x	x					x		x				1
UCIN GEAR		x			x										1
Y1 2M	x	x	x												2
ZERO-4		x												x	3

TABLE 4. Hardware Compatibilities (continued).

ALSA: A HYBRID STRESS FINITE ELEMENT PROGRAM

H. Alaylioglu

TPA, D–605, P/Bag X197, 0001 Pretoria, South Africa

ABSTRACT

ALSA is a general purpose finite element computer program for Accurate Large order Structural Analysis. The program is designed for linear elasto-static and dynamic 2-D or 3-D analyses, and based on the high precision and yet economical hybrid stress-type finite element library developed by the author and his associates. Currently, the ALSA library contains 3-D truss and beam, 2-D triangular and rectangular membrane and plate bending, singly curved and doubly curved shell elements. In the generation of these elements, numerical integrations are completely avoided in order to decrease element generation cost and improve solution accuracy. This is achieved by introducing computerized algorithmic representations of finite element properties and the characteristic arrays, enabling automatic generation of analytically integrated stiffness and mass matrices in a very short time.

Elements of the ALSA library are all compatible, consistent and of correct rank without any deficiency, and associated with only kinematic degrees of freedom. They all exhibit high accuracy and convergence characteristics.

THEORETICAL BACKGROUND

Computational experiences have shown that, for most of the finite element models, bulk of the computing time is taken up by the numerical integration of finite element matrices. This is more pronounced in hybrid stress models because of their dual field property. For this reason, hybrid-type elements are excluded from most of the general purpose finite element programs, although they proved to be superior to their displacement-type counterparts in predicting displacements, stresses and vibration frequencies. The hybrid formulation scheme incorporated in the ALSA program generates element stiffness and mass matrices in simple algorithmic forms, enabling automatic evaluation of the required integrals by a computer, cheaply and exactly.

The hybrid stress model was originated by Professor T. H. H. Pian. The model is based on the modified Hellinger-Reissner principle for which an equilibrating stress field and interelement compatible displacement field are assumed independently. This procedure leads to the element stiffness matrix $[K]$ and mass matrix $[M]$ as follows:

$$[K] = [G]^T[H]^{-1}[G] \quad , \quad [M] = \rho \int_{V_e} [\Lambda]^T[\Lambda] dV_e \tag{1}$$

in which

$$[H] = \int_{V_e} [\Omega]^T[E][\Omega] dV_e \quad , \quad [G] = \int_{S_s} [T]^T[\Gamma] dS_s \tag{2}$$

where ρ and $[E]$ are the density and the elastic compliance of the material, V_e is the volume of element e and S_s is the boundary of volume V_e. In eqn. (2), any i'th row of $[\Omega]$ contains the assumed interpolant for the i'th component of the equilibrating interior stress field. The stress interpolants are usually assumed in a polynomial form with m number of undetermined stress parameters β per element. In this context, an element Ω_{im} in the i'th row and m'th column of $[\Omega]$ can be expressed in the following algorithmic form:

$$\Omega_{im} = P_{im} \, \eta^{A_{im}} \, \xi^{B_{im}} \tag{3}$$

in terms of the normalized co-ordinate variables η and ξ with their exponents A_{im} and B_{im}, and the associated numeric coefficients P_{im}. Furthermore, in eqn. (2), any one row of $[T]$ accommodates the c'th component of the boundary tractions, which is related to the corresponding component of the stress field, at the s'th boundary of the element. Thus the algorithm for an element T_{scm} in the sc'th row and m'th column of $[T]$ can be written as

$$T_{scm} = L_{scm} \, \lambda^{I_{scm}} \tag{4}$$

where L_{scm} is the numeric coefficient related to P_{im}, λ stands for either η or ξ and I_{scm} is the exponent related to either A_{im} or B_{im} depending upon the element boundary. In eqn. (2), $[\Gamma]$ can be expressed in a similar form. Any one row of $[\Gamma]$ accommodates the c'th component of the boundary displacements at the s'th boundary of the element. If f is the number of generalized nodal displacements per finite element, an element Γ_{scf} in the sc'th row and f'th column of $[\Gamma]$ can be expressed as

$$\Gamma_{scf} = \sum_h N_{schf} \, \lambda^{J_{schf}} \tag{5}$$

where N_{schf} and J_{schf} are the numeric coefficient and the exponent of λ for the f'th term of the displacement interpolant at the sc'th row, and h is the number of entities within each term f. In eqn. (2), if an element of $[\Omega]^T$ is designated by Ω_{nj}, for which n=m and j=i, then from eqn. (2), an element H_{nm} of matrix $[H]$ can be written as

$$H_{nm} = \int_{V_e} \sum_i \sum_j P_{nj} \, \eta^{A_{nj}} \, \xi^{B_{nj}} \, E_{ji} \, P_{im} \, \eta^{A_{im}} \, \xi^{B_{im}} \, dV_e \tag{6}$$

after substitution of Ω_{im} and Ω_{nj} according to eqn. (3), where E_{ji} represents the elastic compliance coefficients. Analytical integration of this algorithm is simple. Since $dV_e = a\,b\,t\,d\eta\,d\xi\,d\zeta$ for an arbitrary element whose characteristic lengths are a, b and t, and the normalized local co-ordinates η ξ and ζ vary between 0 and 1, H_{nm} can be integrated analytically as follows:

$$H_{nm} = abt \sum_i \sum_j E_{ji} \frac{P_{nj} P_{im}}{(A_{nj} + A_{im} + 1)(B_{nj} + B_{im} + 1)} \tag{7}$$

Within the computer program, this algorithm calculates the analytically integrated exact form of matrix $[H]$ in a very short time. Once the non-zero terms of the 2-D arrays E, P, A and B (related to the element assumptions) are coded for the $[H]$ matrix-generator algorithm (7), each matrix element H_{nm} is computed within the inner DO loops for the indices i and j, while the outer DO loops for the indices n and m form the lower triangle of the symmetric matrix $[H]$.

An element G_{mf} of matrix $[G]$ in eqn. (2) can be generated similarly. By appropriate substitutions from eqns. (4) and (5) we get

$$G_{mf} = \int_{S_s} \Sigma_s \Sigma_c \Sigma_h L_{scm} \lambda^{I_{scm}} N_{schf} \lambda^{J_{schf}} dS_s \tag{8}$$

where dS_s stands for either a t dη dζ or b t dξ dζ depending upon the element boundary. Since the integration limits for the normalized variables η, ξ and ζ are 0 and 1, the above expression can be integrated analytically as

$$G_{mf} = \Sigma_s \Sigma_c \Sigma_h \frac{L_{scm} N_{schf} S_s}{(I_{scm} + J_{schf} + 1)} \tag{9}$$

It is evident that, this simple algorithm can compute the analytically integrated exact form of matrix $[G]$ very quickly.

The mass matrix $[M]$ is generated next. In eqn. (1), every i'th row of $[\Lambda]$ contains the assumed interpolant for the i'th component of the displacement (or velocity) field. Accordingly, an element Λ_{if} of $[\Lambda]$ (or Λ_{ig} of $[\Lambda]^T$, where g=f) contains the shape function assumed for the i'th component of the displacement field for its f'th generalized nodal displacement. Thereby, an element Λ_{if} of $[\Lambda]$ can be expressed by the following algorithm:

$$\Lambda_{if} = \Sigma_h \Sigma_r R_{ihf} \eta^{C_{ihf}} S_{irf} \xi^{D_{irf}} \tag{10}$$

where r=h, R_{ihf} and S_{irf} are the numeric coefficients, and C_{ihf} and D_{irf} are the exponents. An element Λ_{ig} of $[\Lambda]^T$ can be expressed similarly. By substituting these into eqn. (1), an element M_{gf} of matrix $[M]$ can be written as

$$M_{gf} = \rho \int_{V_e} \Sigma_i \Sigma_p \Sigma_k \Sigma_h \Sigma_r R_{ipg} \eta^{C_{ipg}} S_{ikg} \xi^{D_{ikg}} R_{ihf} \eta^{C_{ihf}} S_{irf} \xi^{D_{irf}} dV_e \tag{11}$$

where p=k=h=r, and the symbolic analytical integration gives

$$M_{gf} = \rho \text{ abt } \Sigma_i \Sigma_p \Sigma_k \Sigma_h \Sigma_r \frac{R_{ipg} S_{ikg} R_{ihf} S_{irf}}{(C_{ipg} + C_{ihf} + 1)(D_{ikg} + D_{irf} + 1)} \tag{12}$$

Algorithms (7), (9) and (12) for generating element stiffness and mass matrices are all independent of element geometry. These exact integration algorithms of the ALSA program generate stiffness and mass matrices of the required elements in a very short time without any computational error.

FIELD OF APPLICATION

Geometrical

ALSA is a general purpose finite element structural analysis program. It can analyse 2-D or 3-D large scale structures containing any combination of trusses, beams, membranes, thin plates and shells with single or double curvatures. For the out-of-core version of the program, there is virtually no limit on the geometrical size of problems.

Materials

The program is primarily intended for linear elastic, isotropic materials. However, the stiffness matrix algorithms of the ALSA program also permit orthotropic material models. Another feature of the program is that, different material models can be used for different element groups of the structure. There can be up to 999 different material models for the structural elements.

Analysis Capabilities

ALSA is capable of analysing linear static and dynamic behaviours of structures encountered in various engineering fields such as mechanical, civil, aeronautical, automotive and ship-building. For static analysis, the program can compute the resulting displacements (translational and rotational), stresses, internal forces and reactions. Vibration and dynamic analysis includes computation of eigenvalues, eigenmodes, harmonic and transient response of the structure.

Loadings

For static load analysis, the program can permit application of a variety of loadings for the structure under consideration. These loadings can be in the form of a point load, line load, gravity load, pressure load, inside load or due to the residual stresses. In a single computer run, the structure can be analysed for a variety of loading cases consecutively. For dynamic response analysis, any type of periodic or transient loads can be applied to the structure.

A pre-processing routine is available in the program for automatic load generation, for each loading case. In the load generation routine, the recurring nodal/elemental loads are generated automatically for those nodes/elements which are within the specified region of the structure.

PROGRAM DESCRIPTION

Method

ALSA is a finite element structural analysis program. The ALSA program library is based on the hybrid stress-type finite elements which are formulated and coded according to the computerized symbolic representations and algorithms given in the first section. The stiffness and mass matrix generator algorithms given by eqns. (7), (9) and (12) generate the required elements without numerical integrations. These algorithms are very accurate, fast and cost-effective.

Another useful feature of these algorithms is that the order of the ALSA elements can be reduced automatically in order to reduce the computer cost even further. This can be performed by the program by declaring the related index numbers of the algorithms corresponding to the unwanted higher order stress parameters and/or degrees of freedom in the input data entries so that the elements would be generated originally only up to the desired hierarchical order. Therefore, it is easy to choose the degree of approximation for the elements which can vary from place to place in the same problem.

The program employs active column storage (skyline) scheme. The structure stiffness matrix in this compacted form is decomposed by using Cholesky factorization for solving the system of simultaneous linear equations in static analysis. For determining the vibration characteristics, extraction of the p lowest frequencies and mode shapes is accomplished by using the updated subspace iteration method based on the simultaneous inverse iteration with a p-dimensional subspace, followed by the Sturm sequence check for verification. In dynamic response analysis, the program uses the modified Newmark algorithm based on a step-by-step direct (implicit) time integration, with controllable algorithmic dissipation, second-order accuracy and unconditional stability.

Type of Elements

Type of elements currently available in the ALSA library are 3-D truss and beam elements, 2-D membrane and plate bending elements of either triangular or rectangular shape, cylindrical shell and doubly curved shell elements. All these elements are of hybrid stress-type and their generations are extremely fast because of their algorithmic coding according to eqns. (7), (9) and (12).

Truss element. The truss element is assumed to have a constant cross-section and is defined by two nodes. The axial displacement varies linearly between the nodes and the axial force remains constant throughout the element.

Beam element. This straight and prismatic element is also defined by its end nodes. Each node may have three translational and three rotational degrees of freedom in and around the directions of the local co-ordinate axes. The axial and torsional displacements are interpolated linearly between the nodes, and the transverse and normal displacements are expressed in terms of the first order Hermite polynomials. The internal stress field is approximated in terms of six independent stress parameters. This element may be used for modelling beams of arbitrary (open or closed) cross-section.

Membrane elements. This plain stress/strain element is available in either general triangular or rectangular shape and is defined by the corner nodes in both geometries. Each node has two translational degrees of freedom, and these translational displacements are assumed to vary bilinearly in the plane of the element. The membrane stress field is also assumed to vary bilinearly, with seven independent stress parameters. In the ALSA program, the membrane element can be combined, if necessary, with the plate bending element of the corresponding shape to yield a membrane-plate bending element, with the combined nodal degrees of freedom, which can be treated as one single element in a finite element modelling.

Plate bending elements. This thin plate element is also available in either general triangular or rectangular shape defined by the corner nodes. Each node is allowed to have four degrees of freedom, namely, the vertical displacement, the rotations around the local in-plane co-ordinate directions and the in-plane twist. The internal displacement field is represented by the Hermite interpolation polynomials, providing C^1 continuity. For both plate geometries, C^0 continuous displacement field is also considered, which is obtained automatically within the algorithms by skipping the every fourth entries of the indices f and g corresponding to the twist degree of freedom. The bending stress field is expressed in terms of 17 independent stress parameters providing complete quadratic variations for the stress components.. From this assumption, 11 and 9 parameter stress fields are obtained hierarchically by the algorithms, corresponding to the bilinear and linear variations respectively for both geometries. Thereby, by combining C^1 or C^0 continuous displacements with the 17, 11 or 9 parameter stress fields, a number of hierarchical plate bending elements become available for both geometries. For triangular (T) geometry the elements symbolized as $T9-C^1$, $T11-C^1$ and $T9-C^0$, and for rectangular (R) geometry the elements symbolized as $R17-C^1$, $R9-C^0$ and $R11-C^0$ are recommended, which are all free from spurious kinematic modes. These elements can be combined, if necessary, with the membrane element of the corresponding shape to yield a membrane-plate bending element.

<u>Cylindrical shell element</u>. The element is thin and defined in cylindrical co-ordinates by four corner nodes of its open planform with subtended angle α and radius r. Six degrees of freedom are considered for each node of the element. These are the three translational displacements in the directions of the local cylindrical axes, the rotations around the in-plane axes and the in-plane twist. The twist degree of freedom is optional as was the case for plate bending elements. In-plane and out-of-plane displacement fields are represented similar to those of the membrane and plate-bending elements. Two different stress field assumptions, with either 18 or 16 independent stress parameters, are available for the cylindrical shell element. However, the 16 parameter assumption should only be used without the twist degree of freedom in order to make the element stiffness matrix of the correct rank.

<u>Doubly curved shell element</u>. The doubly curved shell element is assumed to be thin and defined in curvilinear co-ordinates by four corner nodes of its middle surface with radii of curvatures r_1 and r_2. If $r_1=r_2$, the doubly curved shell element reduces to a spherical shell element. Six degrees of freedom are considered for each node. These are the three translational and two rotational displacements and the twist, similar to those described for the cylindrical shell element. Displacement field representation of the doubly curved shell element is also similar to that of the cylindrical shell. The stress field is expressed in terms of 21 independent stress parameters, providing correct element stiffness rank, and very accurate and economical solutions.

PROGRAM STRUCTURE

ALSA program is written in standard FORTRAN IV language. There are two versions of ALSA. The first version is incorporated with in-core equation solvers and is designed for the efficient solution of small or medium size problems. The second version is incorporated with out-of-core equation solvers. This version of the program can solve large scale problems without any limitation on the size of the finite element model.

The entire ALSA software has a modular structure which contains approximately 25 000 source statements and 200 subroutines. The modularity of the software enables enhancements to be introduced easily in a specified module without affecting other modules. New elements and inclusion of new capabilities can be added to the program as separate new modules. All the program modules are linked together with a centralized data base system.

The user-supplied data input is kept at a minimal level in the form of free and fixed field formats, and extensive input data generation facilities are incorporated in pre-processing modules. These modules perform extensive error checking before the basic computations.

Pre-processors

ALSA program has a variety of pre-processors for automatic generation of nodes, elements and loads for a specified region of the finite element model. These include automatic node numbering, automatic generation of nodal co-ordinates and boundary conditions, automatic mesh generation defining geometrical and material properties and connectivities of the elements, and automatic generation of loads.

Extensive error checking facilities are provided for the user-supplied and generated data inputs, and the program can be set to data checking mode without any execution.

Post-processors

Post-processors of the ALSA program provide prints of the selected results for displacements, stresses, stress resultants, reactions, vibration frequencies and mode shapes, harmonic and transient response of the structure in the form of tables or plots. Computed results can be stored on a data file for further mathematical operations.

HARDWARE COMPATIBILITIES

ALSA program is currently operational on IBM, AMDAHL and BURROUGHS computer systems. However, the program is compatible and hardware independent to the highest conceivable degree due to the standardization of its FORTRAN IV coding. The ALSA software is available in magnetic tapes, both in the binary and in the source codes.

EXAMPLES OF APPLICATION

Basic Tests

All the elements of the ALSA library have been extensively tested by numerous basic test problems and patch tests that have been most commonly used in the literature. These basic tests have shown that the ALSA elements are very accurate, cost-effective and reliable without any deficiency.

Practical Examples from Industry

Name: Automobile body structure.

Brief description: BL ADO 16 Mk II standard production 4 door saloon.

Application: Automotive engineering.

Type of the problem: Static analysis under passenger and luggage loads.

Drawings of the parts: See Fig. 1.

Discretization: Only one symmetrical half of the structure was discretized for two different analyses. For analysis I, the structure between the front and rear axles was discretized by 51 nodes forming 68 beam, plate and shell elements. For analysis II, the complete half of the structure was discretized by 70 nodes forming 95 beam, plate and shell elements.

Types of elements: For analysis I, 41 beam, 17 membrane-plate bending (R9-C^0, T9-C^0), 7 cylindrical shell (CS-16) and 3 doubly curved shell (DS-21) elements were used. For analysis II, 58 beam, 20 membrane-plate bending (R9-C^0, T9-C^0), 14 cylindrical shell (CS-16) and 3 doubly curved shell (DS-21) elements were used.

Number of degrees of freedom: 5 degrees of freedom, i.e. 3 translations and 2 out-of-plane rotations per node.

Band width: 45 for both analyses.

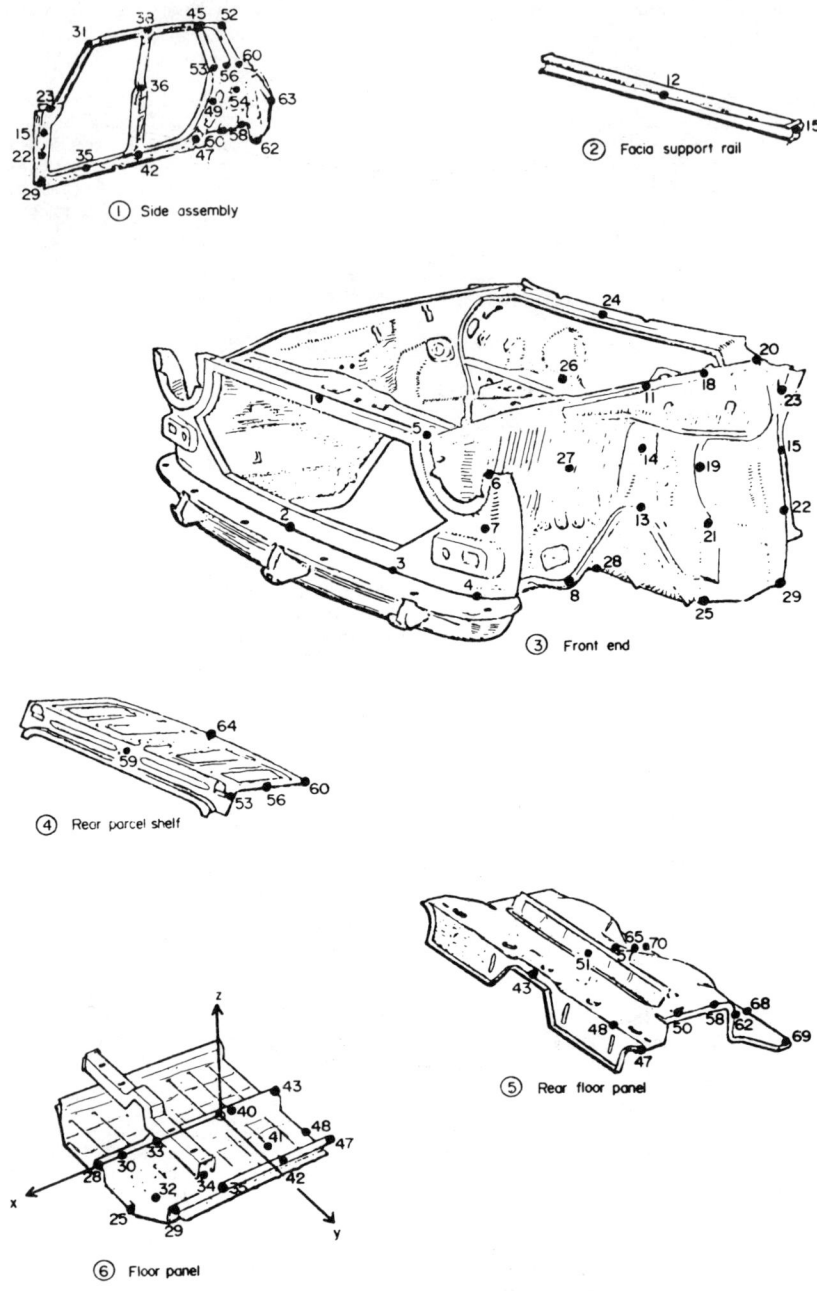

Fig. 1. Details of the subdivision.

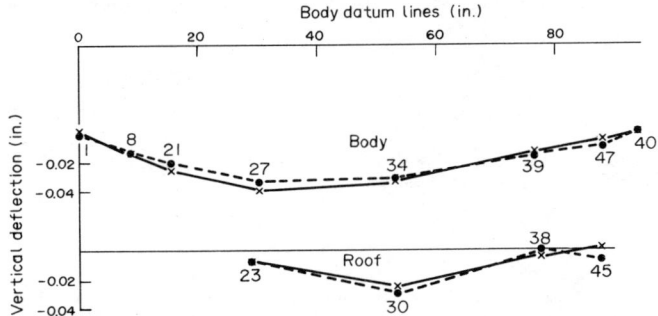

Fig. 2. Vertical deflection along the side of body structure for analysis I. —x—, experiment; —●—, finite element.

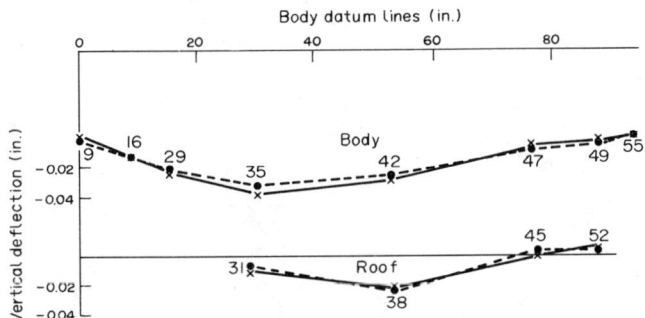

Fig. 3. Vertical deflections along the side of body structure for analysis II - Passenger load. —x—, experiment; —●—, finite element

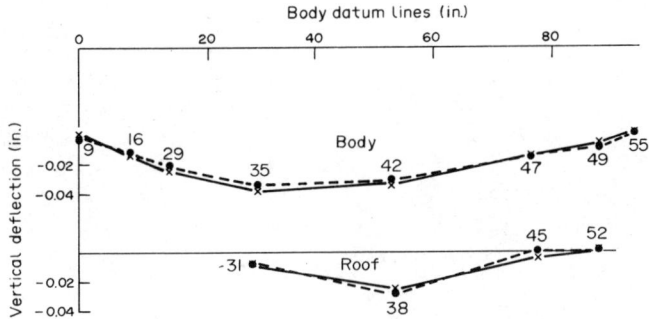

Fig. 4. Vertical deflections along the side of body structure for analysis II, passenger and luggage loads. —x—, experiment; —●—, finite element.

Part of the program and computer used: Static, in-core solution on AMDAHL computer.

Input data: User-supplied and program generated.

Output: Plots of vertical displacements, see Figs. 2-4.

Computation time: 135 and 182 secs of CP time for analysis I and analysis II respectively, in double precision.

REFERENCES

1 Alaylioglu, H. An accurate and economical finite element family for large order structural analysis. ME-1780, MES-363, NMERI, CSIR, Pretoria, SA (1982).
2 Alaylioglu, H. ALSA-General purpose finite element computer program for accurate large order structural analysis: preliminaries. ME-1795, MES-367, NMERI, CSIR, Pretoria, SA (1983).
3 Alaylioglu, H. ALSA-User's manual. RD-CS, TPA, Pretoria, SA (1984).

BEFE: COUPLED BOUNDARY ELEMENT—FINITE ELEMENT PROGRAM

G. Beer

Department of Civil Engineering, University of Queensland, St. Lucia 4067, Australia

ABSTRACT

BEFE is a general purpose program for the static analysis of structures and solids using the Finite Element method, the Boundary Element method or a combination of the Finite Element method and the Boundary Element method. The program allows consideration of nonlinear material behaviour, sequential excavation and construction and time-dependent material behaviour.

The analysis can be two-dimensional (plane strain, plane stress), axisymmetric or three-dimensional. A number of special Elements are included for the anlaysis of shell structures and joints/interfaces. The element library includes solid elements, shell, joint, truss Finite Elements and Boundary Elements.

The program system consists of 4 modules which are completely independent and communicate with each other via a common data base. The modules are: Preprocessor, analysis module, postprocessors including program for graphical display of the mesh and results. BEFE has a conversational input mode where the program requests information as required. Alternatively the input can be supplied through a data file or from a card reader. BEFE has also extensive plot capabilities which include the colour graphics display of results on various types of workstations.

Program BEFE is suitable for the stress and deformation analysis of structures machine components, excavations, foundations, dams, etc. It is particularly suited for problems which exhibit material nonlinear behaviour such as elastoplastic and visco-plastic materials. The program also has particular features which are used in geomechanics such as laminate model, joint elements and sequential excavation.

The program originates from a general purpose Finite Element package to which subroutines for the Boundary and coupled method were added. These subroutines contain 2000 lines of coding. The total coding of the program system BEFE contains about 20,000 lines. A total of 10 man years have been spent in the development of the program system.

Theoretical details have been described in references 1 to 3. The types of Finite and Boundary Elements available are shown in Figs. 1 and 2.

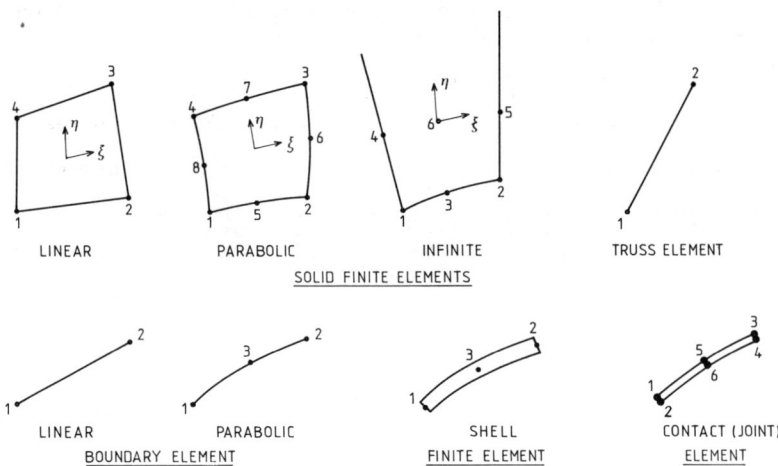

Fig. 1. Two-dimensional Finite and Boundary Elements available in BEFE

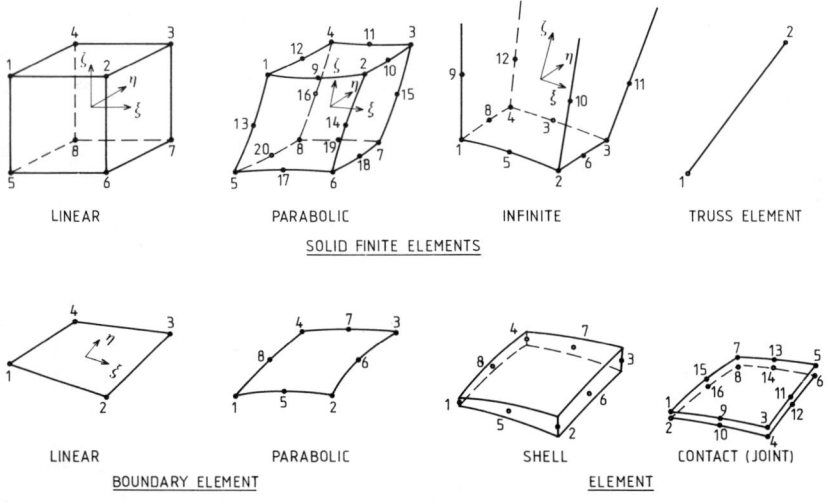

Fig. 2. Three-dimensional Finite and Boundary Elements available in BEFE

STRUCTURE OF BEFE

As mentioned in the introduction the program system BEFE consists of 4 modules which are completely independent *but access a common* data base. The 4 modules are:

1. MESH   Input of Finite Element and Boundary Element mesh: Mesh-generation, error checking.

BEFE: Boundary Element-Finite Element Program

2. BEFE   Analysis module; Solves for displacements and stresses. Gives summary print-out only.

3. PRINT   Detailed print-out of results.

4. BPLOT   Graphical display program which supports a range of devices.

The figure below shows how the different modules communicate with each other:

```
  --------                   ----------                   ---------
    MESH   ------------>  D A T A   ----------------->   PRINT
  --------                   ----------                   ---------

  --------                   ----------                   ---------
    BEFE   <----------->  B A S E   ----------------->   BPLOT
  --------                   ----------                   ---------
```

Each program module accepts input from a permanent file who can be named by the user or alternatively given a default name. This file can be created by using the EDIT utility.

Alternatively the file can be built using a subroutine DIALOG which is available with each module. This subroutine requests information as needed and invites the user to type in data from the terminal. In this way it is not necessary to learn input conventions and formats before using the program. For the input of mesh data a facility exists to correct an existing data file with DIALOG.

The various program modules are called from a command module as required.

The first module which is needed at the beginning of an analysis is MESH. It generates information describing the geometry of the problem, material properties and restraint data. The program has a subroutine for the generation of Finite Element and Boundary Element meshes and joint planes. The information about a particular job is written to the data base and is available for access by the other modules.

The next module needed is BPLOT. It can be used to plot the mesh in plan or perspective and to check for any input errors.

Module BEFE can then be used to specify the loading and to analyse for displacements and stresses. It uses the information in the data base and generates scratch files and files containing results of the analysis such as displacements and stresses. This module only prints out a summary of the results such as max/min displacements and stresses and their location, number of plastic points etc.

Finally a detailed print-out of results can be obtained with PRINT or the results can be plotted in the form of contours, stress vectors, displ. shapes etc. using BPLOT.

ANALYSING PROBLEMS WITH BEFE

It is impossible to present examples of all the capabilities of BEFE here. Some of the capabilities have been demonstrated in reference 3.

An example is given here which serves to highlight the user-friendliness of the system and the ease with which data can be input and results be obtained in a graphical form.

The example presented here involves the three-dimensional elastic stress analysis of a spherical opening in an infinite domain subjected to a vertical stress of unity.

Figure 3 shows a log of the dialog input used to specify one eighth of the Boundary Element mesh. Figure 4 shows the dialog of module BPLOT and the perspective view of the mesh.

```
$ RUN [46,5]MESH

      M E S H    Boundary Element - Finite Element Pre-Processor

    File Name <MESH.CDR> =
    DIALOG INPUT [Y/N] ? Y
    CORRECT EXISTING FILE [Y/N] ? N

    METHOD OF ANALYSIS :
    1    FINITE ELEMENTS ONLY
    2    BOUNDARY ELEMENTS ONLY
    3    FINITE AND BOUNDARY ELEMENTS
    SELECT NO. 2

    TYPE OF ANALYSIS :
    1    PLANE
    2    AXISYMMETRIC
    3    THREEDIMENSIONAL (SOLID ONLY)
    4    THREEDIMENSIONAL (SHELL ONLY)
    5    THREEDIMENSIONAL (SOLID AND SHELL)
    SELECT NO. 3
    ENTER 2 LINES OF HEADING
    spherical opening - 1/8 mesh
    with parabolic Boundary Elements

    INPUT OF NODE COORDINATES

    SCALE FACTOR =1.
    Do you want to define LOCAL AXES [Y/N] ? n
    Default Coordinate System for input is CARTESIAN
    DO YOU WANT TO CHANGE [Y/N] ? Y
    CYlindrical or SPherical coords. [CY/SP] ? SP
    NODE NO. = 1
    R=1.
    ALPHA=0.
    BETA=90.
    GENERATE COORDS [Y/N] ? Y
    END NODE NO.= 5
    R=1.
    ALPHA=0.
    BETA=0.
    NODE NO. = 6
    R=1.
    ALPHA=90.
    ALPHA=90.
    BETA=67.5
    GENERATE COORDS [Y/N] ? Y
    END NODE NO.= 9
    R=1.
    ALPHA=90.
    BETA=0.
    GENERATE COORDS [Y/N] ? N
    NODE NO. = 13
    R=1.
    ALPHA=45.
    BETA=35.33
```

Fig. 3a

```
GENERATE COORDS [Y/N] ? N
NODE NO. = 14
R=1.
ALPHA=22.5
BETA=40.16
GENERATE COORDS [Y/N] ? N
NODE NO. = 16
R=1.
ALPHA=67.5
BETA=40.16
GENERATE COORDS [Y/N] ? N
NODE NO. = 15
R=1.
ALPHA=45.
BETA=17.66
GENERATE COORDS [Y/N] ? N
NODE NO. = 10
R=1.
ALPHA=22.5
BETA=0.
GENERATE COORDS [Y/N] ? Y
END NODE NO.= 12
R=1.
ALPHA=67.5
BETA=0.
NODE NO. =
MORE COORDINATES [Y/N] ?

INPUT  ELEMENT CONNECTIVITY
TYPE OF ELEMENTS AVAILABLE :
1    LINEAR SOLID FINITE ELEMENT
2    QUADRATIC SOLID FINITE ELEMENT
3    INFINITE ELEMENT
4    TRUSS ELEMENT
5    LINEAR BOUNDARY ELEMENT
6    QUADRATIC BOUNDARY ELEMENT
7    INFINITE BOUNDARY ELEMENT
8    LINEAR SHELL ELEMENT
9    QUADRATIC SHELL ELEMENT

ELEMENT NO.= 1
TYPE = 6
ENTER NODE NUMBERS

  1.  =3
  2.  =13
  3.  =7
  4.  =1
  5.  =14
  6.  =16
  7.  =6
  8.  =2
MATERIAL NO.= 1
ELEMENT NO.= 2
TYPE = 6
ENTER NODE NUMBERS

  1.  =5
  2.  =11
  3.  =13
  4.  =3
  5.  =10
  6.  =15
  7.  =14
  8.  =4
MATERIAL NO.= 1
```

Fig. 3b

```
                    ELEMENT NO.= 3
                    TYPE = 6
                    ENTER NODE NUMBERS

                      1. =11
                      2. =9
                      3. =7
                      4. =13
                      5. =12
                      6. =8
                      7. =16
                      8. =15
                    MATERIAL NO.= 1
                    ELEMENT NO.=
                    MESH-GENERATION [Y/N] ? N
                    SPECIFY PROPERTIES
                    MATERIAL NO. = 1
                    DESCRIPTION (< 4 CHAR) ROCK
                    MATERIAL TYPES :
                    1    SOLID THREE DIMENSIONAL
                    2    SOLID PLANE STRAIN
                    3    SOLID PLANE STRESS
                    4    TRUSS
                    5    CONTACT ( JOINT )
                    6    SHELL
                    SELECT NO. 1
                    ELASTIC PROPERTIES
                    MODULUS= 10000.
                    POISSONS RATIO=0.0
                    COEFF. OF THERM. EXPANS. =
                    SPECIFY PROPERTIES
                    MATERIAL NO. =
                    BOUNDARY CONDITIONS
                    ELEMENT =
                    DEFINE JOINTS [Y/N] ?N
                    CUntinue  or STop ? ST
                    FORTRAN STOP
                    *
```

Fig. 3c

DIALOG input for MESH for demonstration example

Figure 5 shows the DIALOG input used for module BEFE to perform the analysis by the Boundary Element method. Note the error recovery after a typing error by the user.

Figure 6 shows a summary print-out obtained from BEFE for a similar problem with 24 elements. The run times shown are elapsed times on a VAX11/780 spent in the various sections of the program. The time noted for the assembly of coefficients includes the time used for the integration of Kernel-Shapefunction products.

Finally Fig. 7b shows a colour contour plot of the distribution of vertical stress in the x-z plane and Fig. 7a the DIALOG input required to obtain the plot.

CONCLUSIONS

A computer program has been presented which completely integrates the Finite Element and Boundary Element methods of analysis.

The program is particularly user-friendly and has powerful pre- and postprocessing capabilities.

Due to space limitations it has been impossible to demonstrate even a fraction of the capabilities of BEFE but it was tried to demonstrate the user-friendliness of

BEFE: Boundary Element-Finite Element Program

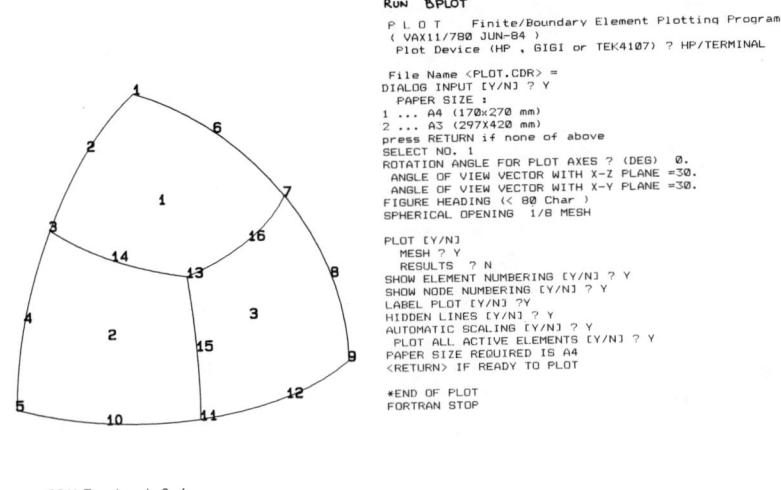

Fig. 4. DIALOG input for BPLOT and plot of the mesh obtained

the system by a small example involving three-dimensional Boundary Elements only.

The program runs currently on a VAX11/780 minicomputer and the graphic display program can drive HP plotters, D.E.C. colour graphics terminals, TEKTRONIX terminals and CALCOMP plotters.

Installation on the following hardware has been completed:

  IBM (VM/CMS)

  CDC Cyber 205 (vectorized version)

  PRIME

Further inquiries with respect to purchase and leasing costs and availability of test versions can be directed to the author.

```
$ RUN [46,5]BEFE


    B E F E    Boundary Element - Finite Element Processor


    File Name <BEFE.CDR> =
    DIALOG INPUT [Y/N] ? Y
    SPECIFICATION OF BOUNDARY ELEMENT REGION
    CHANGE OR INPUT [Y/N] ? N
    SPECIFY LOADING : LOAD CASE (EXCAV.STAGE) NO.= 1
    DESCRIPTION (<60 Char) EXCAVATION
    EXCAVATION PROBLEM [Y/N] ? Y
    NUMBER OF LOAD INCREMENTS = 1
    LOAD TYPES AVAILABLE :
    1   ...   NODAL LOADS
    2   ...   NODAL DISPL.
    3   ...   BOUNDARY TRACTIONS
    4   ...   GRAVITY
    5   ...   THERMAL LOADING
    6   ...   VIRGIN STRESS FIELD
    7   ...   EXCAVATION

    LOAD TYPE NO.= 6
    VIRGIN STRESS FIELD:
    DOES STRESS VARY WITH DEPTH [Y/N]? N
    STRESS COMPONENTS:
    SIGMA-X= 0.
    SIGMA-Y= 1.0        ←——  OOPS   ERROR !
    SIGMA-Z= 0.
    TAU-XY = *    ←———— RECOVER
    VIRGIN STRESS FIELD:
    DOES STRESS VARY WITH DEPTH [Y/N]? N
    STRESS COMPONENTS:
    SIGMA-X=
    SIGMA-Y=
    SIGMA-Z= 1.0
    TAU-XY =
    TAU-XZ =
    TAU-YZ =

    LOAD TYPE NO.= 7
    EXCAVATION:
    DEFINE EXCAVATED FINITE ELEMENTS
    OR BOUNDARY ELEMENTS ON EXCAVATION SURFACE
    ELEMENT=1
    TO=24
    STEP=
    ELEMENT=
    LOAD TYPE NO.=
```

Fig. 5. DIALOG input for BEFE for demonstration example

```
* B E F E *---------VERSION  MAY-84 VAX11/780-------------------   PAGE  10
    UNIVERSITY OF QUEENSLAND - RUN ON  7-FEB-85  AT 16:05:12


    TEST EXAMPLE 3-D B.E. PROGRAM

    EXAMPLE 4 : SPHERICAL OPENING IN INFINITE MEDIUM



    LOAD CASE     1


        S U M M A R Y    OF RESULTS AFTER LOAD STEP     1    (TIME STEP     1)
    MAXIMUM STRESS:

    NORMAL         0.36 @ ELEMENT      6   POINT      1
    NORMAL         0.37 @ ELEMENT      8   POINT      1
    NORMAL         1.85 @ ELEMENT      8   POINT      4
    SHEAR          0.19 @ ELEMENT     22   POINT      1
    SHEAR          0.56 @ ELEMENT     17   POINT      4
    SHEAR          0.53 @ ELEMENT     15   POINT      4

    MINIMUM STRESS:

    NORMAL        -0.38 @ ELEMENT     23   POINT      4
    NORMAL        -0.38 @ ELEMENT     23   POINT      4
    NORMAL        -0.03 @ ELEMENT      1   POINT      2
    SHEAR         -0.19 @ ELEMENT     23   POINT      1
    SHEAR         -0.56 @ ELEMENT     13   POINT      4
    SHEAR         -0.53 @ ELEMENT     19   POINT      4

    MAXIMUM DISPLACEMENTS:

           0.000201 @ ELEMENT     10   NODE     2
           0.000201 @ ELEMENT      5   NODE     1
           0.000997 @ ELEMENT      1   NODE     4

    MINIMUM DISPLACEMENTS:

          -0.000201 @ ELEMENT      6   NODE     2
          -0.000201 @ ELEMENT      8   NODE     2
          -0.000997 @ ELEMENT     21   NODE     2


    RUN TIMES IN SECONDS:

    ASSEMBLY OF COEFF. =     277.97
    REDUCTION OF EQ.   =      87.29
    BACKSUBSTITUTION   =       0.68
    STIFFNESS COMP.    =       0.00
    TOTAL              =     365.94

$
```

Fig. 6. Summary print-out from BEFE

```
$ RUN [46,5]BPLOT

 P L O T    Finite/Boundary Element Plotting Program
 ( VAX11/780 JUN-84 )
  Plot Device (HP , GIGI or TEK4107) ? HP/TERMINAL

 File Name <PLOT.CDR> =
DIALOG INPUT [Y/N] ? Y
  PAPER SIZE :
1 ... A4 (170x270 mm)
2 ... A3 (297X420 mm)
press RETURN if none of above
SELECT NO. 1
ROTATION ANGLE FOR PLOT AXES ? (DEG)
 ANGLE OF VIEW VECTOR WITH X-Z PLANE =80.
 ANGLE OF VIEW VECTOR WITH X-Y PLANE =10.
FIGURE HEADING (< 80 Char )
SIGMA-Z

PLOT [Y/N]
  MESH ? N
  RESULTS  ? Y
  DEFORMED MESH ? N
  DEFORMATION VECTORS ? N


  MARK PLASTIC POINTS ? N
  STRESS VECTORS ? N
  STRESS (STRAIN)  CONTOURS ? Y
NO. OF CONTOUR LINES=5
ANNOTATE CONTOUR LINES [Y/N] ? Y
  COMPONENT OF STRESS (STRAIN) :
1    SIGMA-X
2    SIGMA-Y
3    SIGMA-Z
4    TAU-XY
5    TAU-XZ
6    TAU-YZ
7    PLASTIC STRAIN 1
8    PLASTIC STRAIN 2
    SELECT NO. 3
SHADING BETWEEN CONTOURS [Y/N] ? Y
LABEL PLOT [Y/N] ?Y
LOAD CASE (EXC. STAGE) NO.= 1
HIDDEN LINES [Y/N] ? Y
AUTOMATIC SCALING [Y/N] ? Y
VALUE OF 1. CONTOUR = 0.01
CONTOUR INCREMENT ? 0.300
 PLOT ALL ACTIVE ELEMENTS [Y/N] ?
PAPER SIZE REQUIRED IS A4
<RETURN> IF READY TO PLOT
```

Fig. 7a

Fig. 7b

Fig. 7. DIALOG input for BPLOT to plot contours of vertical stress and (b) plot obtained

REFERENCES

1. Beer, G. Recent Developments in Finite Element Analysis using minicomputers. Proc. Third Int. Conf. on Finite Element methods. The University of New South Wales, Sydney, Australia, 1979.
2. Beer, G. Finite Element, Boundary Element and Coupled Analysis of Unbounded Problems in Elastostatics. *Int. J. Numer. Meth. Eng.*, Vol. *19*, 567-580, 1983.
3. Beer, G. BEFE - a Combined Boundary Element Finite Element Computer program. *Adv. Eng. Software*, Vol. *6*, No. 2, 1983

BEWAVE: PRESSURE WAVE PROPAGATION BY THE BOUNDARY ELEMENT PROGRAM

P. H. L. Groenenboom[*], J. J. De Jong[**] and C. A. Brebbia[***]

[*]PISCES International BV, Groningenweg 6, 2803 PV Gouda, The Netherlands
[**]B.V. Neratoom, The Hague, The Netherlands
[***]Computational Mechanics International, Southampton, UK

ABSTRACT

The boundary element program BEWAVE has been developed for the computation of pressure waves in liquids propagating inside complex three-dimensional structures. BEWAVE computes the transient pressures and velocities arising from explosions or other highly-dynamic flow conditions. Since a variety of boundary conditions has been implemented, it is also possible to compute dynamic, three-dimensional flow of slightly compressible, inviscid fluids.

Two examples of application by BEWAVE in the field of safety analysis of steam generator systems of nuclear reactors will be presented. For this type of application the pressure source is the explosive reaction between water (and/or steam) and liquid metal. With BEWAVE one is able to calculate time histories of pressure and velocity at the structural interfaces.

The interactive colour-graphics package PATRAN^{TM} can be applied for mesh generation and postprocessing of the results at the boundary.

THEORETICAL BACKGROUND

It is well known that for pressure wave propagation and for highly-dynamic fluid flow the effect of the fluid viscosity can usually be neglected. Consequently the fluid dynamics can be described by the scalar velocity potential $u(\vec{r},t)$ at position $\vec{r}$ and time t; the gradient of this function is the fluid velocity. If the velocities remain small in comparison to the sound speed in the medium, the potential satisfies the scalar wave equation in the fluid domain:

$$\nabla^2 u - \frac{1}{c^2} \cdot \frac{\partial^2}{\partial t^2} = \gamma(\vec{r},t) = \gamma(t)\delta(\vec{r}-\vec{r}_s) \qquad (1)$$

Consequently, the engineering problem can be described by the geometry, the physical properties of the medium, the appropriate boundary conditions and initial conditions.

The differential operator ∇^2 is the Laplacian, c the sound speed and γ a source function representing a point source or explosion at position $\vec{r}_s$ inside the domain.

The above differential equation can be transformed into the Kirchhoff integral equation over the boundary Γ:[1]

$$c_o u(\vec{r}_o,t) = -\frac{\gamma(t-R_s/c)}{4\pi R_s} + \frac{1}{4\pi}\int_\Gamma \{\frac{1}{R}(\frac{\partial u}{\partial n})_{tret} + \frac{\vec{R}\cdot\vec{n}}{R^3}(u + \frac{R}{c}\dot{u})_{tret}\}d\vec{r} \quad (2)$$

where $c_o = 0$ if $\vec{r}_o$ outside Ω

$\quad\quad\quad = \frac{1}{2}$ if $\vec{r}_o$ on the boundary Γ

$\quad\quad\quad = 1$ if $\vec{r}_o$ inside Ω

$\vec{R}_s = \vec{r}_s - \vec{r}_o$

$\vec{R} = \vec{r}-\vec{r}_o$

and tret = $t-R/c$.

The interpretation of this equation is that the potential at a certain time t can be expressed in a contribution from the source and to a contribution from the boundary due to the velocity component normal to the surface, and to the potential and its time derivative where all these functions are to be taken at the retarded time "tret". For a rigid boundary the normal velocity $q = \partial u/\partial n$ vanishes.

Starting from given initial conditions for u and $\partial u/\partial n$ on the boundary the solution for u on the boundary can be obtained from the previous values by progressing in time. In addition the velocity $\vec{v}$ is obtained by a direct evaluation of the gradient. Also the pressure may be obtained by

$$P = P_o - \rho\frac{\partial u}{\partial t} - \frac{1}{2}\rho v^2$$

where ρ is the density of the medium and v the magnitude of the velocity.

There exists a solution to Equation 1 if one of the variables u or q is given at the boundary or if a relation between these variables is specified. In addition to the solid-wall boundary condition the following types are available in BEWAVE:

1. non-reflecting opening (radiation):

$$q + \frac{1}{c}\frac{\partial u}{\partial t} = 0; \text{ pressure waves perpendicular to the surface do not reflect}$$

2. constant pressure P_c:

$$P = P_o - \rho\frac{\partial u}{\partial t} - \frac{1}{2}\rho|\vec{v}|^2 = P_c$$

3. prescribed inflow: $q = f(t)$

4. "rupture disc" defined by a solid wall until a certain activation pressure is reached after which a constant pressure boundary condition holds.

Symmetry with respect to one, two or three flat surfaces can be applied via a direct condensation method[2] yielding a significant reduction of computing effort.

FIELD OF APPLICATION

BEWAVE allows for the calculation of the following types of physical phenomena.

- acoustic wave propagation in homogeneous, inviscid fluids (examples: explosions, water hammer, depressurization waves)
- transient,(non-viscous) potential flow

The analyses exclude strong effects due to large variations in density or sound speed and to cavitation. In this respect it should be noted that most liquids can sustain quite strong tension (negative pressures) during short intervals before spall (cavitation) occurs[3].

BEWAVE can be applied to a volume of homogeneous fluid inside arbitrarily shaped, three-dimensional structures. Extension to external flow problems is also feasible.

Since some symmetry properties of the problem can be utilized directly it is also worthwhile to perform two-dimensional or axial-symmetric analyses by BEWAVE.

The loading may be given by a dynamic pressure source inside the domain or by a dynamic boundary condition.

PROGRAM DESCRIPTION

The boundary integral equation (Eqn. 2) can be solved by discretization in time and in space. For the spatial discretization only the boundary needs to be divided into (boundary) elements. Consequently, the following set of equations arises:[1]

$$\tfrac{1}{2} u_i(t) = -\frac{\gamma(t-R_s/c)}{4\pi R_s} + \Sigma_j \{G_{ij} q_j(\text{tret}) + H_{ij}(u_j(\text{tret}) + \frac{R}{c}\dot{u}_j(\text{tret}))\} \quad (4)$$

where u_i is the potential at node "i", q_j the normal velocity at node "j", $R = |\vec{r}_j - \vec{r}_i|$ and tret $= t - R/c$. G_{ij} and H_{ij}^* are the constant influence coefficients, identical to those of the stationary potential problem.

Time is divided into equal steps and the values of u and q at the retarded time are obtained by quadratic interpolation between the appropriate time steps. The most straightforward procedure to obtain results at a new time step consists of interpolation of u(tret) and q(tret) between values solely in the past. This requires the time step to be smaller than the minimum distance between any pair of nodes divided by the sound speed. Unfortunately, this seemingly attractive explicit solution method yields unstable results[4].

The time-stepping procedure applied by the present version of BEWAVE is a "semi-implicit" solution scheme whereby a matrix-equation has to be solved at any time step. Since this matrix only depends on the geometry and the type of boundary conditions, it is constant for most problems. The time step for this solution method must be greater than the maximum distance between any pair of nodes divided by the sound speed. This method yields stable results.

ELEMENT TYPES

The boundary elements of BEWAVE are of a quadratic type both in shape and in functional dependence, i.e. the shape functions and the interpolation functions are quadratic functions of the two local co-ordinates. The advantage of these elements is that a curved surface can be approximated very well and that the number of elements can be kept to a minimum. Both, quadrilateral and triangular elements with 9 resp. 6 meshpoints are available. The elements are discontinuous, which means that the nodal points are inside the elements and do not coincide with the meshpoints (with the exception of the quadrilateral midpoint). A practical advantage of discontinuous elements is that local mesh refinement can be accomplished rather simply, since meshpoints at element interfaces do not necessarily belong to both elements.

PROGRAM STRUCTURE

The input file of BEWAVE consists of fixed format data records with some general parameters, program options, geometrical data, boundary conditions, internal points and source data. The program can run with the following options:

(i)   data checking
(ii) construction of geometry-dependent matrices
(iii) application of the boundary conditions/generation of the solution matrix
(iv) solution in time
(v)   print output,

or any proper combination. If only the boundary conditions are modified with respect to a previous run, phase i and ii does not need to be repeated. If only the source strength varies the calculation can start with option iv.

The geometrical data are the co-ordinates of the meshpoints and the connectivity table. The only restriction to the numbering of both NE elements and NM user-defined meshpoints is that all elements 1-NE and points 1-NM are present. In case of flat, rectangular elements only the corners have to be defined.

The default boundary conditions is a rigid wall; other boundary conditions must be defined in the input.

The co-ordinates of the internal points and of the source, and a table of source strength vs. time must be given as input.

The generation of an input-file is greatly simplified by the use of the preprocessor of the interactive PATRAN^{TM} package. After all meshpoints and elements of a BEWAVE model have been generated, the interactive translator program PATBER generates the complete input-file for BEWAVE.

After the BEWAVE run has been completed the results on the output-file can be used to generate the proper files for the postprocessor-part of PATRAN^{TM} by a reverse translator BERPAT. With PATRAN the user is able to generate the model and to generate contour plots of the potential, normal velocity, transverse velocity and pressure at the boundary of the three-dimensional model in colour graphics. Some examples will be shown with the applications.

The BEWAVE program is written in ANSI-FORTRAN 77 with the exception of just a few machine-dependent (VAX/VMS-specific) statements mainly for performance measurement and file handling. It has a modular structure with about fifty subroutines and it has an overlay-structure for use on computers without virtual memory.

Since the size of the matrices depends strongly on the number of elements of the mesh, variable dimensioning of the arrays is applied throughout the program. Special subroutines for the definition of the loads may be defined by the user and coupled to BEWAVE during the load phase.

HARDWARE COMPATIBILITIES

Since BEWAVE has become publicly available only recently, implementation on VAX/VMS and Gould/SEL are the only ones performed yet. Installations on other mini-computers or on main-frames should, however, be relatively simple.

PATRAN™ is available on many computer systems ranging from Apollo to CRAY; this will be described in a future edition.

The BEWAVE-code and the PATRAN interface are available on magnetic tape from PISCES International and Computational Mechanics.

EXAMPLES OF APPLICATION

Test Case

For the validation of BEWAVE a test case has been defined by a single point source inside a rectangular box. This geometry has been chosen for the reason that an exact solution can be obtained. If the rectangular box is bounded by rigid surfaces the velocity potetial and the flow field can be computed directly from the infinite series of image sources created by multiple reflections in each wall.

Since the propagation velocity c, of the pressure waves is finite, the influence at time t is limited to those image sources that lie within a radius of $c \cdot (t-t_0)$ from any point of the box; t_0 is the initial time.

The box is bounded by the six planes

$$x = 0; \quad y = 0; \quad z = 0$$
$$x = 3; \quad y = 4; \quad z = 5$$

The boundary has been discretized into 32 quadrilateral boundary elements. The mesh can be found in Fig. 1. The sound speed was taken to be 0.2 and the density as 850. No symmetry has been used.

The source is located at position (1, 2, 3) with the strength defined at time t by:

$$\gamma(t) = 0 \qquad\qquad t<0$$
$$= 7.2338 \; 10^{-8} \; t(t-288) \qquad 0<t<288$$
$$= 0 \qquad\qquad t>288$$

From the dimensions of the box and the sound speed a time step of $t = 36$ has been chosen.

A comparison for the pressure at an internal point (x = 1, y = 2, z = 4) between two BEWAVE calculations and the exact solution can be found in Fig. 2. For one of the BEWAVE calculations the exact source function has been used ("analytical"); for the other a quadratic interpolation between the exact values at the time steps has been used ("numerical").

Apart from the shift in time of approximately half a step the agreement with the exact results is quite good. This time shift is due to the quadratic interpolation applied to the initial values of the potential at the boundaries.

Since the source function returns to zero for $t > 288$ the pressure will approach an asymptotic value. By integration of the source function between $t = 0$ and $t = 288$ one obtains the total displaced volume ΔV of the medium. From the compressibility relation the following equation for the asymptotic pressure can be obtained:

$$P_{as} = \rho c^2 \Delta V / V$$

where V is the original volume of the fluid.

With a volume of 60 and a ΔV of 2.88 this asymptotic value becomes 0.1632. The values of the pressure in point (1, 2, 4) at t = 396 are compared to this asymptotic value in Table 1.

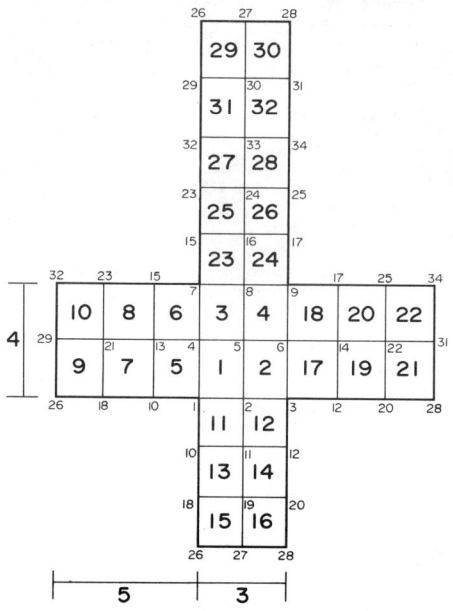

Fig. 1. Boundary element mesh of the rectangular box in folded-out model

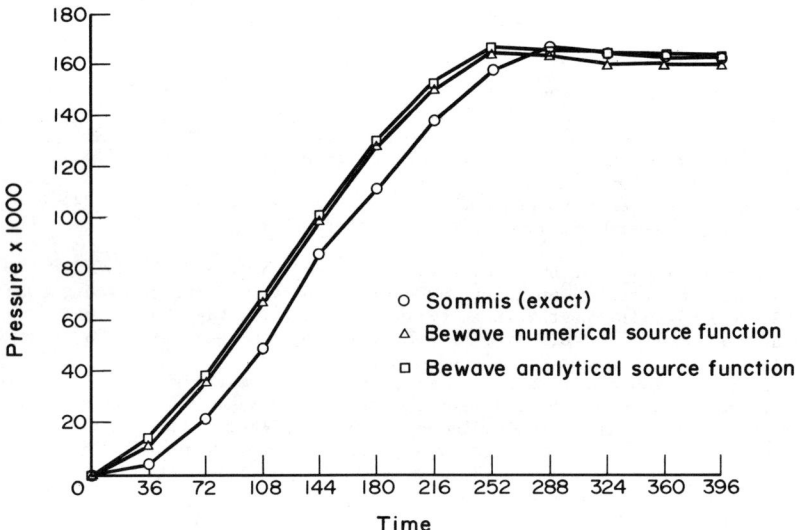

Fig. 2. Pressure at point (1,2,4) for rectangular box with rigid walls

TABLE 1

Method	$p(1,2,4)$ at $t = 396$
"exact"	0.1634
"BEWAVE numerical"	0.1606
"BEWAVE analytical"	0.1640
asymptotic value	0.1632

Practical Examples from Industry

The two examples from industry discussed below are both in the field of the safety analyses in nuclear engineering. They deal with the computation of transient pressure waves in a nuclear steam generator arising from a violent reaction between water and liquid metal.

The final goal of this type of application is to prove the integrity of the steam generator in case of strongly asymmetric loads.

For this type of application the source strength can be identified with (the opposite of) the volume growth rate of the bubble with reaction products (mainly hydrogen gas) generated by the chemical reaction between liquid metal and water. Both geometrical models that will be discussed in this paper are simplified models of the lower part of a straight-tube steam generator. A sketch of this steam generator is included as Fig. 3. Note that it is axially symmetric with exception of the coolant in- and outlet and the pressure relief nozzles. In order to reduce computing costs only the lower part of the steam generator has been modelled for these test calculations with the further simplification that no internal structures are present.

Since it will take about 20 msec for a pressure wave originating in the lower part of the steam generator to reflect at the top and to return, it is reasonable to presume non-reflecting boundary conditions at the lower entrance to the narrow part.

Example 1. A sketch of the BEWAVE model is included as Fig. 4a. The boundary of this model has been divided into two horizontal, circular plates, two conical parts and four cylinders. Each plate is divided into five quadrilateral elements as displayed in Fig. 4b, whereas each conical part and each cylinder is divided into four boundary elements along the circumference. The complete model consists of 34 quadratic, quadrilateral elements.

The origin is located at the centre of the bottom plate. The radius varies between 306, 450 and 316 mm going from bottom to top. The total height is 1582 mm. Since we are interested in asymmetric effects we locate the source off the axis at position: (0,-220,50). The source strength is given by independent calculations on the transfer rate of the reaction.

Without use of symmetry the solution for this model with 306 degrees of freedom takes 25 min and 40 sec of CPU-time on a VAX 11/780 for options (ii) and (iii) together. The solution in time over 16 steps, corresponding to 12 msec takes only 6 CPU-min. These CPU-requirements can be reduced significantly by making use of the symmetry present in this problem.

At the boundary at the height of the source there are significant deviations from the axial symmetry. This can be observed in Figs. 5 and 6 where the pressure along the circumference at $z = 31.67$ mm is given.

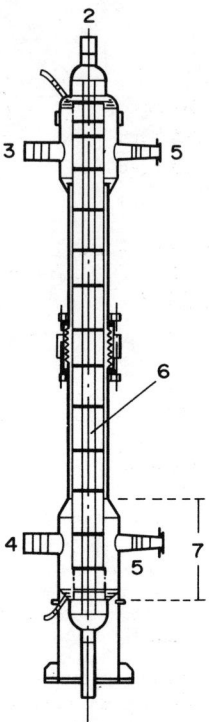

Fig. 3. Sketch of the nuclear steam generator

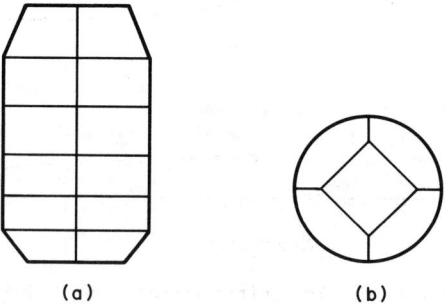

Fig. 4. (a) BE-model 2 for the lower part of the steam generator frontal view). (b) BE-model of the bottom plate

The maximum pressure at the boundary becomes 4.42 MPa at the bottom plate. At the top of the model the deviations from the axial symmetry (due to the source) are negligible. Two-fold symmetry of the problem is retained exactly.

Example 2. In order to study the effect of the presence of the outlet nozzle and the pressure relief nozzle with the rupture disc a second model of the same steam generator has been defined by the geometry and mesh as presented in Fig. 7.

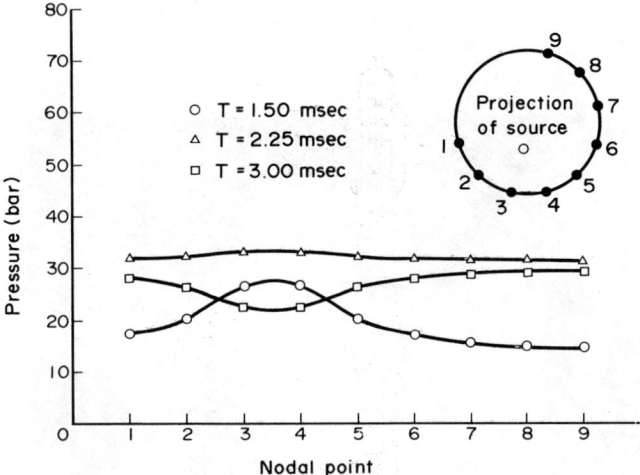

Fig. 5. Pressure profiles along circumference z = 31.67 in model 2

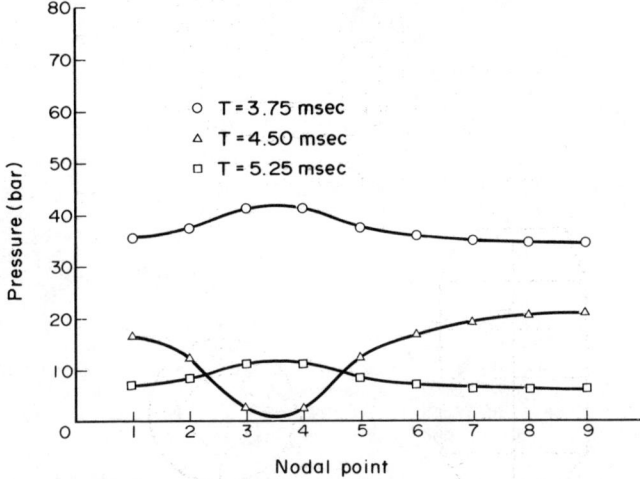

Fig. 6. Pressure profiles along circumference z = 31.67 in model 2

The problem size and consequently computer time has been reduced by a modification of the geometry; the two nozzles are placed diametrically opposed whereas in reality they are at right angles.

From the results of this calculation it has become clear that this distortion of the model will not have great influence.

Consequently the model is symmetric for reflection in the vertical plane through the nozzle axes if the source is also located in this plane. The boundary element mesh has been constructed with help of PATRAN and consists of 23 quadrilateral and 1 triangular element(s) yielding 213 nodes.

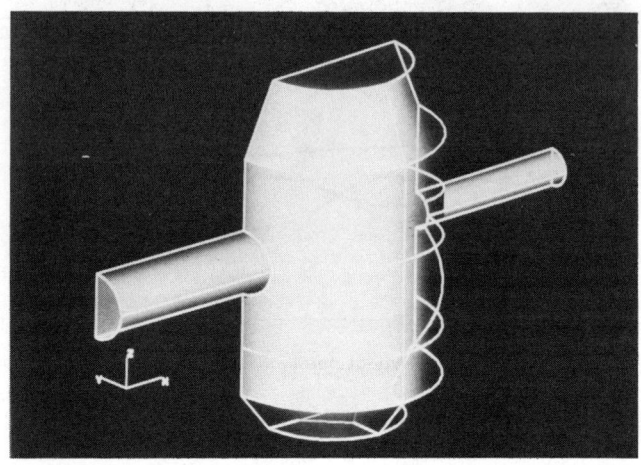

Fig. 7. PATRAN-solid model of the steam generator; the B.E.-mesh is overlaid

The element at the top and the one at the end of the outlet nozzle (to the left in Fig. 7) have non-reflecting boundary conditions, the element at the end of the pressure relief nozzle has a rupture disc condition with an activation pressure of 1.7 MPa; all other elements represent solid walls. The initial pressure is 0.5 MPa and the reaction takes place 50 mm above the bottom plate centre.

For this model the so-called shadow option has been used; the influence between two nodal points must be excluded if the line of sight intersects some structural part in between these points. To this end all elements are divided into small flat triangles that are used to check on possible intersection with every line of sight. Despite the 1138442 calls to the corresponding subroutine the CPU-time for phase ii and iii together does not become higher than 47 min.

Results for the pressure at the boundary are shown by PATRAN-contour plots in Figs. 8 and 9. At 3 msec (Fig. 8) the pressure is almost axially symmetric in the whole model since the pressure relief has not been activated yet.

At 4.5 msec (Fig. 9) the effects of the rupture disc activation is obvious from the strong pressure drop in the pressure relief nozzle.

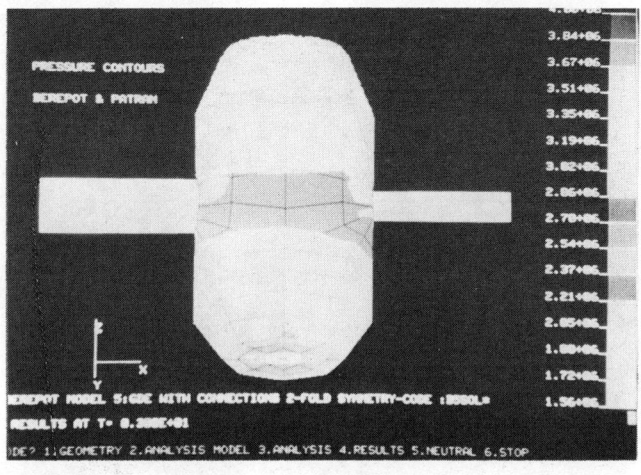

Fig. 8. PATRAN-contour plot of pressure at t = 3 msec

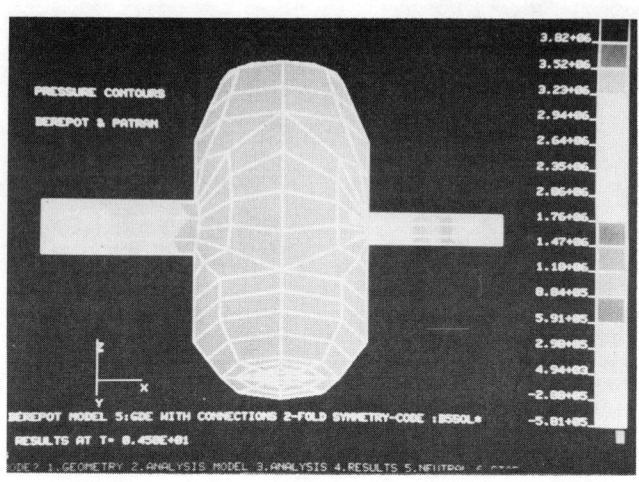

Fig. 9.   PATRAN-contour plot of pressure at t = 4.5 msec

REFERENCES

1. Groenenboom, P. H. L. (1983) Wave Propagation Phenomena. In: C. A. Brebbia (ed.) *Progress in Boundary Element Methods*, Vol. *2*, Pentech Press Ltd., London.
2. Brebbia, C. A., J. C. F. Telles and L. C. Wrobel (1984) *Boundary Element Techniques*. Springer-Verlag, Berlin.
3. Jones, A. V. (1979) Coolant cavitation in dynamic containment loading. *Nucl. Engrg. & Design*, *55*, 197-206.
4. Groenenboom, P. H. L., I. T. Kuijper and J. J. de Jong (1984) Solution of the retarded potential problem and numerical stability. *Proc. 6th Int. Conf. Boundary Element Methods in Engineering*, Springer-Verlag, Berlin

CASTEM: FINITE ELEMENT SYSTEM

A. Combescure*, A. Hoffmann* and P. Pasquet**

*CEA-DEMT, F91191 Gif-sur-Yvette Cedex, France
**CISI, 35 Bld. Brune, 75680 Paris, France

ABSTRACT

CASTEM is a general purpose finite element software for the solution of mechanical and heat transfer analysis for the linear or non-linear problems. It has been developed since 10 years jointly by the mechanical and thermal research department (DEMT) of the French Atomic Energy Commission (CEA) and the CISI which commercializes this system. The CASTEM system is based on the very extensive experience acquired by the CEA engineers, in the main problems encountered in the nuclear industry. These capabilities are continuously upgraded by the mechanical testing sessions performed at the CEA, mainly for the purpose of development and validation of the computational schemes.

INTRODUCTION

The CASTEM system[1,2] is a very modular system. It is composed of a lot of programs which will be described below. The main modules are: ALICE, BILBO, GIBI, INCA, MAYA, PLEXUS, TEDEL, TRISTANA. The independence of these modules makes it possible to select the best suited for the solution of each problem, without running the complete system. But these modules are compatible if necessary and use the same mesh generator and the same post processor. In addition the CASTEM system architecture is particularly efficient in solving non-linear problems.

ELEMENT LIBRARY

The elements used in the CASTEM system are very classical and very easy to use. Some of these are represented in fig. 1. We can see the tetranedron with 10 nodes (3-D) the pentahedron with 15 nodes (3-D), different sorts of beam and pipes (3-D) the triangular with 6 nodes (2-D) and with 3 nodes (2-D and 3-D), the hexahedron with 20 nodes (3-D) the quadrilateral with 4 nodes (2-D) and with 8 nodes (2-D and 3-D). All these elements may be solid elements or fluid elements (except beam elements).

TYPE OF ANALYSIS

CASTEM had a wide range of possibilities. Designed for mechanical engineers,

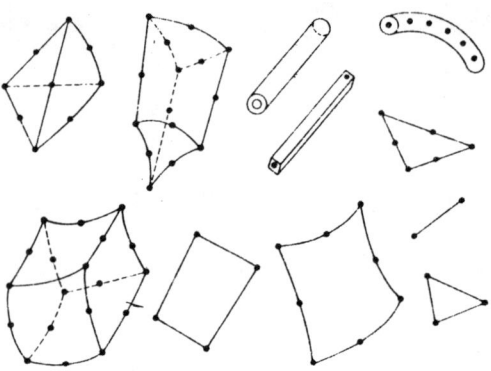

Fig. 1.

the CASTEM system can deal with different phenomena and structures in particular.

- Behaviour of materials:
  Elasticity (compressible or incompressible, isotropic or not)
  Plasticity (isotropic or kinematic hardening, thermoplasticity)
  Viscosity, creep
  More complex models, (cyclic plasticity, arisotropy, concrete ...).

- Fluid - structure interaction.

- Non-linearity connected with geometric deformation model:
  Elastic or plastic buckling
  Large displacements.

- Time history dependencies:
  Vibrations, eigenmodes and frequencies
  Step loads
  Cycles

All these types of analysis can be mixed.

- Geometric shapes:
  Two or three dimensions, axisymmetric
  Structures composed of beams, pipes, plates, thin-wall and thick-wall shells and volume elements, liquid-solid coupling.

THE PRINCIPAL MODULES AND THEIR CAPABILITIES

The general architecture of the CASTEM system is made with one central mesh generation (GIBI), several computing modules (INCA, BILBO, PLEXUS, TEDEL) and some post processors (ALICE, MAYA, TRISTANA).

COCO is a powerful mesh generator able to create models with elements which can have 2, 3, 4, 6, 8, 10, 15 or 20 nodes (see complex structures of fig. 2). We

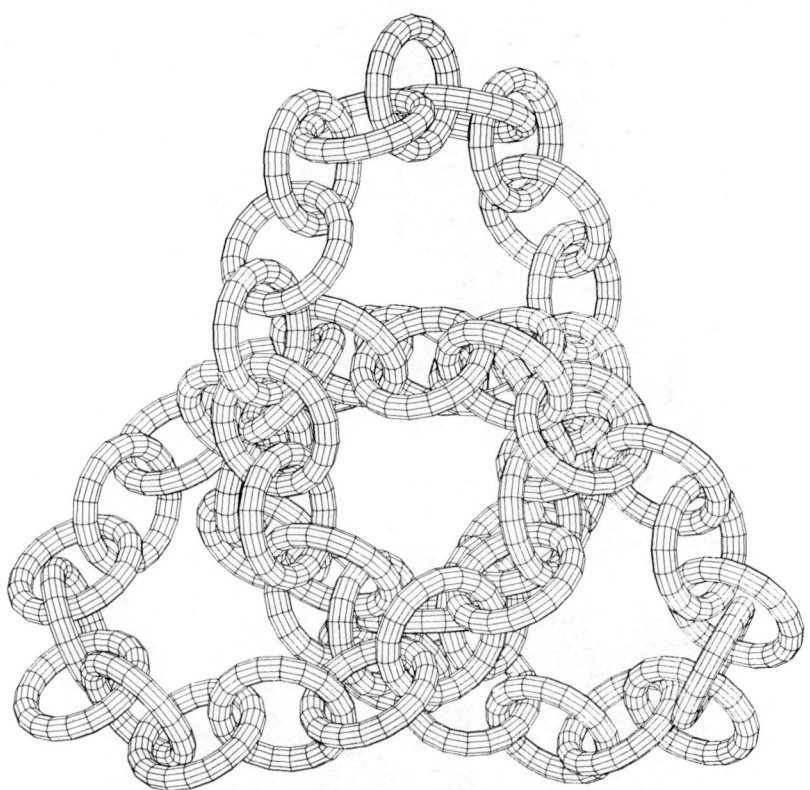

Fig. 2. Type of complex structure which can be generated by GIBI.

can see two examples of meshes created by GIBI superphenix internal structure (Fig. 2) submarine finder (Fig. 3). The main capabilities are:

- the "renumbering" option which allows to minimize the half bandwidth in order to reduce the size of the stiffness matrix,

- the execution in batch or interactive mode. If we work with the interactive mode (with a Tektronix screen) we can use the "help" option which indicates the words we can enter to go on with the generation. In this case we can display the plot on the screen or on a plotting table (Benson or Calcomp),

- the graphic display may be done with or without hidden lines (with zoom effect, windowing, different types of projection). Of course, we can alter, modify, add or suppress elements in the mesh.

INCA[3,4,9] is the module of analysis of plane or axisymmetric structures. There are solid elements, fluid elements, incompressible elements (Hermann formulation) and fluid-structure interaction elements. The types of analyses are:

- linear elasticity, thermo elasticity,
- plasticity with isotropic, kinematic, or cyclic hardening (Chaboche's model),
- thermoplasticity, creep,

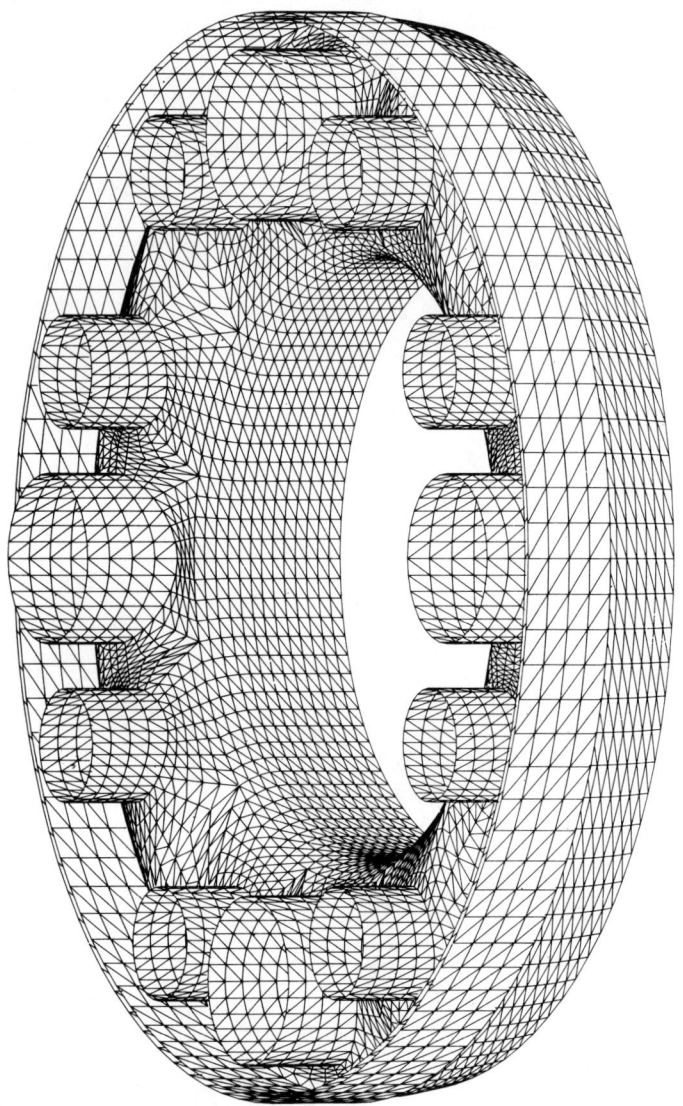

Fig. 3. SUPERPHENIX internal structure. This is a shell structure generated with GIBI for a buckling study with BILBO

- large displacements,
- buckling, postbuckling,
- unilateral contacts

in the static or dynamic domains (with step by step integration).

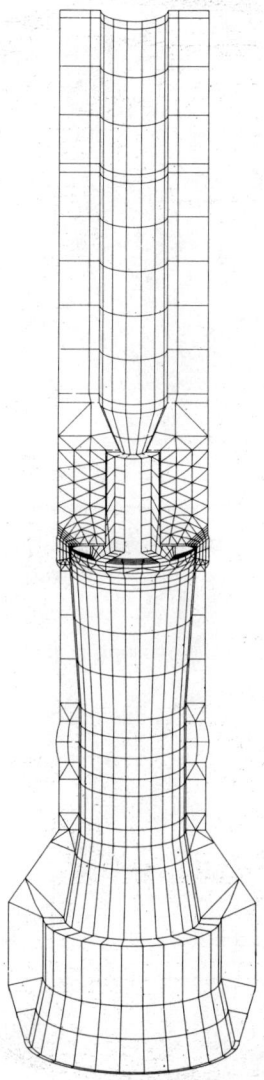

Fig. 4. FUEL ELEMENT, mesh generated by GIBI, 3-D massive analysis carried out by BILBO

INCA is able to solve the eigenvalue and harmonic response problems.

The loadings can be axisymmetric or not (the solution is found by the decomposition of the loading in terms of coefficients of a Fourier's series).

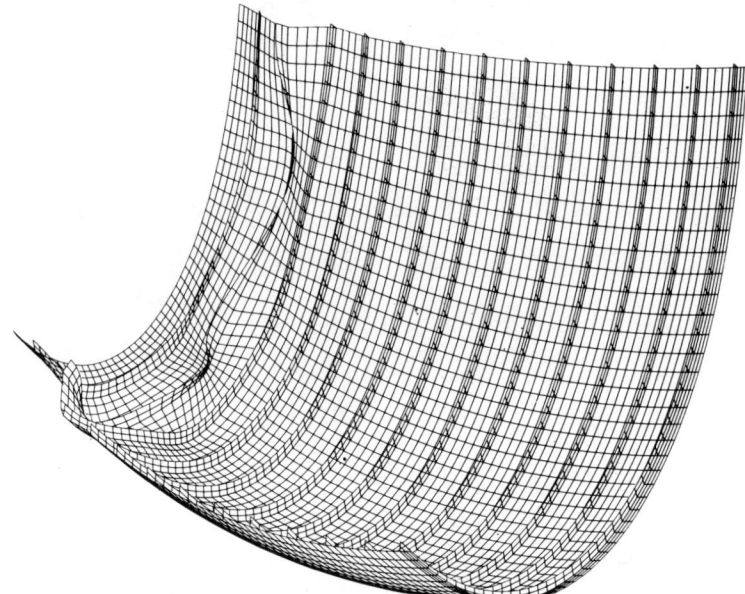

Fig. 5. STIFFENED TORUS, buckling analysis with INCA

Figures 5 and 6 show two application examples of INCA, stiffened torus buckling analysis (Fig. 5) and an imperfect cylinder under axial compression (Fig. 6).

BILBO[3,5,9] can do the same analysis as INCA with a 3-D geometry (with permanent or transient heat transfer analysis). One special element is the thick shell which takes into account the shear stresses. The analysis is possible with the substructuring technique without theoretical limitation on the number of condensation levels.

Just one word on the plasticity model, in order to reduce the computer time, for shell or beam elements we can choose between two formulations. The global model is more economical. The membrane forces and the bending forces are decoupled. The local model is more exact: there are some integration points across the thickness of the shell or the beam. Some typical analysis examples of BILBO are shown in Figs. 7 to 9.

TEDEL[6,7,9] is the module for analysis of piping systems or structural frameworks. The types of material behaviour are the same as in INCA or BILBO a special stress upon the global model for plasticity or creep. TEDEL is very efficient for the whip analysis with non conservative loadings, and is able to perform the modal analysis of acoustico-mechanical vibrations and to study the acoustico mechanical response to various loadings in a pipe with an internal fluid[10]. A typical analysis is shown in Fig. 10.

A special module allows the spectral analysis according to the NRC Regulatory Guide (quadratic combination of stresses) with if necessary different motions of different supports (multi spectral analysis).

PLEXUS[8] is specialized for high-speed dynamic computations (shocks, blasts, impacts) for 2-D or 3-D structures with or without fluids (initial velocity greater than 400 m/s). The mixed Eulerian-Lagrangian formulation is being developed (first in 2-D).

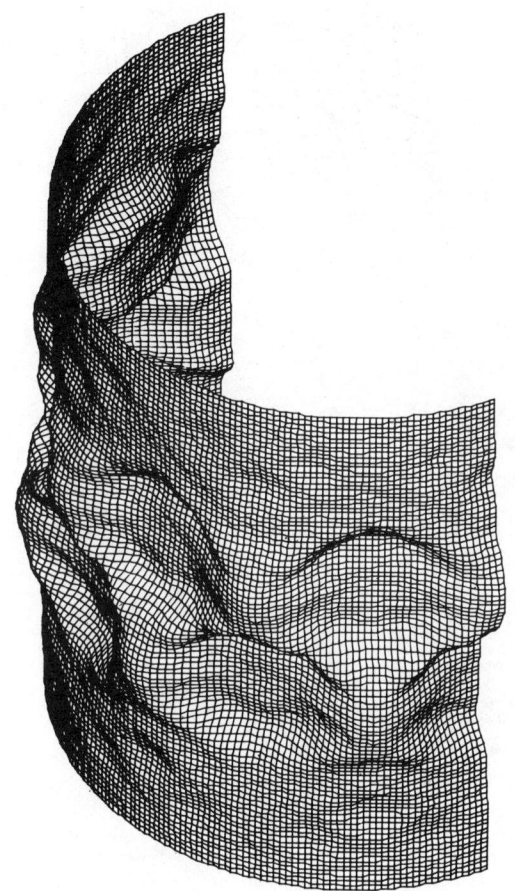

Fig. 6. IMPERFECT CYLINDER under axial compression. Mesh generated by COCO. Imperfect axisymmetric analysis by INCA

For this moment it is a Lagrangian code using the finite element method. The time discretization is explicit. This allows lower costs than with an implicit code when the time step is small. The types of behaviour are various:

- Perfect Plasticity (Von Mises and Drucker - Prager criteria).
- Plasticity with isotropic hardening.
- Specialized model for soil and concrete.
- Sodium water reaction.

Fluids can be viscous or not and anisotropic or not.

In an analysis, the time step is computed by the program according to the geometry and the mechanical datas. The computation of two impact cases are shown

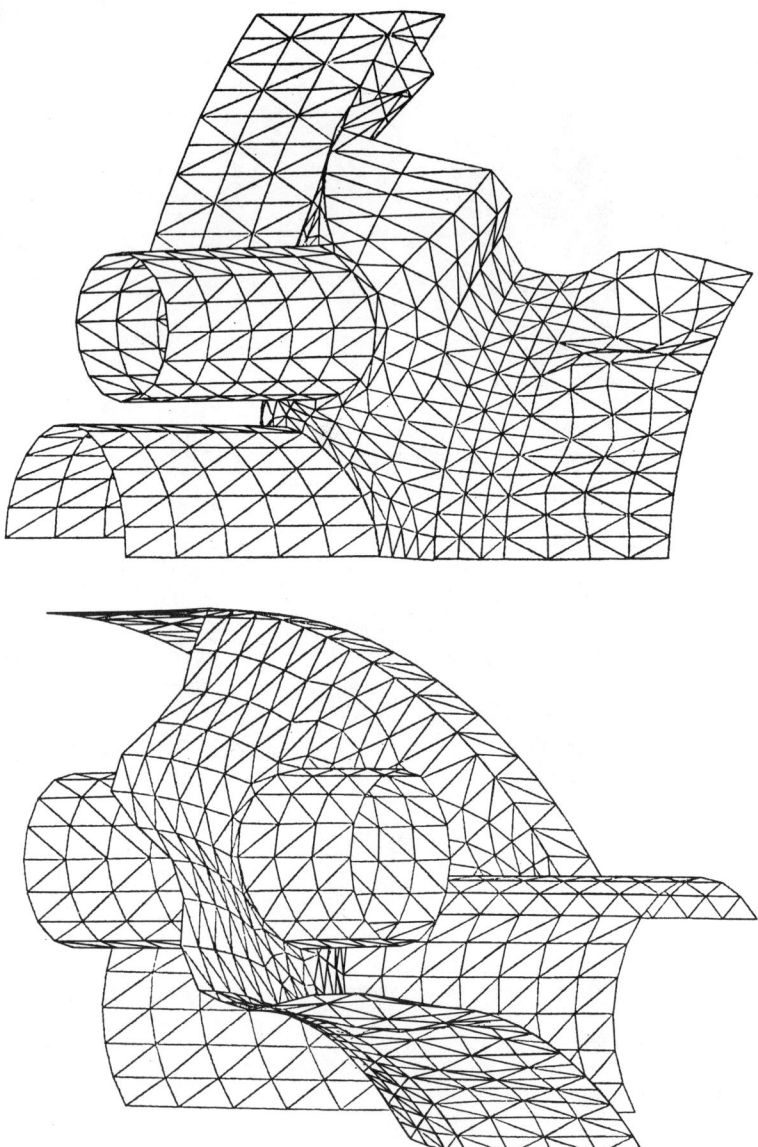

Fig. 7. 3-D buckling analysis with BILBO TORUS, internal structure of the superphenix nuclear reactor

in Figs. 11 and 12.

ALICE is a general interactive and batch graphic post processor for the structures in two or three dimensions. It allows selection and/or combination of results. These can be visualized as:

CASTEM: Finite Element System

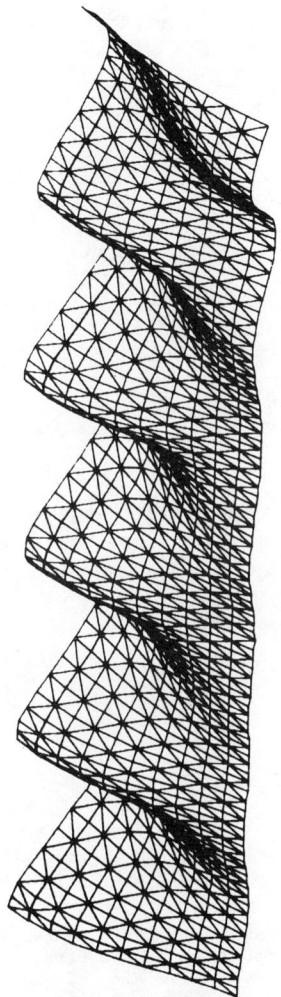

Fig. 8. IMPERFECT CYLINDER under axial compression, calculated by BILBO

- Deformed shapes (with different points of view and hidden lines).
- Iso curves (stresses, displacements and temperatures...).
- Curves of variation (along a line or function of the time or the frequency).

TRISTANA performs modal superposition from results obtained with the other modules using the substructure technique. The eigenvalue problem is solved by the free interface method, in taking into account the influence of neglected modes.

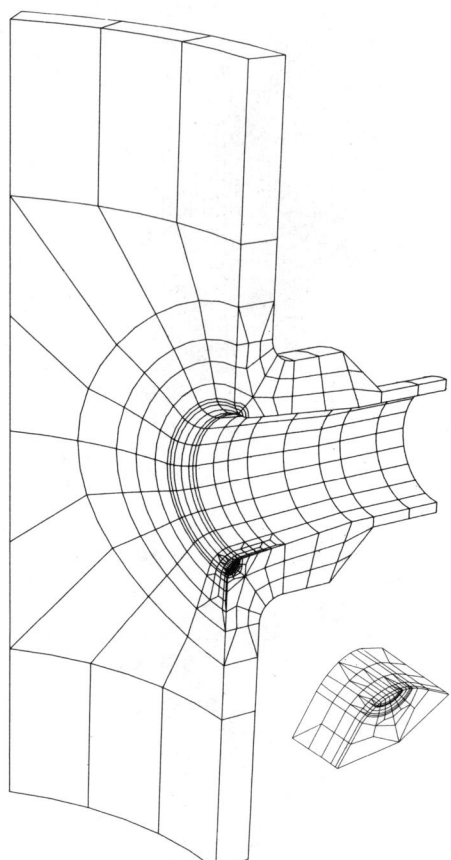

Fig. 9. Outlet nozzle of PWR reactor. Fracture mechanic analysis of a voluntary generated crack, calculated by BILBO

MAYA is a special 2-D post processor for the studies in fracture mechanics (Fig. 13). It allows the determination of the stress intensity factor by extrapolation of displacements in the vicinity of the crack tip and also the evaluation of the Rice integral J.

COMPUTER IMPLEMENTATION

The CASTEM system has been developed on the IBM computer. Now, it is developed on the both systems IBM and CRAY. Its major implementation: IBM/168 and 3033 (CISI network) CRAY (CISI network) CDC 7600 and 6600 CYBER, UNIVAC, IRIS80. Some parts of this system are available on mini computers as VAX, PRIME.

You can access to this system only through the CISI network.

CASTEM: Finite Element System 45

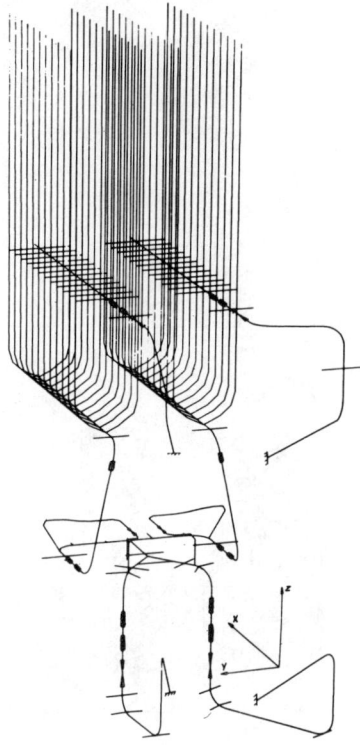

Fig. 10. Seismic analysis of a heat generator calculated by TEDEL

SOME USERS

CASTEM has many users in all the engineering industries (nuclear, civil, naval, aerospace...) as shown in reference 11.

AIR LIQUIDE	METRAVIB
BABCOCK and WILCOX	NEYRPIC
CEA	NOVATOME
CNEN	SACM
CNIM	SNIAS
COMEX	SOCOTEC
CREUSOT LOIRE	STCAN
EDF	STEIN INDUSTRIE
FRAMATOME	TECHNIP
GENERAL ATOMIC	THOMSON BRANDT
JEUMONT SCHNEIDER	BUREAU VERITAS

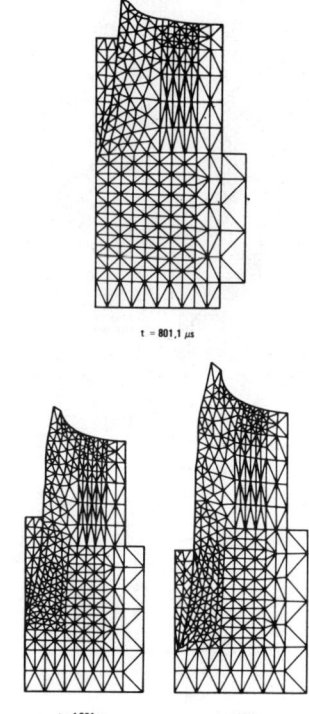

Fig. 11. Impact of a missile in a concrete map calculated by PLEXUS

CASTEM: Finite Element System 47

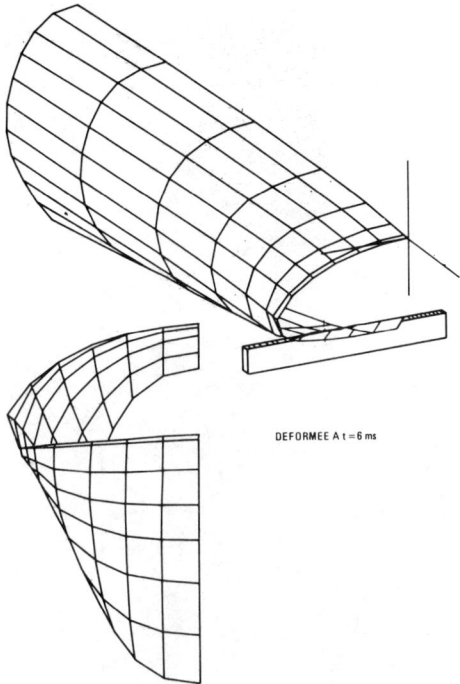

Fig. 12. Pipe impact calculated by PLEXUS

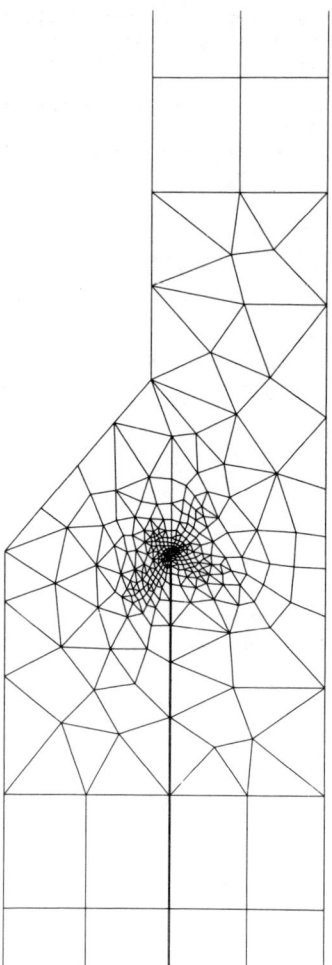

Fig. 13. Crack tip analysis of a fracture mechanics specimen.
Analysis carried out by MAYA

REFERENCES

*1. Hoffmann, A. *et al.* CASTEM - A system of finite element programs, Porto-Alegre, 1978
*2. Hoffmann, A. CASTEM - A general finite element system, CAFEM 1981.
*3. Mezieres, A. *et al.* Post Buckling of axisymmetric and three-dimensional shells, 6th SMIRT 1981.
*4. Chantant, M. *et al.* A solution of unilateral contact problems by means of Lagrange multipler and Frank Wolfe Algorithm, 6th SMIRT 1981.
*5. Combescure, A. *et al.* Non-linear analyses of shells, 5th SMIRT 1979.
*6. Garcia, Jl. *et al.* Studies of Pipe Whip and Impact, 6th SMIRT 1981.
*7. Ricard, A. Tube Collapse Analysis using Finite Element Method, Fenomech'81.
*8. Chavant, C. PLEXUS: A general computer code for explicit Lagrangian Computation. 5th SMIRT 1979.

9. Combescure, A. *et al*. Fluid-structure interaction: A general method used in the CEASEMT (CASTEM) Computer programs. International Conference on Engineering Application of the FEM - 1979 Computers and Structures, Vol. *12*, pp. 421-474.
10. Gibert, R. Methode d'analyse vibratoire des tuyauteries. Revue Francaise de Mecanique no. 79, 1981.
*11. Proceedings of the second users group meeting, CISI, 24 June 1981.

---

*Documents which can be obtained from the authors.

ELASTODYNAMICS (2D): APPLICATIONS OF A BOUNDARY ELEMENT PROGRAM

M. Kitahara* and K. Nakagawa**

Department of Ocean Civil Engineering, Tokai University, Shimizu, Shizuoka, Japan
**Fuyo Data Processing & Systems Development Inc., Tokyo, Japan*

ABSTRACT

The purpose of ELASTODYNAMICS(2D) is to analyze the elastodynamic radiation and/or scattering problems for the piecewise homogeneous elastic body. Especially, this program is suited to elastodynamic analysis of underground structures such as nuclear power plant, oil reservoirs and tunnels in a semi-infinite domain. Of course, ground structures such as a dam or a building are also advantageously treated. Typical application field of this program is the earthquake response analysis of structures for a given earthquake record.

ELASTODYNAMICS(2D) is based on the boundary element method and has the following features:

(1) Quadratic isoparametric element is used in order to calculate the peripheral stress and strain with sufficient accuracy.

(2) Dynamic response is obatined not only for the time-harmonic case but also for the transient case. In the transient analysis, the excitation can be an incident wave with arbitrary time history such as earthquake records.

(3) The effect of a semi-infinite boundary is analytically included by assuming that the scattered wave is a Rayleigh wave on the free surface at a large distance from the structure.

(4) Analytical expression in the low frequency range is introduced in order to have a stable response at low frequency.

THEORETICAL BACKGROUND

The method of analysis is based on the Fourier transformed method. First, we solve the boundary integral equations in the transformed steady-state. Then, we can use the FFT algorithm in order to have the transient solution. The following is the brief description of the method. More detailed treatment is given in references 1-3.

The governing (Navier-Cauchy) equation for elastodynamics has the following form

$$\mu\Delta\mathbf{u} + (\lambda + \mu)\nabla\nabla\cdot\mathbf{u} + \rho\mathbf{b} = \rho\ddot{\mathbf{u}} \tag{1}$$

The Fourier transform pair is defined as follows

$$\left.\begin{array}{l}\hat{\mathbf{u}}(\mathbf{X},\omega) = \dfrac{1}{2\pi}\displaystyle\int_{-\infty}^{\infty} \mathbf{u}(\mathbf{X},t)e^{i\omega t}\,dt \\[6pt] \mathbf{u}(\mathbf{X},t) = \displaystyle\int_{-\infty}^{\infty} \hat{\mathbf{u}}(\mathbf{X},\omega)e^{-i\omega t}\,d\omega\end{array}\right\}. \tag{2}$$

In the Fourier transformed domain, i.e., in the steady-state, the governing equation is reduced to

$$\rho\left[c_T^2 \Delta \mathbf{1} + (c_L^2 - c_T^2)\nabla\nabla + \omega^2 \mathbf{1}\right]\hat{\mathbf{u}}(\mathbf{X},\omega) = -\rho\hat{\mathbf{b}}(\mathbf{X},\omega) \tag{3}$$

where $c_L = \sqrt{(\lambda+2\mu)/\rho}$ and $c_T = \sqrt{\mu/\rho}$. The boundary conditions are

$$\left.\begin{array}{ll}\hat{\mathbf{u}}(\mathbf{x},\omega) = \hat{\mathbf{f}}(\mathbf{x},\omega) & \mathbf{x}\in\partial D_1 \\[4pt] \hat{\mathbf{t}}(\mathbf{x},\omega) \equiv \overset{n}{T}\hat{\mathbf{u}}(\mathbf{x},\omega) \equiv \lambda\mathbf{n}(\nabla\cdot\hat{\mathbf{u}}) + \mu\mathbf{n}\cdot(\nabla\hat{\mathbf{u}} + \hat{\mathbf{u}}\nabla) \\[4pt] \qquad\qquad = \hat{\mathbf{g}}(\mathbf{x},\omega) & \mathbf{x}\in\partial D_2\end{array}\right\}.$$

Furthermore, if the total displacement field $\hat{\mathbf{u}}^T$ is separated into the sum of the incident wave $\hat{\mathbf{u}}^I$ and the scattered wave $\hat{\mathbf{u}}^S$, i.e.,

$$\hat{\mathbf{u}}(\mathbf{X},\omega) = \hat{\mathbf{u}}^I(\mathbf{X},\omega) + \hat{\mathbf{u}}^S(\mathbf{X},\omega), \tag{5}$$

the scattered wave $\hat{\mathbf{u}}^S$ must satisfy the regularity and the radiation conditions:

$$\left.\begin{array}{l}\dfrac{\partial \hat{\mathbf{u}}^{SL}}{\partial r} - ik_L \hat{\mathbf{u}}^{SL} = O(r^{-(m-1)/2}),\quad \hat{\mathbf{u}}^{SL} = O(r^{-(m-3)/2}) \\[8pt] \dfrac{\partial \hat{\mathbf{u}}^{SS}}{\partial r} - ik_T \hat{\mathbf{u}}^{SS} = O(r^{-(m-1)/2}),\quad \hat{\mathbf{u}}^{SS} = O(r^{-(m-3)/2})\end{array}\right\} \tag{6}$$

at infinity, where $\hat{\mathbf{u}}^{SL}$ and $\hat{\mathbf{u}}^{SS}$ are lamellar and solenoidal parts of $\hat{\mathbf{u}}^S$, respectively. Moreover, $k_L = \omega/c_L$, $k_T = \omega/c_T$, and m is the dimension of the space.

Green's (Somigliana's) formula for steady-state elastodynamics is well established, i.e.,

$$\int_{\partial D}\mathbf{U}(\mathbf{X},\mathbf{y})\hat{\mathbf{t}}(\mathbf{y})dS_y - \int_{\partial D}\mathbf{T}(\mathbf{X},\mathbf{y})\hat{\mathbf{u}}(\mathbf{y})dS_y + \hat{\mathbf{u}}^I(\mathbf{x}) = \begin{cases}\hat{\mathbf{u}}(\mathbf{X}) & \mathbf{X}\in D \quad (7)\\ 0 & \mathbf{X}\in D^c \quad (8)\end{cases}$$

where D^c is the complementary domain of D and we rewrote $\hat{\mathbf{u}}(\mathbf{y},\omega)$ and $\hat{\mathbf{t}}(\mathbf{y},\omega)$ as $\hat{\mathbf{u}}(\mathbf{y})$ and $\hat{\mathbf{t}}(\mathbf{y})$ for simplicity. The fundamental solution has the following form

$$\mathbf{U}(\mathbf{X},\mathbf{Y}) = \dfrac{i}{4\mu}\left[H_0^{(1)}(k_T r)\mathbf{1} + \dfrac{1}{k_T^2}\nabla\nabla\{H_0^{(1)}(k_T r) - H_0^{(1)}(k_L r)\}\right] \tag{9}$$

for the two-dimensional elastodynamics and $H_0^{(1)}(\cdot)$ is the zero order Hankel function of the first kind. Furthermore, the double layer kernel $\mathbf{T}$ is defined as

$$\mathbf{T}(\mathbf{X},\mathbf{y}) = \mathbf{U}(\mathbf{X},\mathbf{y})\overset{n_y}{T} \tag{10}$$

ELASTODYNAMICS(2D): Applications of a Boundary Element Program 53

where $\hat{T}^n$ is defined in eq. (4). It should be noted that the fundamental solution in eq. (9) is chosen so as to satisfy the radiation condition in eq. (6). If we take the limit from D^c (or D) to ∂D in eq. (8) (or in eq. (7)), we have the following boundary formula:

$$C\hat{u}(x) = \int_{\partial D} U(x,y)\hat{t}(y)dSy - \int_{\partial D} T(x,y)\hat{u}(y)dSy + \hat{u}^I(x), \quad x\varepsilon\partial D \qquad (11)$$

Necessary information to obtain the solution of eq. (11) for the given incident wave and the given boundary data can be found in aforementioned references in detail.

FIELD OF APPLICATION

Geometrical configuration. This program deals with the two-dimensional elastodynamic response of structures in a semi-infinite or a full space. The geometry of the structure is arbitrary.

Materials. Materials are assumed to be linear elastic ones. Of course, we can analyze the piecewise homogeneous case. Namely, the elastic property of the structure can be different from the foundation. Also, plane strain is assumed.

Analysis capabilities. Typical application field is the earthquake response analysis of structures in (or on) a semi-infinite foundation. The effect of a semi-infinite boundary is analytically included by assuming that the scattered wave is a Rayleigh wave on the free surface at a large distance from the structure. After having the time-harmonic (steady) response, we can calculate the transient response by using the FFT algorithm.

Loadings. The loading is the plane incident wave coming from infinity. It may be a step pressure wave. Time history of the incident wave is arbitrary. Therefore, we can use the observed earthquake record (displacement or acceleration) as the incident wave.

PROGRAM DESCRIPTION

Method. The method is based on the boundary element method (or boundary integral equation method) as described in the theoretical background.

Type of elements. Quadratic isoparametric elements are adopted in order to calculate the peripheral stress and strain in the sufficient accuracy.

Program structure. Language of the program is FORTRAN and the procedure of input of data is quite simple in this BEM program. The subprogram and their relations are briefly shown in Table 1.

Subprograms MAIN01∿MAIN04 are all independent. Input data for MAIN02∿MAIN04 are transferred by disc.

HARDWARE COMPATIBILITIES

Minimal configuration of materials. This program requires card reader, CPU, disc, line printer and plotter.

Type of computers. This program works on FUJITSHU, HITACHI, UNIVAC, IBM or other compatible machines.

Peripherals. CALCOMP plotter package is used.

TABLE 1 Subprograms and their Relations

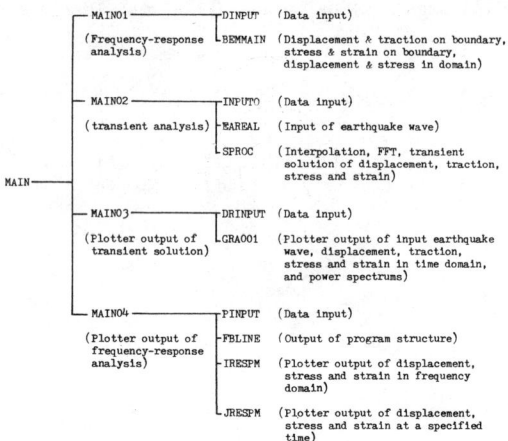

Operating system. Standard operating system on which FORTRAN IV works is used.

Media. Magnetic tape is available.

EXAMPLES OF APPLICATION

Basic Test Analysis. We consider the circular hole with radius a in an infinite elastic body. The number of boundary elements is 24. Figure 1 shows the

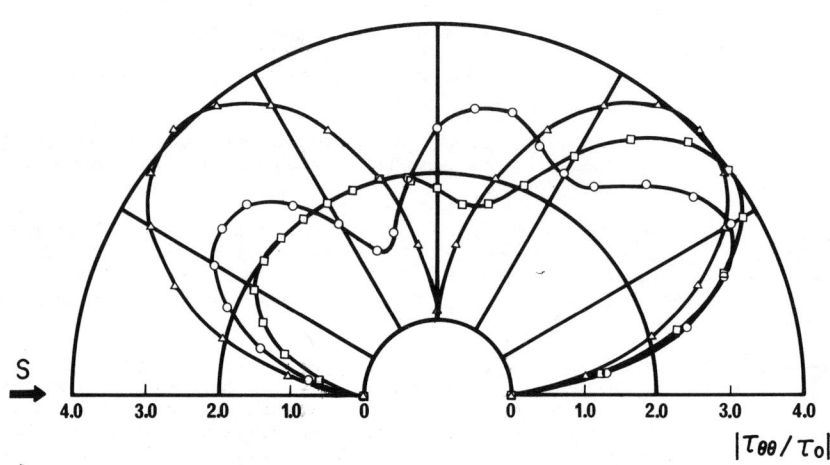

Fig. 1. Distribution of hoop stress $|\tau_{\theta\theta}/\tau_0|$ (——: see reference 4; Δ, ,o: BEM; Δ: $ak_T = 0.1$, : $ak_T = 1.0$, o: $ak_T = 1.5$)

ELASTODYNAMICS(2D): Applications of a Boundary Element Program 55

distribution of hoop stress $|\tau_{\theta\theta}/\tau_o|$ on the boundary for nondimensional shear wave numbers ak_T = 0.1, 1.0, and 1.5. Where τ_o is the stress induced by the incident transverse (S) wave. Figure 2 shows the distribution of hoop stress

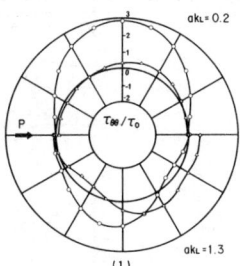

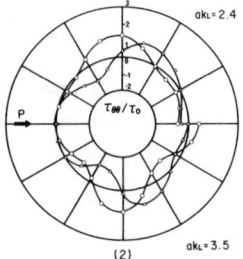

Fig. 2. Distribution of hoop stress $\tau_{\theta\theta}/\tau_o$ (——: see reference 5; O, Δ: BEM; O: real part, Δ: imaginary part)

$\tau_{\theta\theta}/\tau_o$ for ak_L = 0.2, 1.3, 2.4, and 3.5. The incident wave is the harmonic plane longitudinal (P) wave. Figure 3 shows the hoop stress $\tau_{\theta\theta}/\tau_o$ at point θ = 90° for the range of 0 ≤ ak_L ≤ 4. Figure 4 shows the transient displacements on the boundary for the nondimensional time $C_L t/2a$. The incident wave is the longitudinal stress step (P) wave with the intensty σ_o. Figure 5 shows the transient hoop stress at θ = 180°. From these results, we can see that both of the steady-state and transient solutions have good accuracy.

Practical Examples in Industry. We show the dynamic behavior of rock tunnel. In more detail, see reference 8. Figure 6 shows the general view of the tunnel and the location of the measuring instruments. Figure 7 shows the cross-section of that tunnel.

Figure 8 shows the deformation of the tunnel for $L/2R_1$ = 10.0. Where L is the wavelength of the incident wave and R_1 is the radius of arch crown. The incident angle (θ) of the incident S wave is 45°. In this example, constant element is used and the number of elements is 66 on the lining surface. The number of subregions is two.

Figures 9 and 10 show the dynamic strains on the surface of the tunnel for D/L = o.01 and 0.13. Where D is the width of the tunnel and L is the wavelength of the incident wave. Figures 11 and 12 show the dynamic strain amplification factor $\varepsilon_{\theta\theta}/\gamma_o$ for D/L. Where $\varepsilon_{\theta\theta}$ is the dynamic circumferential strain on the surface and γ_o is the strain induced by the incident wave. From Figs. 11 and 12, it can be observed that the dynamic strain amplification factors are almost constant when D/L is less than 0.05. This means that the strain state is almost

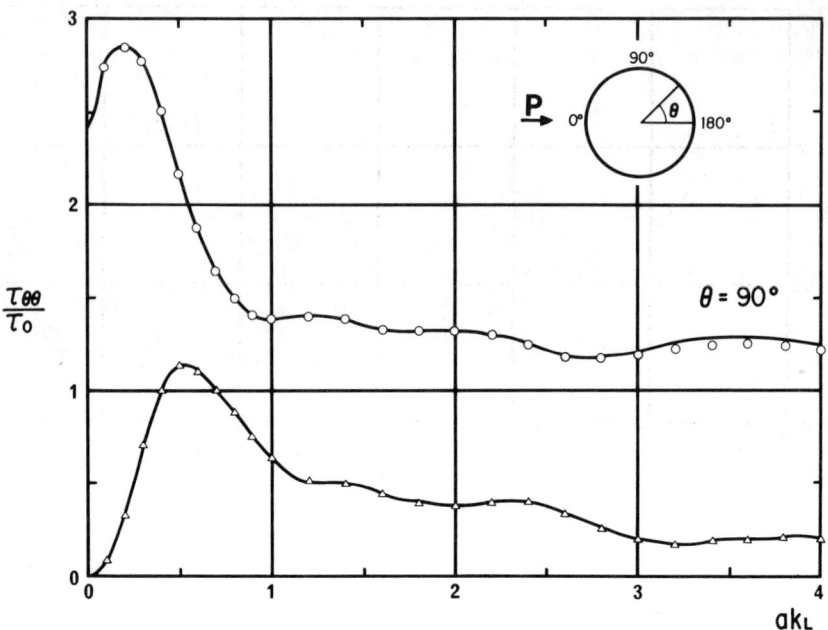

Fig. 3. Hoop stress $\tau_{\theta\theta}/\theta_0$ at $\theta = 90°$ (———: see reference 5; O, △: BEM; O: real part, △: imaginary part)

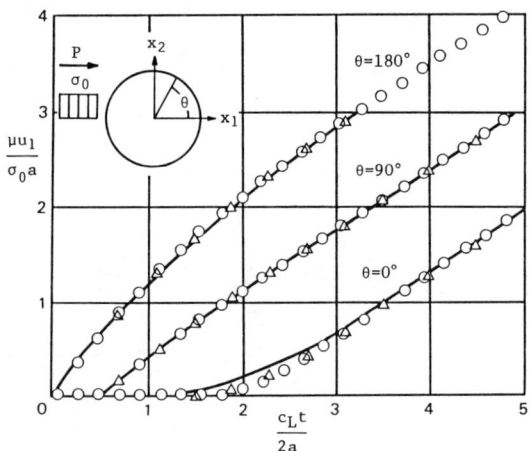

Fig. 4. Transient displacements at $\theta = 0°$, $90°$ and $180°$ (———: see reference 6, △: see reference 7, O: BEM)

static when $D/L < 0.05$. In these examples, quadratic isoparametric element is used. The number of elements is 21 and the number of nodes is 42.

ELASTODYNAMICS (2D): Applications of a Boundary Element Program   57

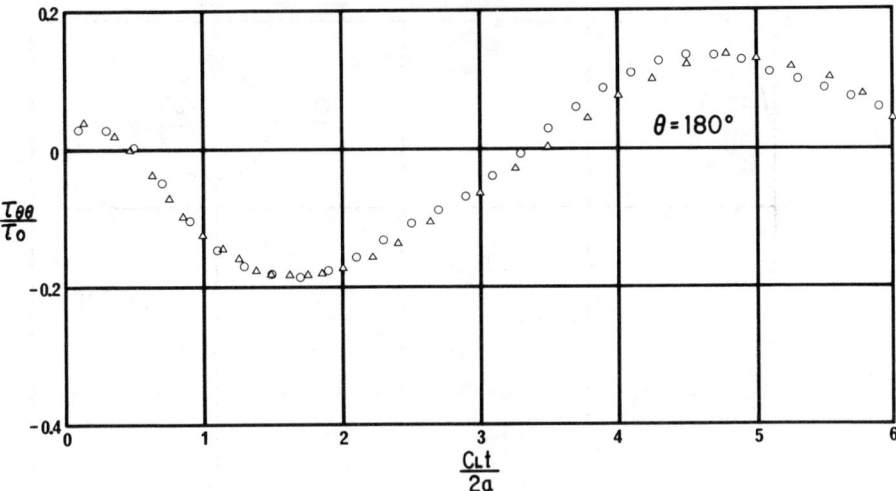

Fig. 5. Transient hoop stress at $\theta = 180°$ ($\triangle$: see reference 7, $\circ$: BEM)

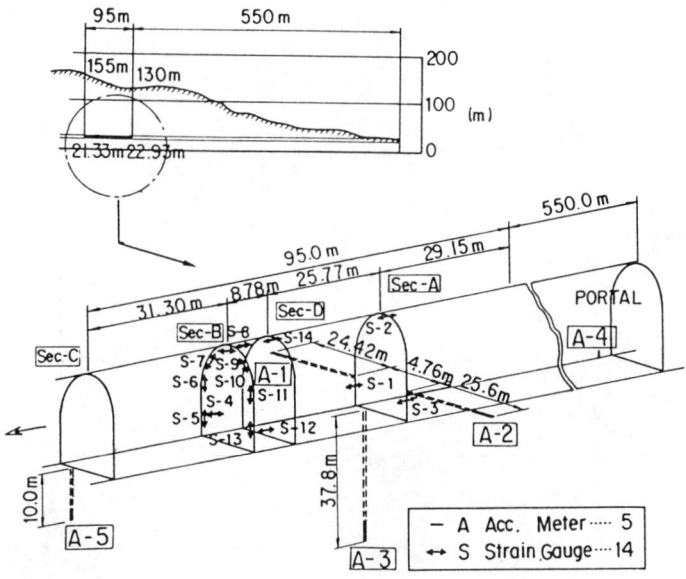

Fig. 6. General view of tunnel and location of measuring instruments

In the last example, the earthquake record is used as the incident wave and the transient analysis is carried out. Figure 13 shows the incident P and S waves. These wave components were estimated from the acceleration records of aftershock in Miyagiken-Oki earthquake. Figure 14 shows the comparison between the calculated dynamic strains and the measured ones at the point S6 on a side wall. In this calculation, quadratic isoparametric element is used. The number of

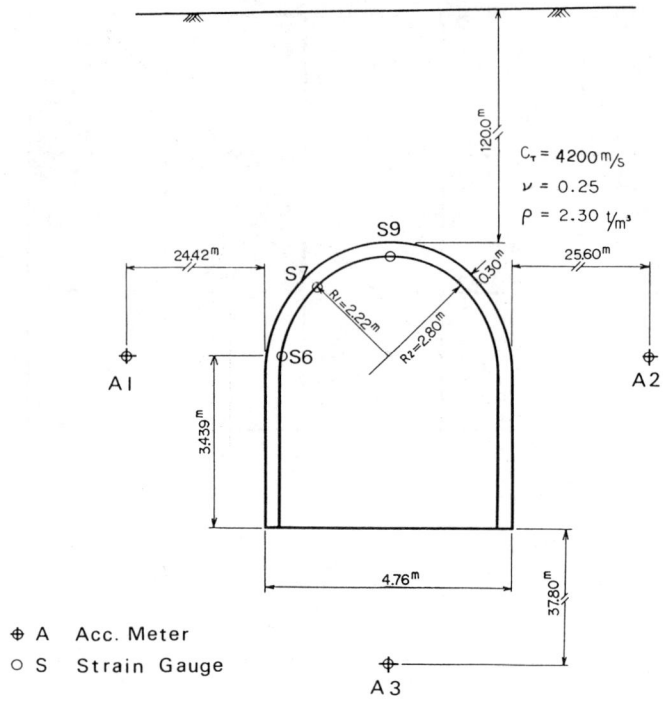

Fig. 7. Cross-section of tunnel

elements is 21 and the number of nodes is 42.

ELASTODYNAMICS(2D): Applications of a Boundary Element Program 59

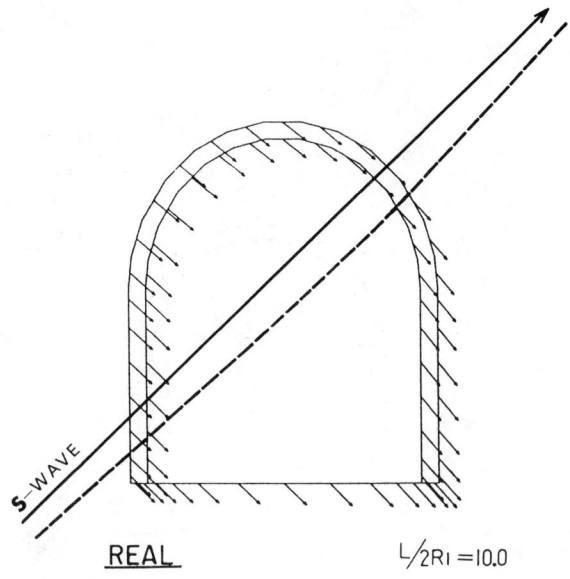

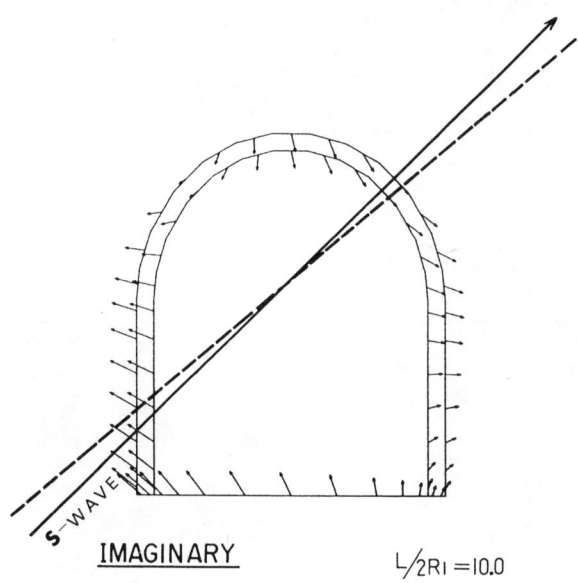

Fig. 8. Deformation of tunnel (angle of incidence: $\theta = 45°$)

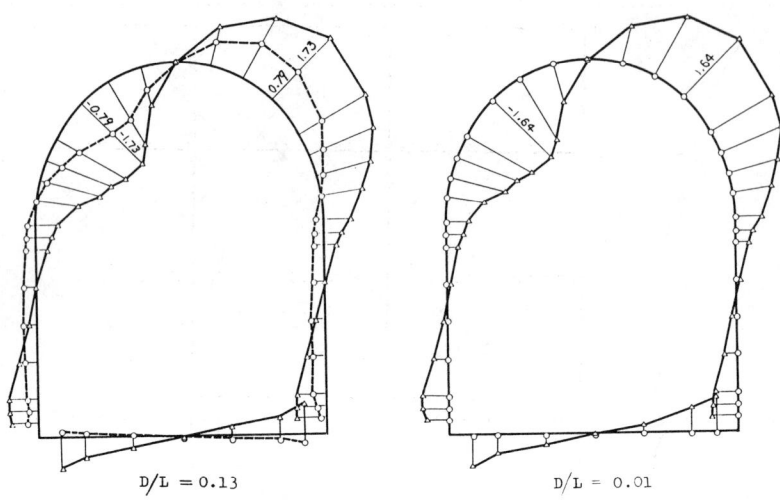

Fig. 9. Distribution of circumferential strain for vertical S wave incidence: θ = 0° (O: real part, Δ: imaginary part)

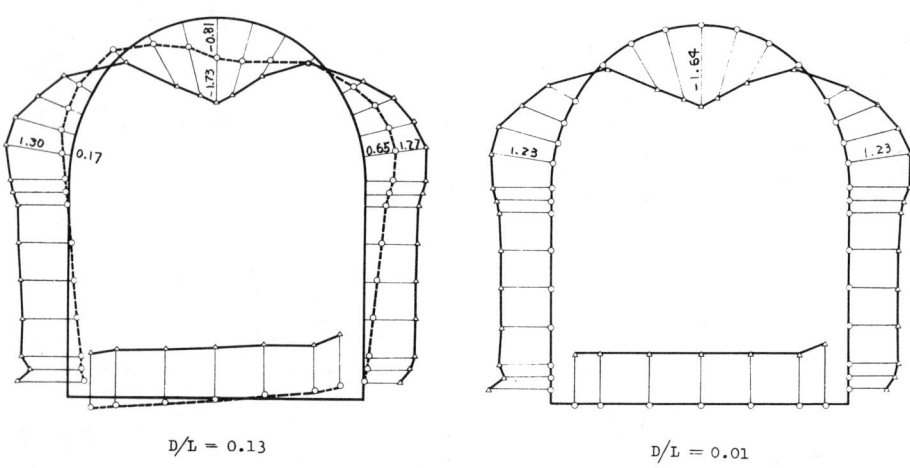

Fig. 10. Distribution of circumferential strain for inclined S wave incidence: θ = 45° (O: real part, Δ: imaginary part)

ELASTODYNAMICS(2D): Applications of a Boundary Element Program 61

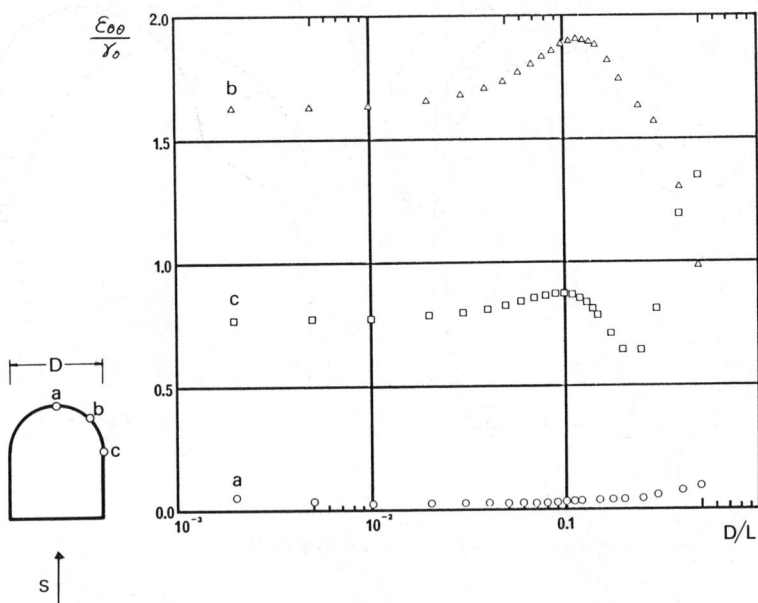

Fig. 11. Dynamic strain amplification factor for $\theta = 0°$

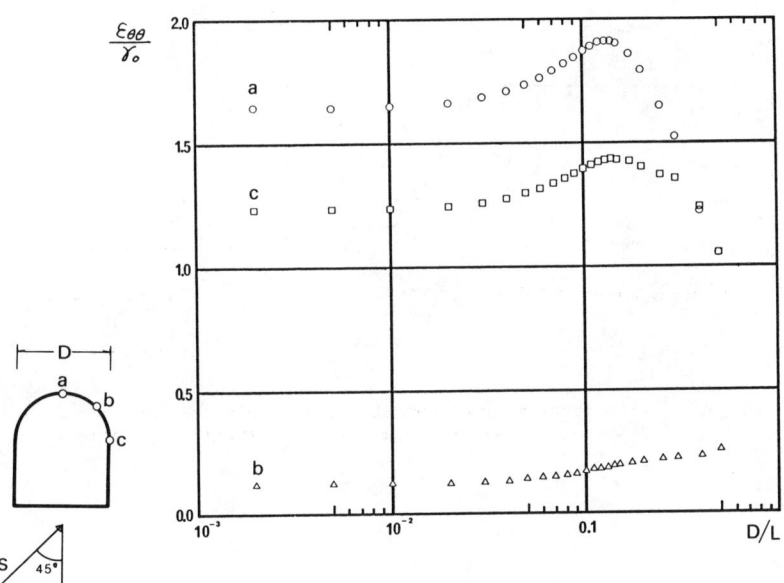

Fig. 12. Dynamic strain amplification factor for $\theta = 45°$

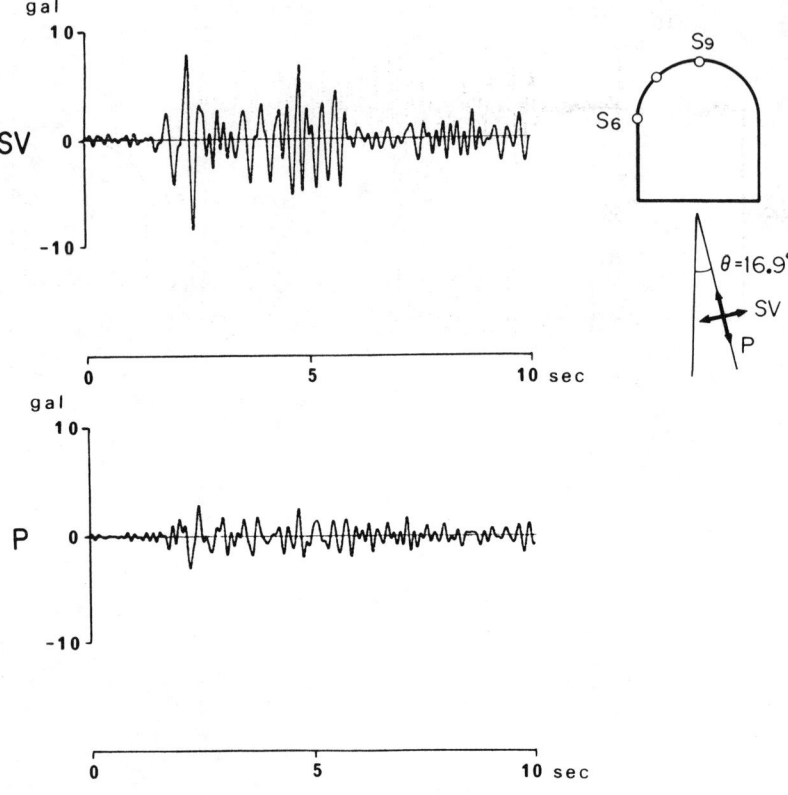

Fig. 13. Incident S and P wave

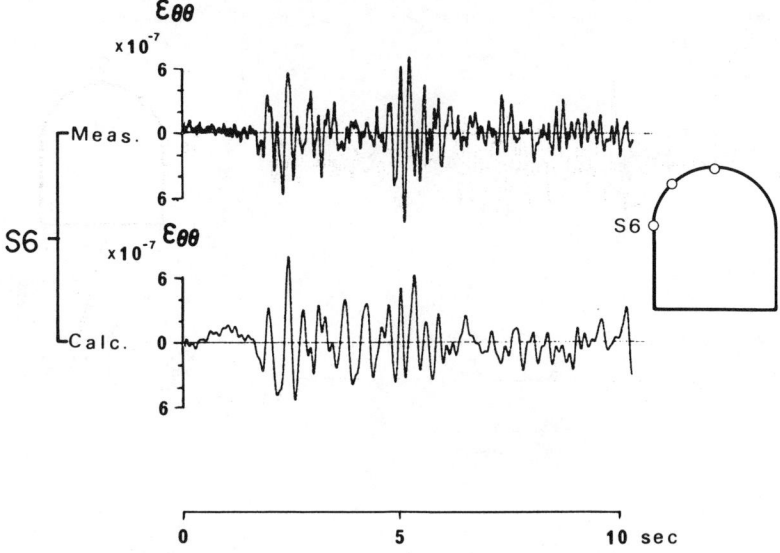

Fig. 14. Measured and calculated strains at point S6 on the side wall

REFERENCES

1. Kobayashi, S. and N. Nishimura (1982) Transient stress analysis of tunnels and caverns of arbitrary shape due to travelling waves. In: Banerjee, P. K. and R. P. Shaw (eds.). *Developments in Boundary Element Methods*, vol. 2. *Applied Science*, pp. 177-21o.

2. Niwa, Y., M. Kitahara and H. Ikeda (1984) The BIE approach to transient wave propagation problems around elastic inclusion. *Theoret. Appl. Mech. 32*, 183-198.

3. Kitahara, M., M. Hamada, K. Nakagawa and Y. Muranishi (1984) Transient wave fields around elastic inclusions in a semi-infinite foundation, *Proc. 6th Int. Conf. Boundary Element Methods in Engineering*, July 3-8, Southampton-New York.

4. Mow, C. C. and L. J. Mente (1963) Dynamic stresses and displacements around cylindrical discontinuities due to plane harmonic shear waves. *J. Appl. Mech., 30*, 598-604.

5. Pao, Y. H. (1962) Dynamic stress concentration in an elastic plate. *J. Appl. Mech., 29*, 299-305.

6. Baron, M. L. and R. Parnes (1962) Displacements and velocities produced by the diffraction of a pressure wave by a cylindrical cavity in an elastic medium. *J. Appl. Mech., 29*, 385-395.

7. Garnet, H. and J. Crouzet-Pascal (1966) Transient response of a circular cylinder of arbitrary thickness, in an elastic medium, to a plane dilatational wave, *J. Appl. Mech., 33*, 521-531.

8. Hamada, M., M. Kitahara, K. Nakagawa and Y. Muranishi (1985) Earthquake

observation and BIE analysis on dynamic behavior of rock cavern. *Proc. 5th Int. Conf. Numerical Methods in Geomechanics*, Nagoya, Japan, April 1-5.

FEMFAM: FINITE ELEMENT ANALYSIS ON DESKTOP COMPUTERS USING THE FEMFAM PACKAGE

J. F. Stelzer

Nuclear Research Centre, KFA, Juelich, D 517 Juelich, Federal Republic of Germany

ABSTRACT

The FEMFAM software comprises four parts: an interactively working preprocessor; a temperature field calculation part for linear and nonlinear, steady-state and transient problems, also considering phase change front propagation; a linear-elastic rigidity calculation part with the elements: truss, beam, plane stress/strain, axisymmetric, bending plate, shell and spatial solid element. The fourth part is a postprocessor for numerical and graphical result representation. The main advantages: pre- and postprocessor fully working in the question- and answer mode, a superior temperature field part, powerful graphical features, dynamic array dimensioning, free format input. In the case of temperature dependent deformations and thermal stresses the temperature field results are automatically transferred to the rigidity calculation part.

STRATEGICAL CONCEPTION AND THEORETICAL BACKGROUND

The FEMFAM software development followed a consequent intention. Some principles were considered to be decisive for a new generation of FEM software. To account some:

(1) FEM is an everyday engineer's tool, therefore, similar to the slide rule, it is best for the engineer to have a computer at his desk-top. He must be free from staying in punching rooms, useless errands to the computer centre, priority problems and JCL,

(2) an engineer must be allowed to concentrate himself on his engineering tasks. A suitable program must work in a way that no computer science is necessary: just switching the computer on and answering questions the program asks. If numbers must be put in then it must be sensible to enter them in a free format. The time necessary to get acquainted with the software must be minimal. High level interactivity is a must. Consequential errors must be checked and reported in a way that is easy to understand,

(3) engineers are men who think visually. This fact gives rise to the need for excellent graphical possibilities,

(4) in today's competitive world and a world which has to save its resources, FEM is a must for medium-sized and small firms, too, which cannot afford a

costly computer centre and the leasing expenses for huge programs. They
should be supplied with perfect software which does not require additional
future costs, and which runs on computers requiring only modest investments.

According to these postulations the existing FEM features and procedures were
screened to select most appropriate software parts. The work started in 1977.
Concerning the hardware, there were not many microcomputers on the market suited
to the proposed task. One of the most promising machines was from Hewlett
Packard, and we decided on this one. By its interactivity-friendly interpreter
technique and excellent graphics, points (1), (3) and (4) were fulfilled
concerning the hardware side. However, on the software side, we had to get along
with the special HP Basic which is very powerful but not transferrable to other
systems. Today, where the environment is more and more dominated by the Unix
system the task to transfer the package to this system has arisen, a task not
yet finished.

FEMFAM utilizes the displacement method. The equation solution is accomplished
using the front method. The rigidity of the package contains, besides a quick
front solver, a subdividing front solver for arbitrary large problems. The
quick front solver is suitable up to a front width of 255. A speciality is the
feature to retain necessary nodes if singularities in the stiffness matrix occur.
In the temperature field part, called FEMFAM-T, for the treatment of nonlinearities
two iteration routines are included which can be called by choice: the direct
iteration method and a complete Newton Raphson procedure.

By using the front method and appropiate external storage memory there are no
limitations in the problem size. The software works economically with the
internal memory, e.g. using the overlay technique.

FIELD OF APPLICATION

The FEMFAM software is especially suited to thermo-mechanical coupled problems.
The temperature part of the package is very powerful. There are several
customers who use the temperature field program only, as they have solely to deal
with temperature problems, like liquid gas equipment factories or manufacturers
of thermal insulation. Therefore, FEMFAM-T may be introduced first. FEMFAM-T
and the rigidity calculation program FEMFAM-F are pure number crunchers fed with
the input of the preprocessor GENFAM.

- *Temperature field calculations with FEMFAM-T*. It can deal with linear and
  nonlinear, steady-state and transient problems. For example, it is possible
  to calculate a 3-D transient temperature field with time-varying internal heat
  sources and convective heat transfer on the surfaces, with heat radiation on
  surfaces and across internal cavities and with temperature dependent
  properties. A temperature field program only needs continuum elements.
  FEMFAM-T has the following: (1) plane, (2) axisymmetric (both quadrilateral)
  and (3) spatial element. The elements can be chosen to be used with linear or
  quadratic interpolation, though the quadratic type is advisable. Thus, curved
  surfaces can be modelled. The quadratic spatial element possesses 20 nodes.

- *Boundary conditions*. The following can be considered: prescribed temperatures
  at certain nodes, i.e. Dirichlet type; and from the Neumann type: (1)
  convection on element surfaces, (2) heat radiation on element surfaces and
  (3) prescribed entering and leaving heat fluxes (e.g. the solar constant).
  Heat radiation across internal cavities can be taken into account and natural
  convection in the cavities, too. It is possible to regard orthotropic
  properties with the thermal conductivity.

- *Nonlinearities*. These concern the temperature dependence of the thermal
  conductivity and, with transient fields, the specific heat capacity. The
  properties must be expressed as functions of the temperature and put in line

by line into the appropriate subprograms. Two examples of these so-called property algorithms can be seen in Figs. 1 and 2. A collection of about 500 property algorithms is delivered with the program. During the calculation for every local element the correct property is calculated. Normally, for the interactive solution the direct iteration routine is recommended. In cases with convergence problems it may be advisable to switch over to the Newton Raphson routine which also is included. It is slower, since, in addition to the stiffness matrix, the tangential stiffness matrix must be established and eliminated which is nonsymmetric. The FEMFAM front solver deals with such matrices, too.

- *Transient temperature fields.* Initial conditions: a start vector with arbitrary temperatures can be taken into account, e.g. the result vector from a former steady-state calculation. Internal heat sources, boundary conditions,

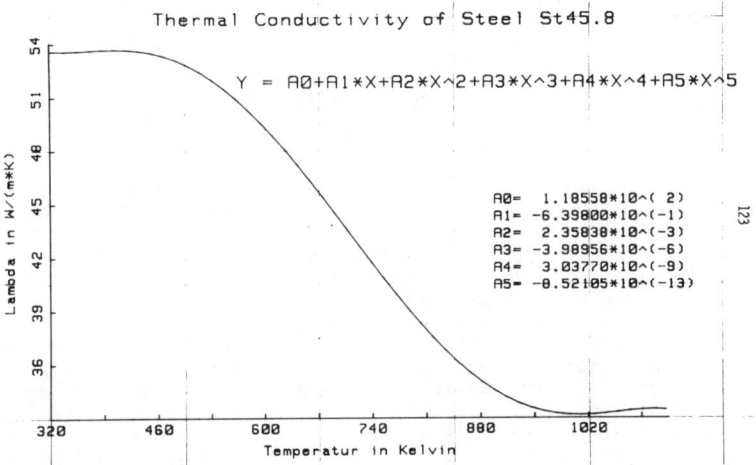

Fig. 1. Example of a property algorithm for the thermal conductivity

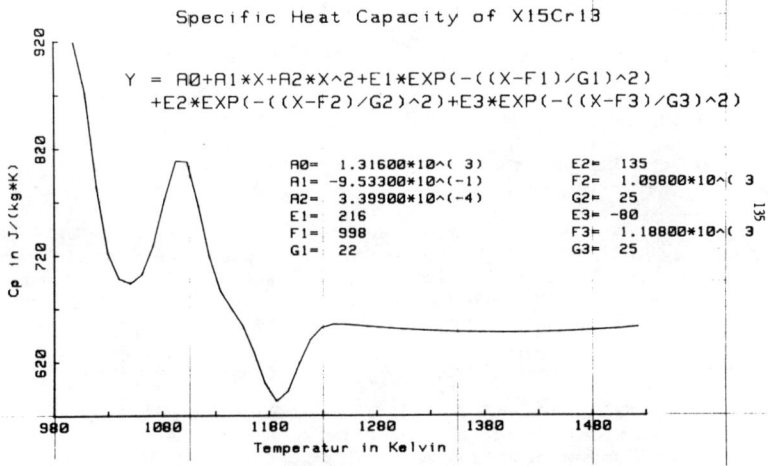

Fig. 2. Example of a property algorithm for the specific heat

ambient temperatures and the time-step width can be changed time-step wise.
Instructions are given on how to relate the geometric and the time
discretization to avoid resulting oscillations. Phase change front propagation
is considered. There are several methods to produce graphical results, see
the postprocessor ERGFAM. The program prints, besides the temperature
listings, the entering and leaving heat fluxes of those surfaces which have
convective heat transfer. These values can be used to determine over-all heat
transfer coefficients (heat transmission coefficients) or heat resistances.
The appropriate procedures are described in the manual. Furthermore, the heat
flux densities are calculated internally at all Gauss points because they can
be used to make an appropriate plot with the local heat flux densities in the
form of arrows. FEMFAM-T is also used for other quasi-harmonic problems, e.g.
for electrostatic problems.

The results of FEMFAM-T can be transferred to FEMFAM-F automatically. Then,
temperature-dependent deformations and stresses can be calculated.

- *Deformation and stress calculation with FEMFAM-F.* This software part considers
linear elastic material properties. The following elements are included: (1)
truss (2- and 3-D), (2) beam (2- and 3-D), (3) plane stress/plane strain
element, (4) axisymmetric element, (5) bending plate, (6) spatial shell, (7)
spatial solid element. Elements (3) to (6) are quadrilateral. They and the
spatial solid element can be chosen to be used with linear or quadratic
interpolation functions. When using the quadratic interpolation, curved edges
and surfaces can be modelled. The quadratic interpolated solids 3-D-element
has 20 nodal points. The different element types can be combined. *Boundary
conditions:* retained nodes and nodes with prescribed displacements in
arbitrary steep planes. *Loads:* nodal load, pressure load, shear load, gravity,
centrifugal load with axisymmetric elements, residual stresses, thermal load
(coupling with the temperature program FEMFAM-T). Consideration of temperature-
dependent properties (Young's modulus, thermal expansion coefficient) by
property algorithms. A lot of such algorithms is found in an appropriate
collection which is delivered with the program. *Deformation energy:* this type
of potential energy is calculated and can be used in a manner which is
described in the manual to solve impact problems and problems of fracture
mechanics. The program works automatically through the prescribed number of
load cases, regarding load factors for different loads. E.g. it can be
instructed that the first load case shall respect all loads, the second one
the thermal loads only, the third one the given pressure loads, the fourth one
the double of the given pressure loads, etc.

Figure 3 shows an example of a property algorithm as used in FEMFAM-F.

THE COMFORTABLE FEMFAM FEATURES

The preprocessor GENFAM and the postprocessor ERGFAM were developed to offer the
user maximum ease of use.

- *GENFAM, the preprocessor.* The above-described program parts, FEMFAM-T and
FEMFAM-F, are number crunch program parts. They work independently from the
user and may run overnight or when the user is absent. On the other hand,
the input program GENFAM and also the postprocessor ERGFAM work through
conversation, guiding the user through the necessary matter.

GENFAM preprocesses the temperature field program FEMFAM-T as well as the
rigidity part FEMFAM-F. In the case of coupling FEMFAM-T and FEMFAM-F, it is
necessary through GENFAM to run again after the temperature calculation to adjust
the mesh to the requirements of the next run. This concerns the different number
of degrees of freedom per node, the physical properties and the loads.

GENFAM works in the inquiry/response mode. It must be specified at the beginning

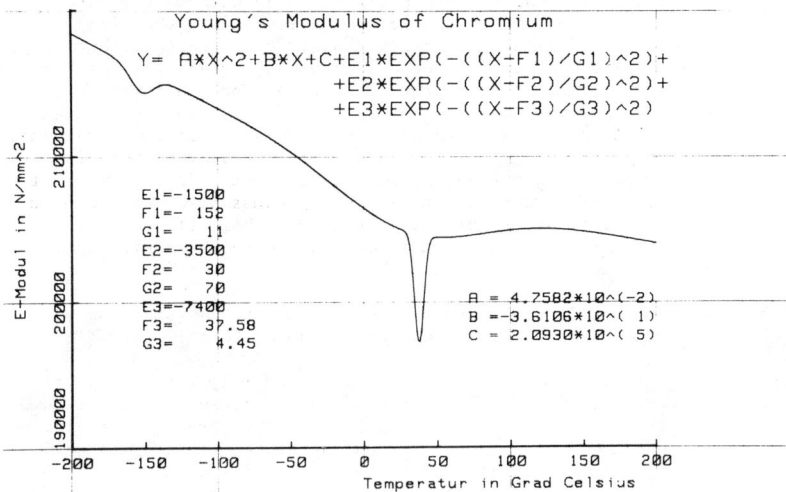

Fig. 3. Example of a property algorithm for Young's modulus

whether the data are to be put in and stored manually; whether starting values, list of nodal points, list of material numbers, node co-ordinates, boundary conditions already exist and, in the affirmative, on which storage device; whether modifications are only to be made on the data already resident in the computer.

If all the data already exists, a large menue appears offering varied possibilities of modifying the mesh, and also: calculation of the storage space required and data check; calling up the mesh generator; input of boundary conditions; generating a graph; front width minimization; mesh transformation, translatory or rotatory; mesh extension by mirroring; combination of two bodies with the possibility of combining as many bodies as desired by means of repetition; insertion or removal of individual elements or nodes. *Calculation of the external storage space required.* This is necessary to provide adequate space for storage. Seven external files are necessary for one rigidity calculation. The arrays are created with record lengths of 256 bytes. The number of records required for each file is printed out. It may thus be seen how many files can be sent to the individual floppy discs or other storage devices.

Data check. This procedure ascertains whether a node number is missing, whether several nodes have the same co-ordinates, whether the same node number appears twice in an element etc.

Mesh generator. Starting out from a number of giant elements, which must be put in by the user with lists of nodal points and co-ordinates, arbitrarily fine and weighted subdivisions are then carried out. In doing so it is also possible to automatically change over from linearly to quadratically interpolated elements, a quality not found with many mesh generators. The operation of the mesh generator is shown in Fig. 4 by means of a simple example. It comprises a machine foundation exposed to asymmetric loads. The final mesh consists of 90 spatial isoparametric 20-node elements (no. 3 in Fig. 4). The plot program also contains the restraints. For generating this mesh the user must only put in the list of nodal points of two elements and 12 node co-ordinates (no. 1). He then uses the mesh generator to subdivide the vertical element nine times, putting in the required weightings. The upper element must be subdivided in the same way and four times in the orthogonal direction (no. 2). A mirroring is then

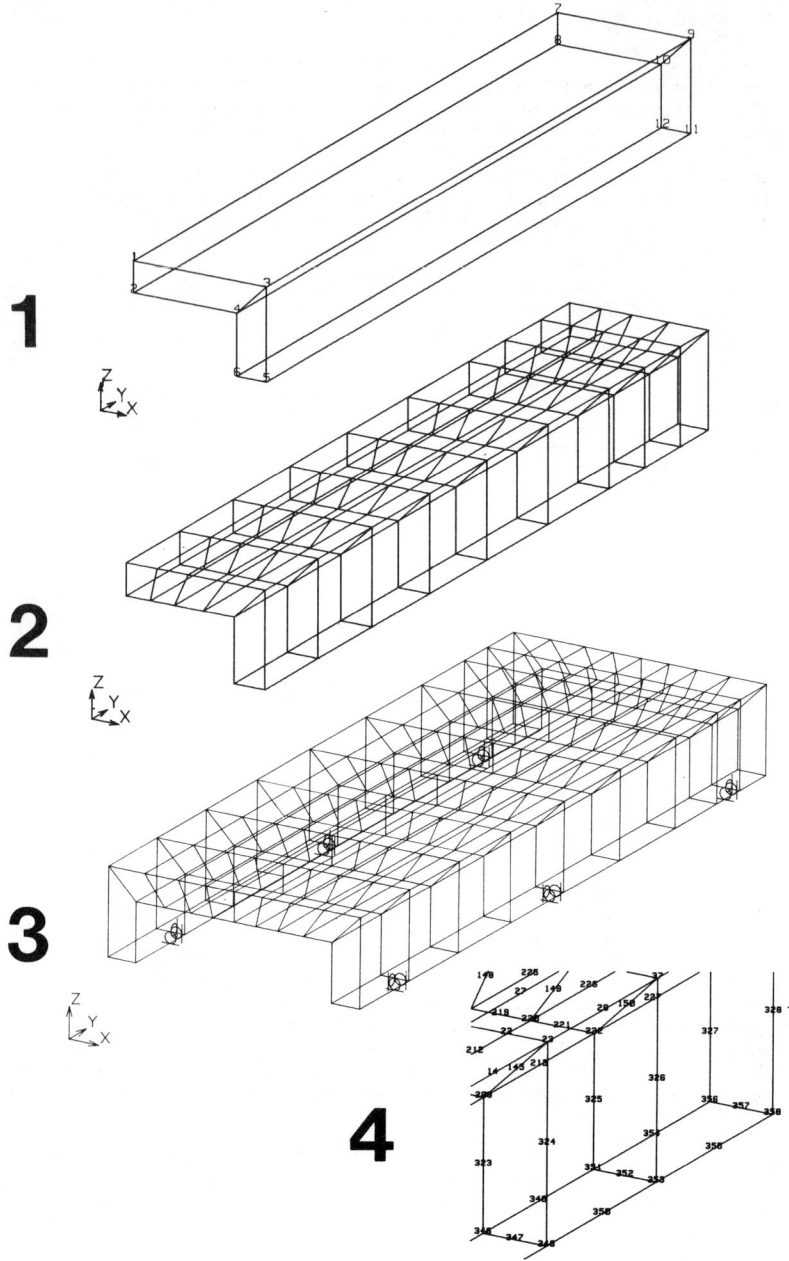

Fig. 4. Steps in the generation of a mesh with GENFAM

- *Mesh generation with weightings.* This plays an important role in models with prescriptions for spatial discretization. This is the case, for example, when calculating transient temperature fields with a sudden change in ambient temperature. In this case, the time step widths must be correlated with the mesh widths. An example is given with the valve housing shown in Fig. 5. The housing is internally exposed first to a cold and then to a hotter fluid causing also the heat transfer coefficient to rise. The original coarse division of the elements can still be seen in the figure with the entire wall consisting of one element layer. A subdivision normal to the wall has been carried out with the weightings for the four layers 1, 2, 3 and 4. All curvatures are included since the subdivisions are made in the natural co-ordinates of the elements. The transformations are effected into the real space using the shape functions. A coupled temperature field and stress analysis of the valve housing was made.

Graphics generation. The program graphics allows the generation of aspects in parallel projection from arbitrary viewing directions. Two angles must be put in, the azimuth and the height inclination. Curved edges are really drawn bent by using the shape functions. The areas or volumes of elements are displayed in their real relative sizes as they are integrated during the program run. The size of the picture is correctly adjusted to the CRT size utilizing the maximum coordinates of the generated aspect. For zooming the cut-out of a picture, the wanted region must be defined by setting a cursor twice at a lower left and an upper right corner of that area. Hidden-line plots can be produced. In Fig. 6 a structure can be seen, left with annexed node- and element numbers, right the hidden-line plot.

Front width minimization. When generating a mesh by hand you can see to it, in connection with the element numbering, that the front width remains as small as possible. When working with an automatic mesh generator or when combining two meshes to one, disadvantageously large front widths are to be expected. The GENFAM front width minimizer continues to change the element numbering until the smallest front width is reached. Thus, in the example of Fig. 4 the front width was diminished from 324 to 240. The consequence is that less external storage is necessary and a shortening of the solution time takes place.

Co-ordinates transformation and combination of two meshes. The best way to show this is to use an example, Fig. 7. The mesh is needed for an impact study. The damage of a big container by a crash on the road was to be examined. The container model is generated in cylindrical co-ordinates. There is the possibility of changing during the input as often as desired from Cartesian co-ordinates to cylindrical ones and vice versa. The lower part of Fig. 7 representing a road section with pavement is modelled separately, too. Finally, the program rotates the container about its centrepoint at an angle causing the centrepoint to be vertically above the impact point. Both meshes are now combined using this point. The program asks for the nodal points of the separate meshes which must be combined to one and, of course, renumbers the nodes and elements.

ERGRAM, the postprocessor. This routine serves for the result output in listings and, most importantly, in graphics, for the temperature fields as well as the deformation- and stress fields. Let us first consider the graphical possibilities with temperature fields.

Graphical result display with temperature fields. A first possibility is to annex the values of the calculated temperatures at the nodes. Other possibilities are: to draw the temperature distribution like mountains over the mesh as a base, drawing isothermal lines for equidistant temperatures or selected ones, or to

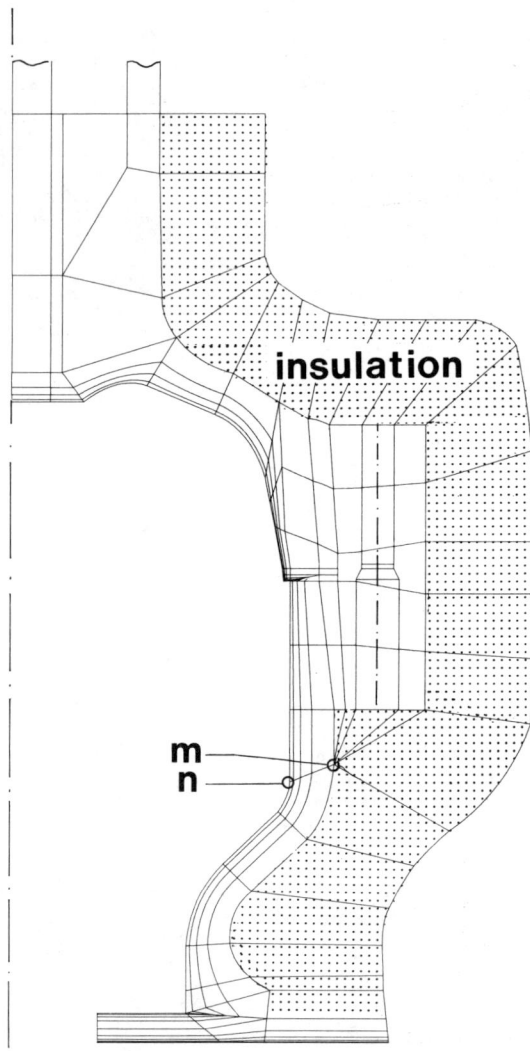

Fig. 5. Mesh of a valve housing with a specially weighted mesh at the inside

draw heat flux arrows at the Gauss points. Some features are shown in Fig. 8. With colour machines there is the option to plot in colours where the spectrum between red (hottest) and blue (coldest area) is applied. With monochromatic screens the respective routine produces grey-tone pictures. In the 3-D case, the isothermal lines or the colour patterns are drawn on the visible surfaces. A primitive and a sophisticated hidden-line procedure are included. The extreme temperature values are printed in a corner of the plot. It is possible to have only interesting parts of the structure plotted. Arbitrary views can be chosen.

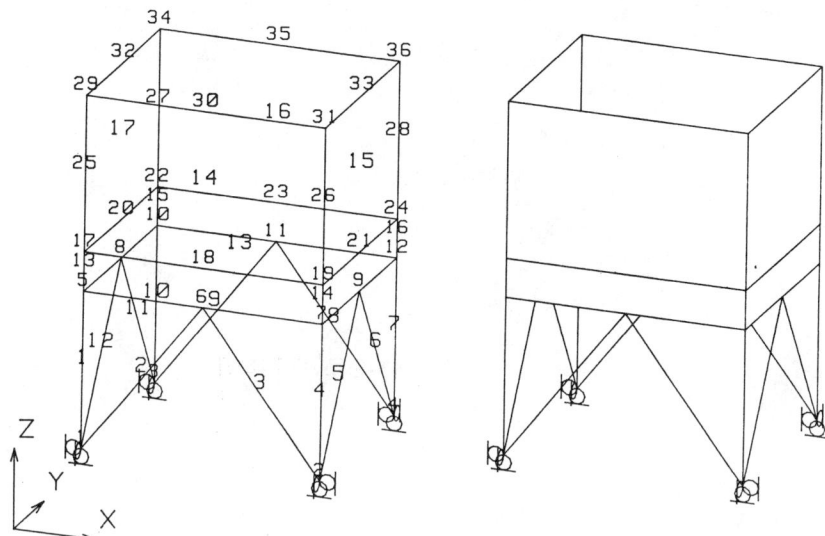

Fig. 6. Example of the hidden-line procedure

Graphical result display with rigidity calculation results. A deformation plot can be generated with arbitrary displacement enhancement. Principal stresses can be plotted as arrows at the Gauss points. For generating contour lines it is necessary first to utilize the stress smoothing routine. Normally, the stresses in the same node point are different depending from which ambient element this node is seen. These values can be listed, and the more they differ the less adequate is the mesh, that means it is too coarse in this region. It is necessary to smooth different values to only one for every node for running the contour line routine. Therefore, the smoothing routine needs to be employed. Arbitrarily chosen detail stresses can be represented: normal-, shear-, principal- or reference stresses. By choice any of these patterns can be called: annexing the stress values at the nodes, drawing stress mountains, arrows at the Gauss points or nodes with the principal stresses, contour lines, grey-tone or colour graphics, with 3-D on visible surfaces. It is possible to do a hidden-line plot. Graphical display of structural parts (zooming) is possible. The extreme values are always written in a corner of the plot.

HARDWARE COMPATIBILITIES

FEMFAM runs on Hewlett Packard micro- and mini-computers of the type 9000, series 200 and 500 and also on the HP9845B. Of course, the calculator type influences strongly the solution time required, as does the configuration, e.g. a floting point processor (FPP) increases the calculation speed considerably, see the following description.

Speed characteristics of different computer types. The most complex element type in the FEMFAM software is the spatial 20-node element which preferably should be used with a Gauss integration order of 3 (27 Gauss points). In the case of a temperature field it is a matrix of order 20, with a rigidity calculation of order 60. During the procedure of a FE program the establishing of the element stiffness matrices is besides the elimination in the front solver the most time consuming feature. The following table shows the time necessary for establishing

74   J. F. Stelzer

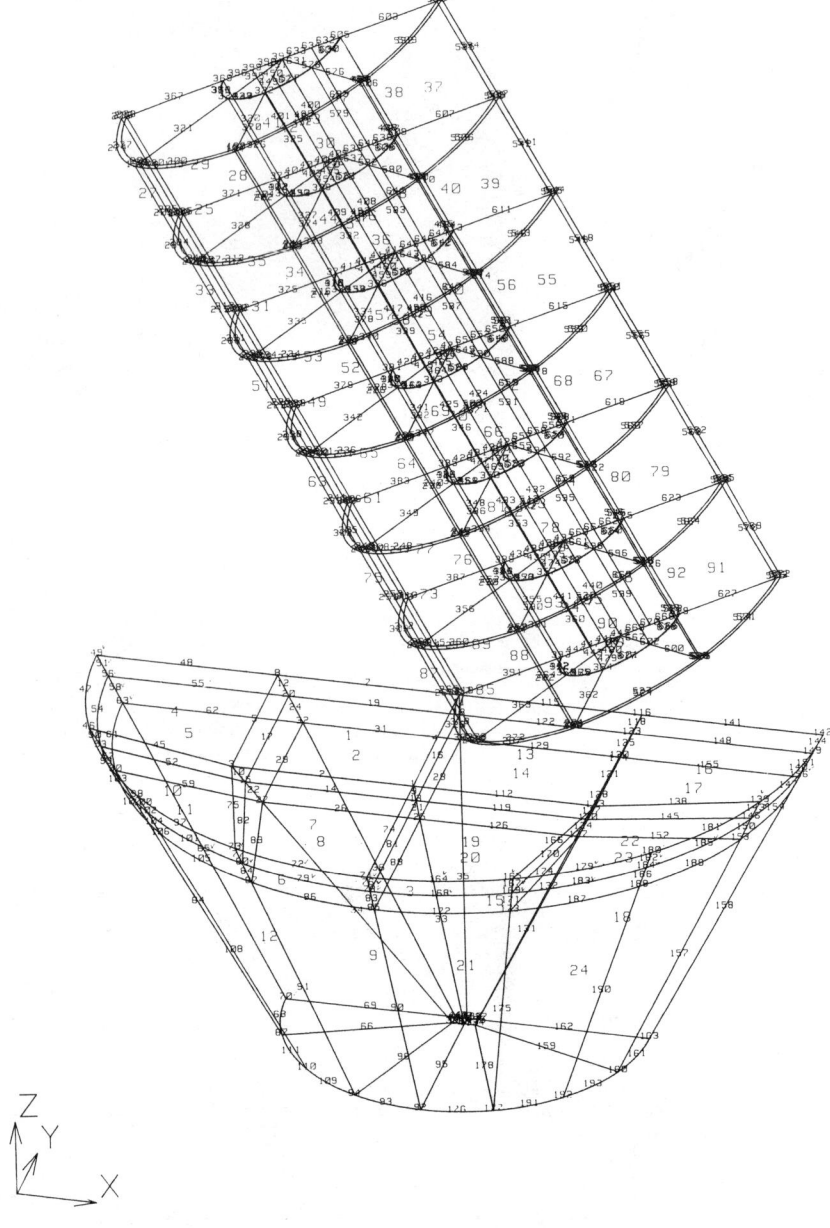

Fig. 7. Example of the combination of two originally single meshes one stiffness matrix.

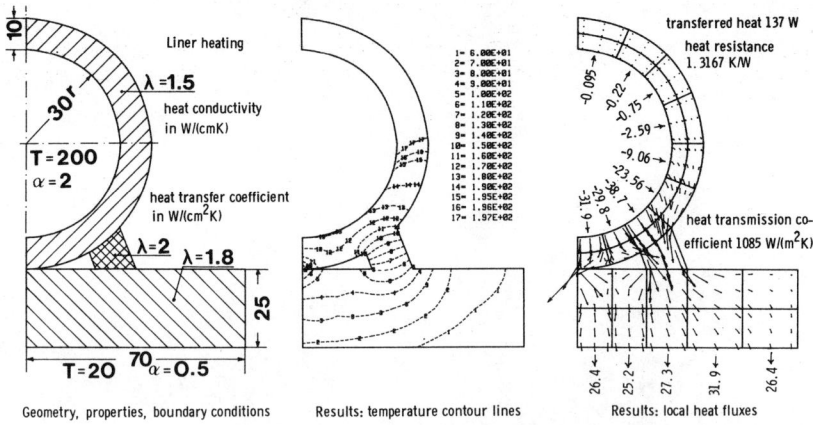

Fig. 8. Example of a plane steady-state temperature field calculation

TABLE Time in seconds required to establish one stiffness matrix
for a 3-D element with 20 nodal points and Gauss
integration order 3

computer type	temperature calculation	rigidity calculation
HP9000 series 500	2.9	22.6
HP9000 series 200 with FPP	10.2	97.1
HP9000 series 200	20.7	165
HP9845B with bit slice process.	36	285
HP9845B	180	1425

The speed of the 9000 series 500 also can be increased by a FPP approximately by a factor 2, but it was not yet measured.

Necessary peripherics. The large amount of data to be processed must be stored interimly on an external device. A Winchester drive and a fast I/O board are recommended. The size of the Winchester determines the size of problems that can be solved. A printer with graphics capabilities is also necessary.

Problem size limitations. There are no limitations from the software. For example, for calculating a problem with 300 3-D elements (20 nodes each) approximately 32 MB external storage capacity is necessary. Depending on the size of the problems a 64 MB or even 132 MB Winchester may be appropriate.

Optional peripherics. A storage medium which can be removed and stored away (disc drive, tape drive) is very helpful to save mesh- and result sets for later use. To receive reproducable plots a black ink plotter is also a must. With a colour screen a colour hard copier is very recommendable, especially the Tektronix 4695. A suitable interface and driver can be supplied by the FEMFAM dealer.

Media. The program is avalable on any kind of disc (3 1/2", 5 1/4", 8") or on data cartridge tape.

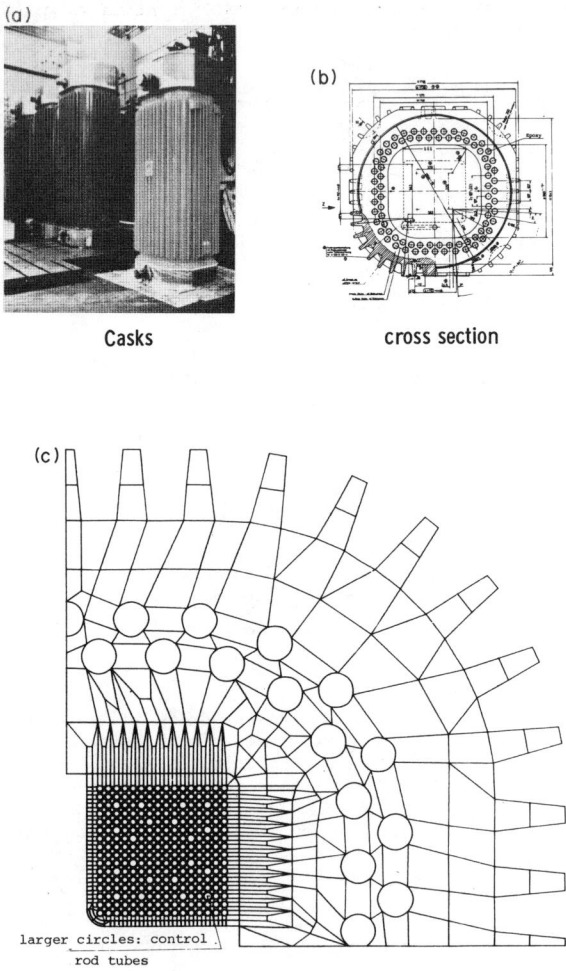

Fig. 9. (a) to (c). Temperature field analysis of casks for spent nuclear fuel

EXAMPLES OF APPLICATION

Nonlinear temperature field calculation.* This deals with the temperature fields in casks for spent nuclear fuel. The *steady-state* temperature distribution across the hottest cross section, the middle plane, was to be calculated. In a second run the time needed for the warming-up of the cask had to be analysed.

Figures 9 (a) to (g) give the appropriate information. In (a) the photograph of some casks is shown. These are the German CASTOR containers manufactured of cast

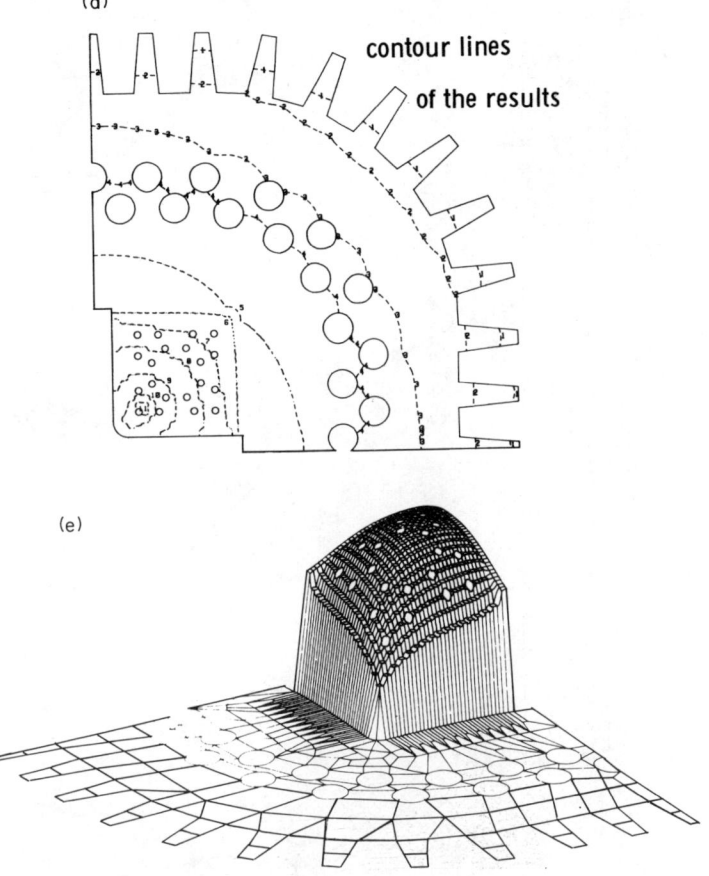

Fig. 9. (d) and (e). Temperature field anaysis of casks for spent nuclear fuel

iron. The drawing of a cross section can be seen in (b). The mesh considers a quarter of the cross section. It consists of 1425 plane elements with 8 nodes each of the quadratically interpolated isoparametric type. There are 4504 nodal

---

*The statements about the consumed time refer to machines without a floating point processor.

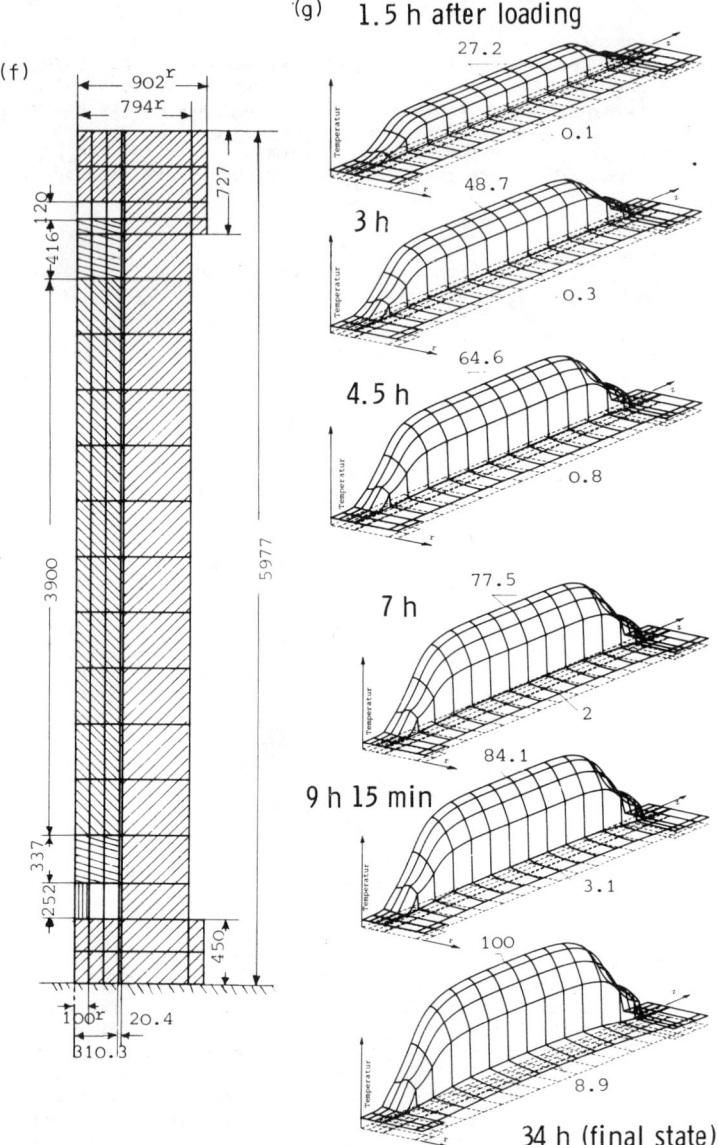

Fig. 9. (f) and (g). Temperature field analysis of casks for spent nuclear fuel

points and an equal amount of degrees of freedom. The front width is 315. Temperature dependent properties were considered, and also the radiation across the gas filled gaps and the natural convection. The problem was calculated with FEMFAM-T on a HP9000 series 500. There were seven iterations necessary using the direct iteration method with a medium error threshold of 0.01%. Approximately 8 hr. calculation time were necessary, including the transfer time to and from the external storage devices. Figures 9(d) and (e) display the results in contour lines and mountains, respectively.

For the *transient* temperature field a simplified axisymmetric mesh was created, Fig. 9(f), consisting of 95 axisymmetric, quadratically interpolated isoparametric elements. The time-dependent temperature development is to be seen in Fig. 9(g). The nonlinearity given by the gas gap (heat radiation) was considered. On a HP9000 series 200 about 1.75 hr. proceeding time were required. There were several types of CASTOR casks examined, for PWR, BWR and high temperature reactor fuel.

Thermo-mechanical calculation of a dump for neutral particles. In the context of a fusion machine of the Tokamak type, an absorber for high energy neutral particles was designed and calculated. It is an application in the nuclear field. Figure 10(a) shows the drawing. The copper plate is crossed by canals with water to remove the heat. Information about temperature distribution, deformation and the stresses was sought for. The discretization of one of the severally repeating wedge-shaped parts with spatial 20-node elements is shown in Fig. 10(b). The model consists of 120 elements and has 805 nodes. The maximum front width for the temperature calculation was 95, for the stress run 285. For the temperature field the establishing of the stiffness matrices lasted 48.6 min (on a HP9000 series 200), the transient temperature field calculation with 7 time steps 145 min, printing included. The rigidity calculation was executed on a HP9000 series 500. The following times were needed: establishing the load vector 4.13 min, of the element stiffness matrices 44.5 min, solving the equation system 88.8 min. Figure 10(b) shows also the results. The picture was produced with ERGFAM. The contour lines of the reference stresses are plotted on the visible surfaces.

Calculation of a rotating anode. This is a rotating target for the Juelich spallation neutron source, the housing of which had to be calculated, see Fig. 11. The housing is loaded by the pressure coming from the cooling water, and in the vertical outer part by a thermal load. This part is the window for the protons. The protons, entering pulsewise and only when the window crosses the beam, depose heat by their counteraction with the matter. It was sufficient to model only a part of the housing, a pie piece, see the model section. It is worked with time dependent heat source vectors. Approximately six revolutions of the wheel elapses until the quasi-steady-state situation is reached. The model comprises 121 spatial 20-node elements. Therefore the details (front width, proceeding time) were very similar to the preceding example and can be omitted. In Fig. 11 the ERGFAM result plots can be seen too.

Calculation of a valve housing. The casing shown in Fig. 12 is the home of a slide valve. If the gate is open the heat radiation from the hot emanating surfaces acts upon some surfaces. A convective cooling shall relieve the situation. The temperature distribution (steady-state) and the deformations and stresses were of interest. For the model 168 axisymmetric elements of the quadratically interpolated isoparametric type were engaged. There are 614 nodes. The temperature field calculation considered the temperature dependence of the properties by property algorithms. The convergence tolerance was 0.001%. The calculation took place on a HP9000 series 200. For establishing the stiffness matrix 4.8 min were necessary. The maximum front width was 33. The iteration required 7 steps. The solution time was 47.6 min. With the following rigidity calculation the front width was 66. A computer HP9000 series 500 was taken. The necessary times: establishing the load vector 1.18 min, the stiffness matrices 2.08 min, to solve the equation system 4.17 min. In Fig. 12 two typical FEMFAM result displays for the temperature distribution are shown. Figures 13 and 14 represent rigidity calculation results: Fig. 13 the principal stresses and Fig. 14 the deformations.

Calculation of a valve plate. With 300 spatial elements it is not a small

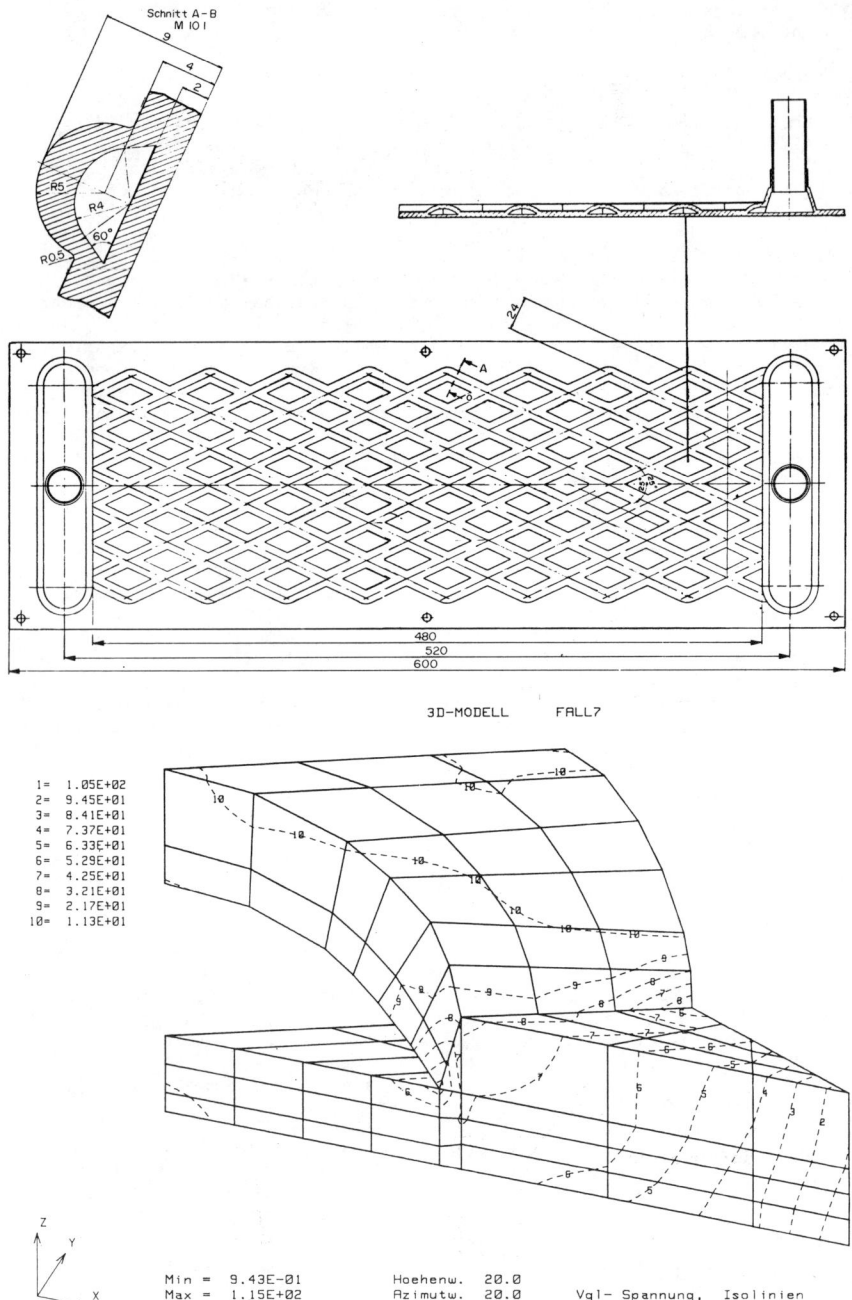

Fig. 10(a) and (b). Thermo-mechanical analysis of a water-cooled plate used as a dump for high energy particles

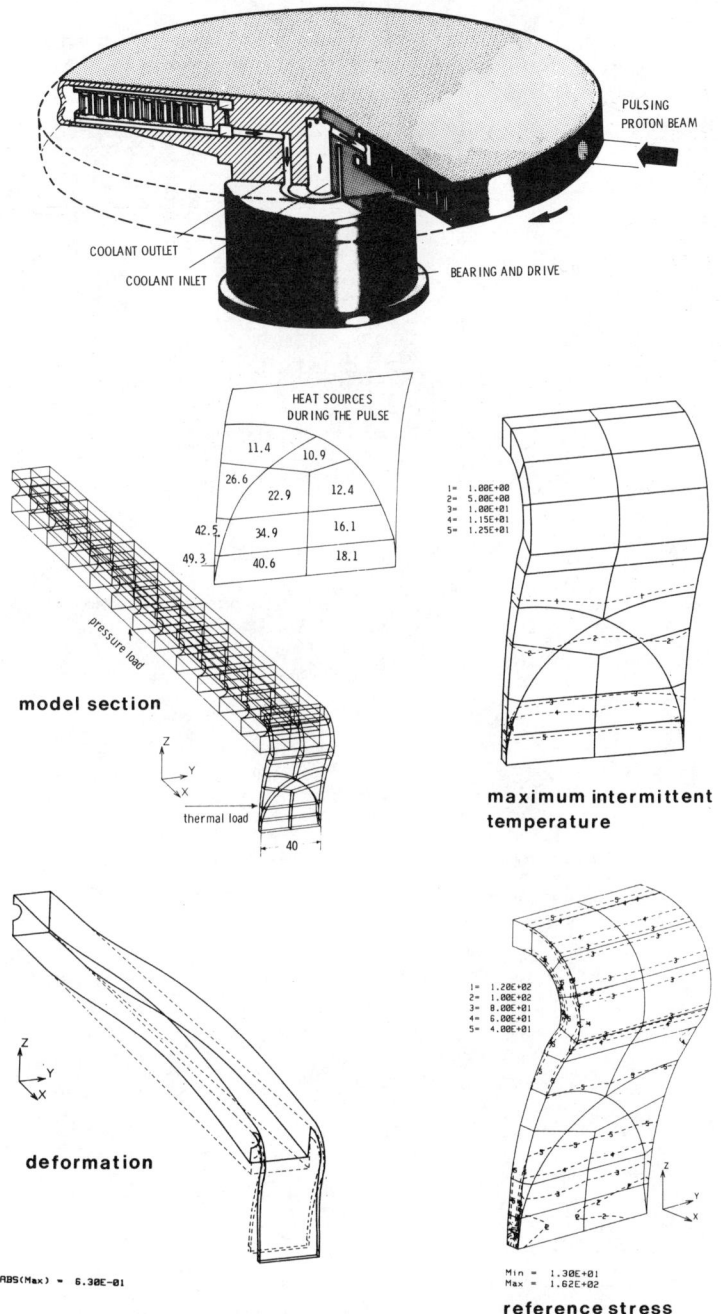

Fig. 11. Calculating the housing of the rotating target of the Juelich spallation neutron source

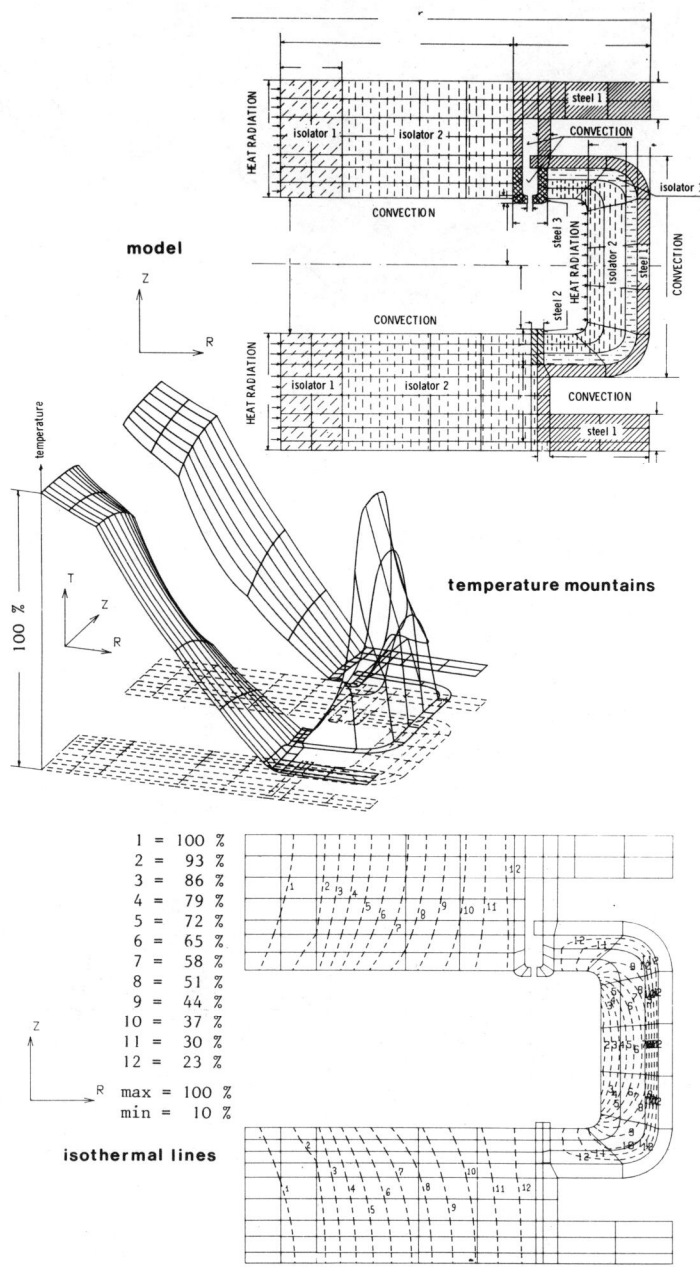

Fig. 12. Calculating a valve housing of a slide valve

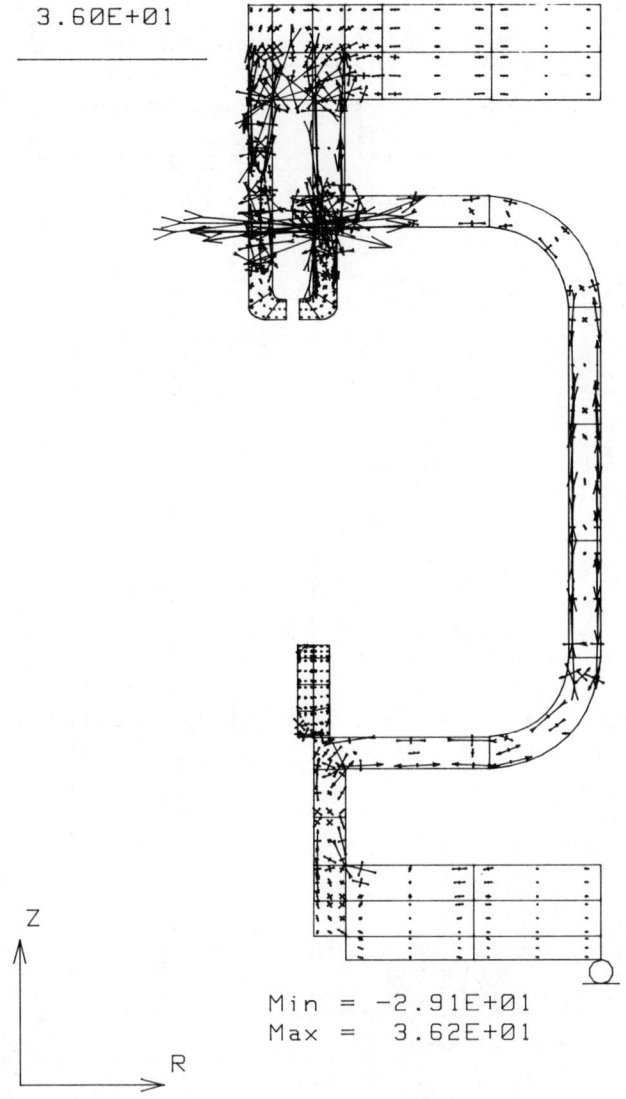

Fig. 13. The principal stresses in the steel parts of a valve housing

problem. Figure 15 shows that pie piece of a valve plate which is on its outer edge exposed to a hot gas flow during the opening period. The time dependent development of the temperatures according to the gradual changing of Neumann boundary conditions on the exhibited surfaces was to be calculated and after that the deformations and stresses. There were 20-node elements applied. For the first two time steps only the outer surface of the region 1 was exposed to the hot environment, for the next two steps regions 1 and 2 etc., thus simulating

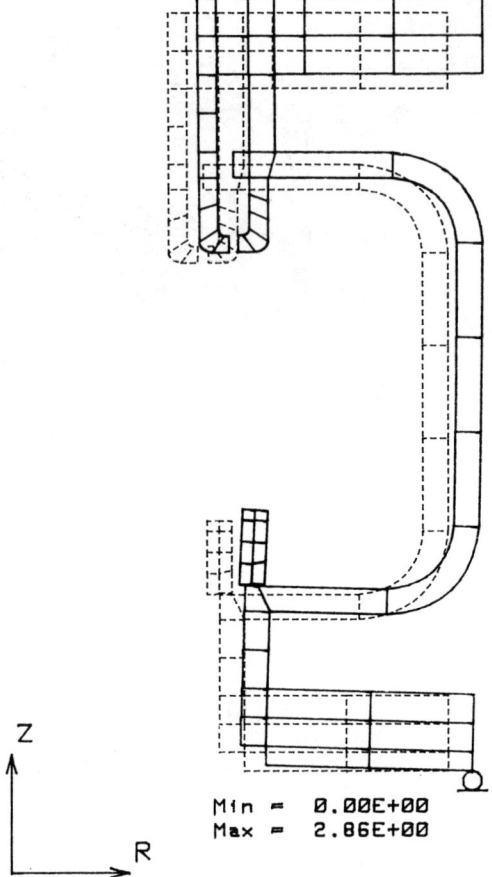

Fig. 14. The deformation of the steel parts of a valve housing

the departing of the plate from its rest position. The internal cavities of the plate are blower cooled. The model had 2003 nodes. The maximum front width for the temperature field was 162, for the rigidity 486. On a HP9000 series 500 the temperature stiffness matrices were established in 14.2 min. The solution time for two time steps was 48 min.

Calculating a sheet design for a railway wagon. This shows just one example where the FEMFAM shell element is used, see Fig. 16.

Calculating a chopper loaded by centrifugal forces. Physisists working in solid state physics need neutrons of a particular wave length. To select the appropriate neutrons choppers are used , the rotational speed of which is correlated to the specific flight velocity of the neutrons required. Figure 17 shows the mesh and the results of a chopper design. It is self explanatory so no more details will be given.

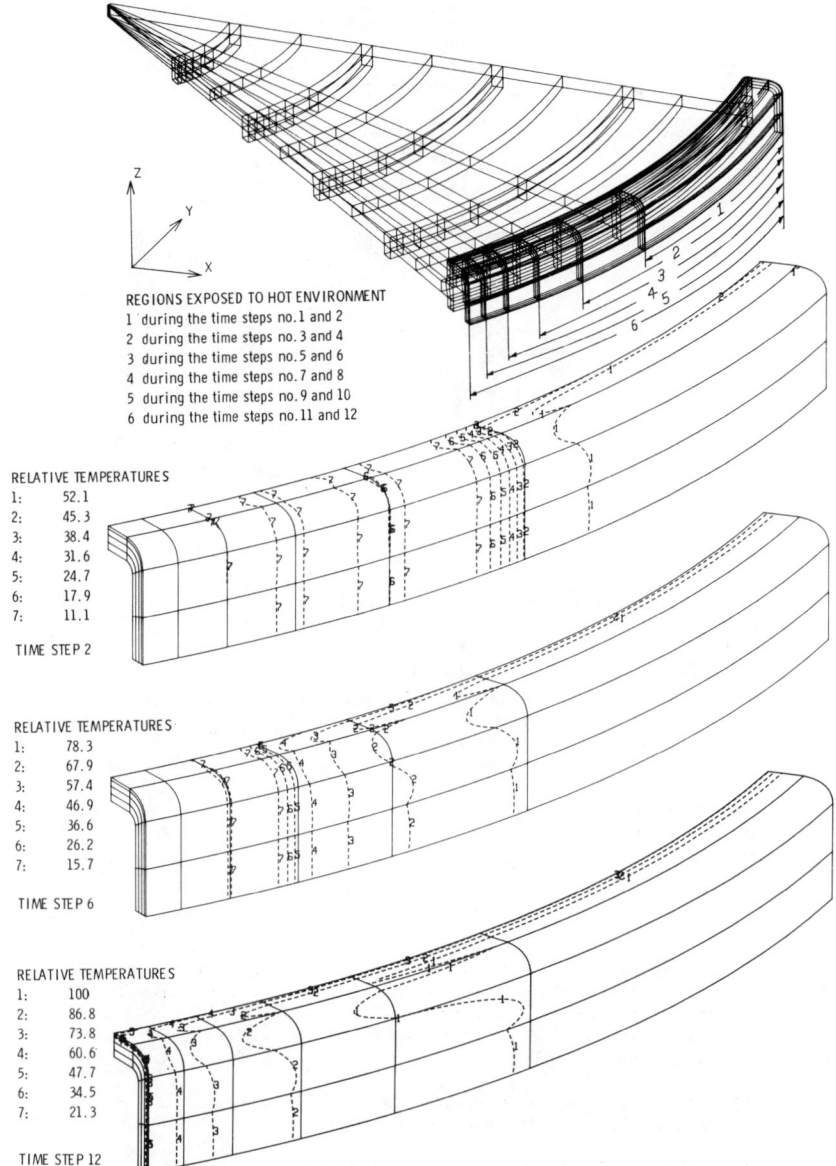

Fig. 15. A thermo-mechanical coupled problem with 300 spatial elements: a valve plate for high temperatures

THE POTENTIAL FENFAM USERS

FEMFAM is an all-purpose program. The customers up to now are from the railway industry, research division of chemical industry, consulting bureaus, manufacturers of vacuum equipment, researchers in medicine technique, liquid gas

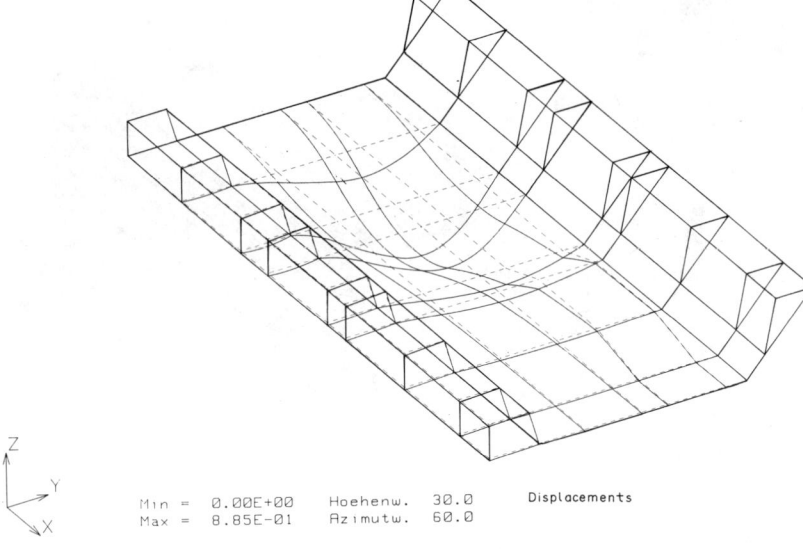

Fig. 16. The deformation of a sheet part of a railway wagon modelled with shell elements

equipment manufacturers, chimney designers, national research establishments, heat insulation designers, manufacturers of vessels and apparatus etc. Even users who have the option to use big computers prefer the incomparably easy way to FE with desktop computers and FEMFAM.

FEMFAM DISTRIBUTION

The software is available from the PROFEM GmbH, Salvatorstr.30, D-51 Aachen.

FEMFAM: Finite Element Analysis 87

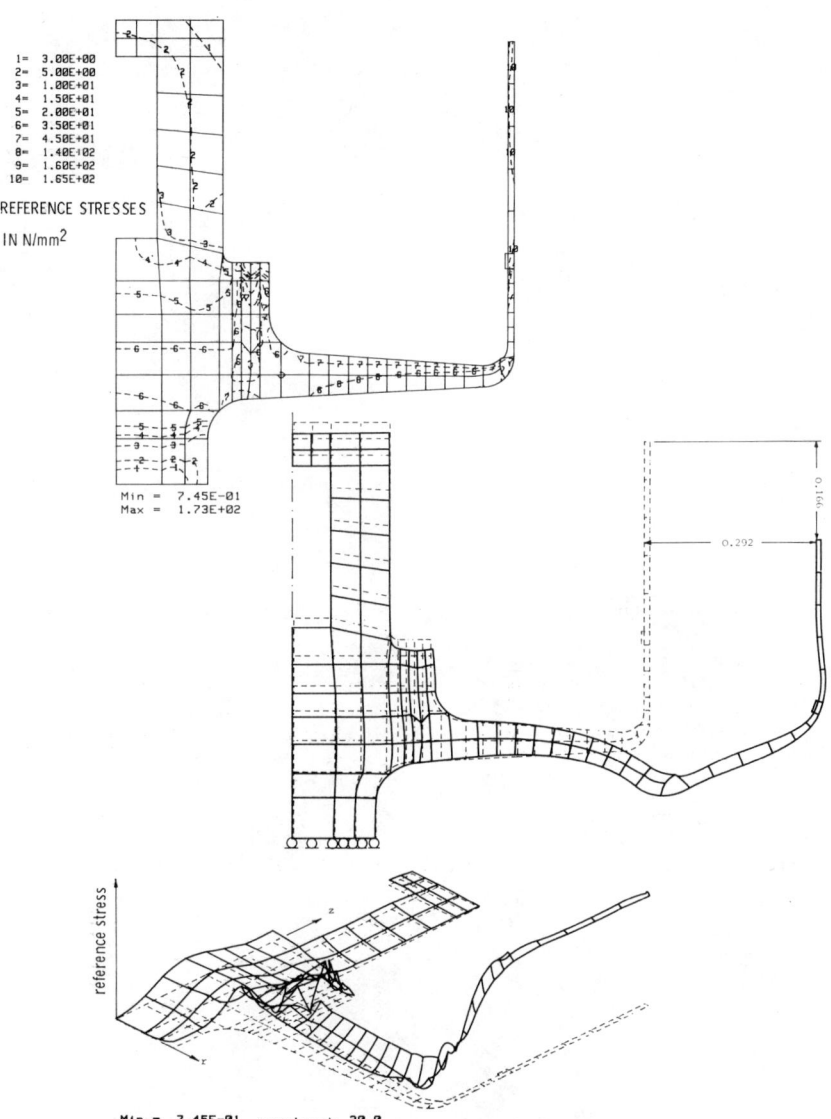

Fig. 17. A chopper stressed by centrigual forces

FEMPAC: AN INTEGRATED FINITE ELEMENT SYSTEM

D. Sundström

FEMPROG AB, Box 26016, 100 41 Stockholm, Sweden

ABSTRACT

FEMPAC provides a wide market with a comprehensive system for finite element analysis.

FEMPAC includes

- an interactive model generator - PRESOL
- the analysis program - FEMSOL
- an interactive results presentation module - POSTSOL.

FEMPAC is used with the same manuals and user procedures on a large variety of computers ranging from very powerful combinations like VAX-FPS164 to personal computers like the IBM PC/XT.

THEORETICAL BACKGROUND

FEMSOL

FEMSOL aims to be an efficient easy-to-use FEM-program for structural analysis. The program is equipped with rapid numerical routines and an efficient data base handler.

Element Stiffness Matrices

For all elements the stiffness matrix is computed from assumed shape functions for the displacements. Numerical integration is used for most of the elements. In order to get improved analysis, reduced integration is used for thick plate and thick shell elements.

Elements with the same stiffness matrix can be grouped to a stiffness group and thus the stiffness matrix is only computed once for these elements.

Local Co-ordinate Systems

Local co-ordinate systems can be specified by nodes and by elements.

The nodal based specification affects the element stiffness matrices and is used for the introduction of nodal constraints at skew boundaries.

The element based specification just affects the presentation of the computed stresses.

Special Transformations

Special transformations are implemented to simplify the solution of complex problems. The master-slave technique enables the handling of stiff zones and coupling of nodes enables the solution of contact problems as shrinkage fit.

Renumbering

In order to minimize the bandwidth FEMSOL offers improvements of two renumbering algorithms

- Collins' direct method
- Rosen's iterative method

The user can control the usage of the two methods. If nothing is specified Collins' algorithm is always performed. The implementation of Collins' method has an out-of-core facility which enables the renumbering of large structures even if virtual memory is not available.

Assembly

The assembled matrix consists of the lower-half band including the diagonal of the global stiffness matrix. If necessary the matrix can be divided into several blocks with equal number of rows. The assembling proceeds element by element. Finally the elastic support contributions are added.

During the assembling procedure care is taken of all constraints and all special transformations. This means that only the active degrees of freedom are assembled. This is also valid for normal rotations of plane parts of shell structures, which are automatically eliminated in the program.

Solution of the Equation System

Since all constraints are taken into consideration during the assembling procedure no further modification is necessary for the solution of the equation system. A Cholesky factorization algorithm with out-of-core facility is used. The routine takes advantage of the profile and thus the zeroes in the band outside the profile are not involved in the computations.

Loading

Consistent loads are computed for pressure, gravity load, centrifugal load and temperature load.

FEMPAC: An Integrated Finite Element System

Data Base

All arrays which are necessary for the further program processing are saved on the data base. This enables an advanced restart capability. The I/O-handling routines communicate with the data base on disc via a buffer in the primary memory. This diminishes the read and write operations on the disc, which is especially important for PC-installations.

Dynamic Analysis, FEMSOL-D

The dynamic analysis is based on mode superposition and covers the following facilities:

- eigenfrequencies and eigen shapes
- forced vibrations
- transient analysis by numerical integration of the modal description of the equations of motion.

The eigenvalue problem is solved by a modern, stable and very efficient algorithm (STLM). It uses Lanczos method on the inverse of a shifted problem.

Heat Transfer Analysis, FEMSOL-T

An additional program package FEMSOL-T solves the transient heat transfer problem.

The conductivity and capacity element matrices are computed from assumed shape functions for the temperature. Numerical integration is used for most of the elements.

The equation system is solved by a Crout factorization. For the time history a backward integration scheme is used.

By analogies of partial differential equations the following problems can be solved

- diffusion
- irrotational flow of an ideal fluid
- electric potential problems

FIELDS OF APPLICATION

Geometrical

FEMPAC is a general package for the analysis of frameworks, membranes, shells, plates and solids in two and three dimensions.

Materials

FEMPAC is used for isotropic as well as anisotropic materials.

A special nonlinear version of FEMPAC is equipped with routines to deal with the following non-linear applications

- large displacements
- elasto-plastic materials

In this FEMPAC version, the heat transfer module can also handle temperature dependent conductivity and heat capacity, occurring e.g. in ceramics.

Analysis Capabilities

The analysis capabilities of FEMPAC include static, eigenvalues, modal shapes, transient dynamic and forced vibrations with modal damping or Rayleigh damping.

Also, a module is optionally included for stationary and transient analysis of heat transfer and other field problems, like electric potential, diffusion, non-frictious flow and harmonic analysis (e.g. the wave equation for a gas).

Loading

The following loadings on the structure can be handled in FEMPAC:

- nodal point loading
- 2-D and 3-D pressure loading
- centrifugal loading
- gravity loading
- temperature loading
- non-zero displacements

Superposition of load cases can be performed, and critical load combinations can be evaluated in the postprocessor.

Boundary Conditions

Boundary conditions can be given as displacement constraints and elastic support. The constraints may be supplied by specifying displacements at nodes as zero or some prescribed quantity. Elastic support can be given for a point, a line (an edge) or a surface, and are consistent with the shape functions.

PROGRAM DESCRIPTION

Method

FEMPAC uses the finite element method.

Library of Elements

- 2- and 3-node beam element for truss and framework structures.
- plane stress and plane strain elements: isoparametric membrane elements with 3, 4, 6 and 8 nodes.
- Thin shell elements with 3 and 4 nodes.
- Thick shell 6- and 8-node elements with constant or variable thickness.
- plate elements: 3, 4- and 8-node elements for thin and thick plates.
- Axisymmetric elements: isoparametric elements with 3, 4, 6 and 8 nodes.
- Axisymmetric shell element: 2-node thin shell element.
- Solids: isoparametric elements with 8, 15 and 20 nodes.

- Stiff elements: Master-slave technique for stiff coupling of nodes.
- Coupling for the simulation of links, contact surfaces etc.

Heat transfer analysis and other field problems are included for the full range for elements.

Program Structure

In PRESOL the user creates interactively at a (colour) graphics terminal a geometric model of the structure, and attaches information about mesh control, material data, boundary conditions and constraints to the geometric entities. The model is subsequently augmented and formatted into a complete input file for the analysis by FEMSOL.

The results computed in FEMSOL include effective stresses, principal stresses and section forces and moments to satisfy the needs of mechanical engineers and the requirements from the building industry.

The interactive postprocessor module POSTSOL uses state-of-art computer graphics techniques to display element models and results. By geometrical selection, sectioning and transformations, the user can display results by contour lines or colour fringes, by vectors, by deformed shapes, by graphs or tables. Also, FEMSOL can itself, through extensive batch-postprocessing capabilities, present selective output, result combination and printer and plotter displays of model, input and output data.

Interfaces to the most important CAD-systems are provided, e.g. through the IGES standard. The user can write his own programs and connect them to FEMPAC. He can then use a library of subroutines available in PRESOL, and thus access and use information about specific bodies and objects in its database. Special preprocessor features are thus easily created.

The whole of FEMPAC is written in Fortran 77, with a minimum of machine-dependent routines, and it is thus easily transferred to new machines.

In order to maximize the ease of use, the package is run from a supervisory command program which handles the database communication within the whole package and calls the different modules according to the demands of the user.

HARDWARE REQUIREMENTS

The basic requirement is FORTRAN 77. FEMPAC has been installed on a large number of computer makes, e.g. VAX, PRIME, Apollo, SUN, HP9000, UNIVAC, CYBER, IBM 43xx, IBM 308x, Data General MV Series, the VAX/FPS 164 combination and recently on IBM PC/XT, AT and a number of machines compatible with those.

FEMPAC is run on a standard colour graphics terminal with colour graphics hard copy facilities. In the PC environment, a high resolution graphics add-on card and an extra high quality colour monitor should preferably be added to the system, although a standard PC colour system may be satisfactory for small scale applications.

Output can also be directed to standard pen plotter.

There are no special requirements regarding the operating systems.

The system is distributed on magnetic media in the form convenient to each type of computer.

EXAMPLES OF APPLICATION

Fatigue in Heavy Duty Equipment

The customer wanted to perform analysis of stress levels after the development of fatigue cracks during the expected service life of the part, a heavy duty front part of an excavator. See Fig. 1.

Fig. 1. Front part of excavator, developing cracks near tooth adapters

The FEM model developed contained 315 solids elements (77 were 15-node elements and 238 were 20-node elements). See Fig. 2.

There were approximately 4800 degrees of freedom and the bandwidth was approximately 750. The whole of FEMPAC was used at a Tektronix 4105 colour terminal with Ink jet plotter 4695. Input data were generated with PRESOL.

A complete FEMSOL computation with a number of load cases took about 2.5 hr CPU time on the PRIME 9950. Output data were displayed in colour graphics with POSTSOL.

For typographical reasons, a pen plotter output is included in this article. (Fig. 3.)

Temperature Distribution in a Chip/Chipcarrier System

This example is taken from the semiconductor industry. The problem was to find the stationary temperature distribution in a semiconductor chip/chipcarrier system when the chip is active. The study was made in an early stage of an industrial research project, based on approximate design data. The FEM-model was generated by PRESOL, and computations performed by FEMSOL's temperature module.

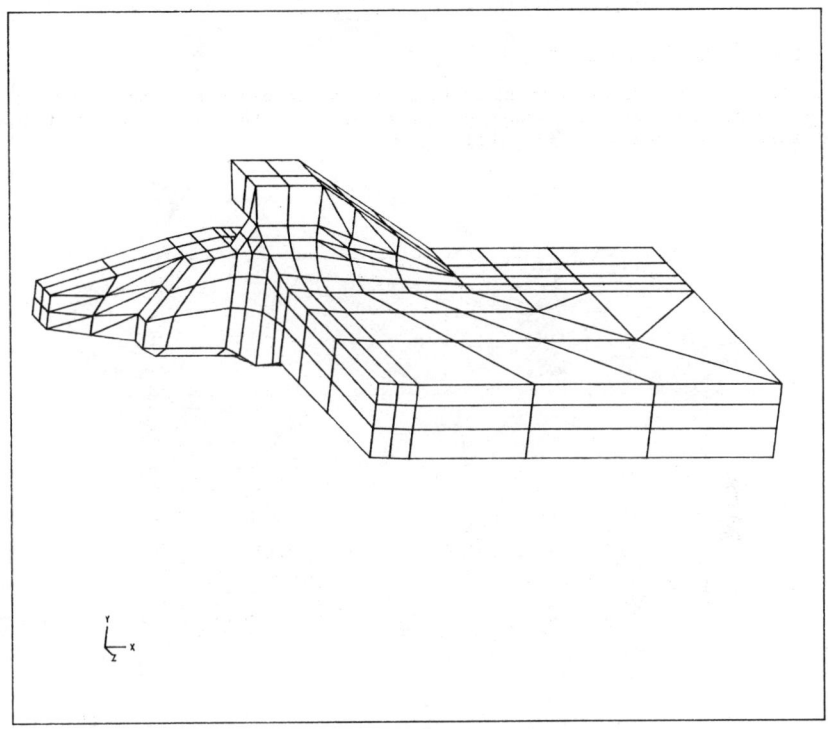

Fig. 2. FEM mesh generated by PRESOL

Type of elements: 8 node isoparametric solids
Number of elements: 288
Number of nodes: 452
Degrees of freedom: 1815
Bandwidth: 119
Total computing time in PRIME 9950: 4 min

No drawing of the chip was presented by the customer. Figure 4 shows the mesh and example of one way to present computational results. Most of the results were however presented in colour ink-jet plots.

Reinforcement Computations for a Silo Construction

The task was to study hoop stresses and bending moments in the outer part of a large concrete structure - a silo built in hard rock (see Figs. 5, 6). The purpose was to find the correct amount and placement of reinforcement. The discretization done by PRESOL is shown in Fig. 7. 312 elements (isoparametric membrane elements with six nodes and beam elements with two nodes) were generated (for half the horizontal cross section). 925 nodes and 1815 degrees of freedom resulted. The bandwidth after renumbering was 222.

Total CPU-time used for a computation comprising four load cases was 900 seconds in a PRIME 9950. For an output example from a pen plotter, see Fig. 8. Most of the output was presented by colour ink-jet plotter.

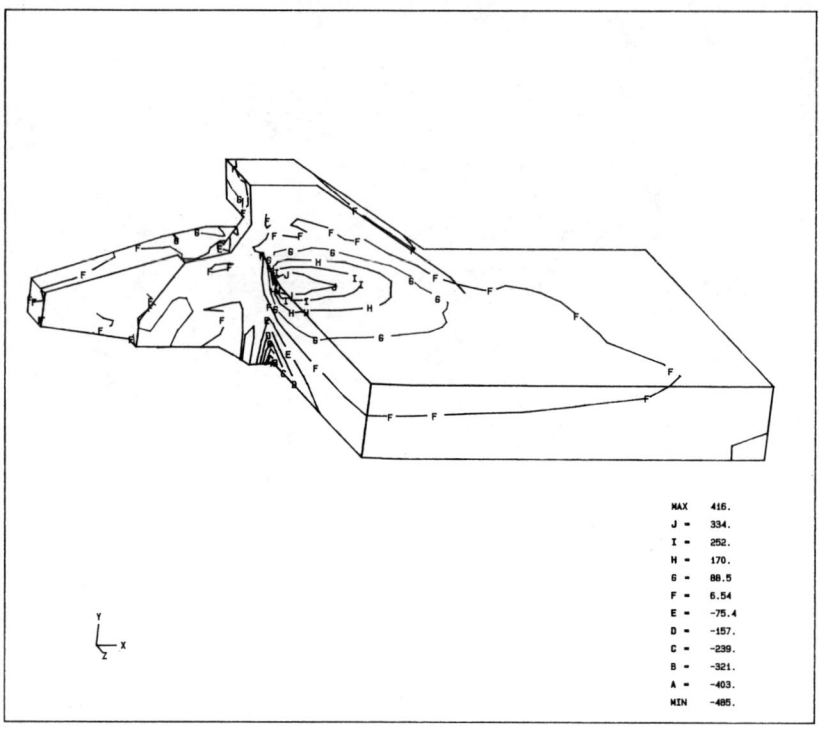

Fig. 3. Pen plotter output from POSTSOL

POTENTIAL USERS

FEMPAC is the ideal tool for companies of all sizes who want to have a very easy-to-use, fast and efficient way to do FEM-analyses of linear models. It should be noted that development of a nonlinear analysis option is under way in 1985. Branches of industry where FEMPAC is already extensively used include offshore, nuclear mechanical, automotive, heavy machinery, building, construction, as well as electromechanical and electronics.

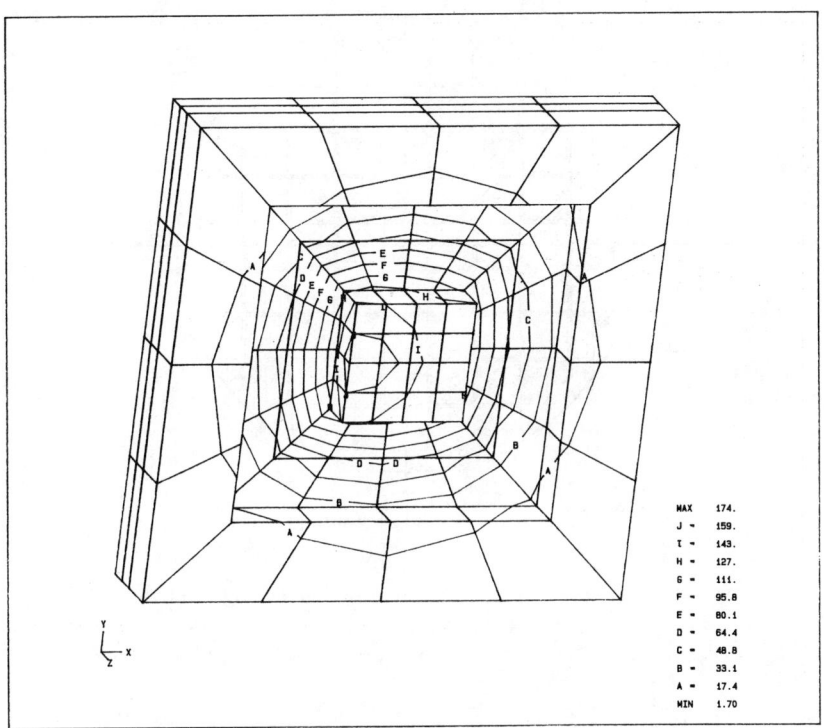

Fig. 4. Temperature distribution in chip/chipcarrier system computed by FEMSOL

Fig. 5. Storage silo built in hard rock

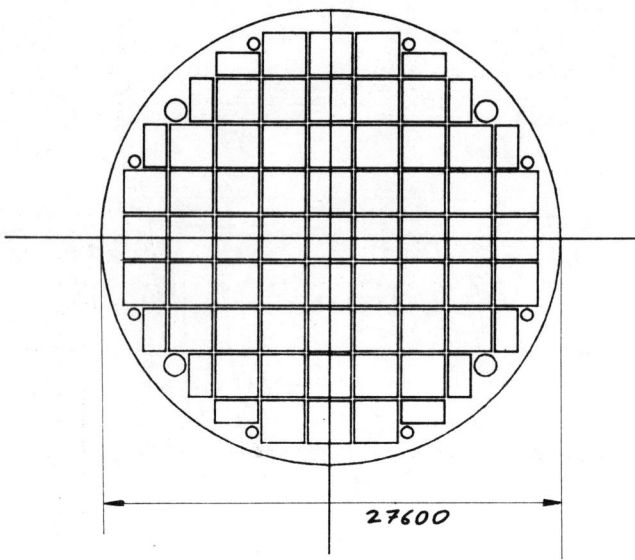

Fig. 6. Horizontal cut through storage silo

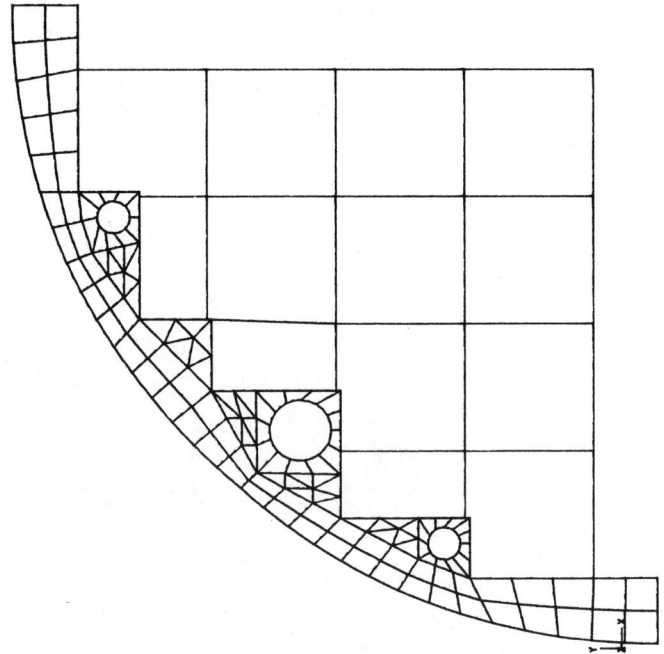

Fig. 7. PRESOL mesh for storage silo analysis

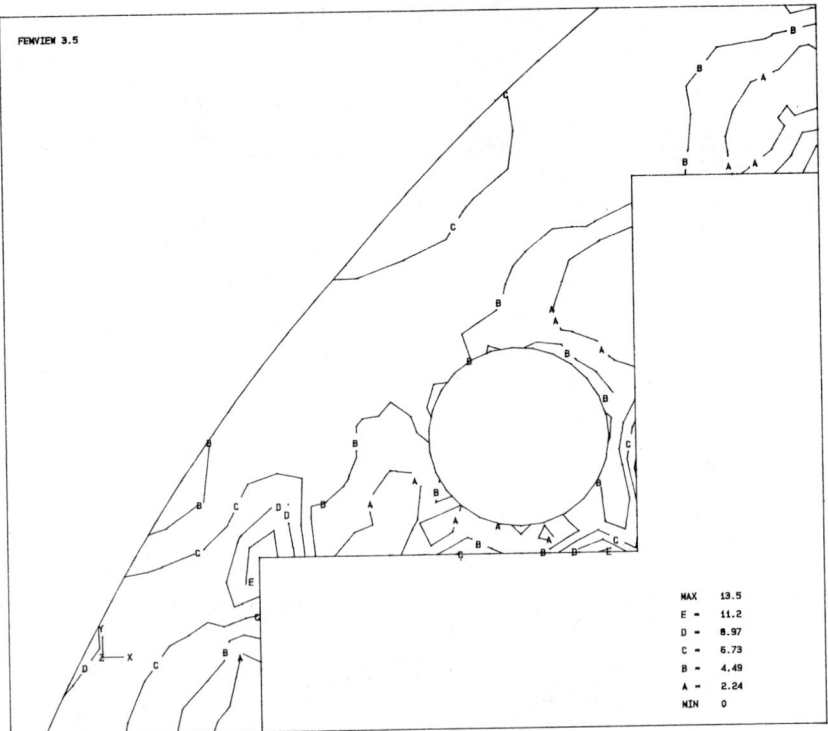

Fig. 8. Pen plotter output of stress levels in part of silo construction

REFERENCES

Zienkiewicz, O. C. The finite element method, Third Edition, McGraw-Hill, 1978.
Collins, R. J. Bandwidth reduction by automatic renumbering. *Int. J. Num. Meth. Eng.* No. 6, 1973, pp. 345-356.
Rosen, R. Matrix bandwidth minimization. *Proc. 23rd Nat. Conf.* ACM Publications. P-68 Brandon System Press, Princebon, New Jersey, 1968, pp. 585-595.
Ericsson, T. and A. Ruhe. The spectral transformation Lanczos method for the numerical solution of large, sparse generalized symmetric eigenvalue problems. *Math. of Comp.*, *35*, 152, 1251-1268, 1980.

FENRIS: FINITE ELEMENT NONLINEAR INTEGRATED SYSTEM

A. Arnesen

A.S. Veritec Veritasveien 1, P.O. Box 300, W-1322 Hovik, Oslo, Norway

ABSTRACT

FENRIS is a nonlinear finite element program designed as a large scale, general package for solving static and dynamic problems,[1,2,3]. The theoretical foundation allows for large displacements, large rotations, large strains and nonlinear behaviour of materials. Application is for structures in general, with special capabilities for analysis of offshore structures.

FENRIS has been designed as a highly modular program system well suited for use in research as well as for engineering application. It is a stand-alone program with its own pre- and postprocessors. However, input to FENRIS and processing of analysis results may also be carried out by use of the interactive pre- and postprocessors of SESAM'80.[4] These programs facilitate automatic generation of mesh, bandwidth optimizer and colour graphics for plot of element mesh and analysis results.

FENRIS has been developed as a joint project between The Norwegian Institute of Technology (NTH), The Foundation for Scientific and Industrial Research (SINTEF), and A.S. VERITEC, a subsidiary of Det norske Veritas. The program is maintained, supported and updated by A.S VERITEC and marketed by A.S VERITEC SESAM SYSTEMS.

THEORETICAL BACKGROUND

The formulation of motion used in FENRIS accommodates for translations and rotations of unlimited size. Large rotations are defined in terms of transformation matrices, rotational vectors are only used incrementally. Both total Lagrangian and updated Lagrangian description are used for the elements, depending on their type. A special feature is that the system analyzed may include rigid parts of finite dimensions.

The equilibrium equation is expressed in terms of a virtual work equation using Green strains and the symmetric Piola-Kirchhoff stresses. The solution of the nonlinear equations assumes a linearized incremental form of the equilibrium equations based on two equilibrium configurations that are close to each other. The program is equipped with a "skyline" block solver that can handle positive definite as well as indefinite systems of equations.

FENRIS utilizes a very general loading concept which allows for arbitrary combinations of different types of loadings such as prescribed displacements, concentrated loads, conservative and non-conservative element loads, inertia loads associated with acceleration histories, buoyancy forces, loadings from current and waves, etc. The variations of the differnet load contributions are defined through separate histories that may be prescribed in an arbitrary manner by the user. Series of standard history functions are also provided by the program.

Different strategies for solution of static and dynamic problems are available in the program.[5,9] Linear static analyses may be carried out with any number of load cases. Solution of nonlinear systems is based on an incremental iterative procedure. Iterations are carried out until equilibrium is attained at each load level. The size of the increments may be prescribed by the user, or it is possible to make use of a facility where the program itself calculates the increments automatically. Automatic incrementation is available both for static and dynamic problems. The automatic algorithm for static problems is based on a hyperplane displacement control method, which may be viewed as a type of arclength method.[5,9] For dynamic problems the time steps may be automatically computed as a function of stiffness and frequency of applied loads.[5,6] The Newmark-β family of time integration schemes are implemented, and both true and modified Newton-Raphson iteration schemes may be used when iterating to equilibrium.

Methods for computation of hydrostatic forces on cable, beam, plate and shell type of structures have been developed.[10,11] A general profile for current loading may be defined and the program calculates and updates buoyancy forces on submerged and partly submerged elements automatically. A method for determination of hydrostatic stability of floating structures has been developed where metacenter and center of buoyancy for rotations about principal axes of the displaced fluid surface are automatically computed. Wave theories for regular and irregular sea states on beam type of structures are also available.[12] A separate module generates the irregular sea state.

FENRIS allows for restarts of computer runs. Large analyses may conveniently be parted into several runs for intermediate check of results. Input parameters may be subjected to changes during such intermediate stops.

FIELD OF APPLICATION

Geometrical

Any type of 2- and 3-D structure (beam, bar, membrane, plate, shell, solid) as well as axisymmetric solid structures and contact problems may be analyzed.

Materials

Material models presently available are:

- Linear elasticity
- Nonlinear elasticity
- Plasticity with isotropic and kinematic hardening
- Overlay technique

Analysis Capabilities

Analysis capabilities of FENRIS:

- Linear and nonlinear statics

FENRIS: Finite Element Nonlinear Integrated System

- Linear and nonlinear dynamics in time domain
- Large deflection and collapse of structures
- Buckling and postbuckling behaviour of plates and shells
- Earthquake response analysis
- Pile-soil interaction
- Contact and collision problems with friction
- Analysis of structures subjected to hydrostatic and hydrodynamic loading (current, buoyancy, waves, added mass and hydrodynamic drag)
- Hydrostatic stability calculation (e.g. launching, upending and setting of jackets).
- Dynamics of anchor lines and flexible risers with possible coupling to fixed or floating structures.
- Different types of bridge analyses.
- Axisymmetric and general analysis of machine structures.
- Space lattice and space frame structures.

Loadings

Load types available are:

- Concentrated nodal point forces
- Conservative and non-conservative element loads
- Prescribed displacements and accelerations
- Inertia loads (gravity)
- Initial strains and stresses
- Temperatures
- Buoyancy forces and concentrated buoyancy volumes
- Current
- Wave loading on slender structures
   . Regular sea (Airy's theory, Stokes 5th order theory)
   . Irregular sea
- Drag and added mass

The different load types may be combined in an arbitrary manner. The variations of the loads are described through separate histories. The program may also read a history record of prescribed displacements from file which have been produced by another program. The program has a special option for smoothing of histories.

PROGRAM DESCRIPTION

Method

FENRIS is based on a displacement formulation of the finite element method.

Type of Elements

The element library of FENRIS presently contains the following elements:

- 2-node cable-bar and beam
- Nonlinear spring and link elements
- Triangular and quadrilateral membranes, plates and shells
  (3-node and 4-node elements)
- 6-node prismatic solid and 8-node solid brick
- Axisymmetric solids
  (3-node triangle and 4-node quadrangle)
- Contact element with friction
- Buoyancy elements without structural stiffness

All elements except for spring and contact elements may have eccentric nodes
(rigid parts at nodes). The plate bending and shell elements are based on the
so-called "free formulation" theory which implicitly satisfies the patch
test.[15,16,17] These elements account for transverse shear deformation.

Program Structure

The program is structured on four different levels, each of which signifies a
certain degree of specialization in the formulation, see Fig. 1. The first level
is designated "system level", and it has to do with data allocation, establishment
and solution of the nonlinear equation system and organization of input and
output. The next level is the "substructure level" which formulates substructures
of different types, such as frames, shells, solids, etc. Associated with this
are attached special application programs, some of which have their own data
generation and postprocessing modules. This level also provides possible links
to other programs, e.g. pre- and postprocessor of SESAM'80. The third level
comprises the finite element library and the fourth level makes up the material
library. The modular structure of the program makes it easy for a user to add

LEVEL 4: MATERIALS LIBRARY

| Linear elasticity | Nonlinear elasticity | Flow theory of plasticity | Overlay model | Concrete |

LEVEL 3: FINITE ELEMENT LIBRARY

Stiffnesses and internal forces:

| 3D cable and bar | 3D beam | 3D membrane | Thin shell | ••• |

Special loading routines:

| Distributed pressure | Hydrostatic forces | Hydrodynamic forces | ••• |

LEVEL 2: SATELLITE PROGRAMS

| Specialized pre- and postprocessors | ⇌ | 3D cable, bar, frame, membrane | 2D and axisym. frame, membrane, shell, solid | Stiffened plate and shell | Solids | Concrete structures | ⇌ | Interface with SESAM'80 |

LEVEL 1: MAIN PROGRAM

| System pre- and postprocessors | ⇌ | Allocation of data storage
Administration of computations
Construction of equations for total system
Algorithms for static and dynamic problems |

Fig. 1. Organization of FENRIS

FENRIS: Finite Element Nonlinear Integrated System

new solution algorithms, element routines, material laws, etc. into the program.

FENRIS has its own batch input module. Input data is read in free format, and a command system initiates the different groups of data. An edited print-out of the input is given, and the program performs extensive checks of the input data. Mesh generation and interactive processing of input are available through the preprocessors of SESAM'80.[4]

The postprocessor of FENRIS prints analysis results such as displacements, element forces and stresses, reaction forces, residuals, norms, etc. Graphical displays and plots of results are available through the postprocessor of SESAM'80.[4]

FENRIS is written in Fortran 77.

HARDWARE COMPATIBILITIES

Minimum Configuration and Material Requirements

The minimum computer configuration is highly dependent on the problem to be solved. Fixed or virtual memory computer of about 1.0 Mb memory and a hundred Mb disc is sufficient for most practical cases, (problem dependent). A magnetic tape unit should be available for permanent storing of model data and results.

Type of Computers

FENRIS is implemented on the following computers, (the oprating systems are indicated in paranthesis):

- VAX 11/750/780/785 (UNIX, VMS)
- NORD 500   (SINTRAN III)
- IBM 30xx   (OS/MVS)
- FPS 164
- CRAY 1   (COS)
- APOLLO   (AEGIS)

Peripherals

The graphics' part of the program (pre- and postprocessors of SESAM'80), has so far been implemented on the Calcomp plotter and Tektronix screens.

Operating Systems

See "Type of computers"

Media

FENRIS is delivered on magnetic tape.

EXAMPLES OF APPLICATION

The examples presented cover some important features of the program in analysis of offshore structures.

Complete Overturning of a Floating Frame[10]

Description of the model. Figure 2 shows a plane frame model of a floating structure. The frame is discretized by a total of 20 beam elements and 18 nodal points. The main geometric and physical data are given in the figure.

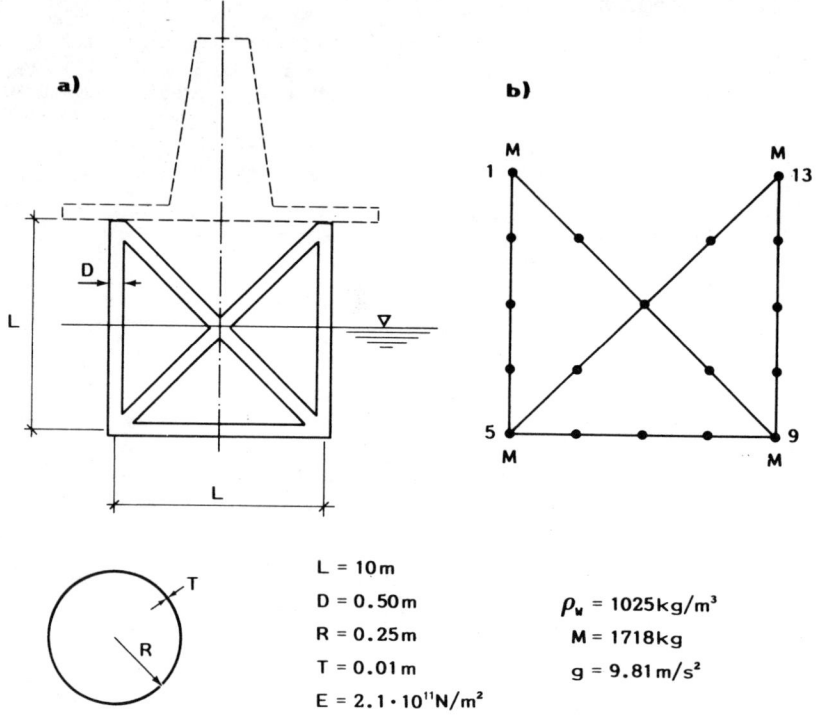

Fig. 2. Floating space frame. (a) Geometry (b) Finite element model

Analysis results. Figure 3 shows the prescribed, partially submerged, initial position of the frame and a sequence of computed configurations after the frame was suddenly released. The response was computed with a nonlinear dynamic algorithm with automatic computation of time steps. The frame is subjected to loads from own weight and buoyancy only. A high degree of mass-proportional damping corresponding to 20% of critical damping in heave motion was introduced.

Some simple checks confirmed that the computed final, stable configuration was the correct one. The present example demonstrates that the present method is capable of solving very large rotational motion of floating structures.

Irregular Wave Loading on a Jacket[12,13]

Description of the model. A jacket of 120 m height at a water depth of 101 m, see Fig. 4, is subjected to loads from irregular waves. Water particle velocities and accelerations have been generated from a wave spectrum described by the significant wave height and the zero up-crossing period. The generation has been carried out by a separate preprocessor of FENRIS. Main geometric and physical data of the structure;

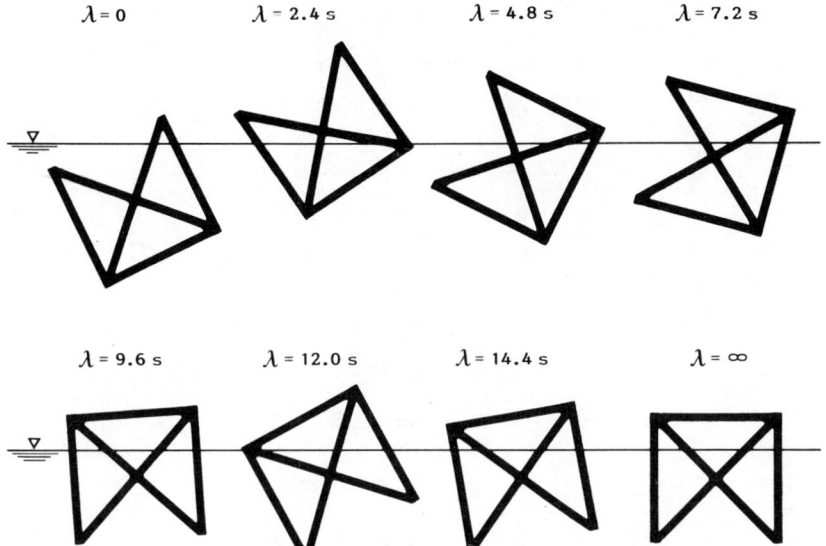

Fig. 3. Sequence of rotated positions of the frame

Number of elements   : 191 beam elements with tubular cross sections
Number of nodes   : 105
Degrees of freedom   : 606
Boundary conditions   : Fixed at bottom nodes
Modulus of elasticity: $2.1 \cdot 10^{11}$ N/m^2
Poisson's ration   : 0.3

Element cross sections:

Legs   : diameter = 1.5 m, thickness = 0.07 m
Bracings   : diameter = 0.75 m, thickness = 0.025 m
Vertical legs: diameter = 1.2 m, thickness = 0.035 m

The water particle velocities and accelerations are calculated at the two nodes of the elements and linearly distributed wave loads are predicted in between.

Analysis results. A wave spectrum of the Pierson-Moscovitz type is used in the present example. The significant wave height is 10 m and the zero up-crossing period is 10 sec. A short simulation of 100 sec duration is made. A time step of 2.5 sec is used in the wave kinematics generation, while a time step of 1 sec is used in the load generation. The generated surface elevation is shown in Fig. 5. The generated wave was applied to the structure parallel to the global x-axis.

The total support reaction (or total wave load) in global x-direction is plotted in Fig. 6. Results are compared with the WAJAC program in SESAM'80.

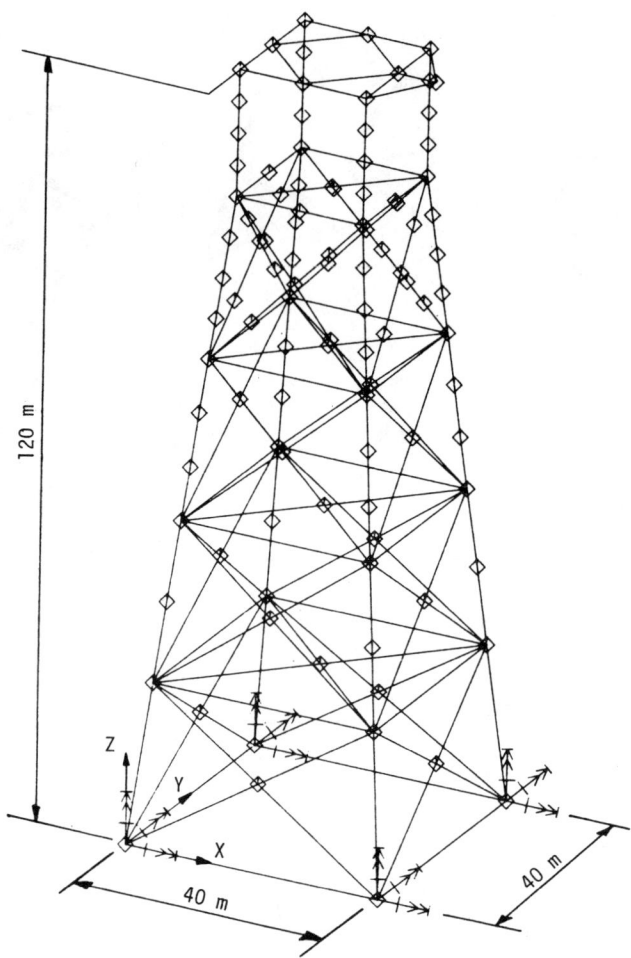

Fig. 4. Model of the jacket

Ultimate Capacity of 3-D System[18]

<u>Description of the model.</u> A 3-D X-braced frame has been analysed to investigate important effects related to the determination of reserve and residual strength of X-braced frames, see Fig. 7. Member dimensions of the frame and other key parameters are listed below. A total of 108 elements are used to model the frame; 8 elements for each of the diagonal braces, 4 elements for each of the horizontal members and 3 elements for each of the vertical legs. Initial deflections (sine waves) are applied to the members, for details see reference 18. The frame is subjected to vertical loads of a total of 120 MN and horizontal nodal loads that are increased until collapse occurs. The loads act at the four corner nodes of the frame, see Fig. 7. The frame is simply supported to ground.

FENRIS: Finite Element Nonlinear Integrated System

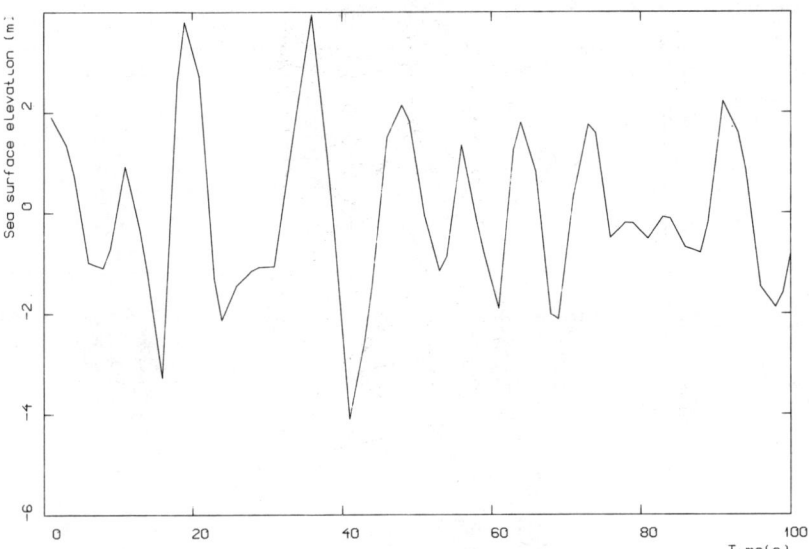

Fig. 5. Sea surface elevation

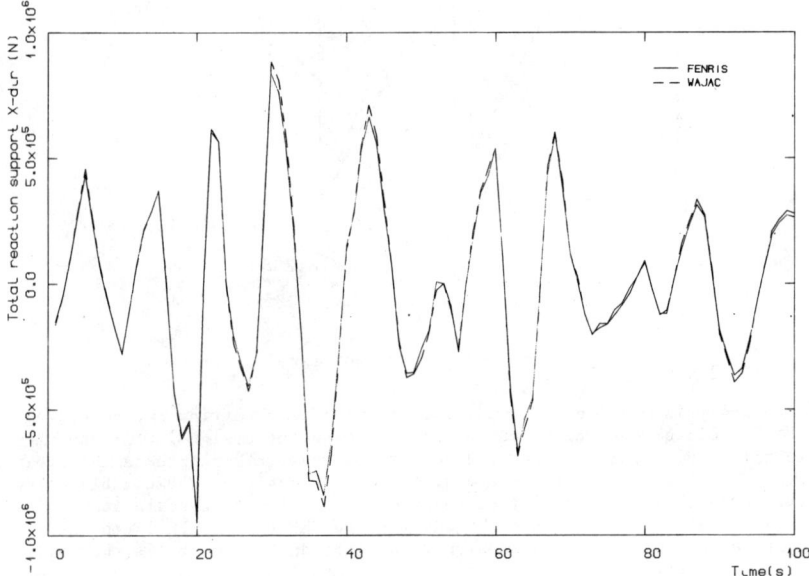

Fig. 6. Total reaction support in x-direction

Member type	Diameter D(m)	Thickness t(m)	Length l(m)	Ratio D/t	Slendern. L/r	Plastic ax.load (MN)	Plastic mom. (MNm)
Legs	2.0	0.060	28.259	33	41	120.67	74.54
Horiz.	1.0	0.040	18.288	25	54	39.80	12.17
Horiz. X-braces	1.0	0.040	25.86	25	76	39.80	12.7
Vertical X-braces	0.508	0.019	33.66	26.7	195	9.63	1.5

<u>Analysis results</u>. The ultimate capacity of the present frame has been thoroughly investigated[18] under different conditions by varying the type of loading, slenderness ratio, initial imperfections and the condition of damaged and undamaged members. Only two out of eleven cases are reported here. See reference 18 for detailing about the analyses.

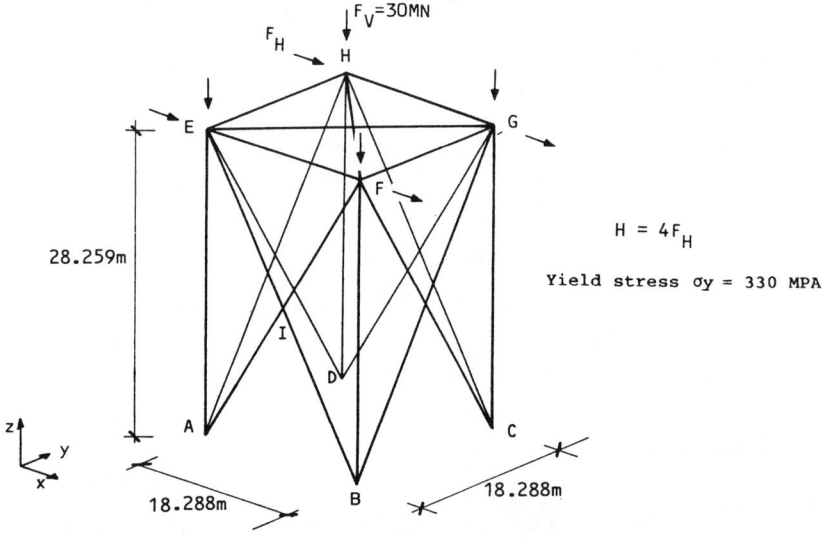

Fig. 7. X-braced frame

A design analysis based on allowable stress was first carried out according to the API-procedure, see reference 18, to determine the design load (resulting horizontal load). This is required before the reserve strength can be evaluated. The evaluation of reserve and residual strength are given in the table below. Reserve strength is the ability of an undamaged system to sustain loads exceeding the design load and is expressed by the measure REF=P_u/P_d. P_u is the ultimate limit state load and P_d is the design load. Residual strength is the ability of the system to sustain loads after a member has failed or been severely damaged. The residual strength is expressed by the factor RIP=P_r/P_u, where P_r is the load that the structure can sustain in a damaged condition. Damaged condition is in the present analysis simulated by removing the member IF, see Fig. 7. Collapse is defined to take place when the system is unable to carry more load due to buckling in compression or yielding in tension.

Condition	Design load (MN)	Collapse load (MN)	REF	RIF	REF*RIF
Undamaged	8.0	16.9	2.11	-	-
Damaged	-	10.6	-	0.63	1.32

Failure mode of the frame is shown in Fig. 8. The failure is dominated by out-of-plane displacements.

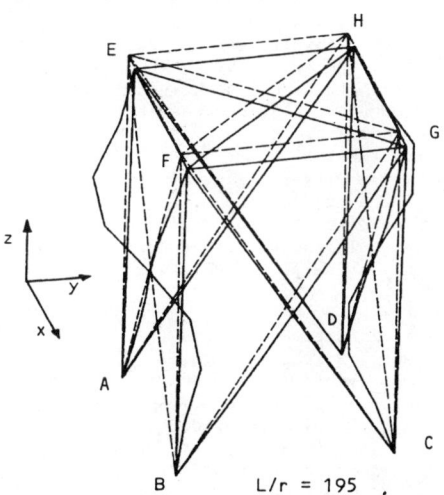

Fig. 8. Failure mode of X-braced frame

Potential Application Areas of FENRIS

The main area of application is within research, civil engineering, offshore, shipping industry. Oil companies, field developers, engineering companies, shipyards and designers and consultants engaged in the corresponding activity are potential users. Other areas such as within automotive, machinery, industry and aeronautics are also potential users of FENRIS.

REFERENCES

1. FENRIS Manuals, Theory-Program Outline - Data Input, NTH, SINTEF, VERITEC, Dec. 1984.
2. Bergan, P. G. and A. Arnesen. FENRIS - A General Purpose Nonlinear Finite Element Program, Proc. on 4th Int. Conf. on Finite Element Systems, Southampton, July 6-8, 1983.
3. Bergan, P. G. Nonlinear Finite Element Analysis by Use of FENRIS, Proc. on 7th Int. Seminar on Computational Aspects of Finite Element Method, (CAFEM-7), Chicago, Aug. 29-30, 1983.
4. SESAM'80, General Description, Veritec, August 1984.
5. Bergan, P. G. and E. Mollestad, Static and Dynamic Solution Strategies in

Nonlinear Analysis. In *Recent Advances in Nonlinear Computational Mechanics*, editors E. Hinton, D. R. J. Owe and C. Taylor, Pineridge Press, 1982.
6. Bergan, P. G. and E. Mollestad, An Automatic Time Stepping Algorithm for Dynamic Problems, Accepted for publication in *Computer Method in Applied Mechanics and Engineering*.
7. Mollestad, E. Techniques for Static and Dynamic Solution of Nonlinear Finite Element Problems. Dr.ing. Dissertation, Division of Structural Mechanics, Report 84.1. The Norwegian Institute of Technology, Trondheim, Norway, 1984.
8. Bergan, P. G. Automated Incremental-Iterative Solution Methods in Structural Mechanics. In *Recent Advances in Nonlinear Computational Mechanics*, editors E. Hinton, D. R. J. Owe and C. Taylor, Pineridge Press, 1982.
9. Simons, J., P. G. Bergan and M. Nygard. Hyperplane Displacement Control Methods in Nonlinear Analysis, in *Innovated Methods for Nonlinear Problems*, edited by W. K. Liu, T. Belytchko, K. C. Park, Pineridge Press, Swansea, 1984.
10. Bergan, P. G. and K. M. Mathisen. Modelling of Hydrostatic Loading and Stability for Coupled Fluid. Structure Problems, In *Numerical Methods in Engineering: Theory and Application*, edited by J. Middleton, G. N. Pande, Balkema Press, Rotterdam 1985.
11. Mathisen, K. M. Doctoral Dissertation, Division of Structural Mechanics, The Norwegian Institute of Technology, to appear in 1986.
12. Hansen, H. T. Doctoral Dissertation, Division of Structural Mechanics, The Norwegian Institute of Technology, to appear in 1986.
13. SESAM'80 Verification and Example Manual, A.S VERITEC, May 1984 and Dec. 1984.
14. Arnesen, A., P. G. Bergan, E. Mollestad and N. Mjøs. Nonlinear Finite Element Analysis of Offshore Structure, *4th World Congress and Exhibit*. 17-21/9-84, Interlaken, Switzerland.
15. Bergan, P. G. and M. K. Nygard. Plate Bending Elements based on Orthogonal Functions, ASCE-ASME Summer Conference, Symp. on New Concepts in Finite Element Methods, University of Colorado, Boulder, Colorado 1981, ASME, Vol. AMD-44.
16. Bergan, P. G., M. K. Nygard and X. Wang. A Class of Quadrilateral Plate Bending Elements, Int. Conf. on Finite Element Methods, Shanghai, China, 1982.
17. Bergan, P. G. and M. K. Nygard. Finite Elements with Increased Freedom in Choosing Shape Functions, *Proc. on Inter. Journal of Numerical Methods in Engineering*, Vol. *20*, pp. 643-663, 1984.
18. Engseth, A. Finite Element Collapse Analysis of Tubular Steel Offshore Structures, Div. of Marine Structures, The University of Trondheim, The Norwegian Institute of Technology, 1985

FIESTA: THE p-VERSION APPROACH IN FINITE ELEMENT ANALYSIS

P. Angeloni, R. Boccellato, E. Bonacina, A. Pasini and A. Peano

ISMES, Bergamo, Italy

ABSTRACT

FIESTA is a computer program for the static and thermal analysis of solid structures based on the p-version of the finite element method. The p-version capability of FIESTA is the result of recent scientific advances concerning the approximation properties of polynomials. In the conventional finite element method the mesh is designed for two purposes: to represent the geometrical model and to control the error of approximation. In FIESTA the mesh is designed primarily for representation of model geometry. The error of approximation is controlled separately through the addition of polynomial shape functions. The user directly controls the desired level of precision by changing one input parameter, polynomial order, to increase the number of degrees of freedom. Alternatively, the polynomial distribution that satisfies the accuracy requirements can be automatically generated on the basis of the error indicator implemented in the program. This brings important benefits to the user; among them greater reliability and reduced cost.

THEORETICAL BACKGROUND

The solutions of most engineering problems cannot be written in terms of simple functions. Consequently engineers use the finite element method to produce approximations of the exact solution. The goal of computation, then, is to produce approximate solutions so that the discrepancy (error) between the computed results and the exact solution is within acceptable bounds.

The error of approximation can be made arbitrarily small by increasing the number of degrees of freedom. Depending on whether the degrees of freedom are increased by mesh refinement or by increased sophistication of the elements, we speak of h-version or p-version of the finite element method. In the conventional approach, h-version, the number and type of shape functions are fixed for each element and the finite element mesh is refined in such a way that the maximum diameter of the element (h) becomes smaller and smaller. Thus, the error of approximation is controlled by the size of the elements.

The distinguishing feature of the p-version approach is that the number and distribution of finite elements is fixed, while the number of shape functions, which are complete polynomials of order p, are progressively increased over some or all elements (see Fig. 1).

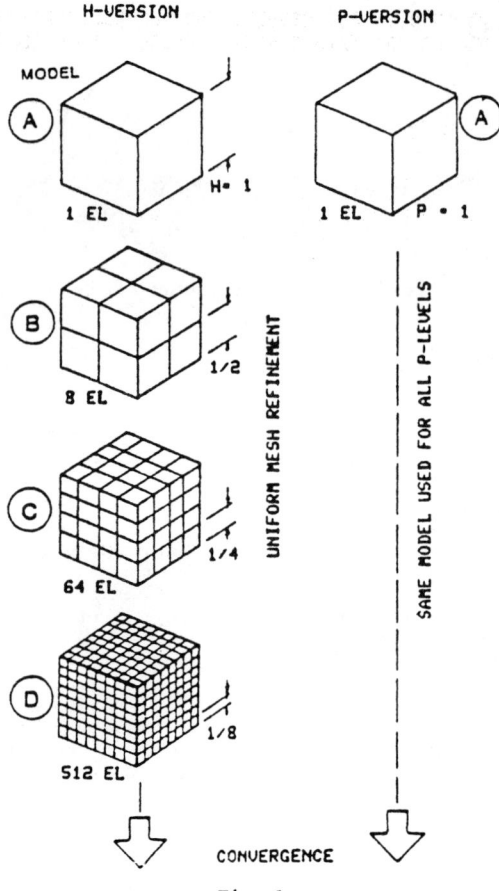

Fig. 1.

Each level of approximation is obtained by adding higher order shape functions to the ones used in the previous level. Therefore the stiffness matrices of lower order elements are embedded in the stiffness matrices of higher order elements (hierarchic property) so that considerable savings are achieved in the integration process.

Theoretical studies and numerical experimentations indicate that the rate of the p-version approach is twice as fast as the rate of h-version when uniform mesh refinement is used (see Fig. 2). The fast convergence rate provided by the p-version leads to considerable savings of manpower because relatively coarse meshes can be used.

Six increasingly sophisticated levels of approximation (p-levels) may be used in FIESTA. The highest level of polynomial approximation is fourth order. Typical shape functions corresponding to the various levels of approximation are shown in Fig. 3.

The first level comprises shape functions which vary linearly along the element sides. Each variable corresponds to a nodal value of displacement or temperature

FIESTA: The p-version Approach in Finite Element Analysis 115

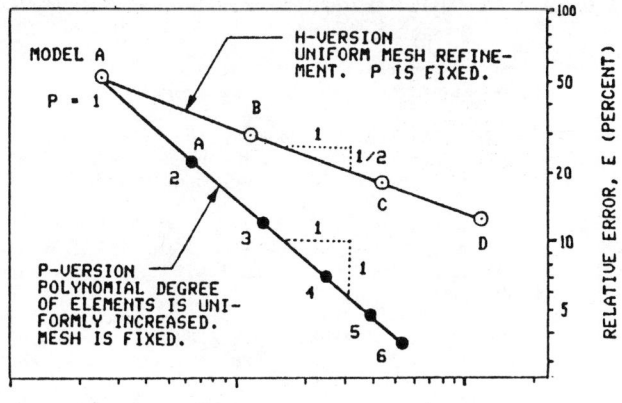

Fig. 2.

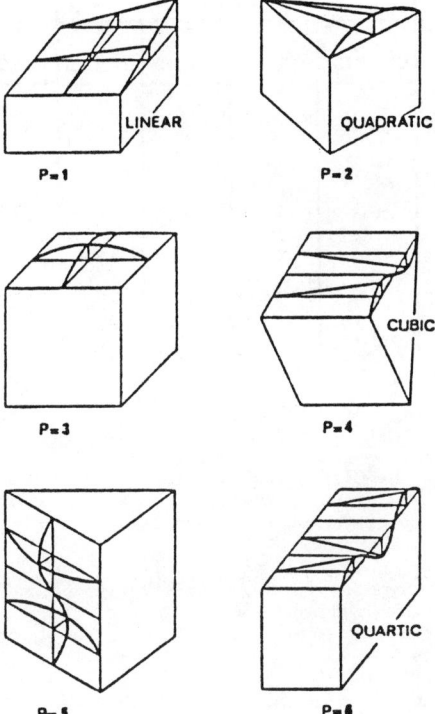

Fig. 3.

and therefore these first level elements are similar to those available in other finite element programs.

The second level of approximation is obtained by adding shape functions that vary quadratically along one element edge and are zero along the other edges. The performance of these elements is identical to that of the well-known quadratic isoparametric elements. The higher levels of approximation in FIESTA represent a unique departure from the h-version in that degrees of freedom are added to elements without the user having to specify more nodes.

In the third level of approximation, for example, each new shape function is zero along all element edges but different from zero on one element face. It varies quadratically along sections parallel to the edges of that face.

Similar sophistication is built into the fourth and fifth levels. Finally, at the sixth level of approximation (the highest level in FIESTA) the shape functions added are polynomials that vary quartically along one edge and are zero along all other edges.

Figure 4 summarizes the number of degrees of freedom for various different levels of interpolation in one hexahedron element. The data indicates that FIESTA is capable of increasing the number of degrees of freedom almost by one order of magnitude over the original mesh.

PLEVEL	DOF/FIELD				DOF/ELEM
	VERTEX	EDGE	FACE	TOTAL	TOTAL
1	8	-	-	8	24
2	8	12	-	20	60
3	8	12	6	26	78
4	8	24	6	38	114
5	8	24	18	50	150
6	8	36	18	62	186

Fig. 4.

The p-level grading is the distinguishing feature of FIESTA that gives the user the freedom to select individually the order of approximation over each element, without any modification of the stored input data.

In addition, the optimal polynomial distribution compatible with the user accuracy and cost requirements can be automatically defined by the program. This is achieved through the computation of an error indicator that orders the available degrees of freedom on the basis of the related contribution to the quality of the solution.

Each automatically selected polynomial distribution is comprised of all degrees of freedom that contribute for more than a given percentage to the quality of the solution.

This means that it is possible to use, in the computations, sequences of almost uniformly-refined models that produce results that can be easily extrapolated up to the asymptotic values.

FIESTA: The p-version Approach in Finite Element Analysis   117

FIELD OF APPLICATION

Geometrical

FIESTA is a computer program for the analysis of 3-D continuum structures. The simplicity of the model in FIESTA provides the flexibility to make changes to the model so that it is possible to evaluate a larger number of alternative designs within time and resources constraints. The FIESTA models require a minimum amount of mesh modifications for a given redesign and reduce the long and generally tedious tasks needed by conventional general purpose programs.

Materials

The current release of FIESTA is capable of representing the linear behaviour of materials with temperature dependence in case of static analysis. The materials may be isotropic, transversely isotropic, orthotropic, as well as generally anisotropic. These material laws allow for the treatment of many difficult problems. For example, applications with laminated materials are well handled by a transversely isotropic description.

Analysis Capabilities

The FIESTA program has been developed for the linear analysis of 3-D continua. Static stress analysis and steady-state and periodic thermal analyses can be executed. Each analysis operates on the same data structure that is completely independent of the type of computation being executed. This allows a lot of saving in data preparation and computer time used in computations.

Loadings

A large variety of loading types are treated by FIESTA. Concentrated forces and fluxes may be applied to both vertex and midsided nodes, as well as anywhere within the element volume. General surface loads and fluxes may be applied. Uniform and variable intensities are available, as well as hydrostatic pressure distribution and fluxes directly ensuing from convective heat exchange. In most of the cases the faces affected by the surface load can be conveniently specified by the surface identification method available in the program. Body forces including weight (gravity) and centrifugal loading can be specified and applied to all or any part of the model. Prescribed displacements and temperatures may be specified as loading conditions. Initial stress distributions can be assumed, for instance, in rock and soil mechanics applications. Thermal strains are computed on the basis of user defined nodal temperature distributions, or temperature distributions directly obtained from the thermal analyses.

PROGRAM DESCRIPTION

Type of Elements

The finite element code FIESTA uses a library of solid elements of various shapes, including hexahedra (bricks), triangular prisms (wedges), tetrahedra and pyramids. The element shapes can have either straight or curved edges. The element shapes and their nodal numbering are shown in Fig. 5. All elements types can be used within the same model. Additionally the joining of elements with different polynomial order is permitted. Complete interelement compatibility and continuity is always assured by FIESTA. The robust properties of FIESTA elements allow model parameters to vary over a much wider range than in the h-version programs.

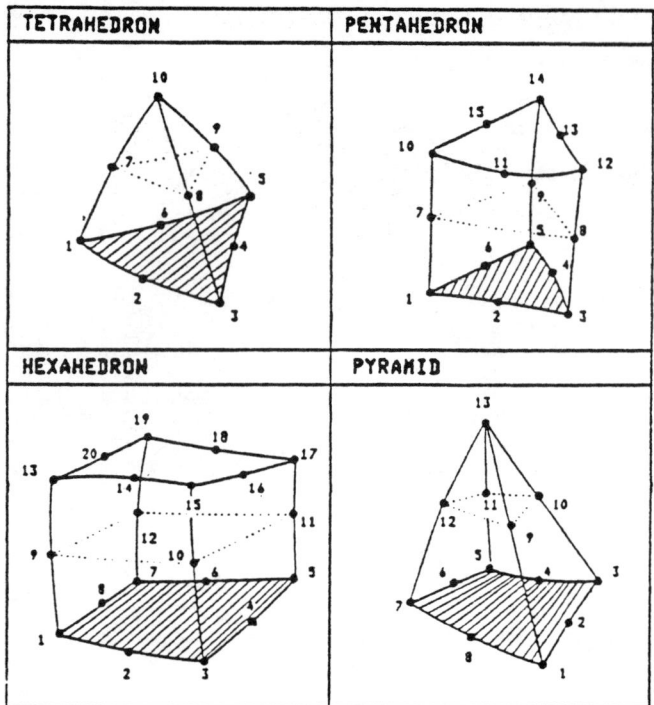

Fig. 5.

For example, Poisson's ratio of .4999, high element distortion (Jacobian ratios up to 10-20), and large aspect ratios (1:50 and higher) will not noticeably downgrade the performance of the models when high p-levels are used (Fig. 6). As a consequence these elements can be successfully employed even in plate and shell applications (Fig. 7). Similarly, beams with high aspect ratios can also be represented.

Program Structure

FIESTA has a highly modular structure on both a macro-level and a micro-level. All the major computational steps have been coded into separable, self-contained components that may be executed by the user as needed. The macrostructure of FIESTA consists of three types of modules: geometric modeling, analysis and output. The geometric modeling module is independent of the type of analysis to be developed. During this phase, a 3-D mesh can be prepared, visualized and checked. The analysis modules perform the computations. The output module, also independent of the type of analysis performed, executes the postprocessing and plotting of the results. Each of the modules described above has, in turn, a microstructure composed of several small processors. Each processor executes a single separate function. The execution sequence of the processors is determined by the order in which the input data is prepared. This attribute is advantageous because it is possible to start the execution (and the debugging) of a segment of data as soon as it is ready, without waiting for the completion of the data for all the modules. Moreover the modular structure permits the most CPU-intensive tasks to be scheduled during the most convenient time without

ASPECT RATIO FREEDOM

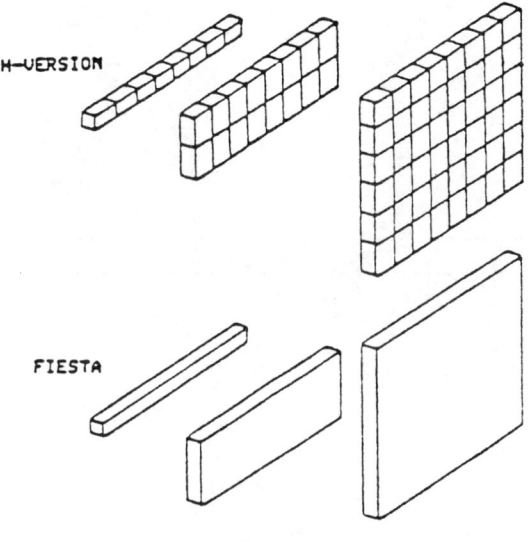

Fig. 6.

any concern for the restart.

FIESTA offers automatic generation schemes to be applied separately to nodes and elements. This uncoupled approach lends itself to the treatment of the most complex geometry details. In such cases it is still possible to apply at least one of the generation methods independent of the other to great advantage. Both generation methods are based on the node number patterns with unique numerical increments in 3 primary generation directions (3 levels). The full power of these incremental generators are appreciated after only minimal use.

The program searches for faces on the surfaces of the model and groups then according to a user defined smoothness tolerance. Each surface is uniquely identified through a number that can be directly referenced to specify in compact form loadings and constraints, as well as areas where output results and plots are required. The surfaces can also be used as a powerful topological debugging tool for the model. Spurious surfaces are in fact identified when there are voids or connectivity errors, or when an incorrect placement of nodes produces undesired kinks or warps in the surfaces.

Executing a complete analysis at the lowest polynomial order (p = 1) provides the most economical and yet comprehensive checkout available. Since a complete solution is obtained, all participating processors are exercised although the desired level of accuracy is lacking. From the reaction and flux balance, magnitude and character of displacements and temperatures, matrix conditioning, etc., most important conclusions about the validity of the analysis can be made.

Furthermore, many internal checks are performed by FIESTA to control the correctness of the finite element model and associated data. The following are the most important: syntax checking of the free format input to detect wrong entries, topology checking to identify inconsistencies, procedural logic checking to identify invalid data or requests, distortion checking to indicate wrong element shapes, etc.

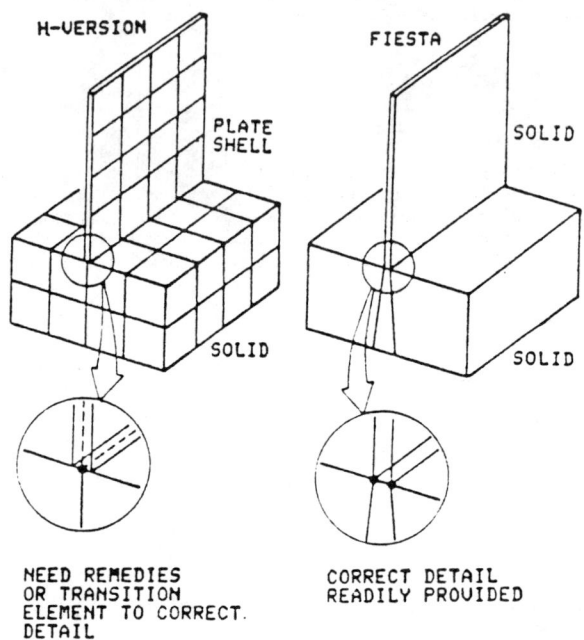

Fig. 7.

FIESTA provides the capabilities to plot from the solution files (1) any desired function along a user defined group of points, (2) any set of contour lines of temperatures, fluxes, stresses, strains and displacements from any part of the structure. A deformed shape plot can be obtained from results of the static analysis. Stress distributions computed along straight lines can be automatically integrated to obtain global resultant forces and moments. This feature is useful for designing the steel reinforcement for concrete structures or for executing particular types of integrity assessments.

HARDWARE COMPATIBILITIES

The FIESTA program has been completely coded using standard FORTRAN 77 so that any installation can be arranged provided that the computer required has a FORTRAN 77 compiler.

The program consists of about 70 thousand FORTRAN statements and is developed and maintained on a 32-bit virtual memory machine. The memory required by the program, which depends on the size of the problem and type of analysis to be executed, is automatically allocated by FIESTA. A standard machine configuration with about 0.5 Mbytes of central memory and more than 20 Mbytes of disk storage, can be enough to run in double precision problems up to about 5000 degrees of freedom.

FIESTA: The p-version Approach in Finite Element Analysis   121

Special versions of the program are available for fixed memory machines that
require a segmentation of the code.

Any type of graphic device can be used to visualize the files produced by the
FIESTA plotting modules. The intermediate neutral plot file generated by the
program can in fact be routed to the various devices by making use of the
utilities delivered together with the code. Both floppy disks and magnetic
tapes can be used as media to deliver the program.

EXAMPLES OF APPLICATION

The Test Case

The test case selected to show the capabilities of the program is the classic
fracture mechanics problem of the semi-elliptical surface crack. The problem is
particularly interesting as the numerical solution can be easily compared with
results available in the technical literature, as well as for the fact that it
highlights the extremely refined level of accuracy that can be obtained using
FIESTA.

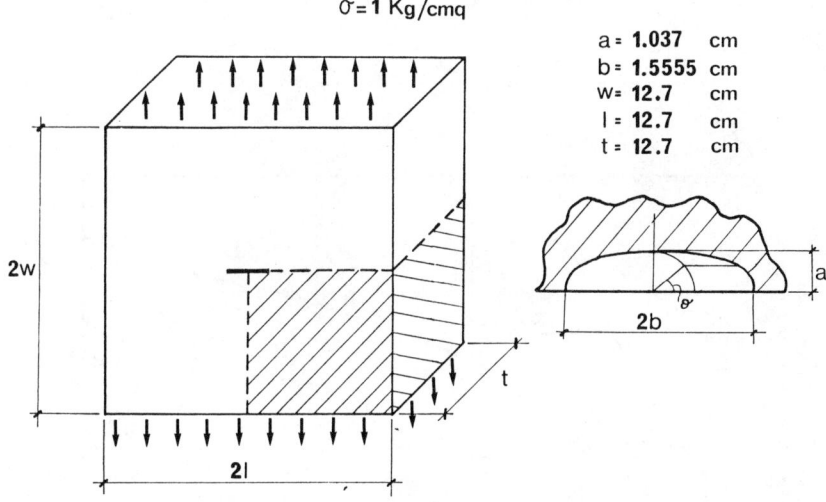

Fig. 8(a).

The problem (see Fig. 8a-b) is solved by using elements whose dimensions, in the
area of the crack, completely span the total length of the crack. Using all
elements at the same level of approximation, a number of degrees of freedom
ranging from 153 to 2241 can be defined. Instead of selecting user defined
polynomial distributions, the computations herewith presented are based on
distributions automatically determined by the program.

Elements of the various levels of approximation are used in the model in such a
way to distribute everywhere the degrees of freedom, according to the "needs" of
the various parts of the structure. Higher order elements are automatically
generated at the crack front, meanwhile lower order elements are progressively
used going away from the critical area. Results of the first computation carried
out with a model comprised of 1209 degrees of freedom are shown in Fig. 9.

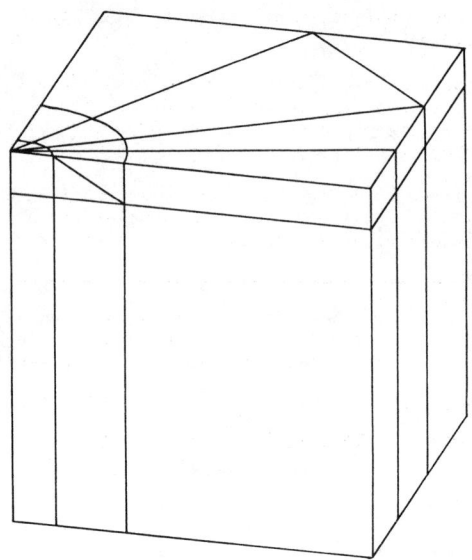

Fig. 8(b).

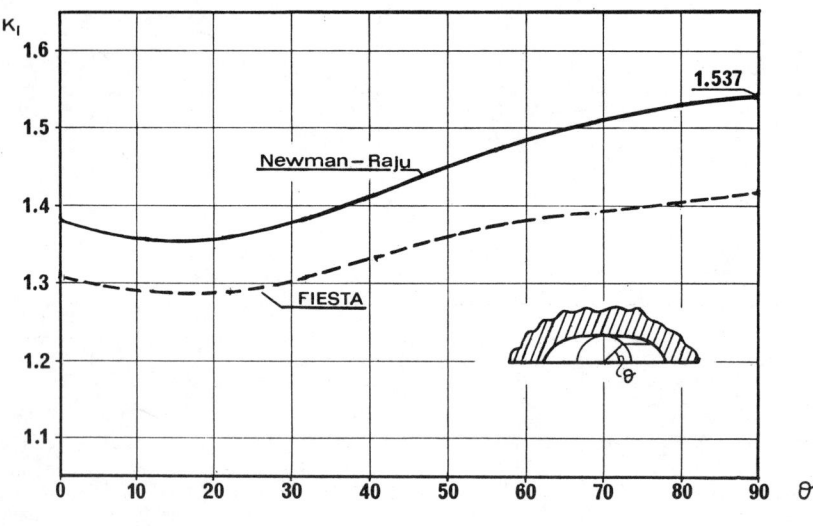

Fig. 9.

The trend of the stress intensity factor computed along the crack front is compared with results of the same problem obtained by the Newman-Raju equation. The stress intensity factors attain the maximum value at $\theta = 90$, and at that location the discrepancy between results is of about 8%. To improve and assess the accuracy of the results, a second computation is executed. Again an automatic polynomial distribution is selected, but in this case only 604 degrees of freedom are used. The new results are presented in Fig. 10 for node location corresponding to $\theta = 0.0$ and $\theta = 90$.

Although separately less accurate, these results, combined with the ones of the previous execution, allow an extrapolation beyond the accuracy of the finite element solution. The intercept value at 1/NDOF=0 (NDOF = ∞) is in fact a good "first guess" of the theoretical solution.

At $\theta = 90$, the extrapolated value of the K_I matches exactly the value given by the Newman-Raju equation. At $\theta = 0.0$ where the smaller radius of curvature makes the model more crude, a discrepancy less than 2% is also obtained.

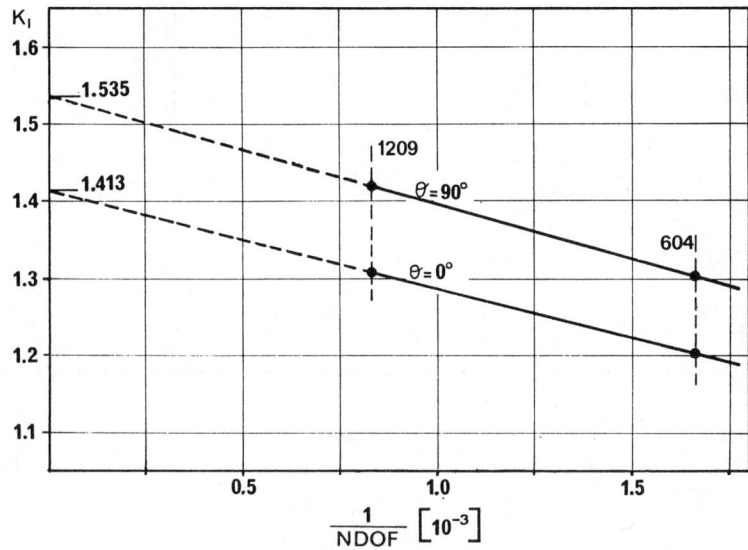

Fig. 10.

Example of an Application in Mechanical Engineering

An example of the possible applications of the FIESTA program in the field of mechanical engineering is now presented. The problem is related to the thermal and structural analysis of a three-ring petrol piston that had shown an unexpected failure in the area of the cooling hole.

A 20° sector of the analyzed structure is illustrated in Fig. 11. The drawing produced by FIESTA shows the external surface of the piston as computed by the program. The finite element mesh corresponding to the same sector of the piston is also shown.

Forty-four elements are used to properly model the geometry of the structure and take into account the areas corresponding to the different materials that constitute the piston. A uniform distribution of cubic order elements is assumed for thermal analysis that is developed with a total number of degrees of freedom of 1095.

The critical thermal distribution obtained from thermal analysis is presented in Fig. 12 where temperature contour lines are drawn on the lateral surface of the

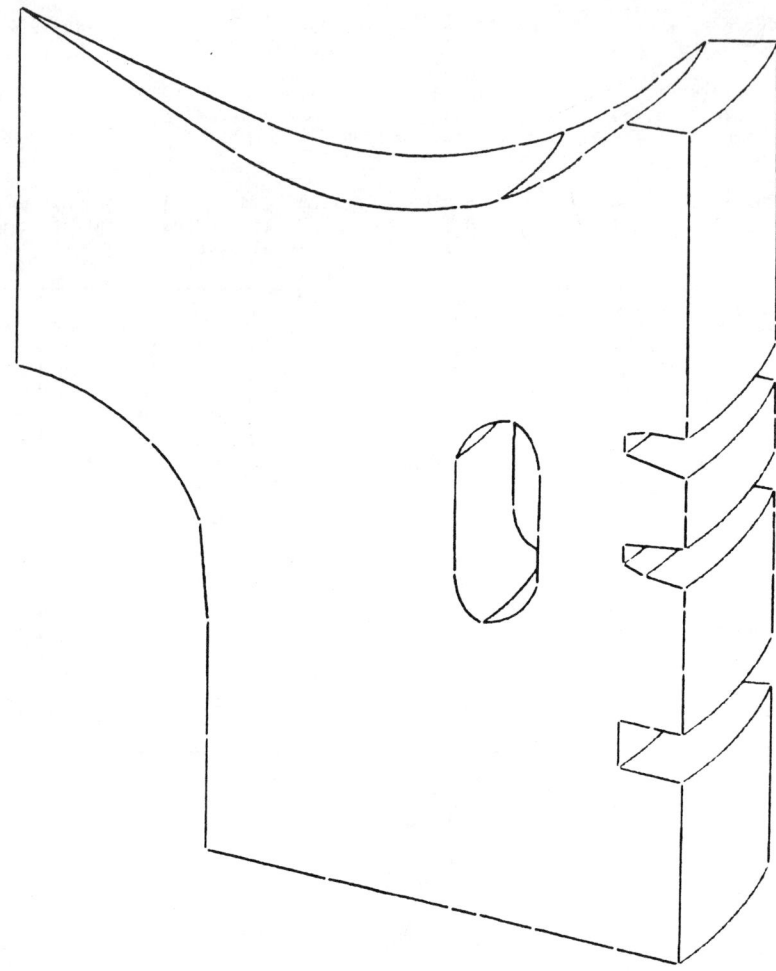

Fig. 11(a).

piston. A refined polynomial distribution is selected for stress analysis. Fourth order elements are used everywhere in the model for a total number of 5811 degrees of freedom. The deformed shape configuration of the piston under thermal and mechanical loadings is shown in Fig. 13. Also shown are the computed stress concentrations that produced the failure.

Example of an Application in Civil Engineering

The possibility of application of FIESTA in civil engineering is demonstrated by the solution of a problem concerning a hollow buttress gravity dam. The structure is mainly investigated to compute the level of stresses produced by the thermal variations that cyclically occur during the year. After a statistical analysis of the measured data, the thermal loadings applied to the dam can be in fact described by mean of periodic functions that are directly treated by FIESTA. The finite element model of the analyzed structure is shown

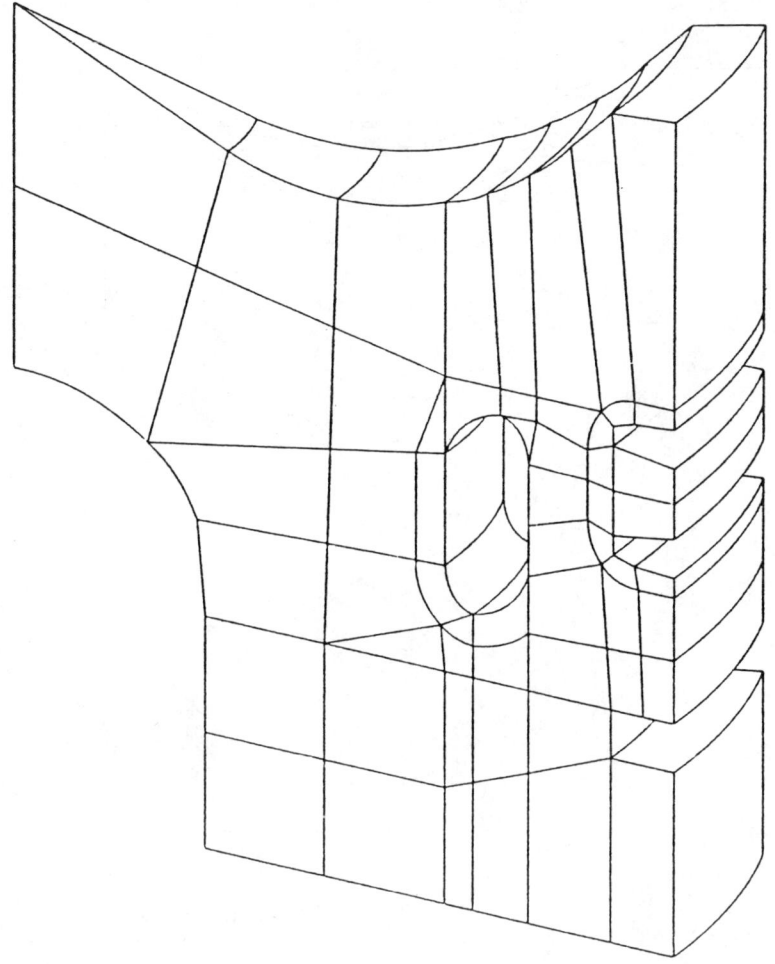

Fig. 11(b).

in Fig. 14. The mesh is comprised of 104 elements that, for symmetry considerations, reproduce half of the buttress only. User defined polynomial distributions of quadratic, cubic and quartic elements are used for a total number of 2308 and 5215 degrees of freedom, for the thermal and structural analysis, respectively. An example of the results of the thermal periodic analysis, is illustrated in Fig. 15(a). The plot shows the contour lines of the May temperature distribution computed on the internal horizontal section of the dam highlighted in the model. The values refer to the temperature deviations measured with respect to the mean yearly ambient temperature.

Figure 15(b) shows the corresponding results of the stress analysis. The contour lines refer to the distribution of the stress component oriented in the direction of the axis connecting the abutments of the dam. The stresses are only due to thermal loadings, as the level of the reservoir in May does not reach the level of the section studied and as the gravity stress components are not shown.

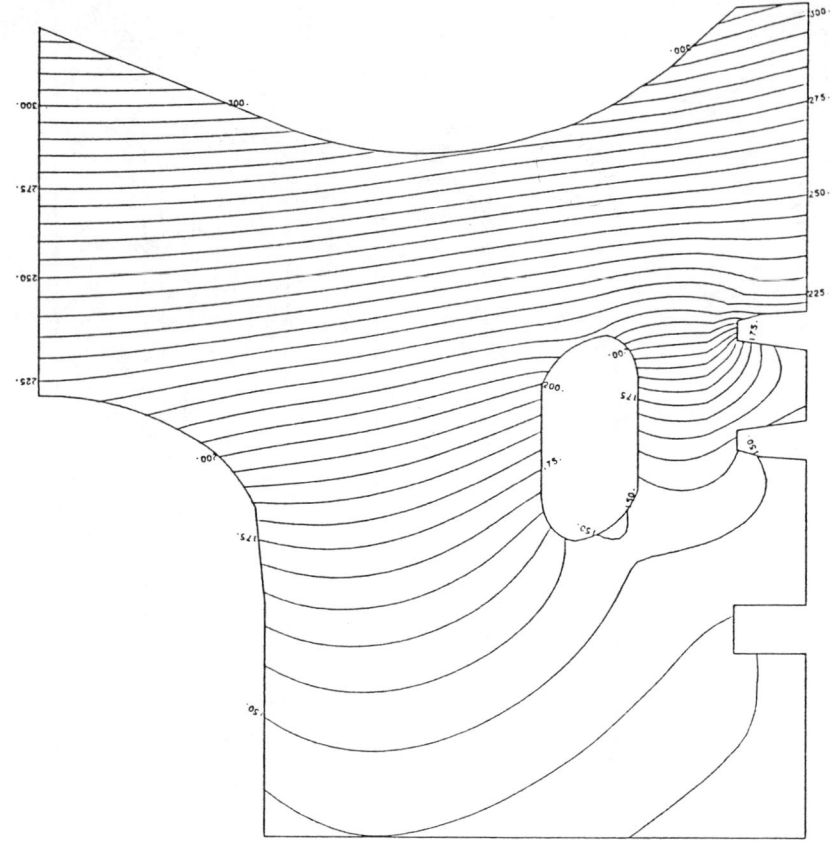

Fig. 12.

Other Fields of Application (see Appendix)

FIESTA features enable it to treat a broad spectrum of applications involving solids, fabricated assemblies, built-up structures, etc. By using 3-D elements all essential features of a model can be represented and therefore the most accurate solutions are obtained. This is especially valuable for intersecting parts, lap joints, welds, and support surfaces which are usually of great interest to the analyst.

The versatile nature of the element makes FIESTA suitable for use in many industries and disciplines. The program has been used especially in mechanical and civil engineering, particularly in the design and analysis of dams, valves, pipe intersections, nozzles, brackets, mechanical components, concrete structures and monoliths and biomechanical applications.

Applications have also been developed for the nuclear and aerospace industries where the extreme accuracy and reliability of FIESTA computations has been particularly appreciated.

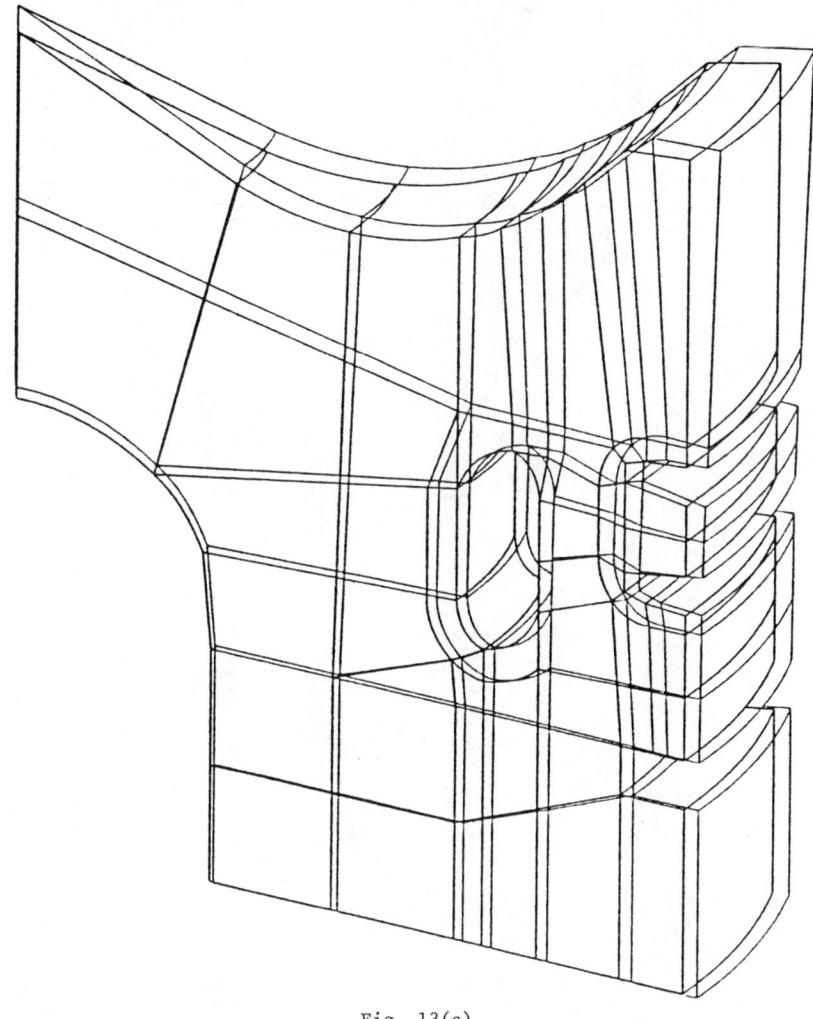

Fig. 13(a)

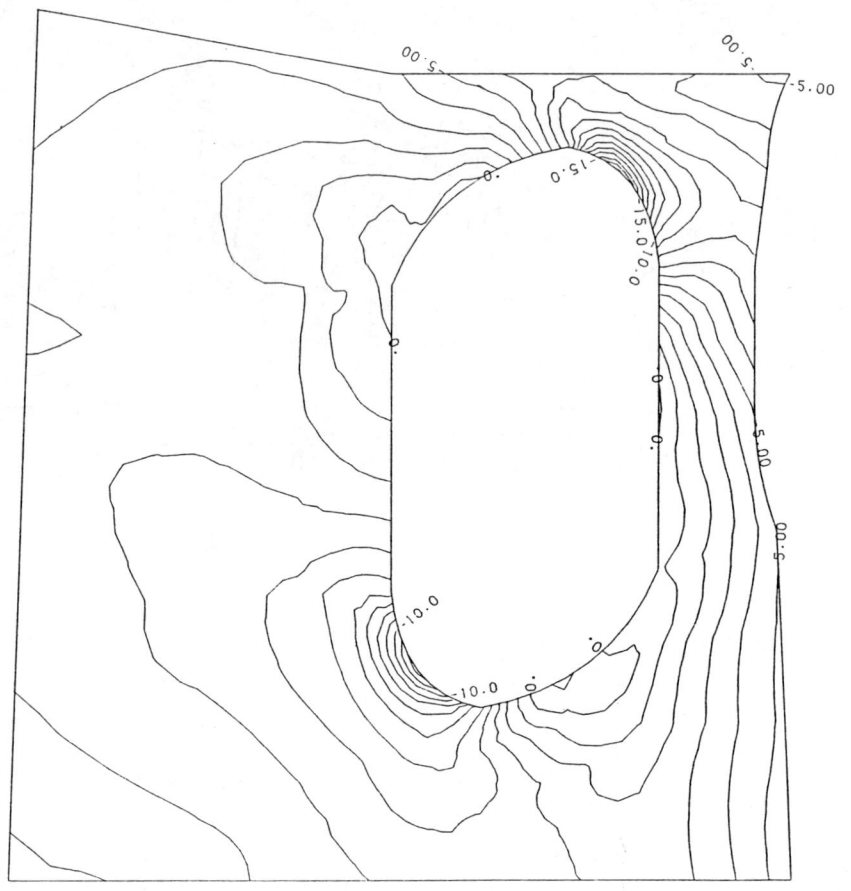

Fig. 13(b)

FIESTA: The p-version Approach in Finite Element Analysis 129

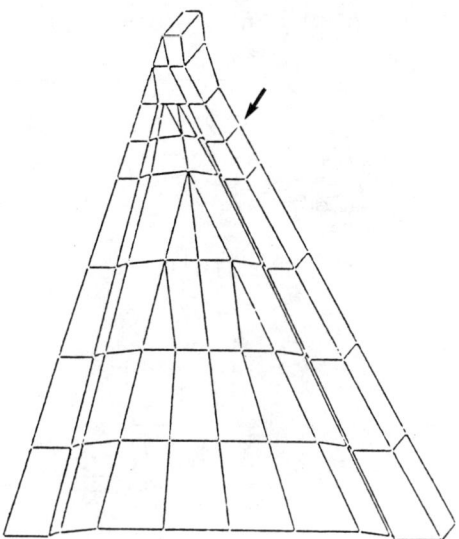

Fig. 14.

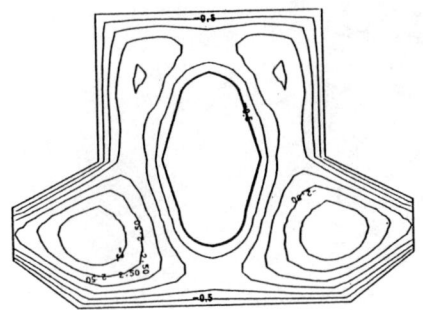 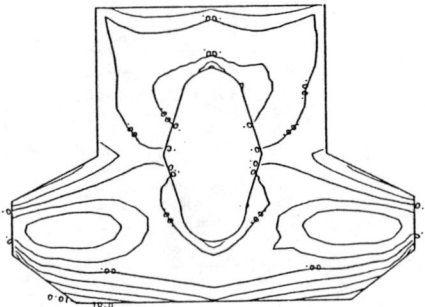

(a)   (b)

Fig. 15.

FIESTA MODELS FOR BALL VALVE ANALYSES

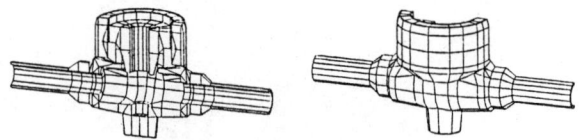

2-INCH BUTTWELDED VALVE

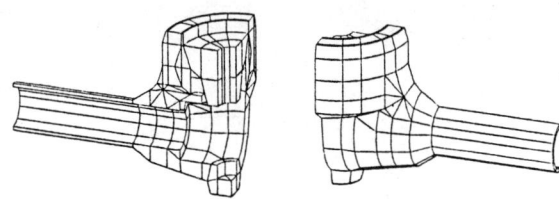

4-INCH BUTTWELDED VALVE

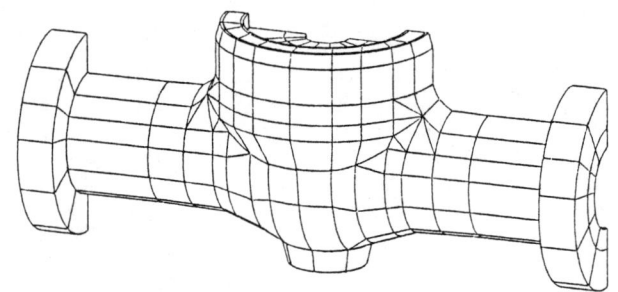

8-INCH FLANGED VALVE

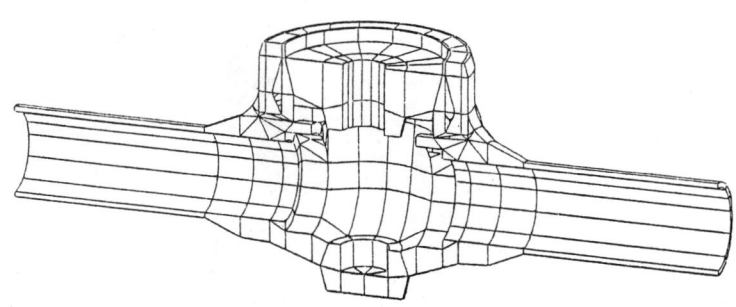

8-INCH BUTTWELDED VALVE

Appendix 1

FIESTA MODELS AND RESULTS FOR THE RESTORATION ANALYSIS OF A 17TH-CENTURY CHURCH IN GUBBIO (ITALY)

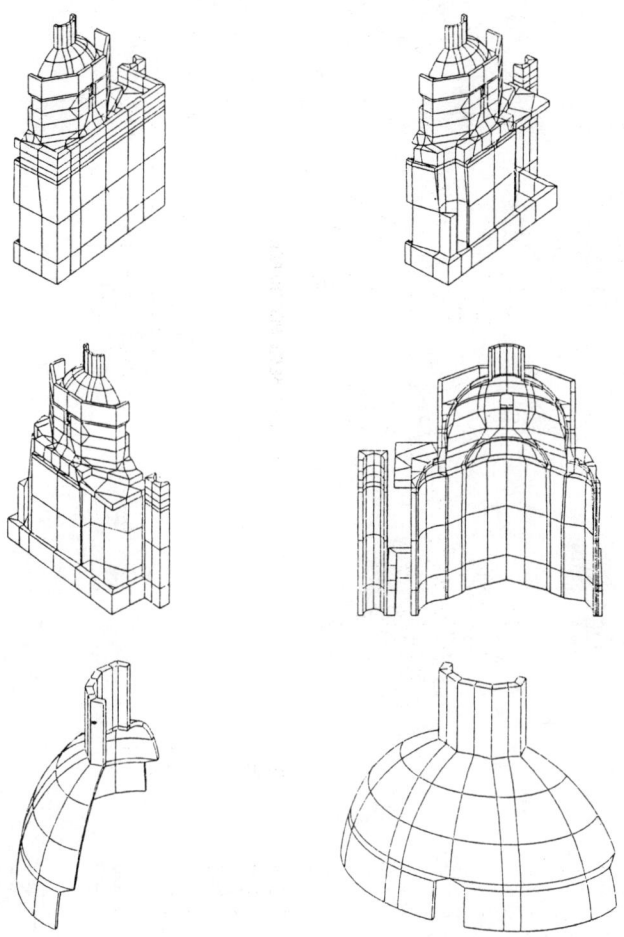

Appendix 2

FIESTA INDUSTRIAL APPLICATIONS

ACTUATOR ARM ANALYSIS

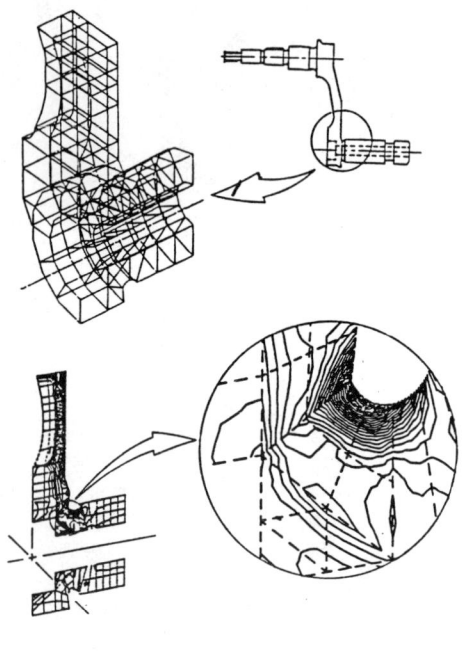

INTERSECTING BORE DETAIL

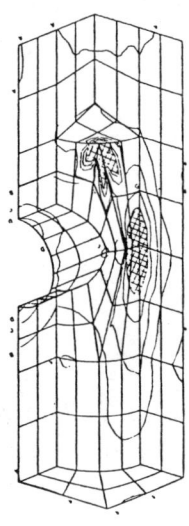

ATTACHMENT BRACKET

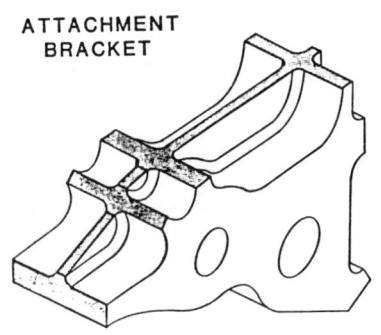

Appendix 3

FIESTA INDUSTRIAL APPLICATIONS

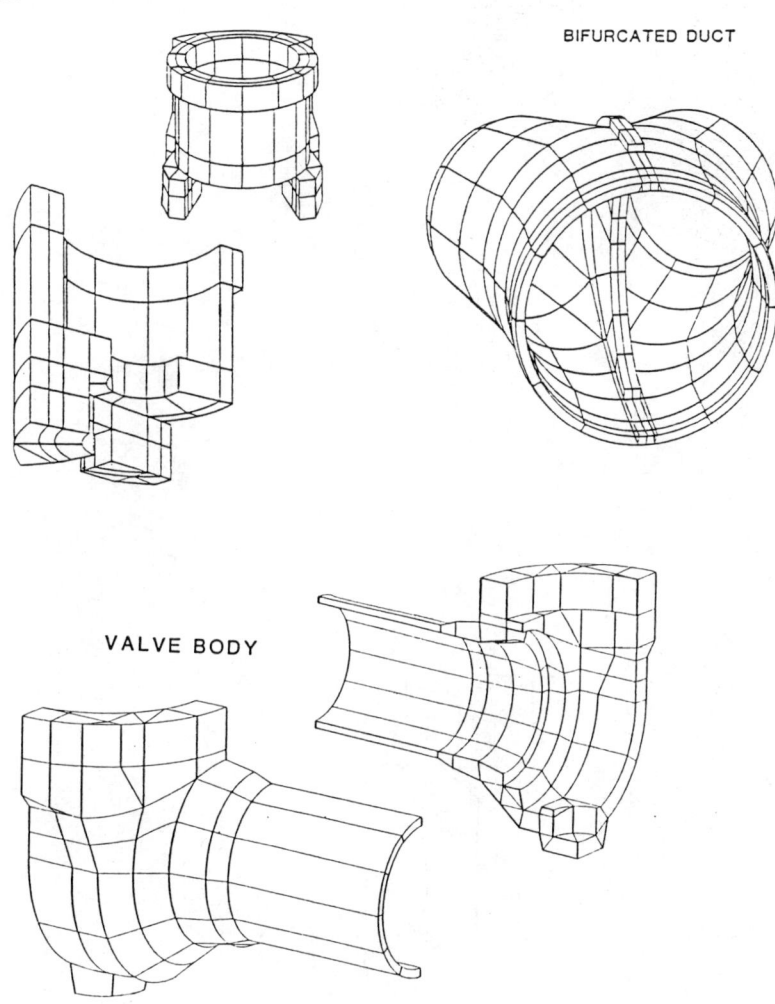

TURBO ALTERNATOR
BEARING STRUCTURE

BIFURCATED DUCT

VALVE BODY

Appendix 4

FIESTA INDUSTRIAL APPLICATIONS

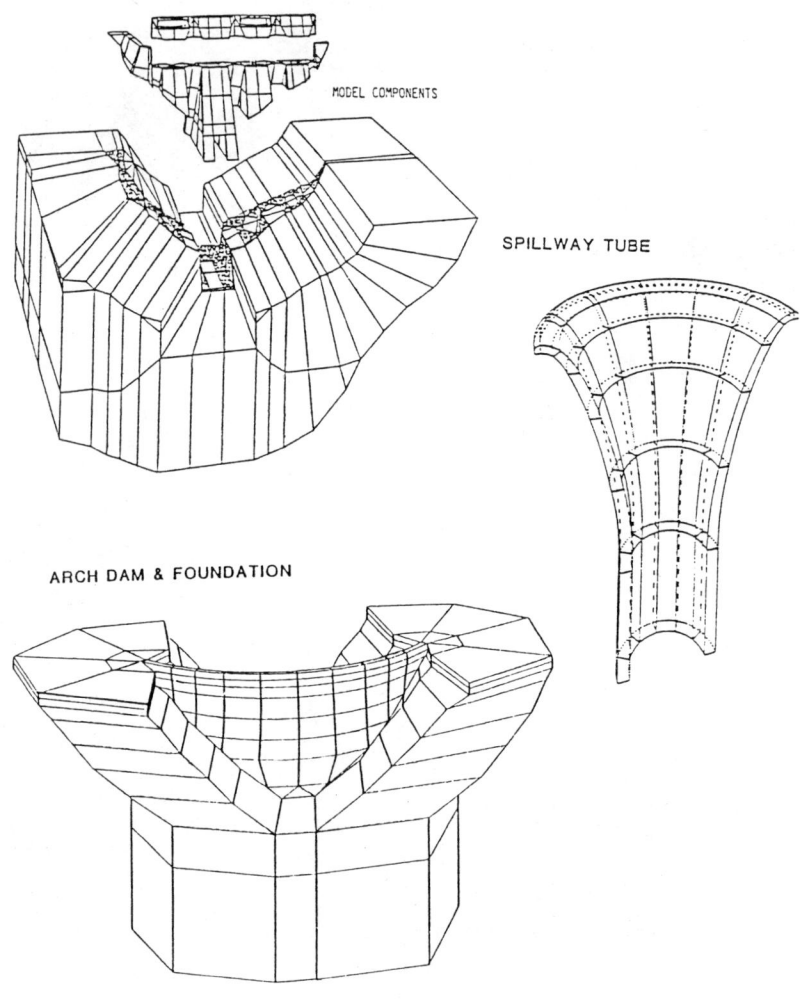

Appendix 5

FIESTA INDUSTRIAL APPLICATIONS

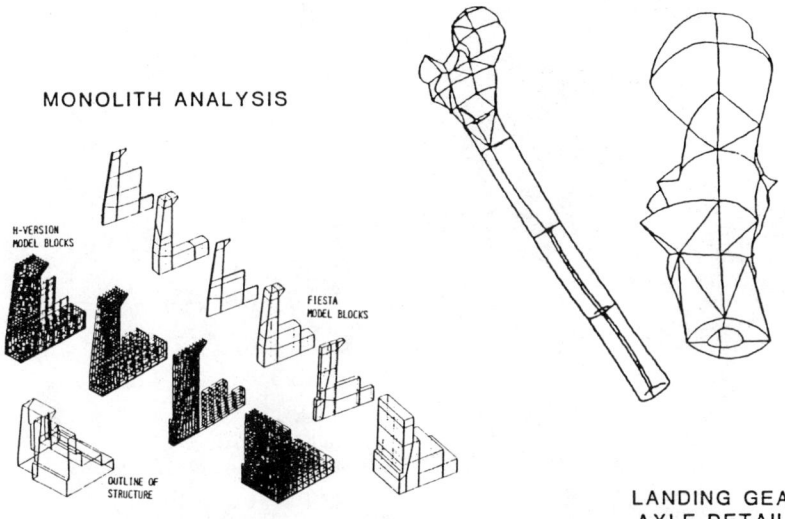

HUMAN FEMUR BONE

MONOLITH ANALYSIS

GEAR CASE ANALYSIS

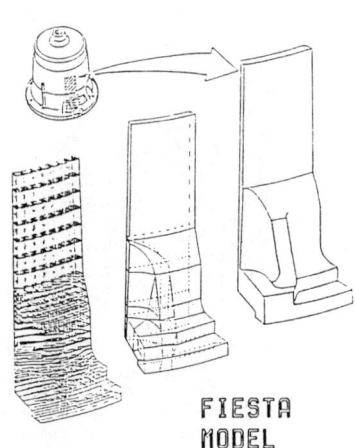

H-VERSION MODEL

FIESTA MODEL

LANDING GEAR AXLE DETAIL

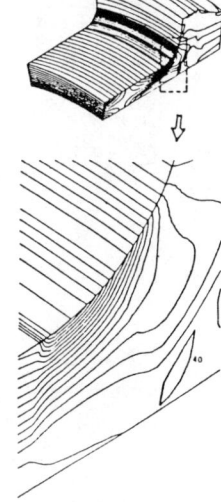

Appendix 6

FIESTA ESTIMATE OF THE SOLUTION IMPROVEMENT FROM P = 1 TO P = 4 FOR A NOZZLE ANALYSIS
REGION WHERE OCTAHEDRAL SHEAR EXCEEDS 100 MPA IS HATCHED

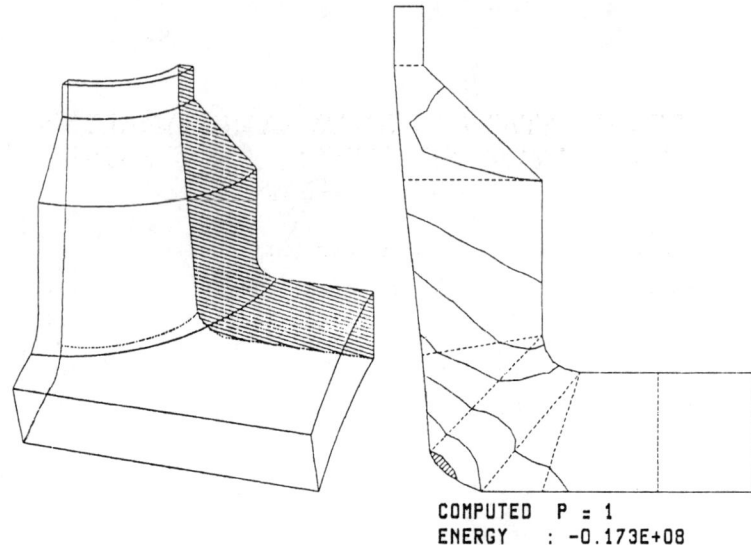

COMPUTED P = 1
ENERGY   : -0.173E+08
CPU TIME :   1

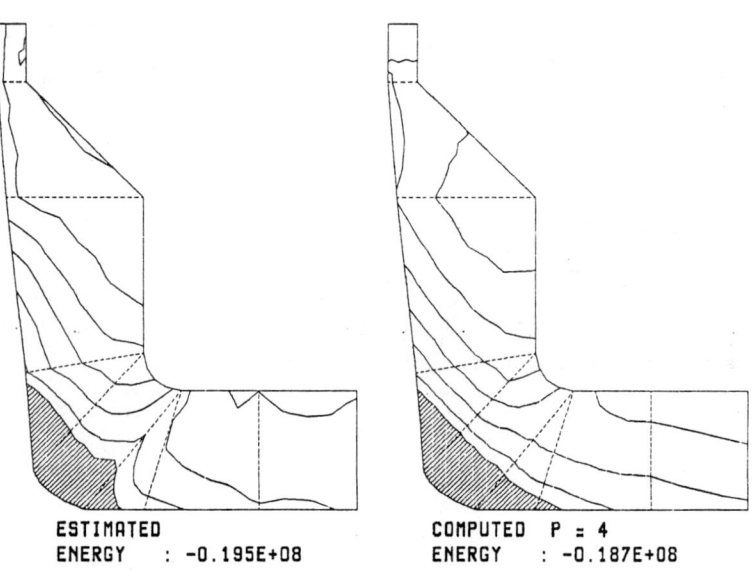

ESTIMATED
ENERGY   : -0.195E+08
CPU TIME :   2

COMPUTED P = 4
ENERGY   : -0.187E+08
CPU TIME :   30

Appendix 7

FLEXAN: STATIC AND DYNAMIC ANALYSIS OF UNDERWATER CABLES AND FLEXIBLE PIPES SYSTEMS

P. A. Schoentgen

CISI Petrole Services, 53 av. Gabriel Peri, BP 83, 92500 Rueil Malmaison, France

I. PROGRAM DESCRIPTION

FLEXAN is a finite element program designed for the study of complex offshore structures the main components of which are cables or flexible pipes.

Its originality lies in the cable element formulation based on catenaries equations. The model may also include buoys, point masses, rigid bodies (platforms) and cables laying partially on the seafloor.

Initially developed at Institut Francais du Petrole (IFP), FLEXAN has been extended and improved by CISI Petrole Services (formerly FRANLAB Informatique) to meet the requirements of an industrial product to be handled by application engineers.

Available on CRAY computers, this powerful program offers a high degree of handiness (easy to handle input, extensive graphical output).

II. THEORETICAL BACKGROUND

(a) Static Analysis

FLEXAN uses a modified Newton Raphson iteration scheme to find the equilibrium configuration of the model. The tangential stiffness matrices of the cable elements are computed iteratively using catenary equations.[1,2]

The hydrodynamic forces acting on an element are computed using the Morison formula with user defined drag and inertia coefficients (C_D and C_M). Together with gravity and buoyancy those forces are averaged along the element and applied as a distributed resultant load.

The two nodes of the element and the direction of the distributed load define the catenary plane.

As far as exterior actions may be considered as constant, this type of element may be very long in comparison with the straight link model generally used for cable analysis.

The need to have a good guess for the initial configuration is also much relaxed with the proposed curved cable element.[3]

(b) Dynamic Analysis

The inertial reactions (mass + added mass) are lumped at nodal points, giving a diagonal mass matrix.

The time integration is performed by means of a multistep predictor corrector method derived from the Adams formula.[4] Together with efficient automatic time step monitoring, this algorithm has good stability properties.

III. FIELD OF APPLICATION

FLEXAN performs static and dynamic, nonlinear 3-D cable analysis.

Cable material is linear elastic and the bending stiffness is neglected (chain like behaviour). The nonlinearities arise from geometrics and kinematics such as large displacements, variable contact with the seafloor and relative velocity squared drag forces.

The loading consists of gravity, buoyancy and hydrodynamic forces due to the current (varying in time and depth) and waves (linear Airy wave) actions.

Sinusoidal or arbitrary motions may also be prescribed at some nodes.

IV. PROGRAM DESCRIPTION

(a) Input

- Free format input with non-positional keywords
- Extended data check and error management
- Simplified enetry for a flexible arch configuration

(b) Output

- Various printed output options
- Extended graphical output (static and dynamic deflections, trajectories, time history curves of displacements velocities, accelerations, tensions).
- Results file for postprocessing
- Interactive graphical postprocessor allowing for curve selection, view angle changes, time scale modification, etc.

(c) Programming

Written in portable FORTRAN 77 language, the FLEXAN source code follows the rules of safe programming: consistent variable names, defensive tests, modularity... The keywords processing has been designed for an easy introduction of additional data blocks as may be required by future developments.

Additional features are regularly implemented without major difficulties.

V. HARDWARE COMPATIBILITIES

(a) The static analysis can be performed on 32-bit microcomputers, although dynamic analysis require more powerful machines presently referred to as "mini" computers (VAX, IBM 4341, etc.).

The memory size depends on the maximum number of d.o.fs to be processed and the amount of graphical data to store during the simulation. Those values are parameters in the source code and could be adjusted to fit the client's installation.

(b) FLEXAN is available for sale in CRAY version (compiler CFT 1.14, operating system COS 1.14) IBM version (compiler FORTVS, operating system VM/CMS release 3) and VAX version (compiler FORTRAN 77, operating system VMS 3.6). An HP9000 (UNIX) version will also be issued soon.

The CRAY version is also available for use through the CISINET service bureau.

(c) Both CRAY and IBM versions include batch plot modules using TATB libraries (CISI product) and generating a neutral plot file (LGI). The plots may be output on any terminal connected to the network. On the sites where TATB are not implemented a postprocessor called FLEXSHOW using normalized GKS routines, provides a wide range of graphical options (including those of the batch modules). Drivers are available for RADIANCE, TEKTRONIX, BENSON.

VI. EXAMPLE OF APPLICATION

Flexible Arch Study (Offshore Industry) (Figs. 1-3)

This is a dynamic analysis of a flexible riser system subjected to current and wave loading. The upper end of the riser is connected to a single point loading buoy, the motion of which is prescribed to the corresponding node of the model. A subsurface buoy allows the flexible pipe to undergo large deflections without hitting the seafloor and prevent excessive loading of the wellhead connection.

The arch is modelled using 10 cable elements. Another long element is used for the anchoring line of the subsurface buoy. In this particular example the flexible pipe linking the underwater buoy to the wellhead is not represented. The total number of d.o.fs is 30.

The wave amplitude is 14.3 m and the period 17.6 s. The water depth is 140 m.

The current velocity varies from 2m/s at surface to 1.5 m/s at bottom.

The simulation was performed during the 60s with an initial time step of 0.001 s (automatically modified - in this case increased - during the simulation).

The computation time was 40.4 sec on the CRAY XMP and 2842 sec on a VAX 750 (CPU times).

Several correlations between the FLEXAN results and full scale measurements on this type of flexible risers have proven the efficiency of the computation method.[6]

Industrial References

FLEXAN has been successfully used by a great number of French and foreign companies among which: ACB, CEA, CNM, COFLEXIP, COMEX, CSG OFFSHORE, EMH, GEMONOD, SEAFLO SYSTEMS,....

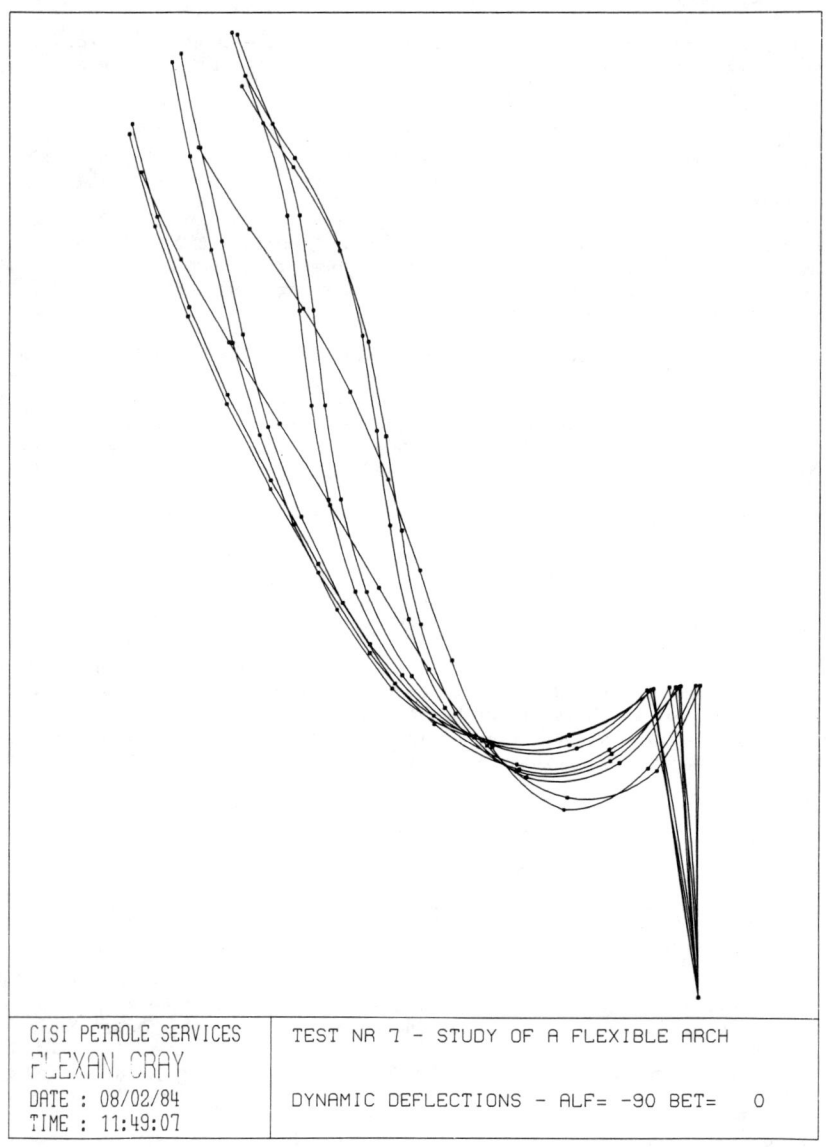

Fig. 1.

FLEXAN: Static and Dynamic Analysis 141

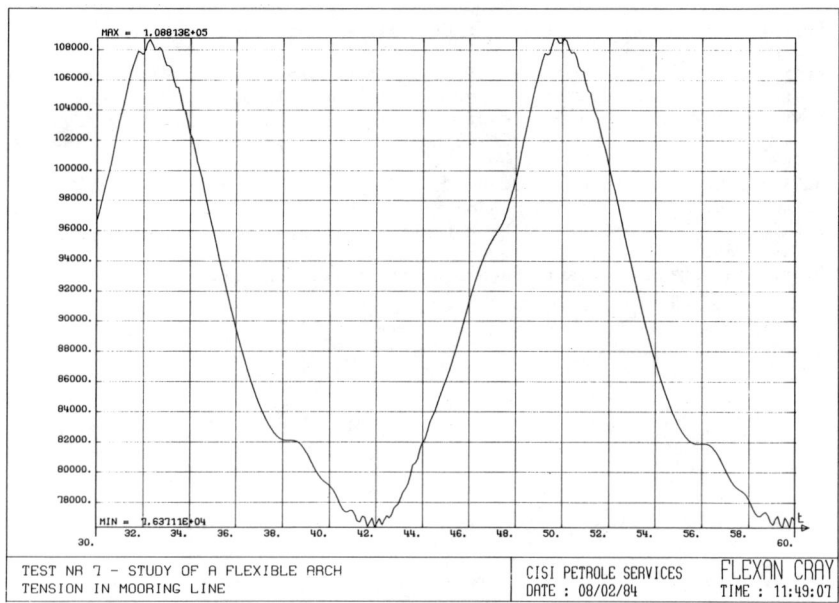

Fig. 2.

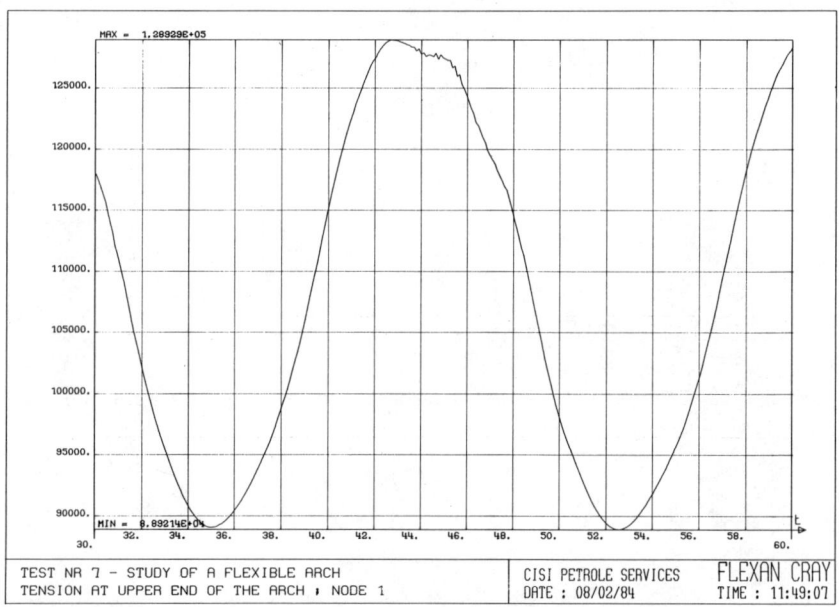

Fig. 3.

REFERENCES

1. Peyrot and Goulois. Analysis of flexible transmission lines. *J. of the Structural Division, ASCE*, Vol. *104*, No. ST5, pp. 763-779, May 1979.
2. Peyrot and Goulois. Analysis of cable structures. *J. of Computer and Structures*, Vol. *10*, No. 5, pp. 805-813, Oct. 1979.
3. Peyrot. Statics and dynamics of offshore cable and flexible pipe systems. *Revue de l'Institut Francais du Petrole*, Vol. *35*, No. 5, pp. 833-848, Oct. 1980.
4. Hall and Watt (editors). *Modern Numerical methods for Ordinary Differential Equations*, Chapter 6, Clarendon Press, Oxford, 1976.
5. FLEXAN CRAY User's Guide, CISI Petrole Services, Marine and Offshore Division, May 1984.
6. Bratu and Narzul. Dynamic behaviour of flexible riser. BOSS 85.

LASSAQ: A COMPUTER PROGRAM FOR LAMINATED ANISOTROPIC STIFFENED SHELL ANALYSIS USING QUADRILATERAL SHELL FINITE ELEMENTS

A. Venkatesh* and K. P. Rao**

*University of Bochum, Federal Republic of Germany
**Department of Aerospace Engineering, Indian Institute of Science, Bangalore–560012, India

ABSTRACT

In many engineering industries such as Aerospace, marine, petrochemical and nuclear industries, shell structures are common. With the advent of fibre reinforced plastic composites, the possibility exists to tailor a structure to carry efficiently the applied loads, leading to higher strength to weight and/or stiffness to weight ratios. Continuum analysis of shell structures made of fibre reinforced composites is complex due to the coupling effects that exist between various modes of deformation. The finite element method proves to be a versatile tool capable of handling such problems which are basically heterogeneous and anisotropic.

This paper presents the application of finite element method to the problem of laminated anisotropic stiffened shell static analysis using a doubly curved quadrilateral shell of revolution finite element. The computer program has been developed by A. Venkatesh, P. V. Ramanamurthy and K. P. Rao at the Department of Aerospace Engineering, Indian Institute of Science, Bangalore. The software written in FORTRAN IV uses the 4 noded shell element with 48 degrees of freedom (d.o.f) with 12 d.o.f. per node. The stiffener elements, which are compatible with the shell elements are 2 noded with 8 d.o.f. per node. The stiffnesses of the stiffener elements obtained as limiting cases of the shell element so that shell-stiffener compatibility is maintained all along the junction. The shell element, which is bounded by two parallel circles and two meridians, uses first order Hermite interpolation polynomials to describe the displacement fields. A nodal solution subroutine is used to assemble and solve the simultaneous equations so as to keep the computer memory requirements small. The computer program has the capability to handle both conventional composites and bimodulus composites (i.e. composites in which lamina mechanical properties in tension are different from those in compression).

THEORETICAL BACKGROUND

A doubly curved laminated anisotropic quadrilateral shell finite element[1] is used along with compatible stiffener finite elements[2] to solve laminated anisotropic stiffened shell problems. The shell element is 4 noded and employs products of 1-D first order Hermite interpolation polynomials for the description of the displacements of the reference surface leading to 12 d.o.f. per node. The contribution of the transverse shear strain energy to the total strain energy of the element is neglected. The thickness of the shell element is assumed to be built up of an arbitrary number of bonded layers each having different thickness, linear elastic orthotropic material properties (conventional or bimodulus) and orientation of principal axes. Full details of the element stiffness generation and application to both conventional and bimodulus composite shells have been presented in references 3-5. A fibre direction governed constitutive relationship for each layer is assumed, based on Bert's model[8] for bimodulus materials.

FIELD OF APPLICATION

Geometry

The software LASSAQ can be used to analyse laminated anisotropic stiffened shells of revolution. The laminated anisotropic stiffeners permissible are to be along parallel circles and/or meridians. As limiting cases, both (1) Annular circular plates stiffened by radial and circular stiffeners and (2) rectangular plates with stiffeners parallel to the sides, can also be analysed. The program can handle positive, zero and negative Gaussian curvature shells which may or may not be complete in the parallel circle direction. The shells considered must not have any curvature of twist.

Materials

The thickness of the composite shell element and the stiffener element is assumed to be built up of an arbitrary number of bonded layers each having a different thickness, linear elastic orthotropic material properties and orientation of principal axes. In the case of bimodulus materials, the constitutive relationship of each layer is assumed to depend on the fibre direction strain.[8] As the constitutive relationship depends on whether tensile or compressive strain exists in each layer, an iterative procedure is employed in the finite element solution of the problem.

Analysis Capability and Loading

The program can handle static analysis of composite stiffened axisymmetric shells under concentrated forces at nodes. Any body forces or pressure loading must be converted by the user into equivalent loads at the nodes and fed to the program. The displacements at all the nodes are printed out. The stresses however are not computed. The input data consists of (1) geometric details such as principal radii of curvature of the shell; (2) the boundary conditions; (3) the mechanical properties of each layer, as well as fibre orientation in each layer. A nodal solution subroutine of Sabir[9] is used for assembly and solution. In this subroutine the assembly and triangulation of the stiffness matrix of the stiffened shell structure occur simultaneously, with the use of auxiliary disc space.

Program Description

The flow chart for the program written in FORTRAN IV is presented in Fig. 1. A brief description of the various subroutines is given below:

MAIN: Reads the details of the mesh, the boundary condition vectors and load vector. Displacements are printed in the MAIN and subroutine SOLVE is called.

SOLVE: In SOLVE, the stiffness matrices of each element (shell and stiffener

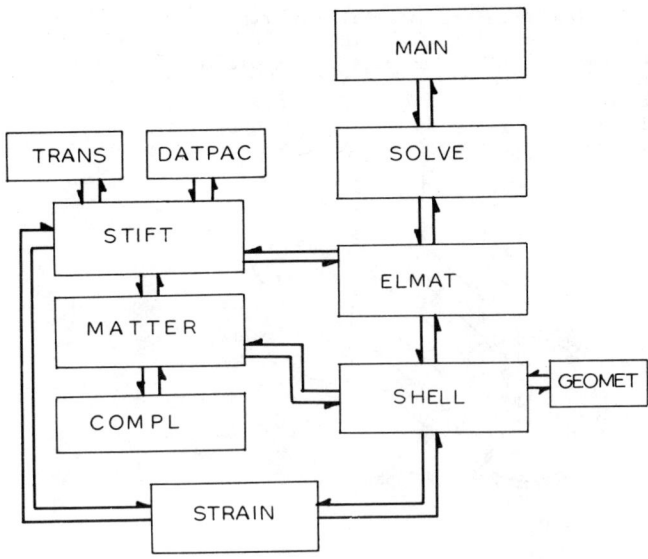

Fig. 1. Linking of subroutines in LASSAQ

stiffness matrices) is first obtained using ELMAT. The assembly and triangulation of the stiffness matrix of the stiffened shell structure occur simultaneously.

ELMAT: Calls SHELL to get the shell stiffness matrix SHE (48,48) and STIFT to get the stiffener stiffness matrix STFST (24,24).

SHELL: Generates shell element stiffness matrix SHE (48,48). The geometry details at the nodes and at Gauss points are supplied by Subroutine GEOMET.

MATTER)
COMPL) : Constitutive relationship is obtained.

STRAIN: Supplies EPSIL matrix at each Gauss point. EPSIL relates 3 membrane strains and 3 curvature changes to the shell element nodal degrees of freedom.

STIFT: Generates the stiffness matrix of the stiffener element.

The program LASSAQ has been run on DEC 1090 computer system at the Indian Institute of Science, Bangalore.

EXAMPLES OF APPLICATION

Test Cases

The computer software developed was used first to solve problems for which analytical or other solutions are available.

(i) Pinched cylindrical shell. A cylindrical shell of isotropic material subjected to two diametrically opposite concentrated loads was analysed (see Fig.

2). The geometrical details, material properties, loading, boundary conditions and the finite element model with 72 degrees of freedom are shown in the figure. The displacements obtained agree well with those in the literature (Table 1).

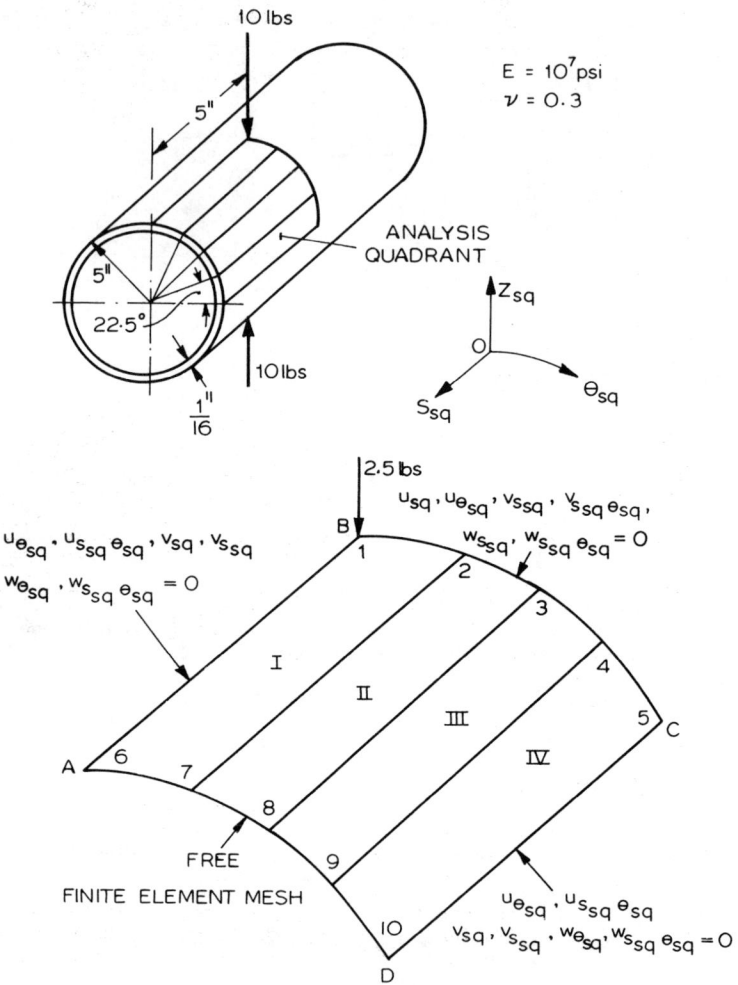

Fig. 2. An isotropic pinched cylindrical shell analysed using four doubly curved quadrilateral shell finite elements

(ii) <u>Open crown hemi-spherical shell</u>. An open crown hemi-spherical shell clamped at a parallel circle and subjected to uniformly distributed moment at the crown is considered next (see Fig. 3). The results obtained using 10 shell elements are in good agreement with those available. Figure 4 shows the comparison of results for both isotropic and orthotropic cases with those of reference 12.

(iii) <u>Clamped orthotropic cylindrical shell</u>. A clamped orthotropic cylindrical shell (see Fig. 5) with

Table 1.

Source	Radial Displacement-B (inches)	Radial Displacement-C (inches)
Yang[10]	−0.0405	0.03670
Timoshenko[11]	−0.04165	0.03830
Present Program	−0.04061	0.03698

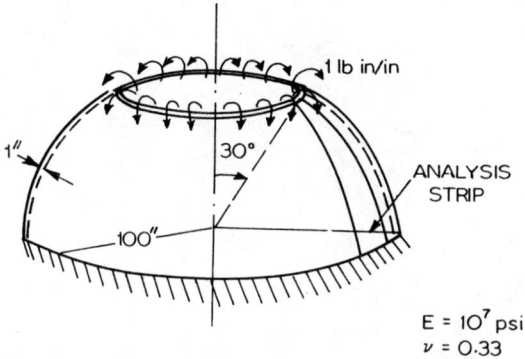

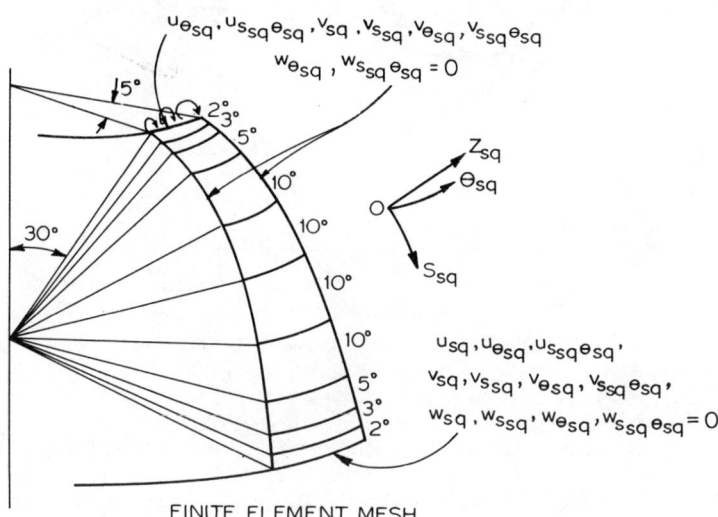

FINITE ELEMENT MESH

Fig. 3. Open crown hemi-spherical shell clamped at a parallel circle and subjected to uniformly distributed moment at crown

$E_s = 7.5 \times 10^6$ psi; $E_\theta = 2 \times 10^6$ psi;
$G_{s\theta} = 1.25 \times 10^6$ psi; $\nu_{s\theta} = 0.25$.

and subjected to internal pressure was analysed using 5 elements to get good results.

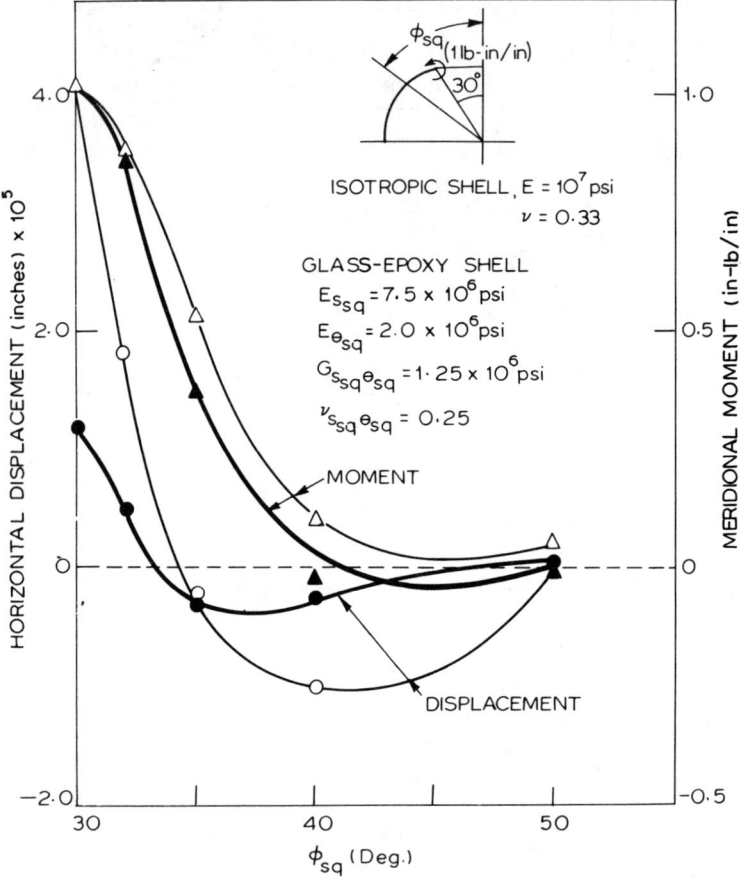

Fig. 4. Comparison of results for open-crown hemi-spherical shell subjected to uniformly distributed end moment at crown (isotropic and glass-epoxy)

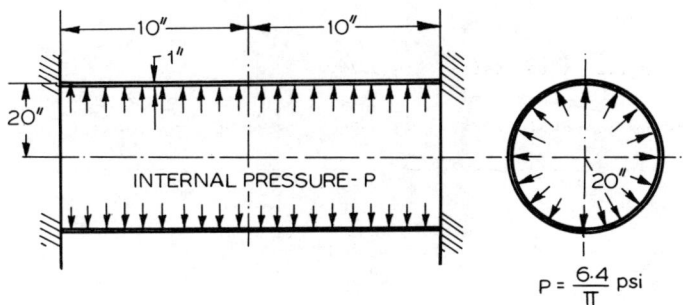

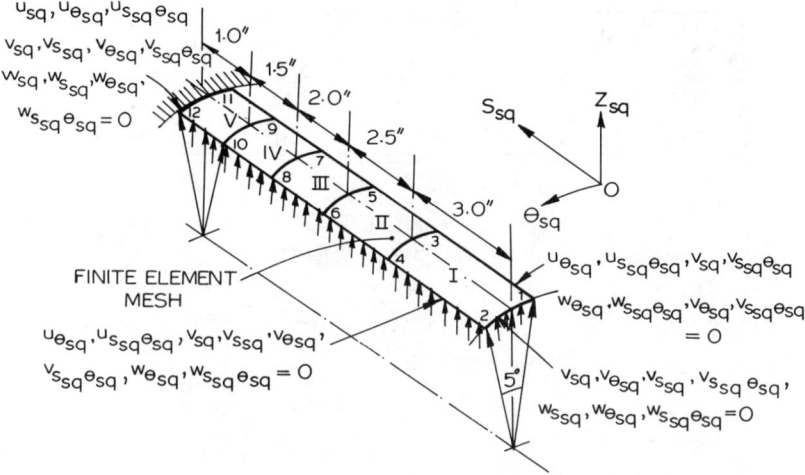

Fig. 5. A clamped orthotropic cylindrical shell subjected to internal pressure analysis using the doubly curved quadrilateral shell finite element

Practical Examples Useful to Industry

(i) <u>Internally pressurized infinite cylindrical shell with periodic stiffeners</u>.
Figure 6 shows the finite element idealization in the analysis strip. In this case 5 shell elements and one stiffener element are used.

(ii) <u>Cantilever cylindrical shell with symmetrically mounted edge stiffeners</u>.
The configuration considered as well as the mechanical properties used are given in Fig. 7. Figure 8 shows the finite element mesh both for the present software (3 x 3 mesh; 160 d.o.f. and 4 x 4 mesh; 260 d.o.f.) and that for SAP IV (7 x 7 mesh; 336 d.o.f. and 10 x 10 mesh; 660 d.o.f.). SAP IV uses a non-conforming faceted Quadrilateral plate/shell element with 6 d.o.f. per node. Present software yields better results compared to SAP IV with lesser d.o.f.

(iii) <u>A Glass-epoxy eccentrically stiffened cantilever cylindrical shell</u>. The configuration studied along with material properties and layup/sequence used are

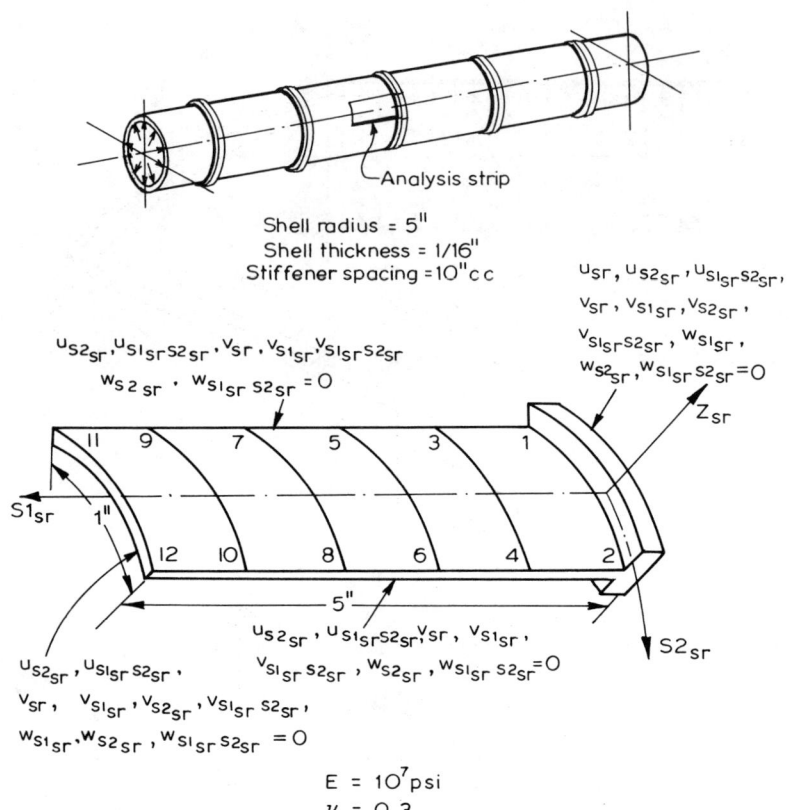

Fig. 6. Internally pressurized infinitely long ring stiffened cylindrical shell

shown in Fig. 9. Convergent solutions were obtained for the mesh shown in Fig. 9.

Potential Users of the Program

The potential user agencies are Aerospace, petrochemical, marine, and nuclear industries. In the aerospace industry, with fibre reinforced plastics, such as carbon-epoxy and kevlar-epoxy, coming in a bigway and shell structures being extensively used, this program can be used for analysis. In petrochemical and marine industries, some fibre reinforced plastics such as glass-epoxy are used as they are non-corrosive. Such shells can be analysed. This program is also applicable to stiffened cooling tower analysis.

ACKNOWLEDGEMENTS

The authors wish to express their sincere thanks to Mr. P. V. Ramanamurthy, now at University of Maryland, USA for many helpful suggestions and the help given in computer programming.

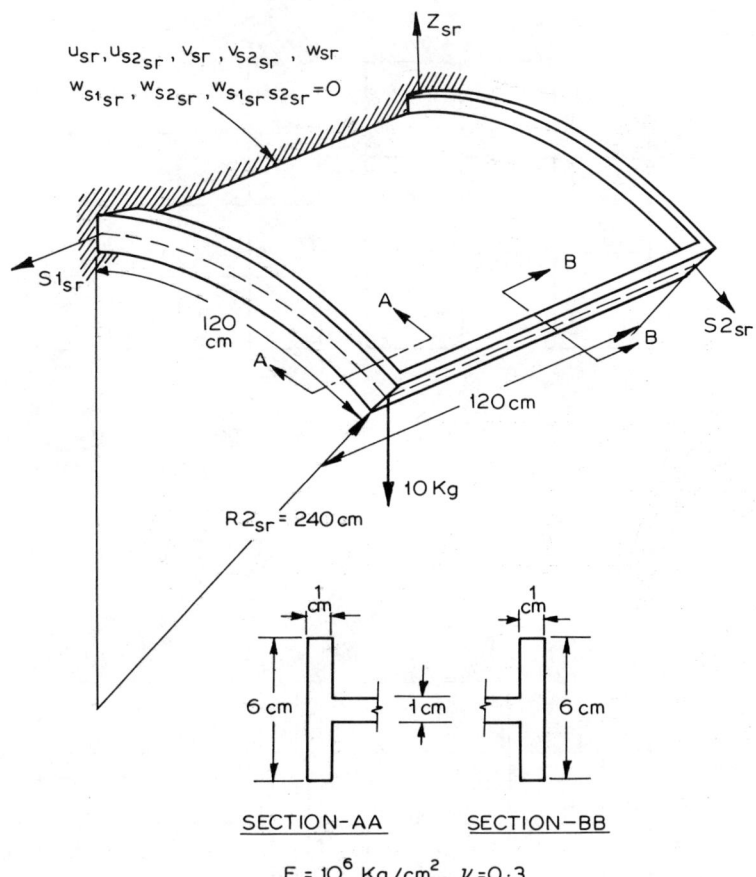

Fig. 7. A cantilever cylindrical shell with symmetrically mounted stiffeners

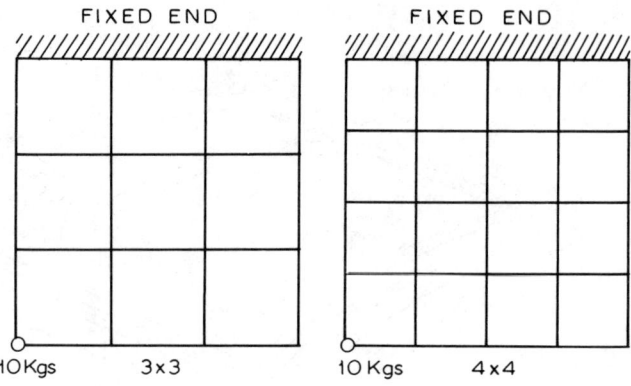

(a). MESHES FOR PRESENT PROGRAM

(b). MESHES FOR SAP-IV

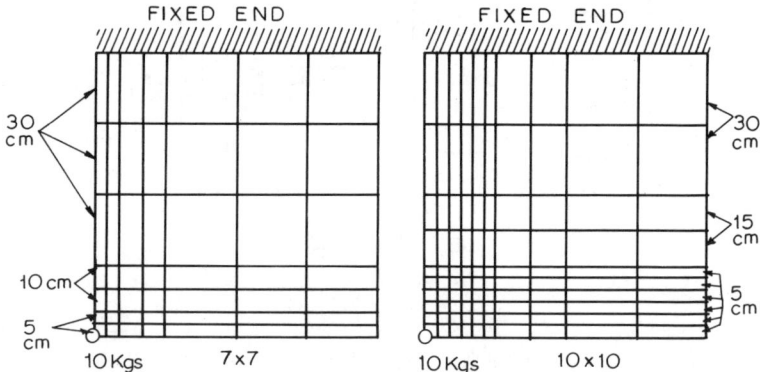

Fig. 8. Finite element meshes for analysis of the cantilever stiffened cylindrical shells (Fig. 3.9 and 3.10)

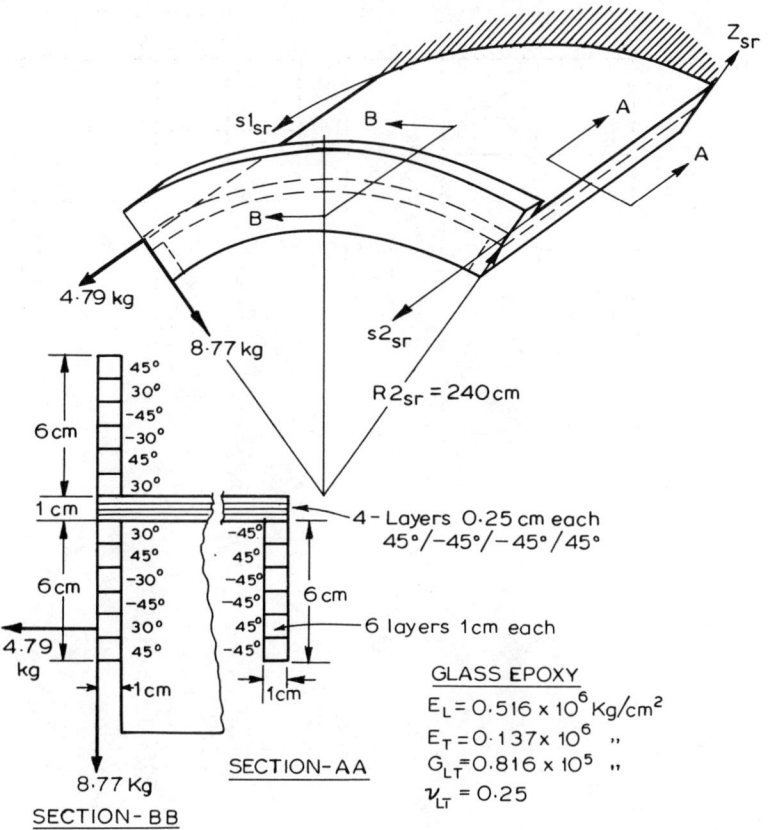

Fig. 9. A glass-epoxy eccentrically stiffened cantilever cylindrical shell.

REFERENCES

1. Venkatesh, A. and K. P. Rao. A quadrilateral layered anisotropic shell of revolution finite element, *Computers and Structures*, Vol. 12, pp. 825-832, 1980.
2. Venkatesh, A. and K. P. Rao. A laminated anisotropic curved beam and shell stiffening finite element, *Computers and Sturctures*, Vol. 15, No. 2, pp. 197-201, 1982.
3. Venkatesh, A. and K. P. Rao. Analysis of laminated shells of revolution with laminated stiffeners using a doubly curved quadrilateral finite element, *Computers and Structures* (In print).

MODULEF: A LIBRARY OF COMPUTER PROCEDURES FOR FINITE ELEMENT ANALYSIS

M. Bernadou, P. L. George, P. Laug and M. Vidrascu*

INRIA, Rocquencourt, BP 105, 78153 Le Chesnay Cedex, France

ABSTRACT

MODULEF is a general purpose finite element computer program developed by the MODULEF CLUB (see Appendix at the end of the paper).

Created by INRIA in 1974, this Club brings together French and foreign universities, and private or public industrial companies with the goal of designing and implementing a library of finite element modules.

Some existing module capabilities include solutions to:

- steady state or time-dependent, linear or nonlinear 2-D, 3-D and axis heat conduction problems

- static or dynamic linear or nonlinear 2-D, 3-D and axis elasticity problems

- elasticity problems for beams plates and shells

- fluid mechanics problems.

The various algorithms and software attributes such as modularity, portability and dynamic memory allocation make the MODULEF library a powerful tool for Research and Development.

Modular structures allow simple modifications and program additions.

Not only one, but several solutions to a problem can be readily implemented, and therefore the relative merits of various approaches can be easily assessed.

An interactive data generation system is available.

It is suitable for automatic mesh generation, generation of boundary conditions and generation of data needed for the main steps used in finite element computing programs.

---

*This is a collective work; it was carried out thanks to D. Begis, J. M. Boisserie, J. M. Crolet, A. Hassim, F. Hecht, P. Letallec, A. Perronnet, F. Pistre and D. Steer.

Furthermore, it has proved to be most valuable for teaching purposes.

THEORETICAL BACKGROUND OF THE PROGRAM

The MODULEF library is a direct application of the theoretical results obtained in numerical analysis in France. The most relevant references are 11, 12, 13, 14.

To write a program from the mathematical formalism requires a design methodology.

For the programming environment, techniques of software development such as top-down design are used. They are based on a common concept: the level of abstraction. As the following figure indicates, we can represent the Modulef structure as an ordered set of abstract machines:

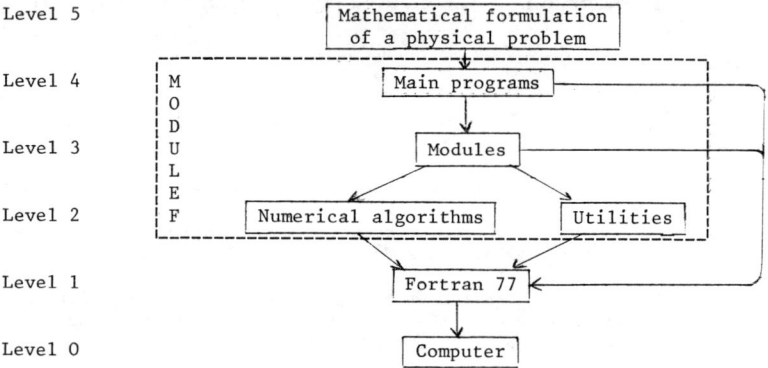

Let's recall two fundamental principles:

- weak levels never reference higher levels,

- each abstract machine provides operators and data structures, but users are unaware how they are implemented.

Structure of the Library

Programmed in FORTRAN 77 the MODULEF library includes about 2500 procedures making 250,000 lines of code. They were designed with great concern for software portability.[1]

The method used to build the library of procedures is a combination of the abstract approach with modular programming.

A new problem can easily be solved. Numerical analysis is used to select an appropriate algorithm. The algorithm is then split into a succession of mathematical operators. Generally, most of the operators are already programmed in the MODULEF library. Each new mathematical operator becomes a computation MODULE which is added to the library.

A module is a set of procedures performing one logical process and communicating with the program through some invariant interfaces called DATA STRUCTURES.[2] So a module transforms input data structures into output data structures.

MODULEF: A Library of Computer Procedures

FIELD OF APPLICATION

The following capabilities are provided within the library[3]:

- the automatic generation and display of meshes;

- the specifications of characteristics of materials or external forces by sub-domains or pieces of boundary;

- the choice of type of the finite element method (e.g., conforming or non-conforming, hybrid, mixed, etc...).

For non-conforming methods, the flow or the stresses can be computed together with temperature or displacement or separately;

- the finite element library contains about 30 elements for heat transfer analysis: 2-D, 3-D and axisymmetric elements; 40 elements for linear elastic analysis are available for isotropic or anisotropic materials: 2-D plane stress or plane strain elements, 3-D and axisymmetric elements, beam, plate and shell elements. In non-linear elasticity 5 elements for hyperelastic compressible and incompressible materials are used for Mooney;Rivlin or Ogden models;

- the solution of linear systems using a choice of several techniques for memory management, depending upon the size of the problem and that of main memory, i.e.;

  • Direct methods (Gauss, Crout, Cholesky) using skyline storage in main memory or secondary memory, or generalized array storage;

  • Iterative methods (relaxation, conjugate gradient algorithms with or without preconditioning (SSOR, ICCG, etc...) or multigrid method);

- the computation of eigenvalues of 2- or 3-D operators using a choice of subspace iteration, Lanczos or QR methods;

- the integration of time-dependent heat equations using multistep, Runge Kutta or Gear methods. These last two select automatically the step size and the order of the scheme (for GEAR) with respect to the stiffness of the data.

- the solution of dynamic problems by means of free vibration modes or multistep methods;

- the determination of plastic or elastic zones of a structure;

- the solution of thermo-elastic problems;

- the computation of velocity and pressure of a plane incompressible fluid flow (Navier Stokes equations);

- the computation of magnetic fields;

- the computation of the effective elastic moduli of composite materials;

- several developments extend the graphics modules to deal with the display of results. Various options exist such as multiple windows views for investigating selected areas of the mesh, isovalues, stresses, deformed configurations...

- the structure of the library allow simple modifications, program additions and new achievements.

HARDWARE COMPATIBILITIES

<u>Computers</u>: Modulef conforms to the FORTRAN 77 standard. The only restrictions are:

- dummy and actual arguments may have distinct numerical types (INTEGER, REAL, DOUBLE PRECISION),

- variables of type INTEGER must be allocated at least 4 bytes of memory.

Modulef has been implemented successfully on Apollo, Bull, Burroughs, CDC, Cray, Data General, Harris, IBM, ICL, Norsk Data, Prime, Univac, Vax.

<u>Peripherics</u>: Modulef subroutines involving graphics use the Benson package, but interfaces can easily be written. Tektronix devices are in current use at INRIA. The GKS standard is to be adopted soon.

<u>Minimal configuration</u>: the core needed is proportional to the number of nodes in the mesh. Problems with about 2,000 nodes have been handled on Apollo DN 600, whose main features are:

    32 bits VLSI CPU

    1 Mbyte main memory

    2 Mbyte display memory

    16 Mbyte virtual memory per process

    158 Mbyte hard disk

<u>Media</u>: Modulef is available in 2,400 ft magnetic tape.

EXAMPLES OF APPLICATION

<u>Introduction</u>

Currently, problems in various engineering fields can be solved using finite element methods available in the MODULEF library.

Solutions can be parameterized to accommodate small variations and save programming time. This feature proved very useful for industrial problems.

Modular programming is the key concept of the library. Intermediate module results make Data Structures. Data Structure handling is transparent to the user, but requires a predefined file organization. Hence some data is duplicated and the user must specify the file environment. A relational data basis, fitted to numerical software, would advantageously replace this file organization, but available systems seem too limited or unsuitable.

Another area of current concern is the simplification of user interface. Patterns, menus or similar techniques for Data input could be helpful. For interpretation and evaluation of results the use of 3-D graphic representations on colour display and animation techniques will be desirable.

2-D and 3-D graphic representation is already provided with MODULEF[4] as shown in Fig. 1. Presently colour display is available for the Apollo computer.

<u>Numerical Comparisons of Modulef Heat Transfer Finite Element Methods</u>

Since the data are stored into the same data structure, one can compare and validate some different methods as conforming, non-conforming, dual methods, used

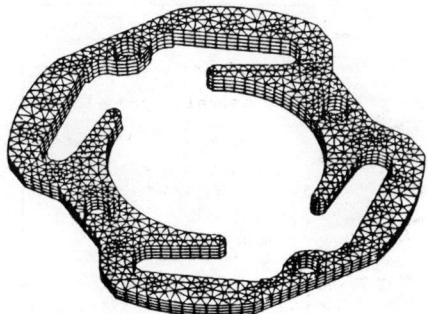

Fig. 1. Mesh of the stator

in order to solve the following heat transfer problem.

Let Ω be the domain of Fig. 2, and let (ρ,θ) be the cylindrical co-ordinates. Then $u_e(x,y) = \rho(x,y)^{1/3} \sin(2/3\ \theta(x,y))$ is solution of:

$$\begin{cases} \Delta u = 0 \text{ into } \Omega, \\ u = u_e|_\Gamma \end{cases}$$

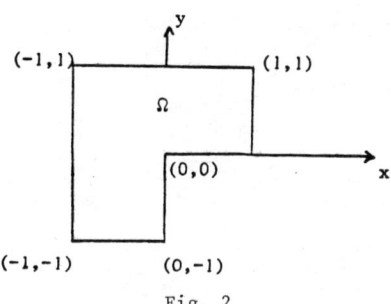

Fig. 2

The goal is to analyse the numerical behaviour of the different approximated solutions obtained by varying the number of degrees of freedom as well as the type of finite element methods. The comparisons are based on the following L^2-relative error

$$ERL = \left\{ \frac{\sum_{i \in \{DF\}} |u_e(i) - u_c(i)|^2}{\sum_{i \in \{DF\}} |u_e(i)|^2} \right\}^{1/2}$$

where $u_c(i)$ means the corresponding calculated solution. One successively compares accuracy, memory occupation and computation time for the different methods.

(i) <u>Accuracy</u>. Figure 3 shows the dependence of ERL on the number of degrees of freedom for the different approximations. With respect to the accuracy, considered methods can be classified as:

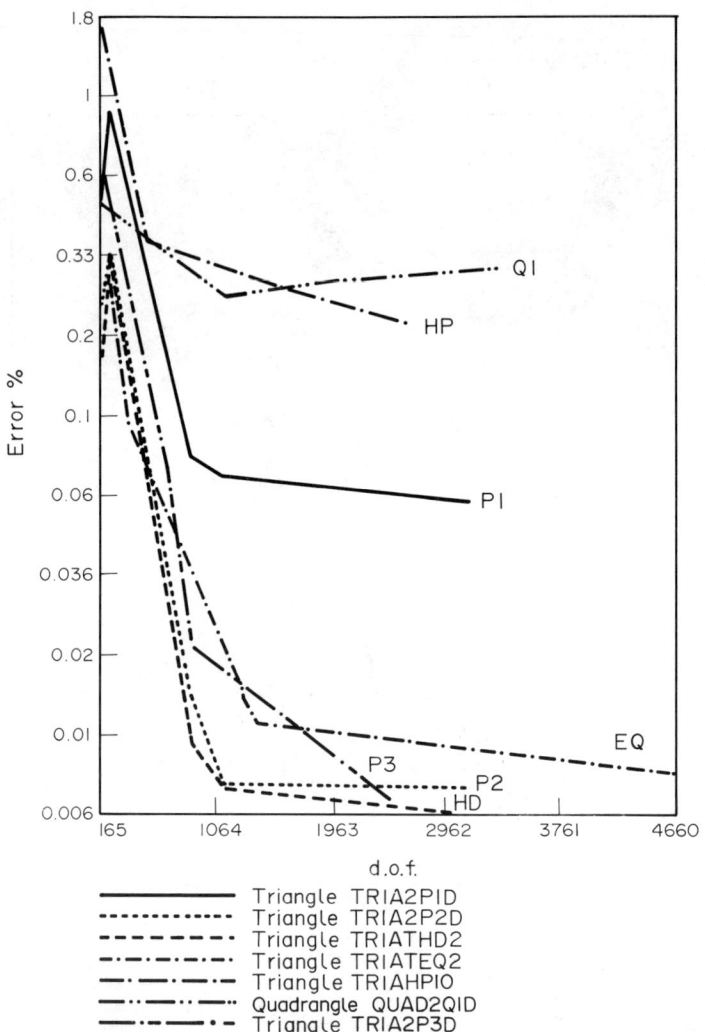

Fig. 3. Accuracy comparisons

good methods	HD: hybrid dual	triangular of degree 2
	P2: lagrangian	triangular of degree 2
	EQ: equilibrium	triangular of degree 2
	P3: hermitian	triangular of degree 3
middle method	P1: lagrangian	triangular of degree 1
bad methods	HP: hybrid primal	triangular of degree 1
	Q1: lagrangian	quadrilateral of degree 1

or, shortly,   HD $\approx$ P2 $\approx$ EQ $\approx$ P3 << P1 << HP $\approx$ Q1

(ii) <u>Memory occupation</u>. One can summarize results of Fig. 4 as

$$HP < P2 \simeq EQ < HD \simeq Q1 < P1 < P3$$

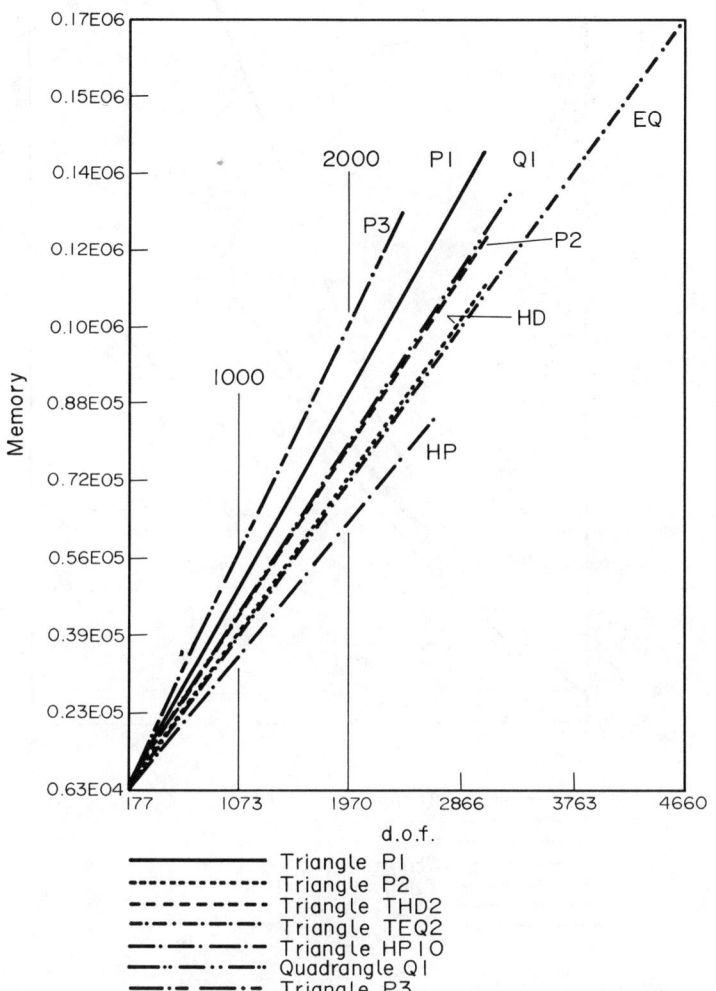

Fig. 4. Comparisons of memory computation

(iii) <u>Computing time</u>. Results are shown on Fig. 5 and can be summarized as

$$EQ < HD \simeq P2 < P1 \simeq P3 < HP < Q1$$

By taking together the three different comparisons one can suggest that P2 or EQ are the best methods for such a heat transfer problem.

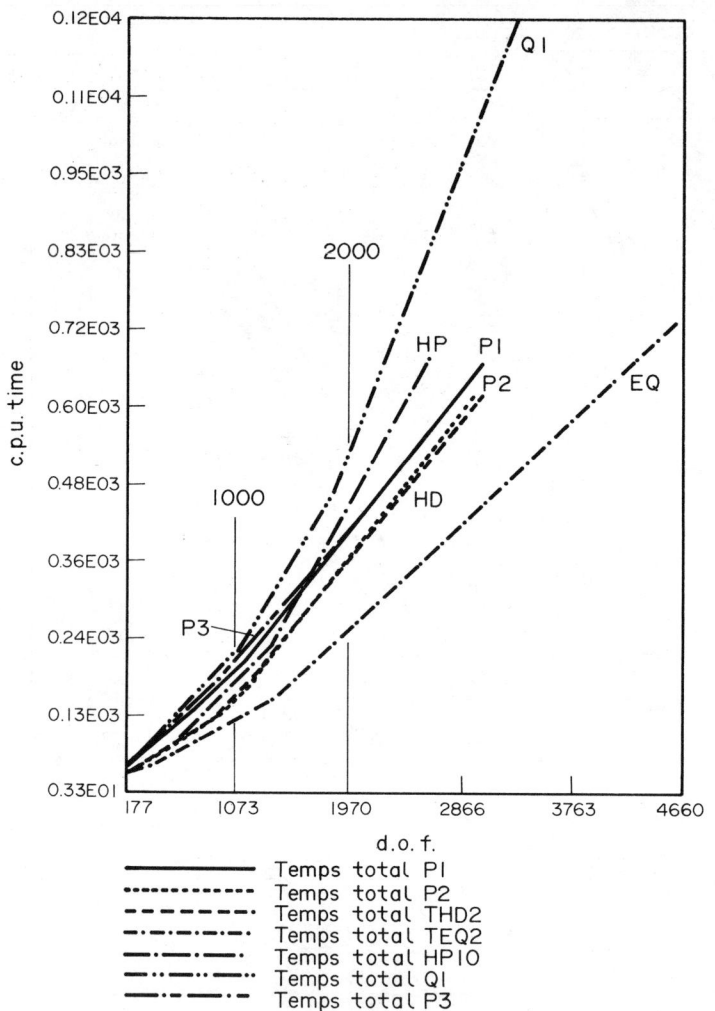

Fig. 5. Computing time comparisons

An Incompressible Finite Elasticity Problem[6]:

Deformations of an elastic tridimensional cylinder made of rubber are obtained corresponding to different loadings. The cylinder is 5 cm height, its diameter is 11.9 cm and it is fixed on its bottom. The strain energy is of Mooney-Rivlin type. The deformed configurations are displayed on Fig. 6.

Computation of Heat Field in the Rotor of an Electric Engine
(joint study with SNCF)

Joule's effect involves heat generation which diffuses into the rotor of an electric engine. Refreshment is produced by circulation of cold air into the

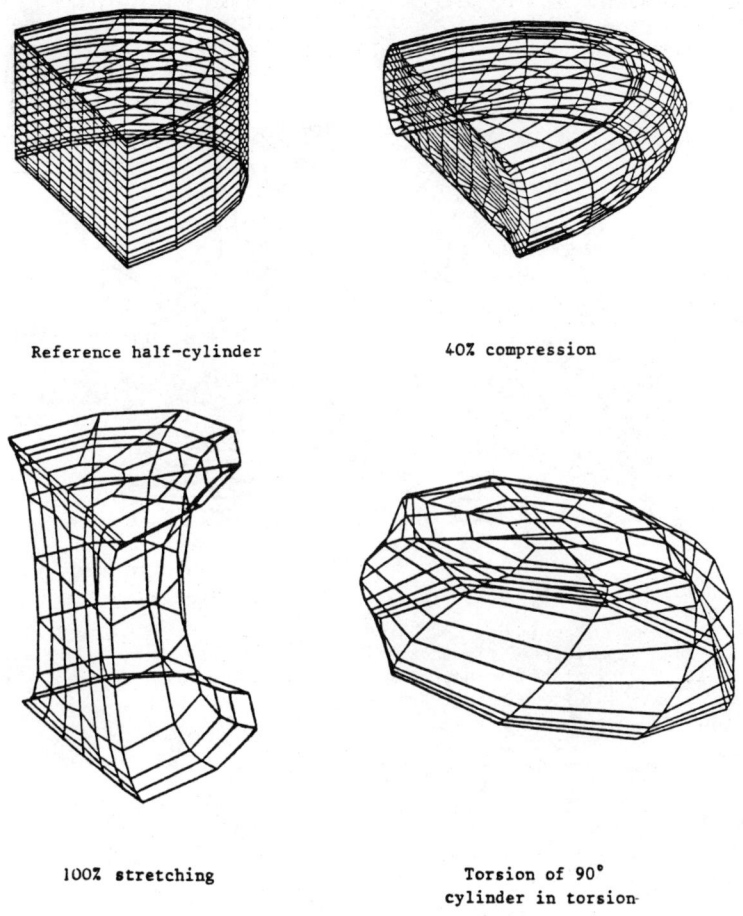

Reference half-cylinder **40% compression**

100% stretching **Torsion of 90°
cylinder in torsion**

Fig. 6. Reference and deformed configurations

cooling circuits as well as outside the rotor. The problem is to compute the heat field in the rotor. Taking into account the length of the rotor and the symmetry of the problem, one only studies a 2-D part of the rotor (Fig. 7).

The equations are:

$$-k_i \Delta u = f_i^\Omega \text{ in } \Omega_i \qquad i = 1 \text{ to } 5;$$

$$u \big|_{\partial \Omega_i \cap \partial \Omega_j} = u \big|_{\partial \Omega_j \cap \partial \Omega_i} \qquad i,j = 1,\ldots, 5;$$

$$k_i \frac{\partial u}{\partial n_i} \bigg|_{\partial \Omega_i \cap \partial \Omega_j} = k_j \frac{\partial u}{\partial n_j} \bigg|_{\partial \Omega_j \cap \partial \Omega_i} \qquad i,j = 1,\ldots, 5;$$

$$k_i \frac{\partial u}{\partial n_i} + g_j u = f_j^\Gamma \text{ on } \partial \Omega_i \quad \Gamma_i \qquad i = 1 \text{ to } 5; \; j = 1 \text{ to } 3;$$

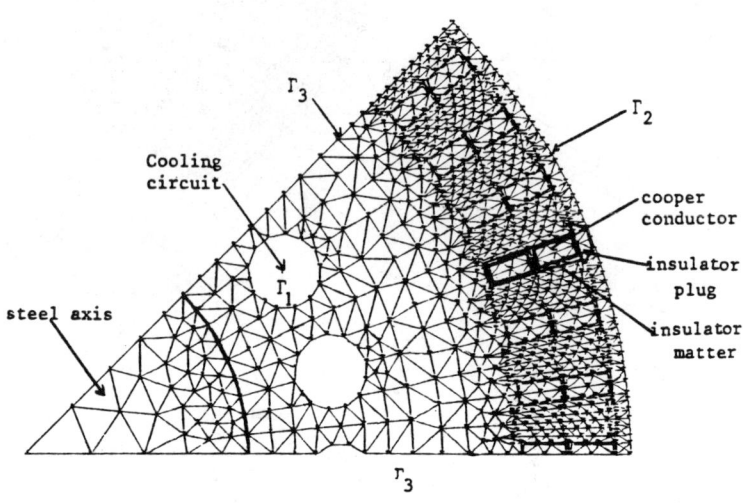

Fig. 7. Triangulation of the rotor

where u is the temperature field in the rotor, Ω_1 = steel axis, Ω_2 = silicon steel sheets, Ω_3 = isolation plug, Ω_4 = isolating matter, Ω_5 = copper conductor, k_i = conductivity in Ω_i, g_j = heat transfer coefficient on Γ_j, f_i^Ω = density of power on Ω,

$$f_j^\Gamma = g_j \, u_j \text{ with } u_j = \text{temperature outside of } \Gamma_j.$$

Here $f_i^\Omega = 0$, $i = 1, \ldots, 4$; $f_5^\Omega = 3.10^6$; $f_3^\Gamma = g_3 = 0$ (Γ_3 = symmetry axis) $f_j^\Gamma = 10^3$, $g_j = 50$, $j = 1, 2$; $k_5 = 1000 \, k_4$.

Among the difficulties, one needs to underline the geometric complexity of the rotor and the great variation of conductivity of copper with insulator matter. Corresponding temperature field is displayed on Fig. 8.

A Biomechanical Problem in Connection with Total Hip Replacement
(joint study with St. Louis Hospital, Paris)[7].

Total hip replacement is now a routine implant and is generally successful. Occasionally, some years following the operation a loosening affecting the acetabular cup is observed. In this case the patient needs to be urgently reoperated.

Numerical simulation method using the Modulef library can provide the main stresses in the different components of the fitted acetabular cup as well as the stress vectors at the interfaces between the different materials (alumina or polyethylen/cement/bone).

The results explaining the loosening phenomena are in agreement with the clinical observations. Different steps of this study can be visualized on Fig. 9 to 12.

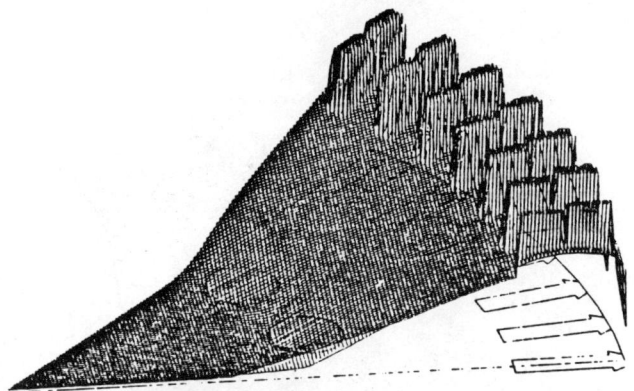

Fig. 8. Visualization of the temperature field

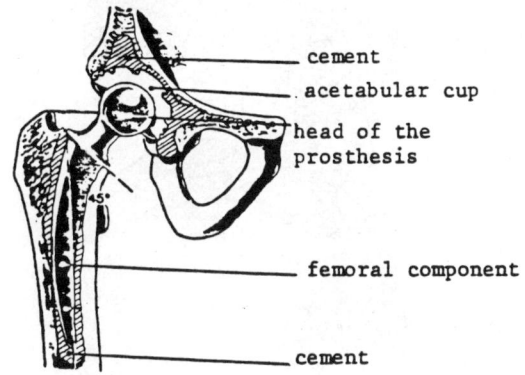

Fig. 9. Total hip replacement

Numerical Simulations of an Arch Dam[8,9]
(joint study with EDF)

One considers the project of Grand'Maison arch dam studied by COYNE and BELLIER, shown on Fig. 13.

One has to take into account the effects of:

(i)   the thermal loads;
(ii) the hydrostatic pressure;
(iii) the self weight.

Two different modelizations have been used:

- a 2-D model derived from linear thin shell theory of W. T. Koiter;

- a 3-D linear elastic model.

Both methods give very good stress distribution and free vibration modes which

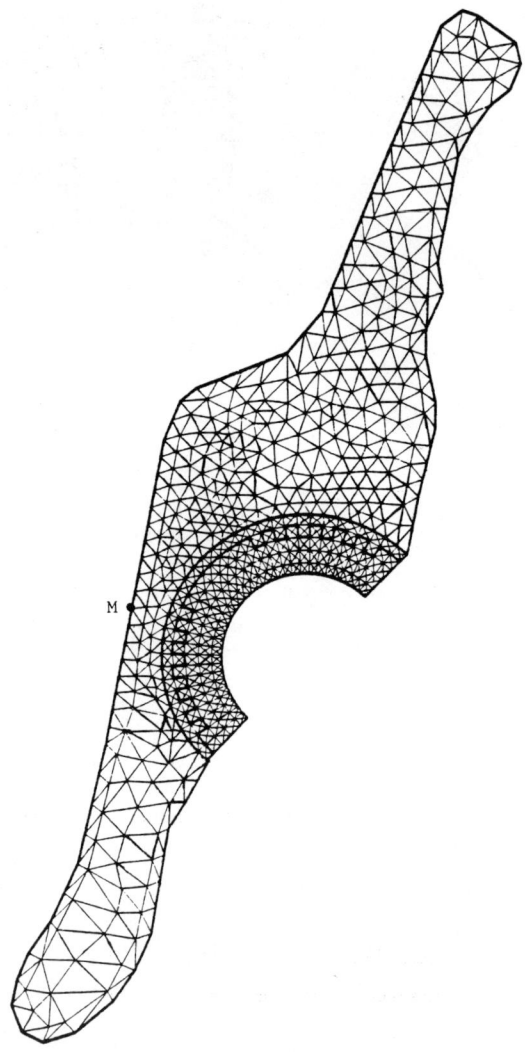

Fig. 10. Mesh of the vertical iliac bone section

are qualitatively in good agreement with experimental results measured into similar arch dam.

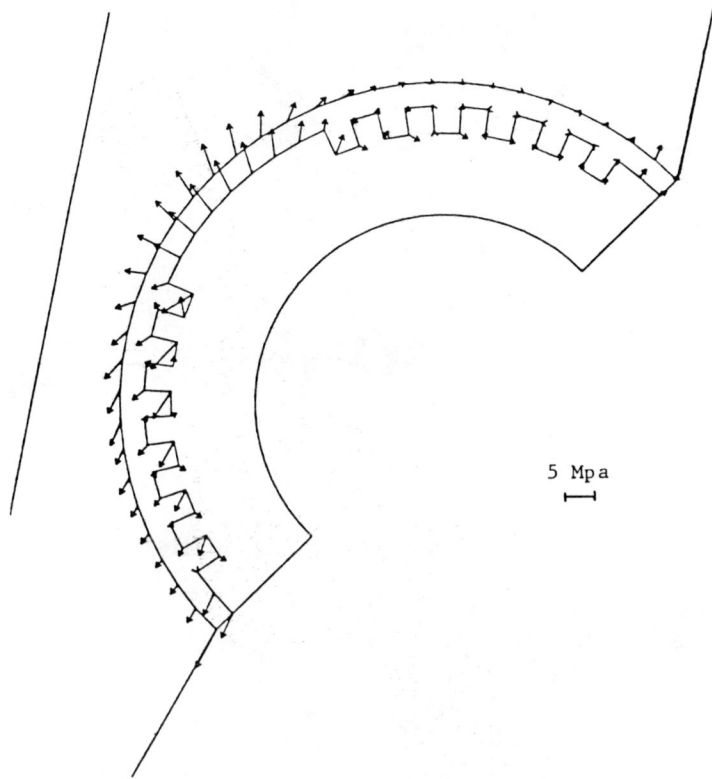

Fig. 11. Stress vectors at the interfaces for a polyethylen cup

- Comparison of free vibration modes with experimental results issued from existing simular arch dam are very suitable.

- Comparison with a 3-D approach shows a good agreement of results.

Navier Stokes Equations for Incompressible Viscous Fluids

Several methods are implemented in the Modulef library:

(i)   a non-conforming P1 method using a zero divergence basis[10];

(ii) a method which combines finite elements for the space discretization and alternating directions for the time discretization. The splitting effectively decouples the two main difficulties, the nonlinearity and the incompressibility. The nonlinearity is solved by a least squares and conjugate gradient method[11];

(iii) a Q2 conforming method for the flow velocity, where the pressure is a discontinuous function linear by quadrilateral, and we build a zero-divergence local basis[5].

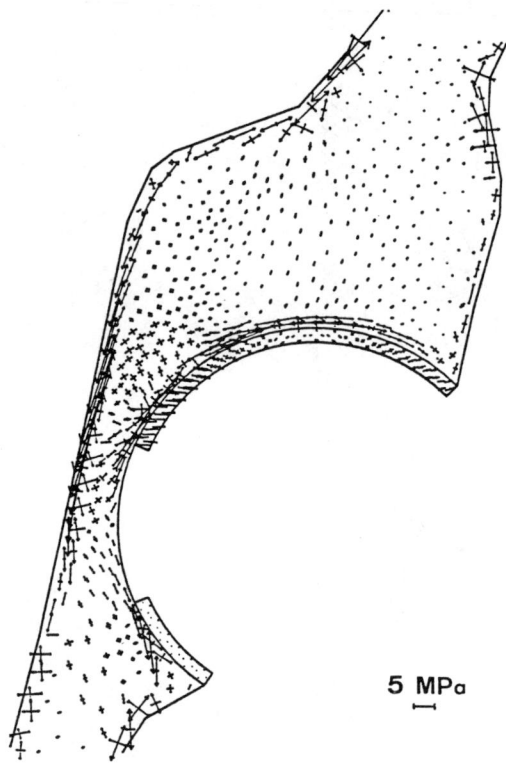

Fig. 12. Main stresses for a normal acetabulum

Two numerical methods have been implemented: the least squares method for the steady equations and the method of characteristics for the time dependent equations. The main value of this last method is that it makes possible the solution of the Navier Stokes equations with large Reynolds number in the least CPU run time. We used these methods to compute the flow and the pressure in the following problem of a channel with a step.

At the intake, we have a fully developed laminar flow profile with Umax = 1.

The two methods yield the same good results for a Reynold's number up to 200, but only the method of characteristics converges at Re = 500. Figure 16b shows the line at Re = 500 computed by the method of characteristics.

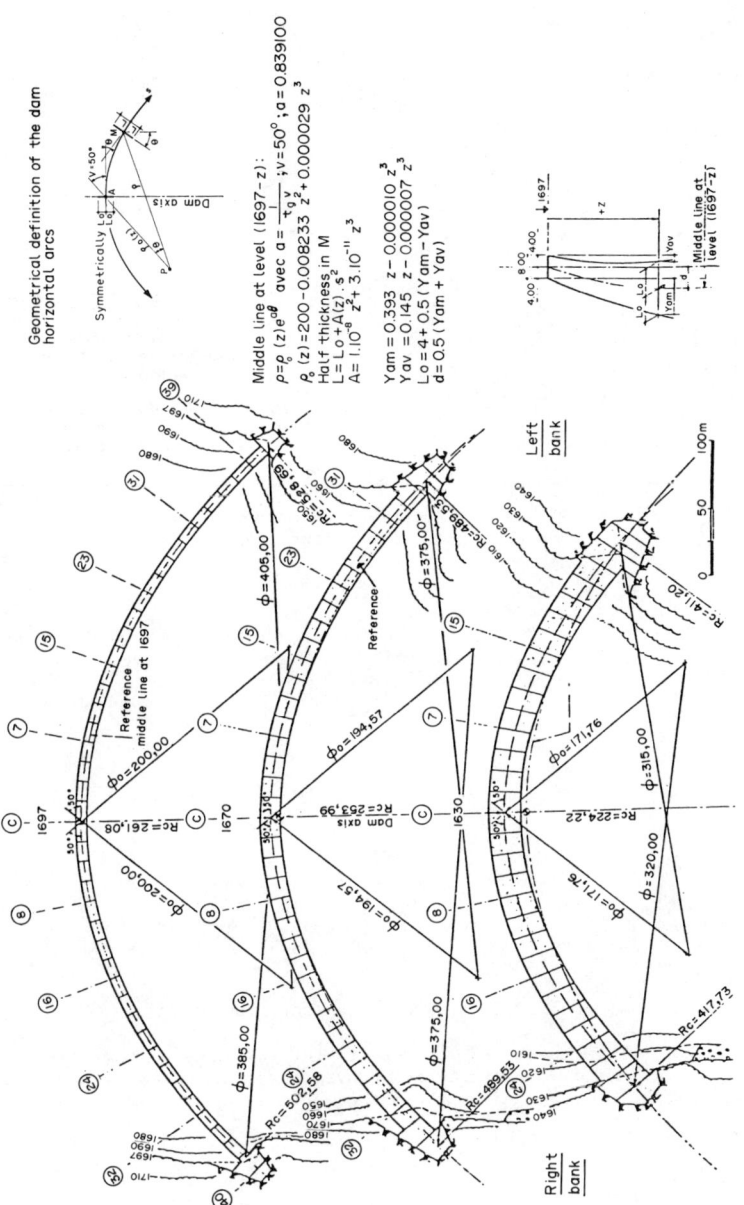

Fig. 13. Geometric definition of the dam - Upper horizontal sections

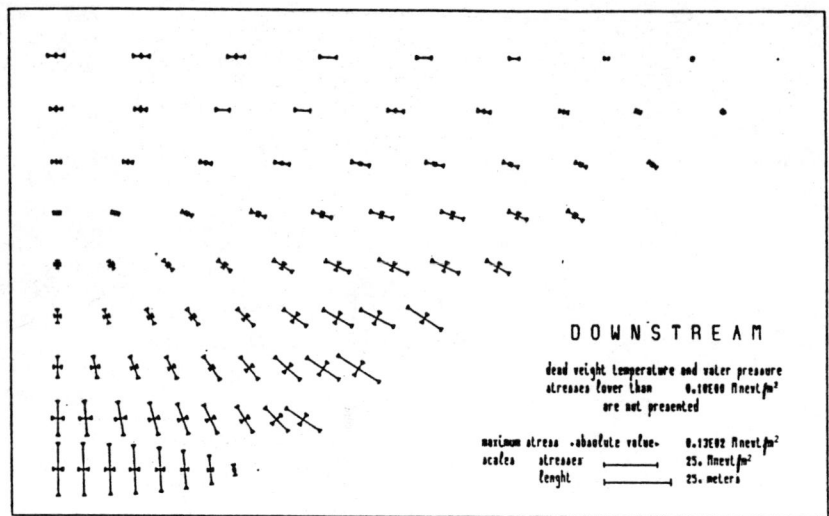

Fig. 14a. Stress distribution on downstream face
(32 Argyris triangles)

Fig. 14b. Stress distribution on upstream face
(32 Argyris triangles)

MODULEF: A Library of Computer Procedures

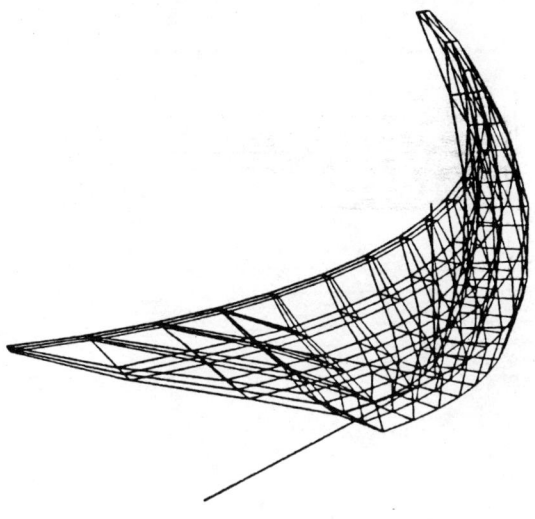

Initial structure

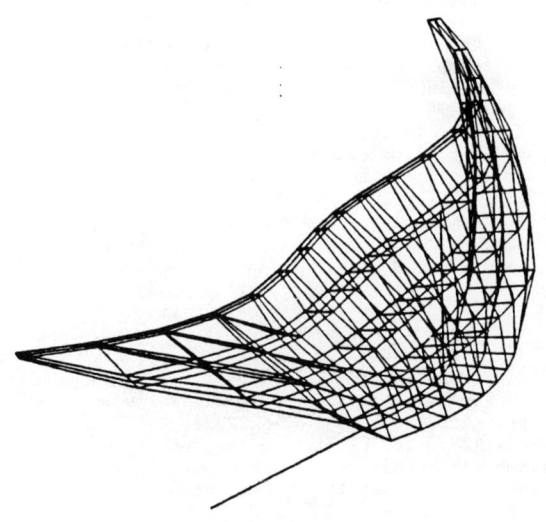

Deformed structure
(the ratio of deformation is 1000)

Fig. 15. Visualization of the deformation from a 3-D approach

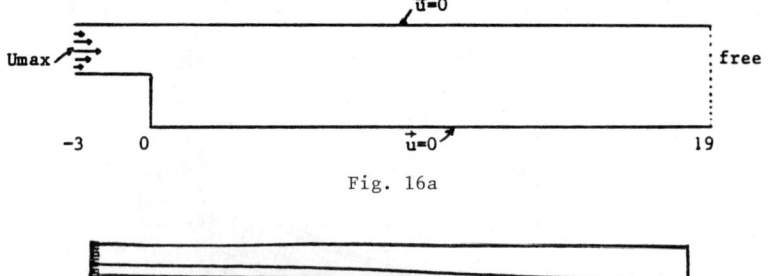

Fig. 16a

Fig. 16b. Characteristics method (Reynolds = 500.0)

REFERENCES

1. George, P. L. and M. Vidrascu. Guide d'utilisation et Normes de programmation, Rapport technique INRIA no. 42, October 1984.
2. Perronnet, A. Description des structures de données du Club MODULEF, Février 1979, brochure Modulef no. 2.
3. Présentation du Club MODULEF, Version 84, Mai 1984.
4. Begis, D., P. L. George and F. Pistre. Présentation générale des mailleurs de la bibliotheque MODULEF, Journées sur la Génération Automatique et la Visualisation des maillages, Décembre 1982, INRIA.
5. Hecht, F. Construction d'une base de fonction P_1 non conforme à divergence nulle dans R^3, RAIRO, *Analyse numérique/Numerical analysis*, Vol. *15*, no. 2, 1981, pp. 119-150.
6. Le Tallec, P. and M. Vidrascu. Une méthode mixte pour le calcul en grandes déformations de solides élastiques, Bulletin de liaison Lab. des Ponts et Chaussées, mai-juin 1982.
7. Bernadou, M., P. Christel and J. M. Crolet. Simulation numérique des contraintes aux interfaces prothèse de hanche-os, in *Computing Methods in Applied Sciences and Engineering*, North-Holland, Amsterdam, 1984, pp. 381-400.
8. Bernadou, M. and P. L. George. Comparison between two and three dimensional approaches for the analysis of an arch dam, not yet published.*
9. Bernadou, M. and J. M. Boisserie. The finite element method in thin shell theory. Application to an arch dam. Birkhauser Boston Inc., 1982.
10. Thomasset, F. and P. Caussignac. Equations de Navier Stokes bidimensionnelles, modules NSNCEV, NSNCPR, NSNCST, TRSD, Mai 1984, Brochure Modulef no. 36.
11. Glowinski, R. Numerical methods for nonlinear variational problems, (Second Edition) Springer Verlag, New York, 1983.
12. Ciarlet, P. G. 1978. The finite element method for elliptic problems, North Holland, Amsterdam.
13. Duvaut, G. and J. L. Lions, 1972. Les inéquations en mécanique et en physique, Dunod, Paris.
14. Glowinski, R., J. L. Lions and R. Tremolieres, 1978. Numerical analysis of variational inequalities, Amsterdam, North-Holland.

---

*To be requested directly from the authors.

APPENDIX: STRUCTURE AND OBJECTIVE OF THE MODULEF CLUB

Structure of the Club

Currently the MODULEF Club with its 112 members is composed of:

- 29 French industrial companies
- 5 foreign industrial companies
- 52 French universities or research laboratories
- 26 foreign university laboratories

The rules of the Club dictate that exchanges between members are solely of scientific nature.

Objectives of the Club

The main objectives of the MODULEF Club are:

- to expand the finite element library using the latest results of theoretical and numerical research in applied mathematics, and industrial experience in solving large and practical problems.

- to bring together laboratories interested in the same topic to join efforts in determining the optimal programs and methods.

- to promote the exchange and sharing of each member's knowledge.

- to validate new methods and compare them with those already implemented.

On the computer software side, fulfilling these objectives requires:

- standardization of programming

- portability of the programs

- development of computer tools within a coherent multicomputer set.

- full documentation and maintenance of the MODULEF library.

MSRC-RB: 3-D ELASTOPLASTIC FINITE ELEMENT PROGRAM

Gua Youzhong* and Lu Jiayou**

Institute of Mathematical Science, Academia Sinica, Wuhan, China
**Institute of Water Conservancy and Hydroelectric Power Research, Beijing, China*

ABSTRACT

This program presents a numerical model which takes into account the discontinuities of medium. The discontinuities are simulated by eight thin nodes 3-D isoparametric elements. The medium is represented by 3-D elastoplastic collapse elements. The stress, displacement and plastic zone can be calculated.

THEORETICAL BACKGROUND

Discontinuities are divided by discrete elements with established stiffness matrices based on their constituent equation. On the other hand, the medium involving orthogonal discontinuities can be treated as a pseudo-homogeneous material. It is not necessary to set discrete elements one by one. Within linear range, it is treated as an elastic medium. When discontinuities appear as a result of an increase in tensile or shear stress which exceeds their respective threshold, plastic yielding takes place.

So, in theory, the material shall be elastic below the threshold of plasticity and plastic beyond.

FIELD OF APPLICATION

Geometrical: Eight nodes 3-D isoparametric element.

Material: The material and discontinuities are assumed to be linear elastic and elastoplastic.

Analysis Capabilities: Static analysis.

Loading: Concentrated forces, pressure, body force are considered.

PROGRAM DESCRIPTION

Method: Finite element method.

Type of Elements: 3-D element.

Program Structure: Free format input, Fortran language, new developments can be introduced.

HARDWARE COMPATIBILITIES

Configuration: This program is active on M-160H computer.

Type of Computer: The program can operate successfully on any standard computer with a Fortran compiler.

Peripherals: A plotter is useful for displaying the output data.

Operating system: Any of the standard operating systems are acceptable.

Medium: The program can be transferred between computers by magnetic tape and floppy disk.

EXAMPLE OF APPLICATION

Test Case with Detail Description: For checking this program, the thick tube loaded with uniform pressure was calculated (Fig. 1). The theoretical solution of an elastoplastic thick tube can be seen in some standard references. The material parameters are:

$$E = 2 \times 10^6 \text{ kg/cm}^2,$$

$$\mu = 0.25,$$

$$R_t = 2000 \text{ kg/cm}^2,$$

$$T_s = R_t/\sqrt{3} = 1154.7 \text{ kg/cm}^2.$$

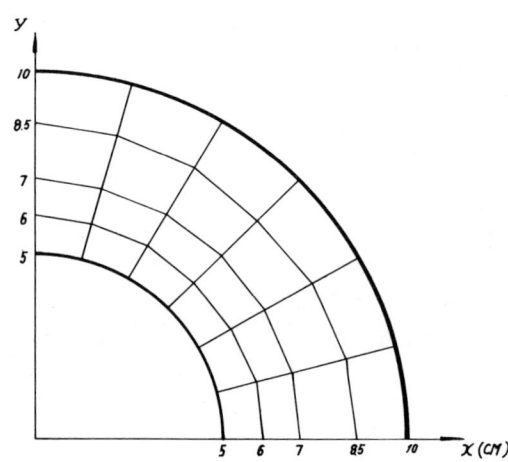

Fig. 1. The finite element mesh of thick tube

When $\phi = 0$, $C = R_t/\sqrt{3}$, in Drucker-Prager criterion and K can be expressed as follows:

$$\alpha = \tan\phi/\sqrt{9 + 12 \tan^2\phi} = 0, \quad K = 3C/\sqrt{9 + 12 \tan^2\phi} = C = R_t/\sqrt{3}.$$

Thus, the Drucker-Prager criterion,

$$\alpha I_1 + \sqrt{J_2} - K = 0,$$

becomes the Mises criterion,

$$\sqrt{J_2} - K = 0.$$

The inner and outer radius are 5 cm and 10 cm respectively. The results obtained from theoretical solution and from this program are shown in Fig. 2. It can be seen the results of FEM are in agreement with theoretical solution.

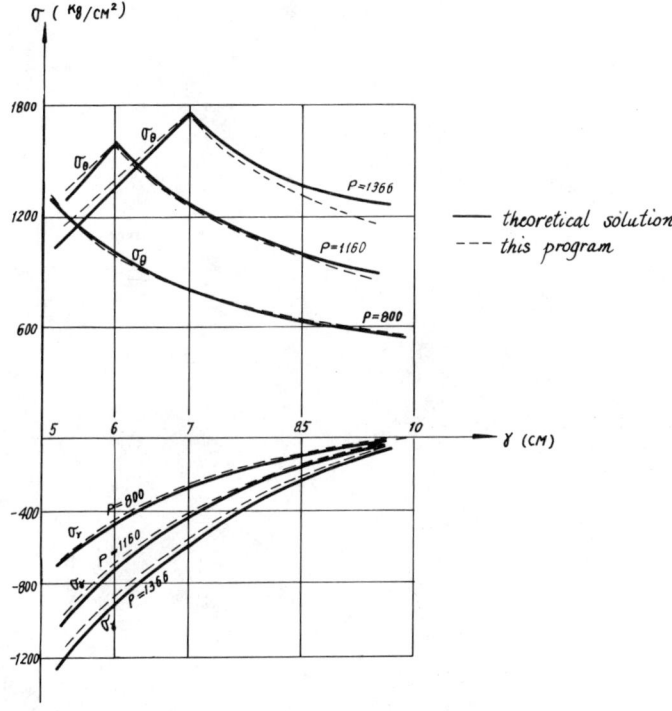

Fig. 2. The results obtained from this program and from the theoretical solution

OSTIN: A COMPUTER PROGRAM TO PERFORM THE SEISMIC ANALYSIS OF RIGID STRIP FOOTING ON 2-D ZONED VISCOELASTIC SOILS ON FREQUENCY DOMAIN

R. Abascal

Department of Mechanical Engineering, University of Seville, Spain

ABSTRACT

The use of finite element models consisting of boundless horizontal soil layers based on a rigid rock may lead to nonrealistic results for soil-structure interaction problems. In this paper a computer program that is able to analyze the dynamic behaviour of surface or embedded rigid strip footings when the subsurface soil topography is arbitrary is presented. The frequency domain formulation of the Boundary Element Method is used. Typical applications of the program are the computation of dynamic stiffness matrices and the analysis of the seismic response of strip footings.

THEORETICAL BACKGROUND

The Boundary Element Method (BEM) is well suited for the kind of problem in hand because of its ability to model infinite media.

In this paper the BEM is used to model a non-homogeneous viscoelastic soil. Each homogeneous subregion is discretized into straight line constant boundary elements (Fig. 2) and the compatibility between adjacent subregions enforced. The formulation used to compute foundation compliances is presented first.

Using the integral representation, the following equation for boundary point y of region R_1 (Fig. 1) may be written,

$$c_i^k(y)\, u_i(y) = \int_{s_2+s_3+s_4} \left[U_i^k(x{:}y)\, t_i(x) - T_i^k(x{:}y)\, u_i(x) \right] ds(x) \tag{1}$$

where x are the boundary points to which the integral extends, $u_i(x)$ and $t_i(x)$ are displacement and traction components at x, $U_i^k(x{:}y)$ and $T_i^k(x{:}y)$ stand for displacement and traction components of the fundamental solution at x when the unit point load is applied at y following the k direction, and c_i^k is a coefficient that depends on the geometry of the boundary at y ($c_i^k = 0.5\, \delta_{ik}$ for smooth boundary). The integral over s_4 is zero according to the radiation conditions, and boundary s_3 doesn't exist in the case of Fig. 1.a.

Similarly for a boundary point of region R_2

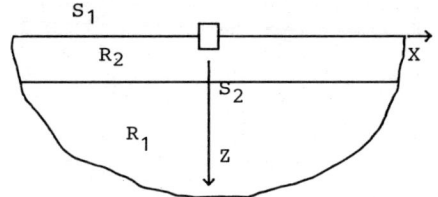

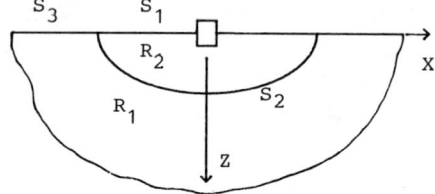

Fig. 1. Schematic models

Fig. 2. Discretization

$$C_i^k(y)\, u_i(y) = \int_{s_1+s_2} [U_i^k(x:y)\, t_i(x) - T_i^k(x:y)\, u_i(x)]\, ds(x) \qquad (2)$$

Since T_i^k, U_i^k, t_i and u_i satisfy the regularity conditions, for increasing distance to the load zone, the parts of s_1 and s_2 in Fig. 1.a, and s_3 in Fig. 1.b that are far from the foundation have little influence on equation (2) when it is written for nodes in the soil-foundation interface or its vecinity. Consequently, one may neglect the influence of those parts and extend the boundary discretization of s_1 and s_2 in Fig. 1.a only to a certain distance from the foundation. The same may be done for Fig. 1.b taking into account elements on s_3 only up to a certain distance from the soil deposit R_2.

In order to compute the foundation compliances, equation (2) is written for all nodes of the boundary element model. Enforcing compability and equilibrium along boundaries between adjacent regions, imposing zero traction conditions along the soil free surface, and prescribing displacements combatible with foundation rigid body motions at the soil-foundation interface one obtains a system of equations which solution gives the tractions over the elements at the soil-foundation interface. The resultant of these tractions for different rigid body motions gives the foundation stiffness matrix and its inverse the compliance matrix.

The second problem studied in this paper using the BEM formulation for non-homogeneous media is the analysis of the motion induced on foundations by incident P and SV waves coming from the far field. Diffraction problems dealing with infinite or semi-infinite regions are usually formulated decomposing the total displacement and stress fields into two parts. One is the free (undisturbed) field $[u^{(f)}, \sigma^{(f)}]$ and the other the scattered field $[u^{(s)}, \sigma^{(s)}]$. For the non-homogeneous half-plane of Figs. 1.a and 1.b the (f) will exist only for region R_1 and will be composed of the incident waves and the waves reflected by the free surface of a uniform half-plane having the properties of region R_1. The total field will be:

$$\left. \begin{array}{l} u(x) = u^{(f)}(x) + u^{(s)}(x) \\ \sigma(x) = \sigma^{(f)}(x) + \sigma^{(s)}(x) \end{array} \right\} x \in R_1 \tag{3}$$

$$\left. \begin{array}{l} u(x) = u^{(s)}(x) \\ \sigma(x) = \sigma^{(s)}(x) \end{array} \right\} x \in R_2 \tag{4}$$

The formulation for the case of Fig. 1.b will be presented first. Using the integral representation for the scattered field on R_1, one may write for points on s_2 or s_3,

$$c_i^k(y) u_i^{(s)}(y) = \int_{S_2} [U_i^k(x:y) t_i^{(s)}(x) - T_i^k(x:y) u_i^{(s)}(x)] ds(x) +$$

$$+ \int_{S_3} [- T_i^k(x:y) u_i^{(s)}(x)] ds(x) \tag{5}$$

that may be written as

$$c_i^k(y) u_i^{(s)}(y) = I_{s_2}^{(s)} + I_{s_3}^{(s)} \tag{6}$$

The total displacement for a point on s_1 or s_2 as part of region R_2 is

$$c_i^k(y) u_i(y) = J_{s_1} + J_{s_2} \tag{7}$$

where J represents integrals with the same kernel of I but referred to region R_2, $u^{(s)}(x) = u(x)$ and $t^{(s)}(x) = t(x)$.

In order to be able to enforce the compability and equilibrium conditions of the total field along s_2, equation (6) will be written in terms of total and free fields.

$$c_i^k(y) [u_i(y) - u_i^{(f)}(y)] = I_{s_2} - I_{s_2}^{(f)} + I_{s_3} - I_{s_3}^{(f)} \tag{8}$$

where $^{(f)}$, $^{(f)}$ and $I_{s_2}^{(f)}$ are known. The integral $I_{s_3}^{(s)} = I_{s_3} - I_{s_3}^{(f)}$ is:

$$I_{s_3}^{(s)} = - \int_{S_3} T_i^k \cdot (u_i - u_i^{(f)}) ds \tag{9}$$

The boundary s_3 in the above integral extends to infinity, however when the distance to the soil deposit increases the total field tends to be equal to the free field. Due to this fact plus the regularity conditions of T_i^k the parts of

s_3 that are far from the soil deposit have little influence on equation (9) when it is written for nodes near the foundation. Consequently the discretization of s_3 will only extend to a certain distance from the soil deposit.

To complete the solution of the problem one only has to use equations (6) and (8) plus the equilibrium and compatibility conditions along s_2 to form a system of equations that may be solve for any general boundary conditions at s_1 and s_3.

When the soil profile is that of Fig. 1.a the equations are very similar. For region R_1 and points on s_2 one may write

$$c_i^k(y) \left[u_i(y) - u_i^{(f)}(y) \right] = I_{s_2} - I_{s_2}^{(f)} \tag{10}$$

For points on s_1 or s_2 as part of R_2

$$c_i^k(y) \, u_i(y) = J_{s_2} + J_{s_1} \tag{11}$$

Everything is done as in the previous case. The only difference is that integrals that tend to zero when getting far from the point of reference have to be neglected now for boundaries s_1 and s_2.

FIELD OF APPLICATION

Geometrical

The solids to be analyzed should be of bidimensional geometry and their boundary being represented by means of straight segments (Fig. 2).

The computer program incorporates the possibility of symmetry according to one or two axes.

Materials

For the representation of the properties of the materials a linear-viscoelastic model is used making use of the principle of correspondence, which implicates, in the frequency domain, the use of complex wave velocities, calculated from the real value and from a damping coefficient β. For example the shear modulus is calculated as follows:

$$G_c = G_r \, (1 + 2i \, \beta), \quad i = \sqrt{-1} \tag{12}$$

The existence of areas of the material with different properties is also considered.

Analysis Capabilities

The computer program was thought for the analysis of Soil-Structure Interaction problems in the frequency domain using the substructures procedure. The calculation of the stiffness compliance matrix of massless rigid foundation, on the surface or embedded in a non-homogeneous half-space of any geometry, is found in its most direct applications, just as the response of massless foundations to incident waves of various types (kinematic interaction). At present it contains P and SV waves, the incorporation of another type of wave being immediate.

In spite of being particularly suited for the above mentioned use, the computer program permits the analysis of all types of homogeneous as non-homogeneous solids, of linear or linear-viscoelastic properties and bidimensional geometry, under certain tractions/displacements boundary conditions or an incident wave; the fields of displacements and tractions on the boundary being calculated for each frequency.

Loadings

The excitation is represented through certain boundary conditions in displacements and/or tractions; or else by means of up to two incident waves, P or SV, of variable amplitude and angle of incidence.

At the present it is possible to solve several load cases simultaneously. In the case of symmetrical geometry, symmetrical and skewsymmetrical load cases can be solved simultaneously which results in a significant saving of calculation time facing the analysis of real problems.

PROGRAM DESCRIPTION

Method

The method used has been the Boundary Elements in the frequency domain, whose efficiency for the analysis of infinite or semi-infinite domains has been extensively tested.

The calculation of the stiffness matrix of rigid strip foundations is attained through the application of unitary displacements, as a rigid body, and the calculation of the resultant of the tractions produced upon this application. The response of rigid foundation to incident waves is attained solving the simultaneous solution of four load cases; the first three corresponding to displacements as the rigid body of the foundation and the fourth to null displacement of it, all these cases having zero tractions prescribed on the free surface. Once the resultants are known $\{R_1\}$, $\{R_2\}$, $\{R_3\}$, $\{R_4\}$, the displacements $\{u\}$ of the rigid foundation is calculated solving the following system

$$\begin{bmatrix} R_1 & \vdots & R_2 & \vdots & R_3 \end{bmatrix} \{u\} = -\{R_4\} \tag{13}$$

once $\{u\}$ is known the load cases are combined in order to obtain the real field of displacements and tractions on the boundary.

Type of Elements

As a consequence of the formulation used it is only necessary to discretize the boundary of the bidimensional solids being studied. The said boundary will be discretized in linear elements whose geometry is defined by means of linear interpolation of the coordinates of the extreme points. Along side them the field variables are represented by means of a single value (constant shape function) associated with the midpoint of the elements (Fig. 3).

The integration of the fundamental solution along the boundary elements, in the case of the point of application of the concentrated load being away from the element of integration, are attained numerically through a Gauss quadrature using a number of integration points that can be defined by the user. In the case of the application point of the load being within the integration element the solution of the different integrals are explicitly programmed.

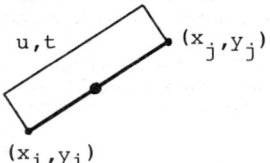

Fig. 3. Element geometry and shape function

Program Structure

The computer program is prepared to run in all types of computer having medium or large capacity, having been divided into eight overlays, the greatest of which can take up approximately 34 kbytes of instructions the rest of the central memory remaining available for an array which is organized by a series of indices according to the dimensions of the current problem. In this way are stored all the data that has been read or calculated throughout the computer program and that may be necessary at any moment. The solution of the system of equations, just like its assembly, is attained within the auxiliary memory.

The first overlay consists of the reading out of the geometrical data of the elements and the properties of the different subregions into which the material is divided, the possibility of automatic generation of the geometrical data of the elements existing; and with it only being necessary to supply the coordinates of one of the symmetrical parts if the said properties exists.

The second overlay reads the boundary conditions of the problem with the possibility of automatic generation existing. If the calculation required is the stiffness matrix of a foundation or the rigid body displacement of it due to incident waves, it is not necessary to read the boundary conditions as they are automatically generated through the program. The overlay also achieves a preprocessing of the matrix of coefficients of a type that remain subdivided in the auxiliary memory in blocks, in such a way that it can be assembled and solved in the available central memory.

The third overlay takes care of the necessities of the auxiliary memory creating two disc-files of sequential access and another two of random access. The two first ones are used to store geometrical characteristics and the points of integration of the different elements and as an auxiliary file; the other two are used to store the matrix of coefficients to be solved at any moment and to store the elemental matrix corresponding to the symmetrical parts should there be any.

The fourth and fifth overlays attain the assembly and calculation of the matrix of coefficients.

The sixth overlay controls the resolution and prints the results. The seventh solves the matrix of coefficients. The eighth controls the additional operations to be accomplished in the case of incidence of waves.

The language used for programming has been the FORTRAN 77.

HARDWARE COMPATIBILITIES

Minimal Configuration Required

The structure of the computer program previously described makes the minimum configuration that is necessary to the central memory about some 60 kbytes and

2.5 Mbytes of auxiliary memory, to solve problems of a medium order. (Some 100 elements and 4 subregions), which allows mini-computers to be used.

Its programming on computers of large capacity does not present any problems since it would merely be necessary to increase the dimensions of a small number of arrays, automatically signalling the memory.

Type of Computers and Other Hardware

At the present there are two versions of the program. One in a minicomputer HP-1000 and the other in a VAX 11/780, both are similar, so the problem of the compatibility of the hardware does not arise.

Peripherics

Hard disc unit.

Operating System

The only thing required is that it supports the FORTRAN 77.

Media

The computer program is disposable on a magnetic tape. (Version of VAX 11/780).

EXAMPLES OF APPLICATION

Test Case

As an example to test the results obtained by means of the computer program OSTIN, the problem of the diffraction of a cylindrical inclusion of waves coming from the infinite, is shown in Fig. 4.

The discretization has been achieved using 21 boundary elements on half circumference making use of the problem symmetry. The values obtained for the modulae of the displacements in two points of the circumference are plotted versus the frequency and compared with the exact solution obtained by Pao and Mow, for the cases of P and SV waves, in Fig. 5. It can be seen that the agreement between them is excellent.

The values of the parameters used have been, for the inclusion: shear modulus 16, density 1; and for the full space 4 and 1 respectively. The radius of the inclusion being 1, and the Poisson modulus of both being 1/4.

Practical Examples in Industry

For an example to be applied, the analysis of Soil-Structure Interaction problem is here shown. For this, the variation with frequency of the compliance of a rigid surface foundation on an alluvial valley of semielliptical shape beneath which exists a half-space (Fig. 6) is presented. Besides, the rigid body displacements induced by waves impinging on this foundation will be shown.

This is a common problem in the seismic studies necessary for calculating buildings of a great responsibility such as Power Plants.

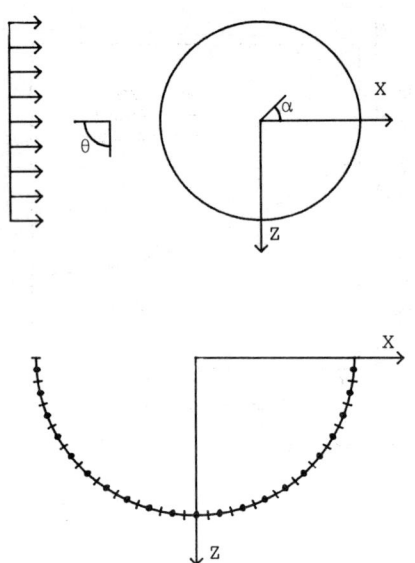

Fig. 4. Elastic Inclusion. Wave incident

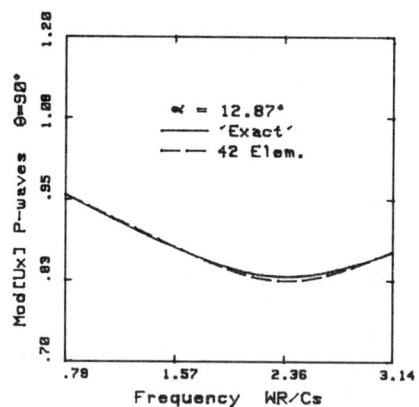

Fig. 5a. Displacements on the interface of the inclusion

The discretization used consists of 51 boundary elements and two subregions of different properties (Fig. 7), having made use of the symmetry.

The geometrical characteristic magnitudes of the problem are: half-width of the foundation B, major semiaxis of the ellipse D and minor semiaxis H.

In Fig. 8 the evolution of the real and imaginary parts of the vertical compliance F_z, corresponding to the vertical displacement, is represented versus the dimensionless frequency $\omega B/C_{s1}$ (ω = excitation frequency, C_{s1} speed of S-waves in the halfspace) for the values $D/H = 4$; $H/B = 4$ and $RC_s = C_{s1}/C_{s2} = 2$

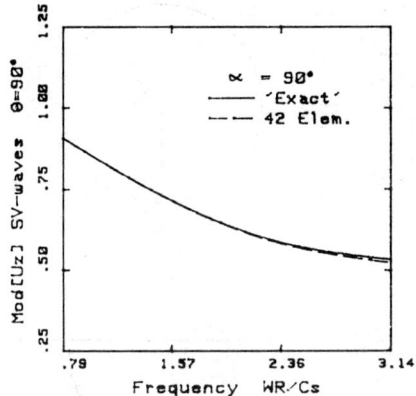

Fig. 5b. Displacements on the interface of the inclusion

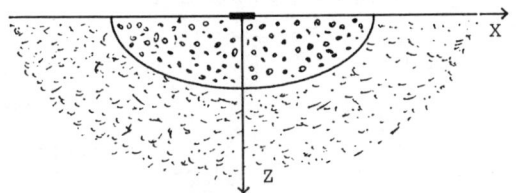

Fig. 6. Alluvial valley

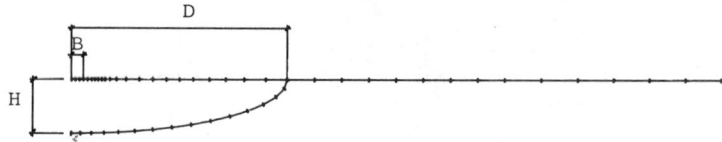

Fig. 7. Discretization of the alluvial valley

(C_{s2} = speed of S-waves in the alluvial valley); the Poisson modulae of both, halfspace and valley, being 1/4, and having used a percentage of damping of 5%.

In Fig. 9 the modulae of the vertical and horizontal rigid body displacements of the foundation, are represented, for P-waves (θ = 30º) ans SV-waves (θ = 15º) respectively. The results are presented normalized by the free-field displacement; being the parameters of the problems identical to those in the previous example.

The computer program OSTIN allows for analyzing more generic problems than the previous one with buried foundations and with a stratum of diverse shape.

Potential Application Areas

- Soil-Structure Interaction.
- Wave analysis.

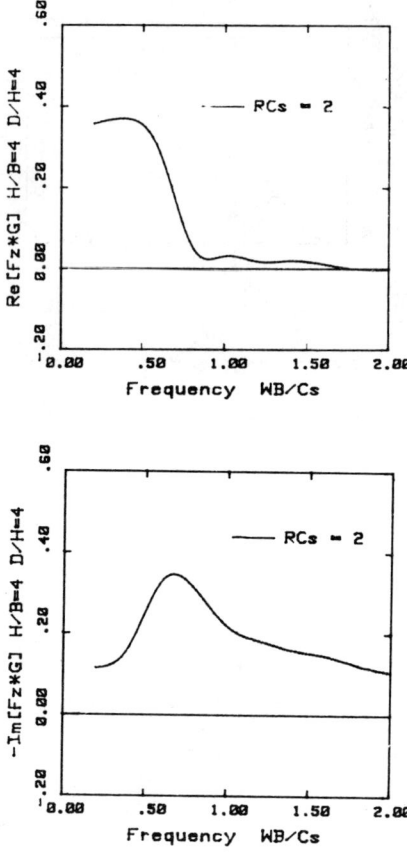

Fig. 8. Vertical compliance of the rigid strip footing

- Tunnels.
- Dynamic analysis in the frequency domain.
- Effect of the topographical profile on seismic analysis.

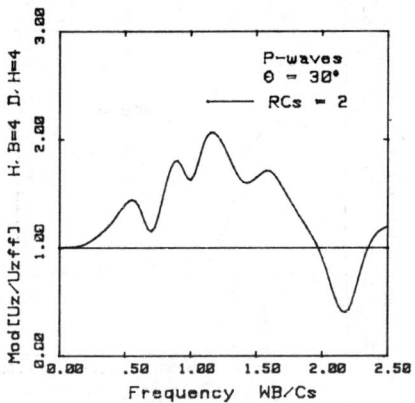

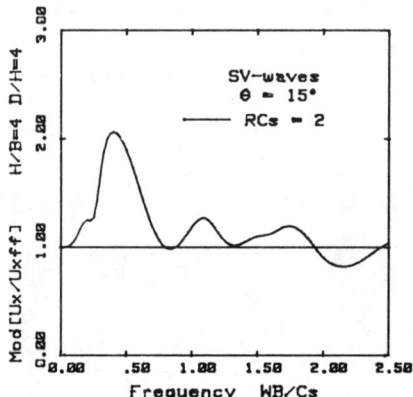

Fig. 9. Rigid body displacements on the foundation in wave analysis

RAPS: A PLOT PROGRAM FOR TESTING OF THE MODEL AND FOR PLOTTING OF THE RESULTS OF FINITE ELEMENT CALCULATIONS

D. Koschmieder and J. Altes

Institut für Nukleare Sicherheitsforschung der Kernforschungs anlage Jülich GmbH,
Postfach 1913, D-5170 Jülich, Federal Republic of Germany

INTRODUCTION

The large quantity of data occurring in finite element computations is related to both the description of the structure as well as the results achieved. A graphic representation is most suitable for the efficient handling of these data. It is therefore usual to couple pre- and postprocessors to the FE program.

The preprocessor should be designed to enable a rapid and effective error diagnosis of the structure to be computed. The error routines built into the FE software systems often prove to be insufficient since they can carry out element tests but no structure tests. Thus there are for example element specifications which are logically possible within the structure, but not intended, e.g. missing or overlapping elements. This will not be detected by the error routines. A lot of computing time and manpower can be saved if the structure is examined thoroughly with respect to freedom from errors before the actual cost-intensive computer runs.

Plot programs which reproduce the large quantities of data in such a way that a comprehensive survey of the results can be rapidly obtained are also necessary for evaluating and representing the results of FE computations.

Such a plot program which offers both extensive possibilities of testing the structure (preprocessor) and of evaluating results (postprocessor) is described in the following. It is known as RAPS (Räumliches ASKA Plot System - 3D ASKA Plot System).

RAPS offers various possibilities of representing 2- and 3-D structures with freely selected angles of observation and drawing scales. The parallel perspective is used in projecting the model on to the drawing plane.

The results of static and dynamic calculations, such as displacements, stresses, temperatures, cracks and eigenforms, can be variously represented as plots of deformed structure, isolines, principal stresses or crack patterns. Two additional types of diagram are also implemented:

1. The results of time-dependent calculations can be drawn as a function of time.

2. The results can be plotted in a section through the structure defined by the

nodal points.

There are two existing versions of the program: on the one hand a batch version in which all plot data are processed without any possibility of intervention on the part of the user. If the user e.g. wishes to see the structure from a different viewing angle then he will have to restart the program. Microfilm plotter and paper plotter (e.g. CALCOMP) are available as output media. On the other hand there is an interactive version which enables the user to develop or change the picture in dialogue with the computer at the display screen. Great emphasis was placed on a user-friendly data input. Interfaces are currently available for hardware from the following companies: HP, RAMTEK, RASTER TECHNOLOGIES and APOLLO DOMAIN. During program development attention was paid to keeping the largest part independent of hardware so that only one subroutine would have to be correspondingly modified for matching to a graphic terminal.

RAPS was developed for the FE systems ASKA and SMART. Beam, plate, shell and solid elements can be processed. Additional elements can be easily incorporated. In the meantime interfaces have been established for ADINA, SAP IV, SAP V and NONSAP. It is also possible to match the program to other FE systems.

FORTRAN 77 is applied as the programming language. Input of the control data is unformatted. The storage capacity required depends on the size of the field dimensions (number of elements to be plotted, nodal points, loading cases etc.) and is between 1 and 2 Mbytes. Importance was attached to short computing times, which has a particular effect in the hidden-line algorithm. RAPS is being continuously further developed (colour graphics, reducing computer times).

With the corresponding hardware (e.g. terminals from RAMTEK, RASTER TECHNOLOGIES) colour graphics can be used very effectively with RAPS. For example, the visible surfaces of the elements can be filled in with colour so that the observer no longer has the impression of a wire model but rather of a solid 3-D structure. The use of colour also enables results to be presented more clearly, e.g. stresses or temperatures can be plotted as a function of the intensity of colour (isoshading). RAPS currently runs on the following computers and operating systems:

        IBM 3081   under VM/CMS

        IBM 3033   "   MVS

        IBM 3033   "   TSS

        APOLLO DOMAIN

        VAX

The plot system is distributed by the Gesellschaft fur Strukturanalyse (GfS), Wermutsbrunnstr. 15, D-5100 Aachen, tel. 02408/7067.

USE AS PREPROCESSOR

Both the whole model (Fig. 1) as well as individual areas (sectors) (Fig. 2) can be depicted with RAPS. There are three possibilities of defining the sectors:

1. If the FE system permits the whole structure to be divided into individual element groups then these groups can be represented individually or several combined together.

2. The sector can be restricted by co-ordinates.

3. After drawing the whole structure the required sector can be localized on the display screen with the aid of the graphic cursor.

If required, all the nodal points occurring in the plot can be identified by a

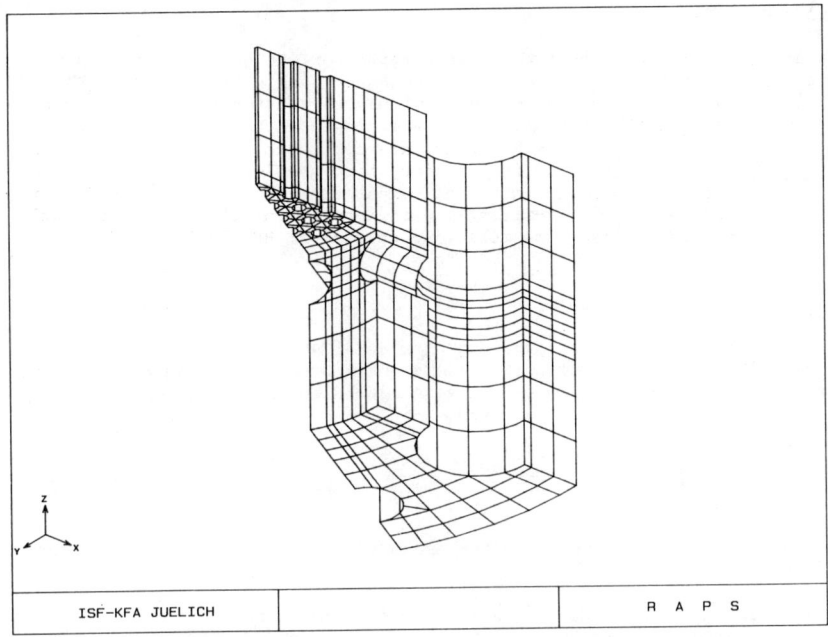

Fig. 1. Part of a prestressed concrete reactor pressure vessel of a high temperature reactor

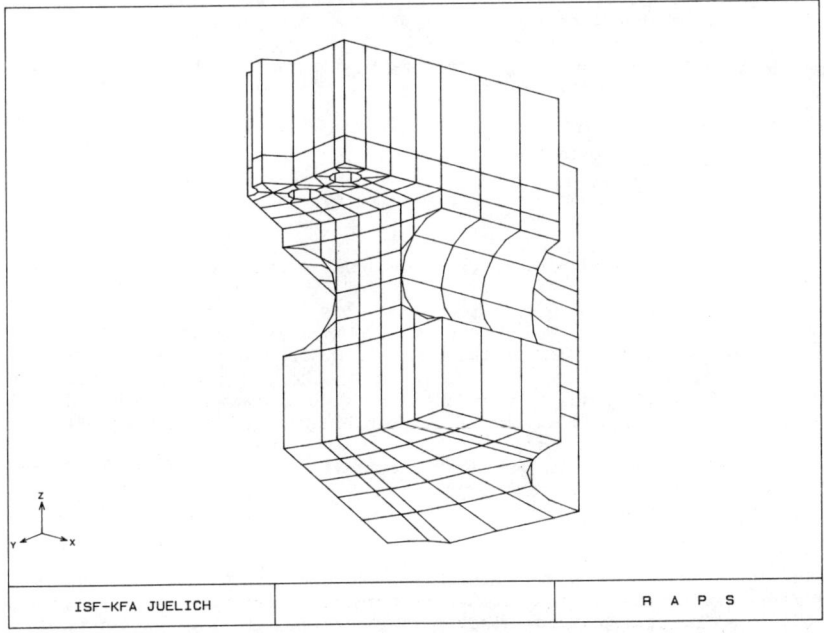

Fig. 2. Detail of the prestressed concrete reactor pressure vessel model shown in Fig. 1

symbol and/or their number.

It is absolutely essential in testing the structure that the input boundary conditions are also checked. All nodal points having suppressed, external or prescribed degrees of freedom can therefore be identified in RAPS.

Viewing Angle

The structure can be viewed from any angle. For this purpose angles of rotation and tilt from $-360°$ to $+360°$ must be input.

System of Co-ordinates

In every picture a system of co-ordinates can be optionally drawn in the bottom left-hand corner. The three unit vectors positioned vertically on top of each other are thus projected into the image plane (Fig. 1). The length of the projected vectors provides information about the ratio of length to width to height.

Scales

Three possibilities are available corresponding to the different requirements of the users:

1. In each individual picture the same scale is used in both directions of the drawing plane so that the proportions are retained for each viewing angle.

2. A different scale can be used for each drawing direction in order to better exploit the drawing space available. However, information about the ratio of dimensions is thus lost.

3. The same scale is used for all combinations of angles so that the pictures display the same proportions in spite of different viewing angles.

Possibilities of Representation

The options described above can be applied to the following methods of representation:

1. Line plot. In this representation the boundaries of each element are drawn.

2. Line contour plot. With this representation it is possible to plot all lines only defined once in a model or part of the model. In the case of 2-D structures one thus also has the possibility of testing for missing or incorrectly defined elements in addition to the possibility of drawing the external boundaries and the cavities. The line contour plot for a 2-D (rotational symmetric) structure is shown in Fig. 3a and in Fig. 3b the line plot. It can be seen that an error in the topology has been made at the location shown by the arrow. In the line plot this cannot be established. This option can also be used to represent the boundary lines of 3-D structures. If desired the contour lines can be divided into visible and invisible lines.

3. Surface plot. All the surfaces of a structure only defined once are drawn in the case of a surface plot. This type of plot represents a possibility of testing 3-D structures for missing or incorrectly defined elements. Figure 4a shows that the model represented as a line plot in Fig. 4b has a cavity in

RAPS: A Plot Program   195

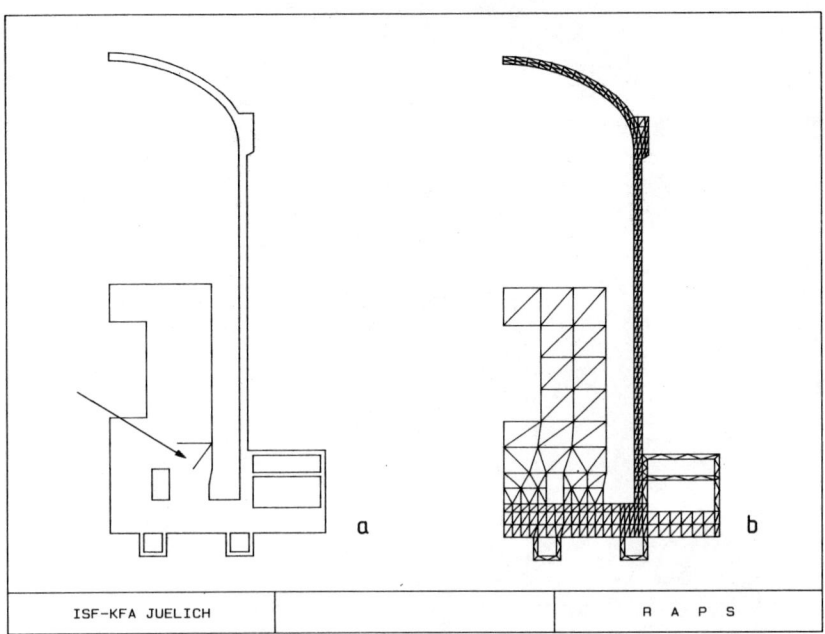

Fig. 3. Line contour plot (a) and line plot (b) of a rotational symmetric model

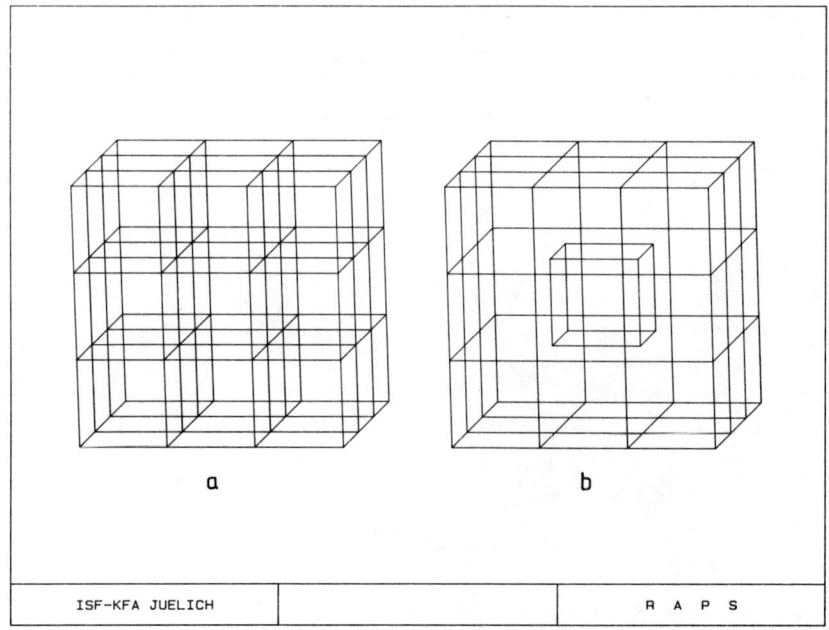

Fig. 4. Line plot (a) and surface plot (b) of a 3-D structure

the middle or an element in the middle has not been defined. This cannot be seen from the line plot.

4. <u>Hidden-line plot</u>. RAPS offers the possibility of producing plots in which the invisible parts of the structure are not represented (Fig. 5) or are shown as dashed lines (hidden lines).

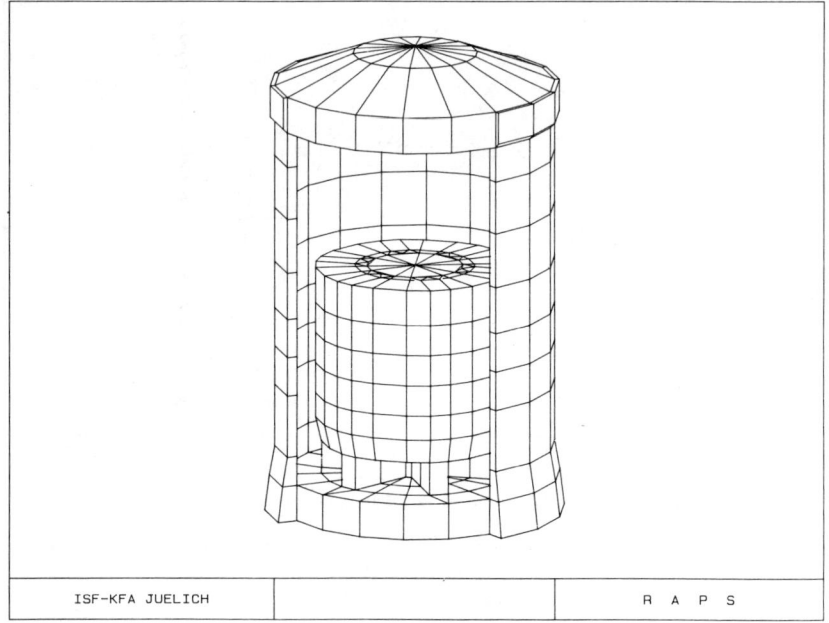

Fig. 5. Hidden-line plot of a 3-D model

USE AS POSTPROCESSOR

The following methods of representing results have been implemented in RAPS to date:

- plot of the structure deformed by load
- plot of isolines on the visible part of the model
- plot of the principal stresses
- plot of crack patterns
- combination of the first four possibilities
- plot of results as a function of time
- plot of results of sections cut through the FE model.

<u>Plot of the Deformed Structure</u>

The structure deformed by static or dynamic load can be represented by all the plot options described above. Since the deformations are always so small in relation to the dimensions of the model that they would not be visible in the plot, they have to be enlarged. There are two possibilities of achieving this enlargement; on the one hand with the aid of a constant factor with which the deformations are multiplied, and on the other hand by normalization to the maximum deformation for which a certain length can be predefined.

A deformed system is represented in Fig. 6 as the hidden-line plot. The undeformed structure can also be thinly backed.

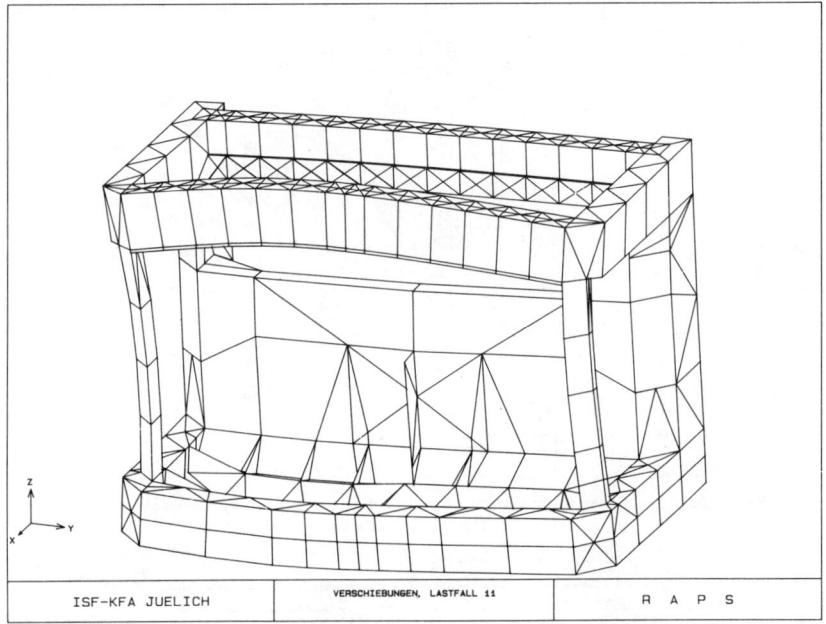

Fig. 6. Plot of a deformed structure

In the case of colour terminals, different colours can be assigned to the deformed and undeformed structures.

Plot of Isolines

A further possibility of representing results is to draw isolines. For greater clarity, the isolines are only drawn on the visible surfaces of the model (Fig. 7). The values for which the isolines are to be generated can either be predefined by the user or automatically localized by the program. In this latter case equidistant values between the minimum and maximum of the results are formed.

In the case of colour terminals, different colours can be used for the individual isolines so that e.g. tensile and compressive stress areas or the stress-free line can be represented by different colours. This considerably increases the clarify of the results depicted. In addition isoshading can be used, to plot e.g. the different values of stresses or temperatures by changing the colour intensities.

Plot of Principal Stresses

RAPS enables the principal stresses to be represented 3-D in the form of arrows giving information about the direction and size. This can be selected either for all the nodalpoints or only the visible ones. If the arrows point towards the

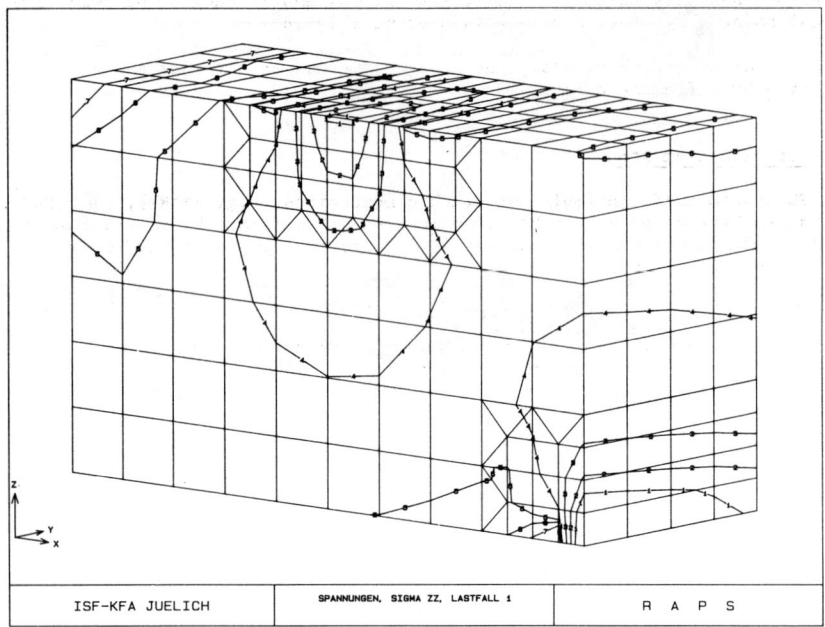

Fig. 7. 3-D structure with stress isolines on the visible parts of the model

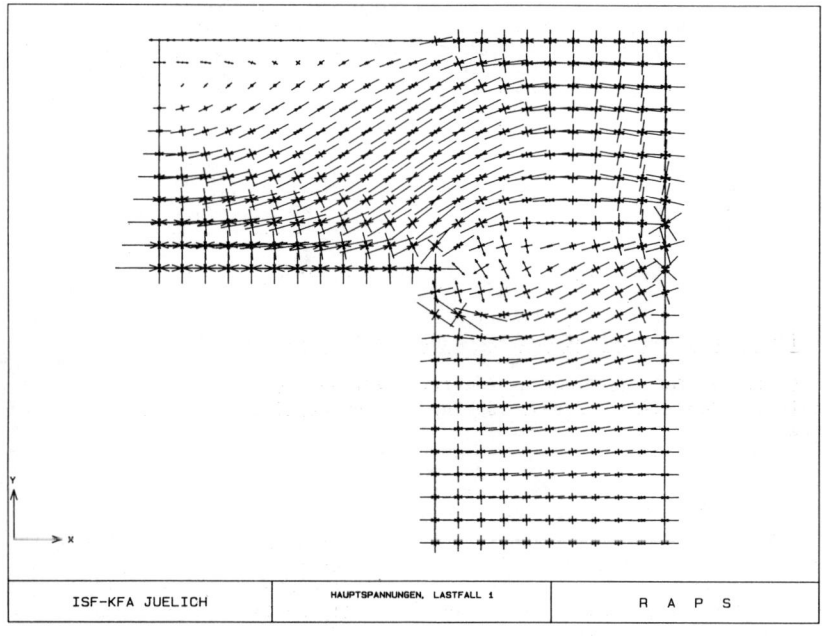

Fig. 8. Representation of principal stresses

nodal point then this indicates compressive stress and if they point away from the nodal point then tensile stress is present (Fig. 8).

In the case of colour terminals, tensile and compressive stresses can be represented by different colours.

Plot of Cracked Elements

If the FE system used can implement crack computations (e.g. SMART), then the elements displaying cracks can be drawn in a shrunken form. Vectors are drawn in the node points where cracks occur and if desired the type of fracture can be written on them (Fig. 9).

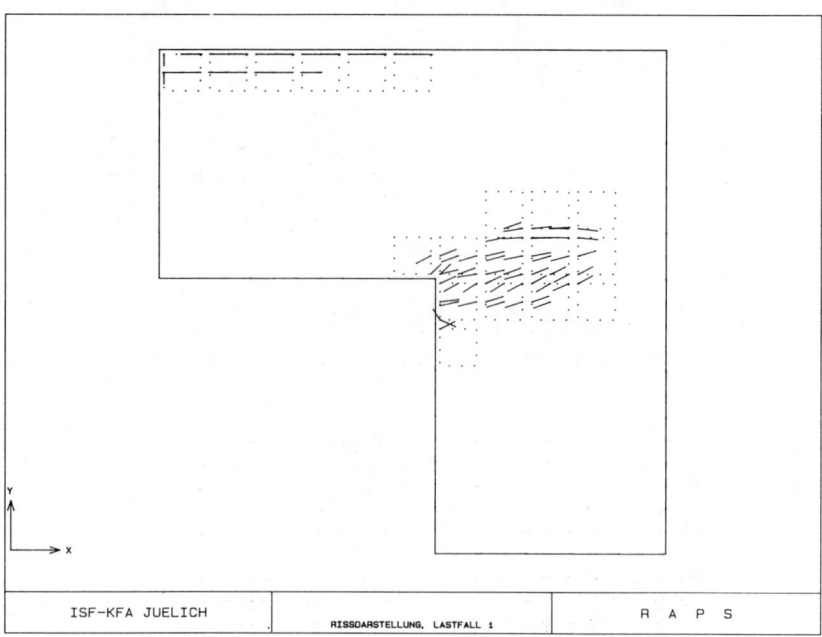

Fig. 9. Plot of a crack pattern

Combination of the Methods of Representing Results Described Above

The possibilities for representing results described above can be combined in any way required. For example stress isolines can be applied to the deformed structure.

Plot of the Results as a Function of Time

In evaluating the results of time-dependent processes (e.g. creep, vibrations) diagrams can be drawn in which the results are represented as a curve for one or more nodal points as a function of time. The axes can be selected as linear, logarithmic or log-log. The axes are automatically scaled, but this can also be preset by the user (Fig. 10).

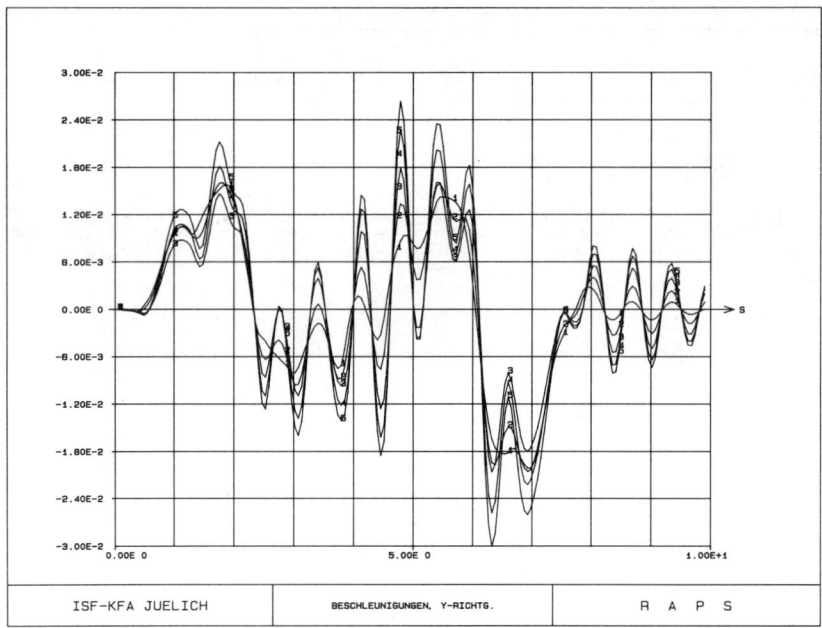

Fig. 10. Plot of results as a function of time

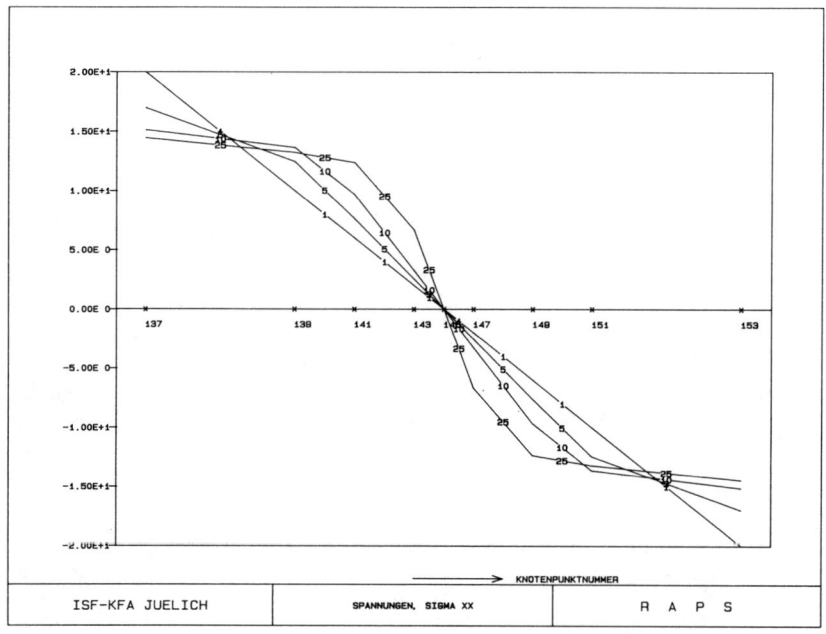

Fig. 11. Plot of creep stresses in a section through the FE-model

Plot of Results of Sections Cut Through the FE Model

The results can be plotted in sections defined by selected nodal points. The axes are automatically scaled but the user can preset the scaling of the y-axis (Fig. 11).

REFERENCE

Koschmieder, D. and J. Altes. RAPS - Ein dreidimensionales Plotprogramm zum Test und zur Ergebnisdarstellung von Finite-Element-Berechnungen Jül 1596, August 1980, Kernforschungsanlage, Jülich.

ROBOT: PROGRAM FOR LINEAR ANALYSIS OF AXISYMMETRIC STRUCTURES

I. Páczelt

Technical University, Department of Mechanics,
H-3515 Miskolc, Egyetemváros, H-3515 Hungary

ABSTRACT

ROBOT is a comprehensive computer program for linear elastic analysis of axisymmetrical structures subjected to axisymmetrical loading.

The program is based on the finite element displacement method, so that it has great versatility for modelling complex structures composed from many different parts and materials. Both 2-D axisymmetric and shell elements as well as some special elements are available. A great variety of structures can be analyzed including segmented, branched shells of revolution with various meridional geometries, wall constructions and stiffeners. Temperature-dependent material property conditions may range from homogeneous isotropic to nonhomogeneous orthotropic. Five classes of loads are possible, i.e. mechanical line loads applied at nodal circles, pressure loads distributed over surfaces, centrifugal loading, body forces due to axial acceleration and distribute thermal loads arising from temperature distribution over the shell surface and through the shell wall thickness. Any compatible set of kinematic boundary conditions may be specified. One of the main advantages of the code is the provision for realistic engineering details, such as interface coupling constraint, internal eccentric rigid link, elastic foundation, rib reinforcings and three types of spring elements. Though the code is basically intended for linear problems, there is an option for performing the nonlinear frictionless unilateral contact analysis of two axisymmetrical bodies by means of quadratic programming technique.

The ROBOT is actually not a single program but a collection of four modules operating on a unified data base. A typical problem might be solved by calling in a specified order the individual modules which can communicate only via the data base. In this way the program has a restart capability. The program has been facilitated by a thorough data-checking system. Emphasis in the design of the system has been placed to ease of data generation, efficient solution techniques and options for obtaining clearly arranged output. Data allocation within the program is performed dynamically, so that there are essentially no restrictions on the sizes of any arrays; instead, the restrictions arise entirely out of the need to be able to store all the data in-core at the same time. The programming language is FORTRAN. The ROBOT consists of nearly 16,000 statements in 175 subroutines. The amount of core required, largely depends on the program modules being executed. Sixty-four kbyte is sufficient for the overlayed modules and maximum 64 kbyte for the program's data. The low core requirement does not practically restrict the program capacity and in most cases 50 Mbyte disck is sufficient.

The program is implemented on CDC and on VIDEOTON R11 computer.

The program is documented as user's, programmer's and theoretical manuals.

Since 1980 the program has been used for engineering calculations and for research.

THEORETICAL BACKGROUND

The Finite Element Programming System is based on compatible displacement of elements. For modelling of the rotationally symmetric shell structures eleven different kinds of technical shell elements can be applied.

They are constant thickness walled homogeneous symmetrically three-layered plate, cone (including the axe), or cylinder elements (1-3 type elements).

Furthermore, constant thickness walled homogeneous or symmetrically built-up three-layered or dissymetrically built-up two-layered, linearly varying thickness walled plate, cone, cylinder, truncated cone (including ring form plate), torus (including sphere), shell (given by the equation of the meridional cone section), shell, with C^1 continuity (given the meridian assymptotically by spline function in form of $R = R(Z)$ or $Z = Z(R)$, R is the radius, Z is the axe) with either radial or axial element stiffeners which can be constant or varying cross sectional. Matching the middle surfaces of plate or shell elements, only the C^1 continuity is assured but extra terms of the approximation polynomials can be taken into consideration as well. For instance, in case of torus element denoting the tangential displacement co-ordinate by u and the normal co-ordinates by w, the approximation is

$$\begin{bmatrix} u \\ w \end{bmatrix} = \begin{bmatrix} 1 & s & 0 & 0 & 0 & \sin\theta \\ 0 & 0 & 1 & s & s^2 & -\cos\theta \end{bmatrix} a + \begin{bmatrix} \underbrace{\ldots s^{n+1} \ldots}_{NPU} & 0^T \\ 0^T & \underbrace{\ldots s^{k+2} \ldots}_{NPW} \end{bmatrix} \hat{a}$$

where θ is the angle between the n normal of the middle surface and the axe Z. a and $\hat{a}$ are constants, s is length.

The extra constants $\hat{a}$ are eliminated at the element level. In case of the elements 1-3 the stiffness matrices and the generalized nodal loading vectors are determined in closed forms. The material of homogeneous one layer shell is either isotropic or orthotropic. Material constants are temperature dependent. They are determined from given data by linear interpolation.

Temperature can be varied linearly along the thickness and along the middle surface. The temperature distribution is given as input.

Distributed pressure loadings and the accelerations in direction of the axe Z can vary linearly.

Kinematical loading effects either from direct prescriptions of given nodal points or from bilateral contact problems (for instance overlaps).

These loadings are taken into consideration at the element level one by one and at last the solution can be obtained for arbitrary combination of the basic

ROBOT: Program for Linear Analysis of Axisymmetric Structures

loadings and the kinematic prescriptions.

Program gives possibility to consider the so-called eccentric joints, when given nodal circles have constant distances during the deformation. By these the isoparametric elements can be linked to thin-walled shell elements which give more accurate results near disturbances.

Contact problems without friction are solved by quadratic programming based on a modified Wolfe method. Rigid body movements between bodies in contact can be allowed.

FIELD OF APPLICATION

Axisymmetric bodies in axisymmetric strain state, thin-walled shells.

Material is linear, isotropic or anisotropic. Homogeneity is supposed per element.

Analysis capabilities: static

Loading possibilities:
 4 different kinds of pressure
 2 different kinds of acceleration (in Z direction), rotating, temperature, kinematic loading and 10 different distributed loadings along lines.

Unilateral contact.

PROGRAM DESCRIPTION

Finite element method

Type of elements:

  axisymmetric solid,
  axisymmetric plate,
  axisymmetric shell elements,
  spring elements.

The ROBOT programming system consists of four different program which can be run one by one but with increasing order number.

First program reads the geometrical data of nodal circles, makes the necessary automatizations and determines the primary unknowns of the FEM mesh, second program determines the element stiffness matrices, the nodal loading vectors and prepares the stress calculations, third program solves the linear equation system and the fourth program makes the combination of the basic loadings, calculates the generalized displacements and stresses. The program's language is FORTRAN IV. There is possibility to extend the element library, to match pre- and postprocessors to the program etc.

HARDWARE COMPATIBILITIES

Type of computers: CDC
  VIDEOTON R11
  VIDEOTON SzM52
  minimal configuration
  128 kbyte
                                      70 CORE

Peripherics: 50 Mbyte disc
  50 Mbyte disc

Operating system: MASTER
 VIDEOTON special
Media:
 magnetic tape magnetic tape

NUMERICAL EXAMPLES

Example for test case:

Strength analysis of a flywheel. The structure on Fig. 1 was modelled by a ring i.e. curviform beam and thin-walled shells. Loading occurred from rotation of $\omega = 460.07$ rad/s and overlapping of 0.1205 mm between nodal circles 2 and 3. Elastic constants were Young modulus $E = 2.05 \cdot 10^5$ MPa and Poisson's ratio $\nu = 0.3$, mass density $\rho = 7.8 \cdot 10^{-9}$ Ns^2 mm^{-4}.

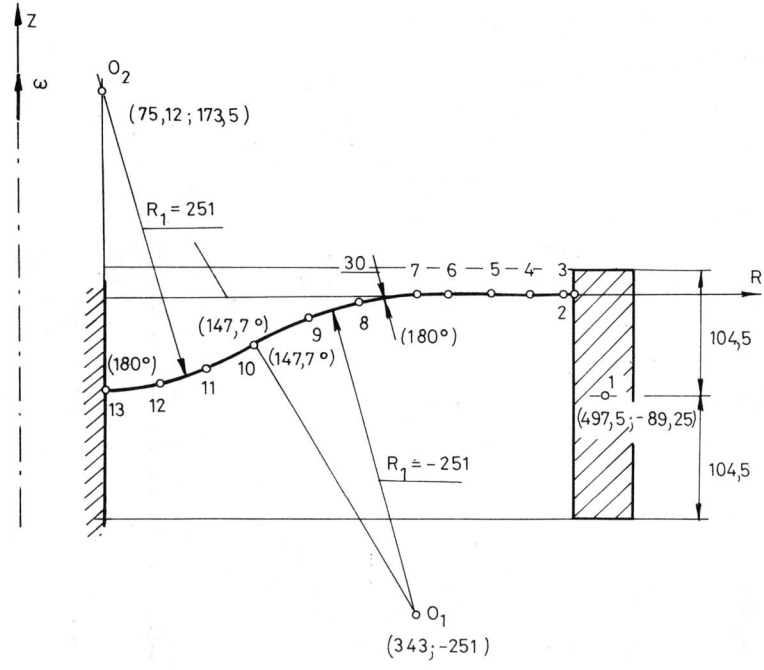

Fig. 1. Flywheel and the finite element mesh

In centre of gravity of the ring the radial displacement was $u_r = 0.925$ mm, the axial displacement was $u_z = 1.107$ mm and the angular rotation was $\beta = -5.99 \cdot 10^{-3}$ rad.

In the clamping cross-section (nodal circle 13) of the wheel-balancing disc the Mises equivalent stress was 272.7 MPa on the outer and 291.9 MPa on the inner side. Tangential stress in the ring was $\sigma_\varphi = 654.62$ MPa. Maximum Mises equivalent stress in the disc occurred along the nodal circle 8, with the value of 445.5 MPa.

ROBOT: Program for Linear Analysis of Axisymmetric Structures 207

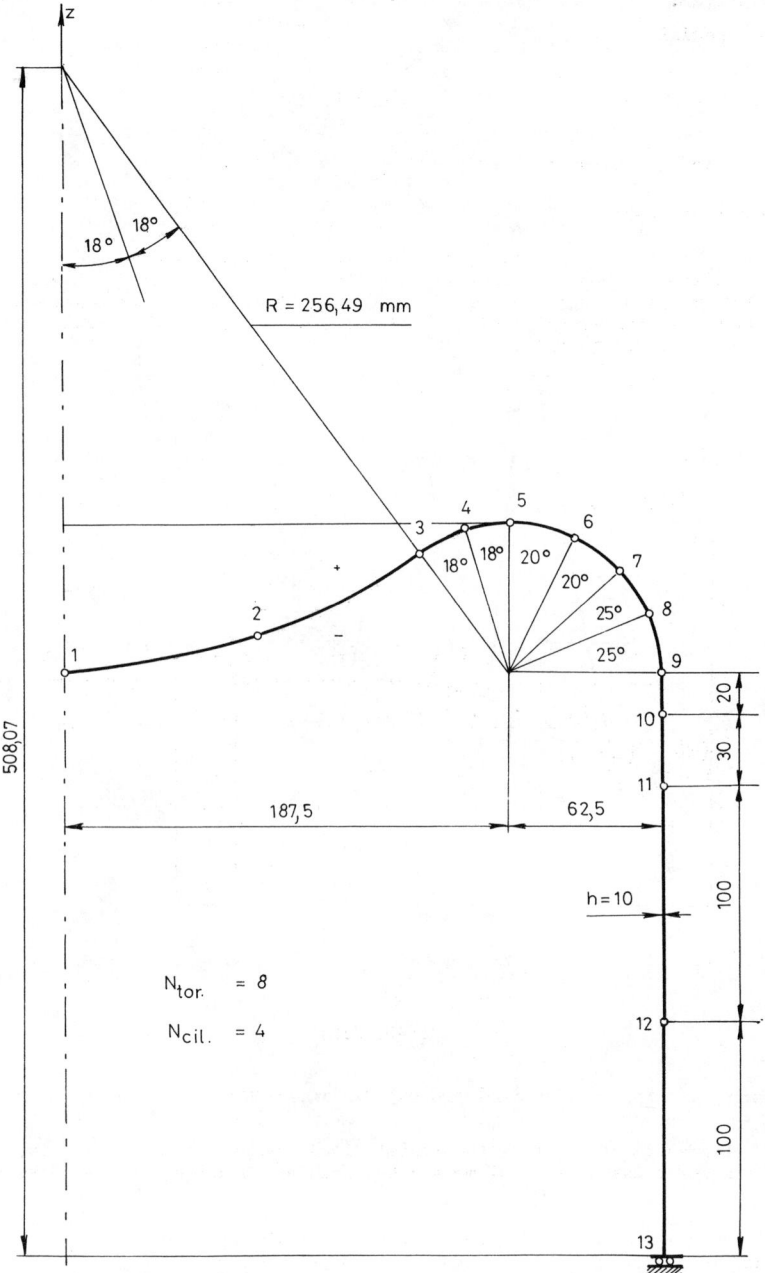

Fig. 2. The syphon tank bottom and the finite element mesh

Practical examples. Example 1:

Figure 2 shows the bottom part of a syphon tank. Material constants are
$E = 2.0 \cdot 10^5$ MPa, $\nu = 0.3$. The inner p pressure is 1 MPa. The torusoidal part is
divided into $N_t = 8$ torus and the cylindrical part into $N_c = 4$ cylinder elements.

The problem was solved by the order increase of the approximating polynomial.
(NPU = 5 and NPW = 5). On Fig. 3 the continuous line shows the calculated
equivalent Mises reduced stress distribution along the inner, and the broken
line shows the same along the outer side. The disruptions along the element's
boundaries were practically zero.

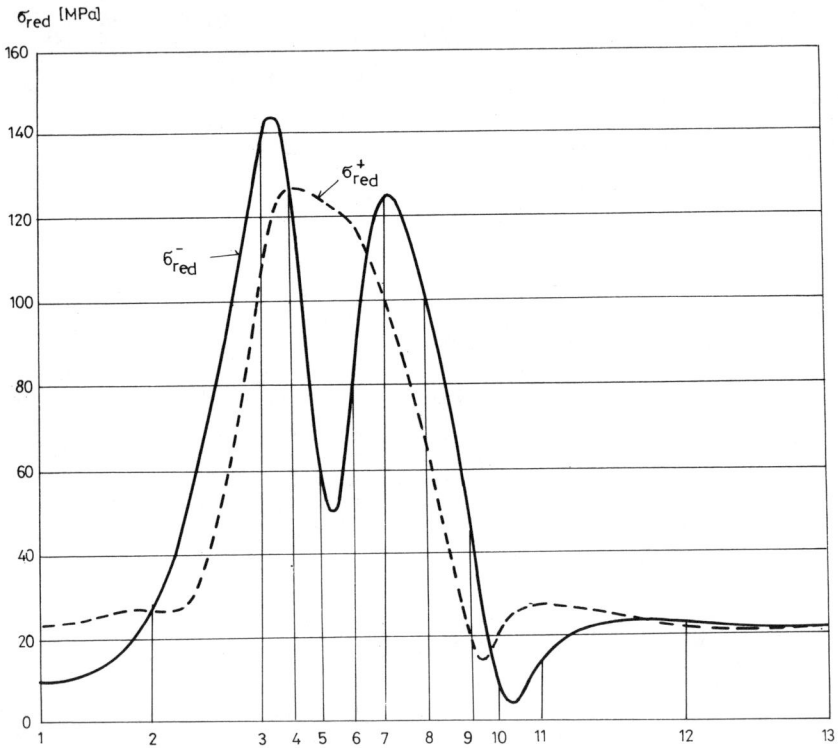

Fig. 3. Reduced stresses along the inner and the outer superficies

The example proves the effectiveness of the order increase. The problem was
solved with less, $N_t = 4$ and $N_c = 3$ elements as well but with the same
increased polynomials. However, the disruptions in stresses along the
neighbouring elements were everywhere less than 1%.

Example-2:

The strength analysis of a heat exchanger joining was carried out by two
different finite element modelling. The wall thickness of the structure is
small compared with the radial dimensions, so its parts can be considered as a
thin-walled shell structure (Fig. 4).

ROBOT: Program for Linear Analysis of Axisymmetric Structures

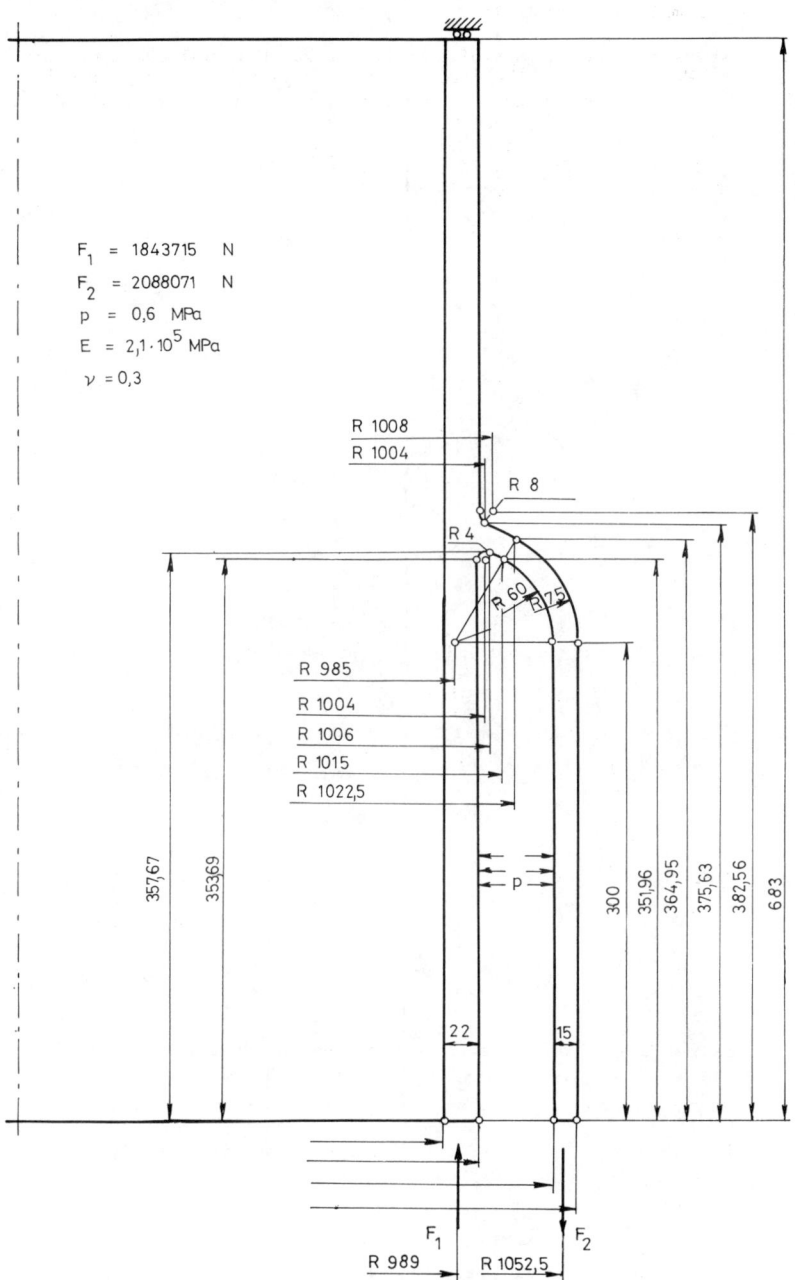

Fig. 4. Part of the heat exchanger

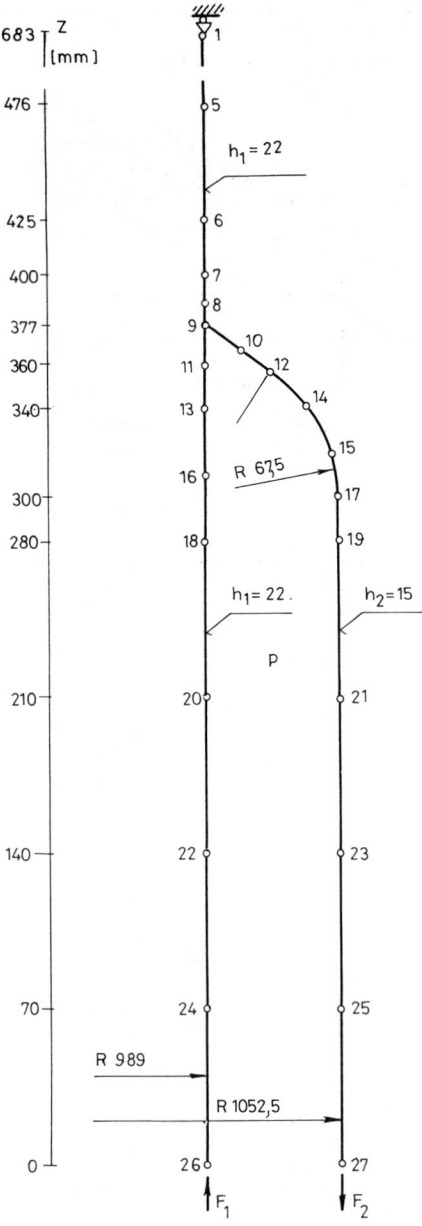

Fig. 5. Finite element mesh from shell elements of the heat exchanger

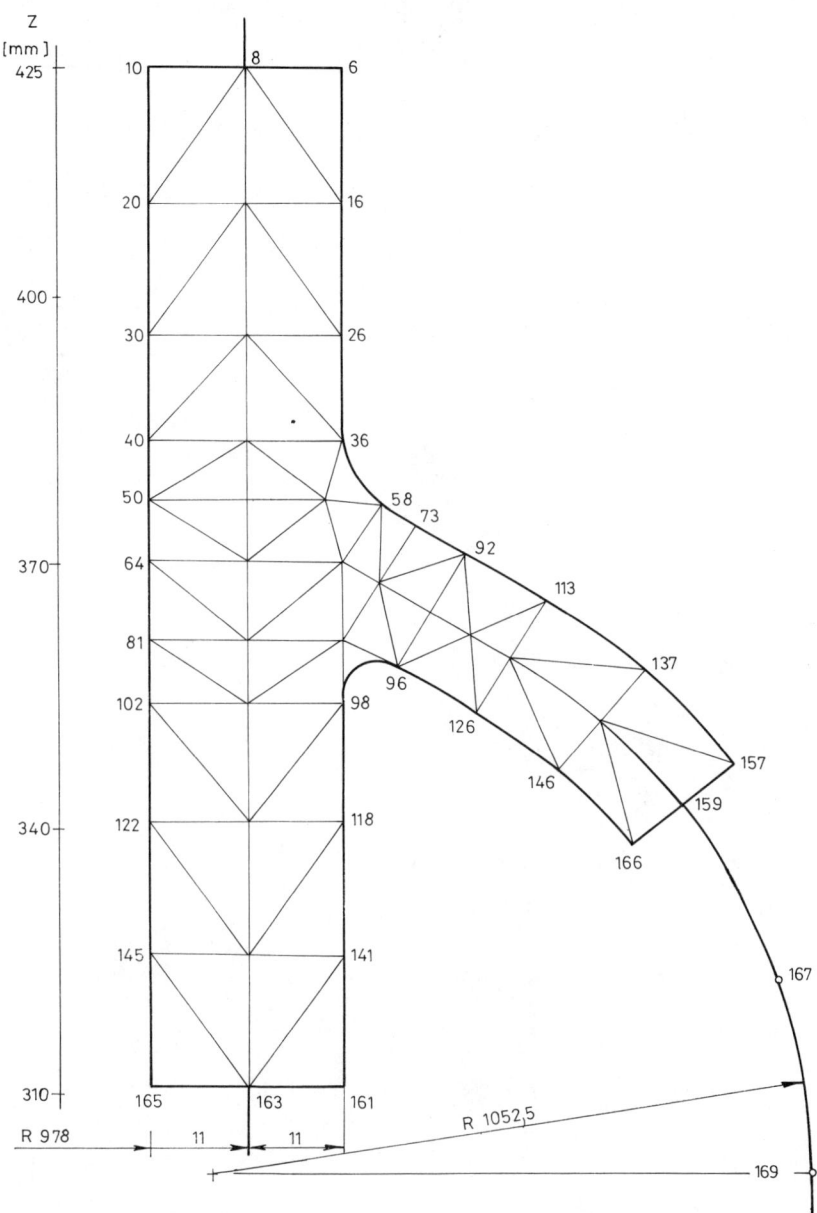

Fig. 6. Finite element mesh from shell and isoparametrical elements of the heat exchanger

The first model consists only of thin shell elements (Fig. 5) while the second composite model builds-up beside the shell elements spatial ring elements (Fig. 6). The equivalent Mises reduced stress calculated by the program are shown in Figs. 7 and 8.

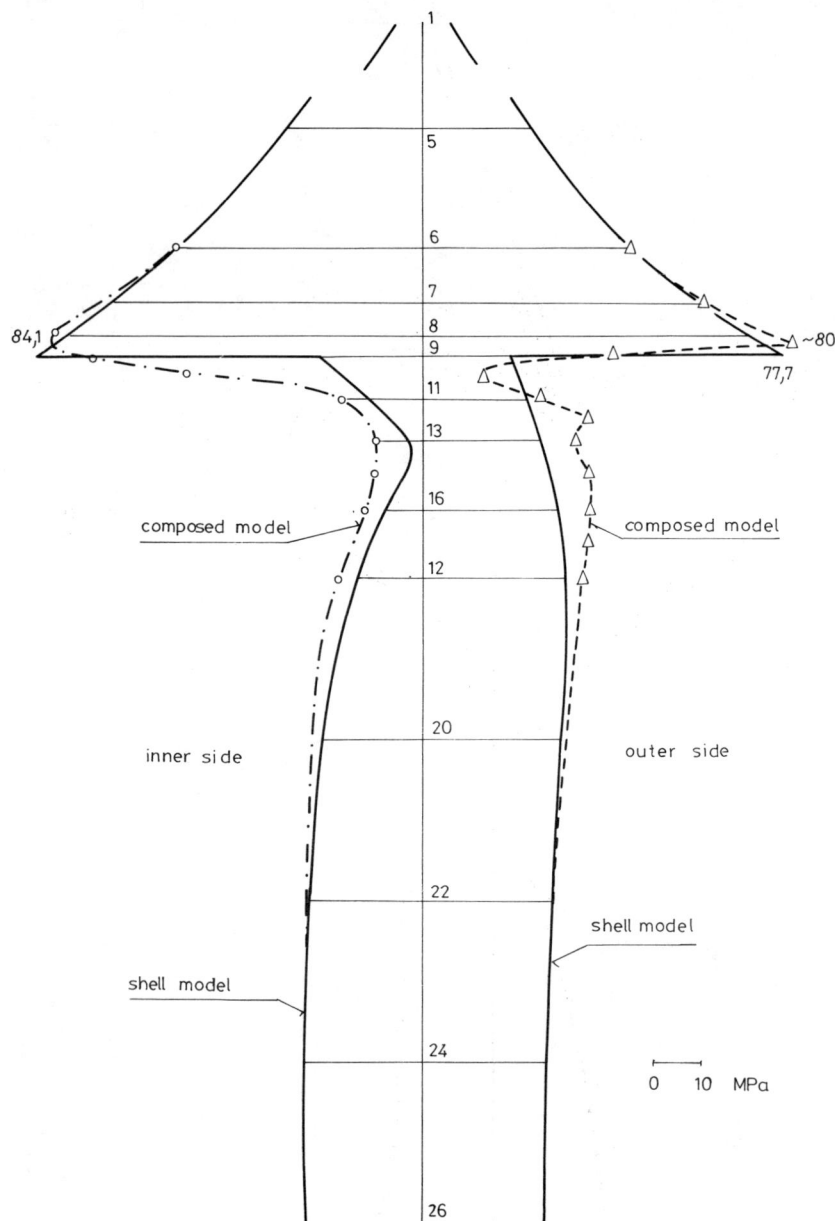

Fig. 7. Reduced stress distributions in the case of the heat exchanger

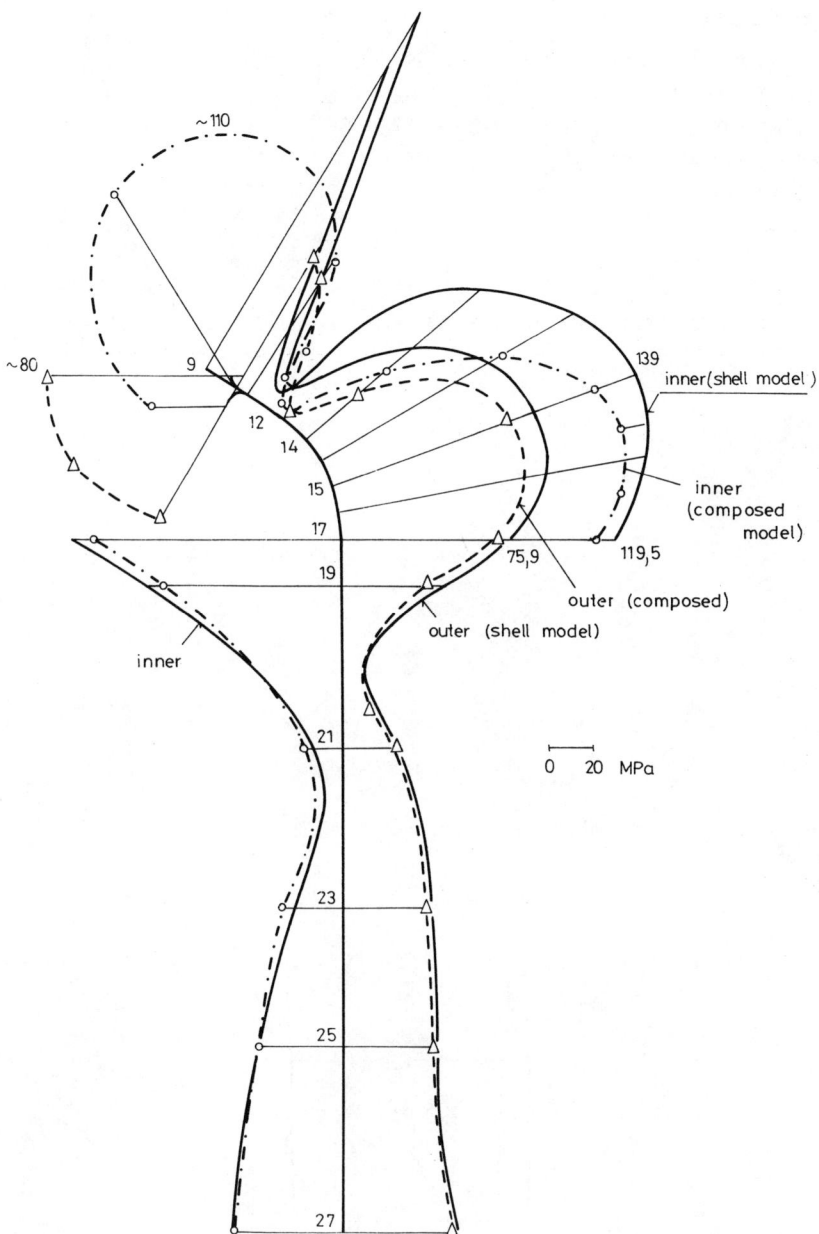

Fig. 8. Reduced stress distributions in the case of the heat exchanger

Composed Model

Number of nodal circles	178
Number of elements	81
Shell elements	17
Isoparametric elements	64
Basic loading cases	2
Number of unknowns	351
Bandwidth	62
Number of blocks	18

Running time (Job TIME) 5' 42' SzM52 Videoton Computer

SAMKE: FINITE ELEMENT SYSTEM

S. Maksimović

Aeronautical Institute of Belgrade, 11133 Žarkovo, Niška b.b., Yugoslavia

ABSTRACT

The current version of the SAMKE system is briefly described. SAMKE is an established computer system based on the finite element method for: stress analysis, heat transfer analysis and analysis problems of fracture mechanics. The use of the program in some interesting applications is pointed out.

INTRODUCTION

SAMKE is general purpose finite element program for analyzing actual problems encountered in aerospace, mechanical and many other industries. In order to cover as many situations as possible in one facility, SAMKE was created as a general system, with a large element library covering 2- and 3-D structures. The element library consists of a full set of modern multiorder isoparametric solid, membrane, beam, shell and crack elements.

Because of generality of scope required to deal with the variety aircraft components in existence, the system is suitable in many application areas outside the aircraft industry.

FIELD OF APPLICATION

The structural systems to be analyzed may be composed of a combination of a number of different structural elements. Analyses can be made in one, two or three dimensions including axisymmetric element options.

Material Behaviours

The material library consists of general anisotropic materials along with isotropic elastic, elastic or orthotropic, laminated composite materials. All materials are temperature dependent. Material properties are specified in the MATER processor. Program COMP determines elastic properties of fibrous composite materials. Program MLAYER determines equivalent: membrane, bending, membrane-bending and shear elastic properties-laminated plate/shells. These programs are compatible with SAMKE.

Analysis Capabilities

SAMKE is a computer program which determines: stresses, strains, displacements and reactions of general structures subjected to arbitrary forms of loadings. Augmenting the static capability are packages for heat transfer (SAMKET) and problems of fractures mechanics (SAMKEF). SAMKET program can be employed in linear and nonlinear, steady-state and transient heat transfer analysis. Nonlinear conduction and boundary convection and radiation conditions can be taken into account. SAMKET can be used as an independent analyser for transient or steady-state heat transfer problems, or as a pre-processor to provide temperature load case data for the statics programs.

SAMKEF can be too used as an independent analyser for problems of fracture of mechanics. Once finite element solution has been obtained, the values of the stress intensity factor can be extracted from it. Three approaches to the calculation of stress intensity factor in SAMKEF are used:

- the direct method[1]
- the indirect method[2] and
- the J-integral method[3,4]

It is well known that the J-integral formulated by Rice[3] is one of the best methods for analysing fracture structures. The path-independent J-line integral is defined as

$$J = \int_\Gamma (W dX_2 - \sigma^{ij} \frac{\partial U_i}{\partial X_1} n_j \, ds) \qquad (1)$$

Unfortunately, J-integral is path dependent for cases which include elastoplasticity or thermal stress terms or loadings along the crack face. An integral which retains path independence in these cases[4] has form

$$J^* = \int_\Gamma (W dX_2 - \sigma^{ij} \frac{\partial U_i}{\partial X_1} n_j \, ds)$$

$$+ \lim_{r \to 0} \int_{A_0} (W \frac{\partial U_i}{\partial X_1} - \frac{1}{2} \frac{\partial \sigma^{ij}}{\partial X_1} \frac{\partial U_i}{\partial X_1} - \frac{\partial}{\partial X_3} |\sigma^{i3} \frac{\partial U_i}{\partial X_1}|) dA \qquad (2)$$

where A_0 is the area inside any contour away from the crack tip region. For linear thermoelastic materials eq. (2) can be expressed in simple form[4].

$$J^* = \int_\Gamma (W^* dX_2 - \sigma^{ij} \frac{\partial U_i}{\partial X_1} n_j \, ds) + \frac{E \alpha}{1-2\nu} \int \varepsilon_{ii} \frac{\partial \theta}{\partial X_1} dA \qquad (3)$$

and hence

$$J^* = (1 - \nu^2) K_I^2/E \qquad (4)$$

The results of J^* - integral are not sensitive to mesh size, a coarser mesh may be used to save time and cost computation. The terms in equations (1) - (4) denote; Γ is any contour from the lower crack face leading anticlockwise around the crack tip to the upper face, s is the arch-length along the contour, σ_{ij} is the stress tensor, n_j is the unit normal vector, X_1 and X_2 are the local co-ordinates such that X_1 is along the crack, W is the strain energy density and K_I is the stress intensity factor of the interaction of mechanical and thermal loads.

PROGRAM DESCRIPTION

SAMKE is an established computer system based on the finite element method for the stress analysis of complicated structures; heat transfer analysis and fracture mechanics analysis.

Element Library

The available elements are shown in Fig. 1. The program SAMKE contains the following element types:

- 3-D truss element
- 3-D beam element
- plane stress and plane strain element
- 2-D axisymmetric solid
- 3-D solid
- variable number nodes thick shell and 3-D element
- thick/thin shell plate or shell elements
- thin shell elements
- special singular elements for analyses problems of fracture mechanics.

SAMKE claims a special capability in regard to thin plate and shell analysis and the availability of the "semi-loof" elements. Thick/thin plate and shell elements are degenerate from solid isoparametric elements and allow through the thickness shear deformations.

PRE- AND POST-PROCESSING CAPABILITIES

For the efficient practical use of a finite element program effective pre- and post-processing capabilities can be most important. The program allows one to:

- digitize elements and nodes of model from drawing
- select elements, nodes or element type with or without node numbers
- display of the structure with or without node numbers
- generate a symmetric mesh by reflection about an arbitrary plane in rectangular (or cylindrical) co-ordinates
- both undeformed and deformed structures can be viewed interactively on any type of graphic units such as shown in Fig. 2
- the geometry may be renumbered to reduce the bandwidth and profile before its use with the main processor

The same graphical capabilities of program are given in reference 5. The program SAMKE has extensive data-checking procedures. The program checks for correct data format on input, and sophisticated cross checks and performed before analysis can proceed.

HARDWARE COMPATIBILITIES

Graphical capabilities provide many options for verification of model and loads. The mesh and selected elements can be plotted or displayed to verify the input and considering the calculated results (the displacements, the stresses, the temperatures,...) can be displayed in effective manner. Typical hardware

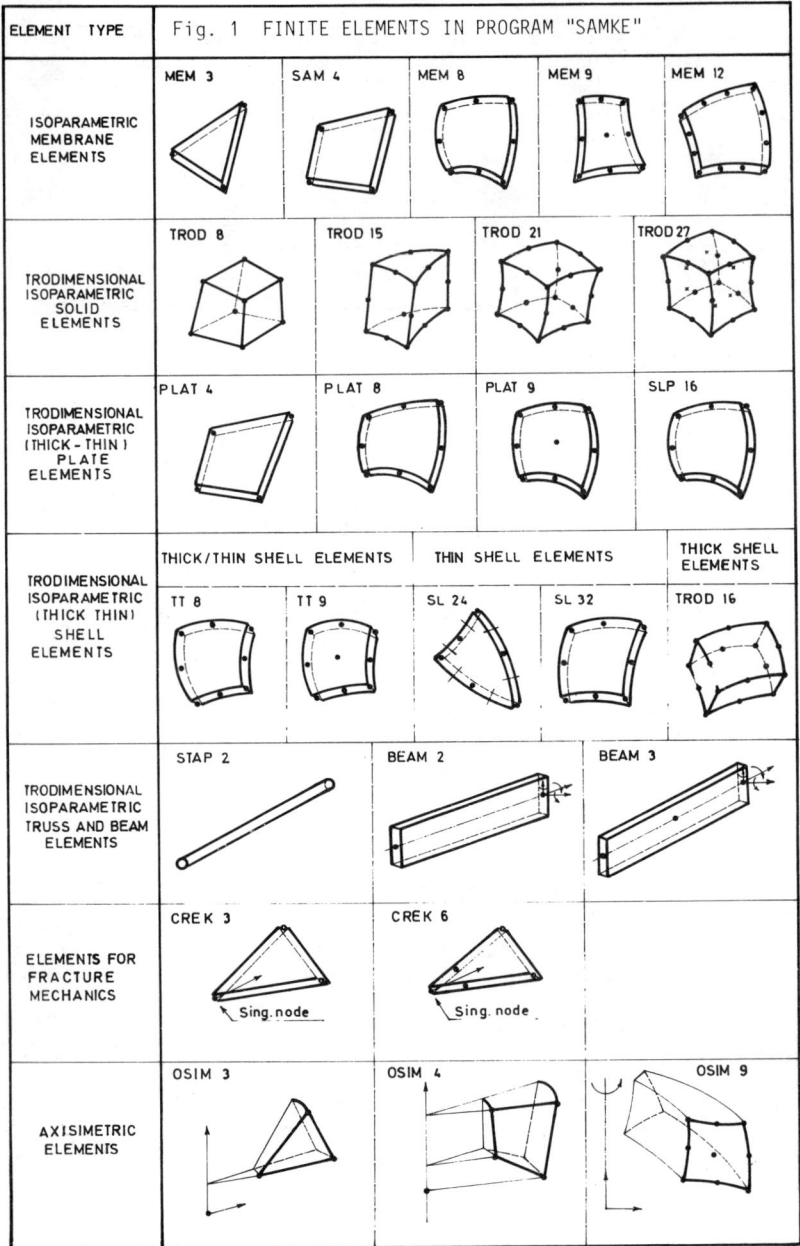

Fig. 1. Finite elements in program "SAMKE"

configuration of effective using SAMKE system is shown in Fig. 2.

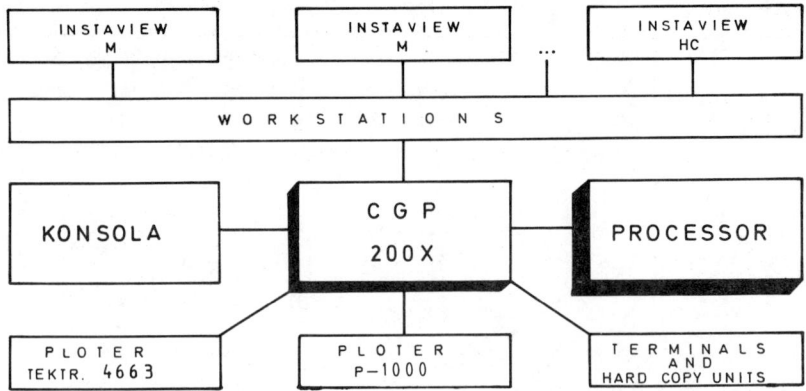

Fig. 2. Computervision system Designer V

There are two types for graphical representation of structural geometry and results: plotters and visual display units (VDU).

EXAMPLES OF APPLICATIONS

The first problem considered is the plate with an insuled circular hole and a radial crack subjected to transient heat flow, Fig. 3. The Crank-Nicolson scheme is used for temperature profile of transient heat flow in the plate by using standard 8-node (MEM8) isoparametric finite elements. Figure 3b shows the transient stress intensity, due to rapid changes in temperature. The maximum value of the stress intensity factor is about three times higher than that for a steady state. The finite element model utilized in this example with a typical mesh pattern is shown in Fig. 3c. Two types of elements were used. The 6-node collapsed singular element (CRAK6) is used around crack tip (see Fig. 1). The standard 8-node isoparametric element (MEM8) is selected in the regions away from the crack tip. The following material properties of maraging steel are employed; the tensile strength σ_B = 2000 MPa, $E = 1.9 \times 10^5$ MPa and coefficient of thermal expansion $\alpha = 10.08 \times 10^{-6}$ $^oC^{-1}$.

The next example treats a problem stress analysis for nose wheel leg of current interest aircraft. Figures 4 and 5 shows the discretization of structure. For this purpose two types of finite elements are used: 3-D 8-node elements for solid (TROD8) and 4-node membrane elements (SAM4). This problem has ab-ut 2500 degrees of freedom. The computational time is 42 min (CPU) on computer VAX 11/780. Detailed results of this problem are given in reference 6.

The same aspects for analysis of composite structures are given in references 7 and 8.

CONCLUSIONS

SAMKE is a general-purpose finite element program for analysis of complicated structures, with special pre- and post-processing facilities. Current work is centred on extension of program to include options for elastic stability and material/geometrica- nonlinearity.

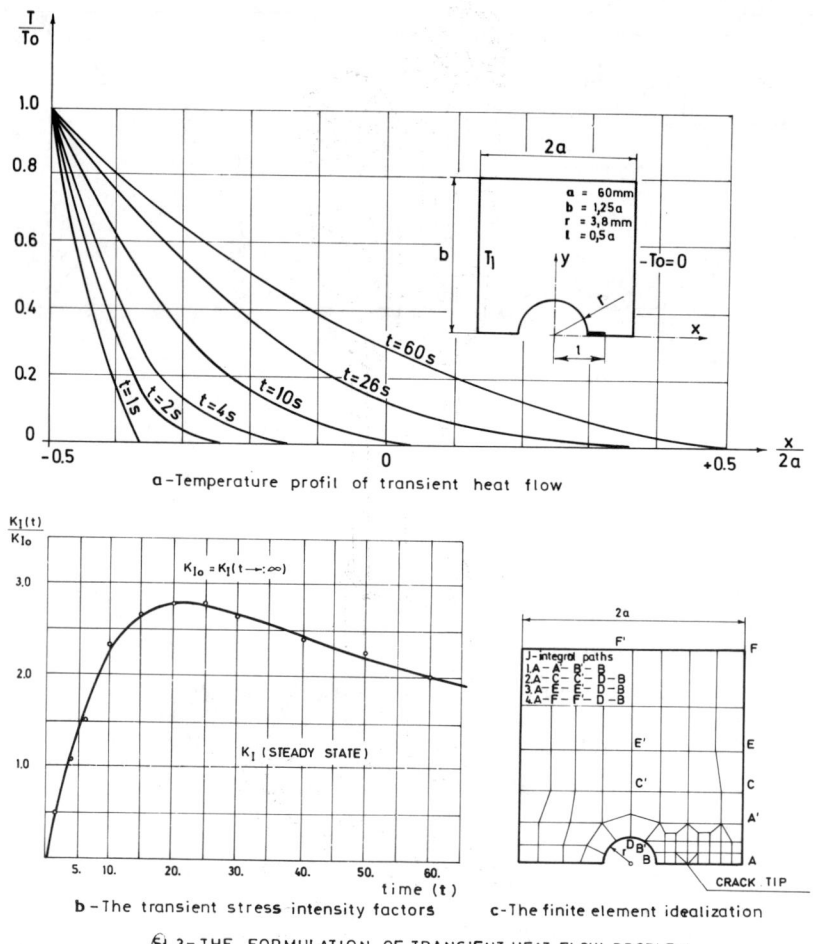

Fig. 3. The formulation of transient heat flow problem

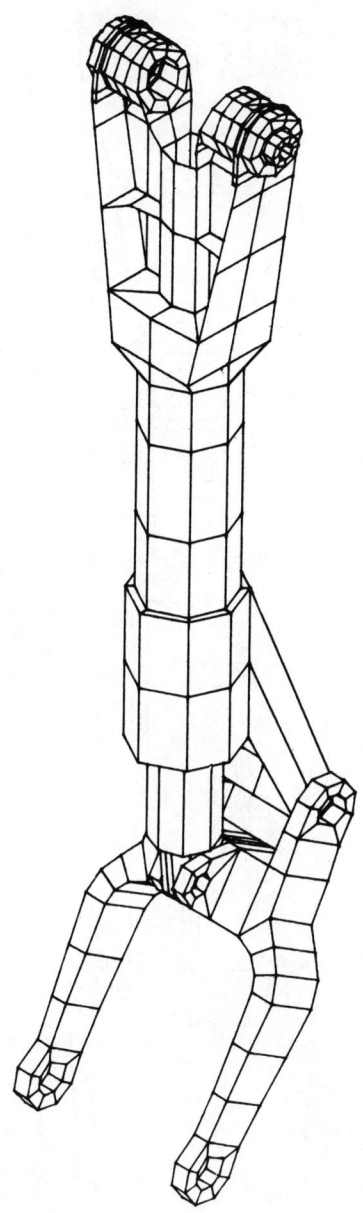

Fig. 4. The nose wheel leg of aircraft

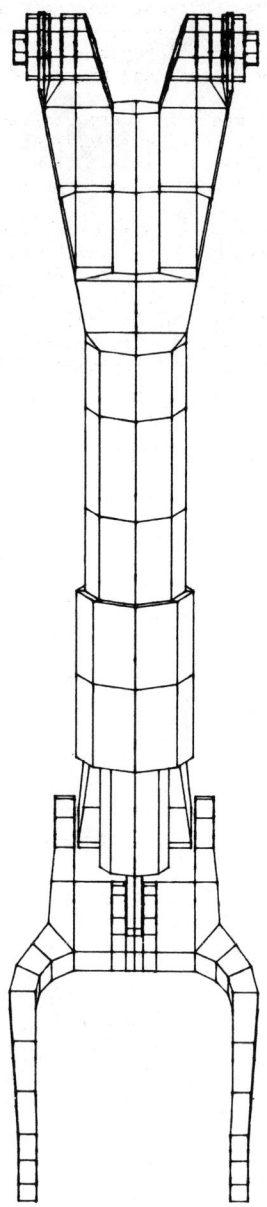

Fig. 5. The nose wheel leg of aircraft

REFERENCES

1. Benzeley, S. E. Representation of Singularities with Isoparametric Finite Elements, *IJNME*, *8*, 1974, p. 537.

2. Barsonum, R. S. On the Use of Isoparametric Finite Elements in Linear Fracture Mechanics, *IJNME*, *10*, 1976, pp. 25-37.
3. Rice, J. R. A Path Independent Integral and the Approximate Analysis of Strain Concentration by Notches and Cracks, *J. Appl. Mech. Trans ASME 35*, 1968, pp. 379-386.
4. Maksimović, S. Finite Elements in Thermoelastic and Elastoplastic Fracture Mechanics, Proc. 3rd Int. Conf. on NUMERICAL METHODS IN FRACTURE MECHANICS, 25-30, March, 1984, Swansea.
5. Nedić-Krstić, M. Graphical Visualization of program SAMKE, Report VTI (in preparation).
6. Arsić, V. Structural analysis of nose wheel leg...., Raport VTI, V4-1365-P.
7. Maksimović, S. Elastoplastic Analysis of Fibrous Composite Shells Using 'Semiloof' Finite Elements, Proc. 2nd. Int. Conf. on Composite Structures, 14-16 Sept. 1983, Scotland
8. Maksimović, S. The Finite Element Analysis of the Stress Concentration in Fibrous Composite Plates and Shells, Fourth World Congress and Exhibition on Finite Element Methods, 17-21 September, 1984, Interlaken, Switzerland.

STDYNL: A CODE FOR STRUCTURAL SYSTEMS

B. A. Ovunc

University of Southwestern Louisiana, USL 40172, Lafayette, LA 70504, USA

ABSTRACT

The main skeleton of the code STDYNL for structural systems is composed of a preprocessor, a processor and a postprocessor. In turn, each processor is formed by independent modules for the generation of specific items. During the data preparation of a specific problem, the preprocessor leads the solution process to the selection of proper driver routine for the given specific problem. The driver routine assembles all the required modules with minimum freedoms depending on the type of the problem. Thus the execution of the given problem is directed to specific modules with minimum freedoms rather than to the general routines with unnecessary data and computations and superfluous freedoms. The code STDYNL is a medium capability general purpose program in which most of the modules are the results of the individual formulations proper to the code STDYNL, such as: characteristic matrices for curved elements, iterative procedures for the structures with geometrical nonlinearity, linear and nonlinear, elastic-plastic analyses of high strength steel frameworks, dynamic analysis of frameworks with constant and variable moment of inertias and dynmaic analysis of plates by continuous mass matrix method, effect of member axial force and soil-structure interaction on the natural circular frequencies and on the modal shapes, buckling of structures, dynamic response time histories of continuous mass frameworks, boundary elements for plane stress and for plate bending. Moreover the regular features such as: support settlements, known displacements, temperature variations, wide supports etc., and regular modules such as: various finite elements for plane stress, plate bending, shell, etc., are also included in the code STDYNL. Due to its modular nature, the code STDYNL can be easily adapted to microcomputers. Each independent module can be executed separately by using the full capacity of the microcomputer and the outcome can be stored in the corresponding location of the database. For the most efficient core assignment the sizes of the arrays in the modules are entailed during the execution of each specific problem. Thus the code STDYNL is problem oriented rather than program oriented. Various structural systems have been analyzed by the code STDYNL.

METHODS OF ANALYSIS

Some of the significant methods particular to the code STDYNL are related to geometrical nonlinearity, plastic design, continuous mass matrix method and application of complex variable theory to the boundary element method.[1,2]

Geometrical Non-Linearity

Various approaches have been developed for the analysis of structures with geometrical nonlinearity.

In the first approach the basic idea is to perform a standard linear analysis under the action of a given set of external loads and then calculate the member end forces by using the deformed geometry. If the member end forces at a joint are not in equilibrium with the given external loads, the out-of-balance forces are applied on to the deformed geometry to yield another set of deformations and forces. If the new member end forces do not satisfy the joint equilibrium, the linear analysis continues with the latest geometry and with the latest out-of-balance forces. This procedure is repeated until the equilibrium is reached at every joint. For the buckling of the structure, the original external loads are gradually increased and the equilibrium status is established at each time by following the process described above. The magnitude of the external loads causing the divergence in the unbalanced forces, in other words, producing excessive deformations at the joints, is considered as the buckling load of the structure.[3,4,5,6]

In the recently developed method for the geometrical nonlinearity, the equilibrium equations of an infinitesimal element are satisifed at any point on the deformed configuration of the structure. At an arbitrary point on the element the strains and the stresses are along the Eulerian axes system, whereas the displacements u and v are referred to the Updated Lagrangian axes system. The axial and transversal displacements u and v are written in terms of a new variable ξ,

$$\xi = y_u + u(\xi)$$

as follows,

$$u = u(\xi)$$

and

$$v = v(\xi)$$

By using the differential geometry, the normal strain is expressed in terms of the displacements as,

$$\varepsilon = \varepsilon_o - \eta k_o (1 + \varepsilon_o)$$

where

$$\varepsilon_o = \frac{(1 + (v')^2)^{\frac{1}{2}}}{1 - u'}$$

$$k_o = \frac{v''}{(1 + (v')^2)^{3/2}}$$

The member stiffness matrix is obtained in terms of the displacement functions. The displacement functions $u(\xi)$ and $v(\xi)$ are assumed in series form of ξ. The coefficients of the series are determined from the equilibrium equations and the boundary conditions. An iterative procedure is used to determine the actual deformed configuration of the structural system.

Continuous Mass Matrix Method

In the continuous mass matrix method the equations of motion are satisifed not only at the nodal points as in lumped or consistent mass matrix methods but at any point of the structural system. In continuous mass matrix method the equations of motion are written as,[9,10]

$$[K_{dyn}]\{d\} = \{F(t)\}$$

where, $[K_{dyn}]$ is the dynamic stiffness matrix.

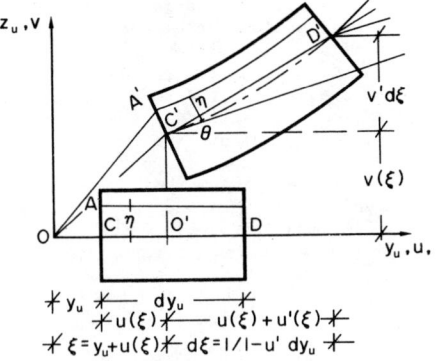

Fig. 1. Deformations

In space a member has four independent vibrations: vibrations due to axial displacements, torsional rotations and bending in two orthogonal planes. For instance, the spatial part of the deflection function for the bending in vertical plane can be written as,

$$Z(y) = \{\phi\}^T\{C\}$$

where, $\{\phi\}$ is the vector of interpolation functions and $\{C\}$ is the vector of integration constants.

The interpolation function for beams with constant moment of inertia varies depending on the cases: without any effect,[9,10] with the effect of member axial force only,[11] with the effects of member axial force and soil-structure interaction.[12,13] For beams with variable moment of inertias, the interpolation functions are expressed in terms of Bessel functions.[14] Interpolation functions are also developed for in-plane vibration of plates.[15] The dynamic member stiffness matrix for each of the above cases are obtained by using the Lagrangian dynamic equation and the corresponding interpolation functions. The dynamic stiffness matrix for the structure is determined from those of the members through code numbers.[9] The forced vibration of the structures is investigated either by modal analysis or by numerical integration.[16]

Boundary Element Method

The application of complex variable theory to the plates under in-plane or transversal loads provides a unique solution if the boundaries of the plates can be expressed in terms of a single parameter, or if the boundaries can be transformed by conformal mapping into one which can be expressed in terms of a single parameter. An approximate solution has been given for plates whose boundaries can neither be expressed by a single parameter nor be transformed by conformal mapping.[17,18] The plates whose boundaries can not be mapped conveniently are divided into elements. Only the points along the common boundaries adjacent to two elements are discretized and the tractions at these discrete points are considered as the unknowns to be determined. The member characteristic matrices are obtained by means of the contour integrals on the two complex potential functions. The unknown tractions at the discrete points along the common boundaries are determined from the continuity of the displacements at these discrete points.

The analysis is based on the determination of two complex potential functions per member whose expressions are uniquely obtained from the stress conditions of the member. Therefore there is no need to select any interpolation function. The accuracy improves when the sizes of the elements increase. The plates having their boundaries at infinity do not require any special treatment. The computer code is the same as the one for finite element method, except the member stiffness matrix, the load vector and the back substitution modules need to be modified. Since only the boundaries adjacent to two elements are to be divided to discrete points and the elements are to be of largest size possible, the number of unknowns, the required storage area and the CPU time are very small compared to those of finite element method. The number of terms in the series for the conformal mapping functions must be large enough to represent the mapped boundaries of the elements properly. The corners of the elements are somewhat rounded due to the limited number of terms considered in the conformal mapping functions.

FIELD OF APPLICATION

The code STDYNL contains so far the following type of elements: truss, beam and curved elements for plane and space frameworks, triangular, rectangular, trapezoidal, isoparametric finite elements for plane stress, plate bending and shells and boundary elements for plane stress and plate bending. Linear and nonlinear elastic and elastoplastic materials are considered in the analysis.

The analysis capabilities can be summarized as follows:

i. linear and geometrically nonlinear static analysis including temperature variation, support settlements, known displacements, wide supports, beams with variable moment of inertias, effect of shear deformations for deep beams, effect of member axial forces,

ii. dynamic analysis based on lumped mass, consistent mass and continuous mass matrix methods. Frameworks and plates with constant and variable moment of inertias under timewise continuous and discontinuous externally applied dynamic forces, support motions, earthquake, including the effects of member axial force and the soil-structure interaction,

iii. buckling states are determined either from the geometrical nonlinearity or from the free vibrations including all the effects described in the geometrically nonlinear or dynamic analyses,

iv. the disturbances causing the deformations in the structures may be position or time wise continuous and discontinuous externally applied loads of any form, support settlements, support motions, temperature variations and residual stresses.

DESCRIPTION OF THE CODE STDYNL

The main skeleton of the code STDYNL is composed of:

1. preprocessor, providing the input data to processor,
2. processor, performing the analysis,
3. postprocessor, providing the output of the processor.

Although the processor is the main analysis routine, there may be some overlapping of preprocessor and postprocessor with the processor.

STDYNL: A Code for Structural Systems

1. PREPROCESSOR is the part of the code where the given structure is described to the machine by two types of data.

    a. EXTERNAL DATA which describes,
        i. type of the structure: truss plane or space frame, plate, shell or any combination of these, in order to eliminate superfluous freedoms,
        ii. type of the analysis: static: linear, nonlinear, etc., dynamic: steady state, transient, modal analysis, direct integration, various effects,
        iii. the geometry of the structure, boundary conditions, constraint,
        iv. externally applied disturbances: loads, settlements, support motions, temperature variations, etc.

The external data feeding may be interactive and conversational type with double checking on the input data.

    b. INTERNALLY COMPUTED DATA are obtained by the modules which generate:
        i. the meshes,
        ii. joint co-ordinates, numbering of the joints and members,
        iii. code numbers array, which minimizes also the bandwidth,
        iv. element axes transformation matrices,
        v. element characteristic matrices,
        vi. system characteristic matrices, which are stored in single dimensional arrays with minimum bandwidth.

The internally computed data may be checked, modified, if necessary. Part of the internally computed data may be considered as overlapping with the processor.

2. PROCESSOR is composed of modules for:
        i. solution for unknowns, which is obtained from the system characteristic matrices in single dimensional arrays by using direct solution algorithms based on Gauss elimination, Choleski factorization, skyline reduction or iterative solution algorithms for finding the eigenvalues,
        ii. back substitution of the resolved unknowns into the element characteristic matrices in order to determine the required states at any point of the given system.

3. POSTPROCESSOR consists of displaying on the screen or printing on hard copies the results as numerical values or graphs. By assigning a proper value to the related parameters any intermediate or final results can be stored in the database for their interpretations. The results can be checked, if needed, the data stored in the preprocessor can be modified and the execution can be restarted from the first point affected by the modification.

A specific driver routine related to the type of the structural system is selected by the first data of the external data part of the preprocessor. The specific driver routine for a specific system type assembles the necessary modules to analyze the type of system in consideration. For instance, the specific driver routines DYNTR2, DYNFR3, DYNPLN are the simplified forms of DYAN for the general purpose dynamic analysis. DYNTR2, DYNFR3 and DYNPLN are for dynamics of plane truss, space frame and in-plane vibration of plates, respectively. The users must be able to recognize the type of his system in order to select the appropriate driver routine. Otherwise, he can use a more general routine at the expense of extra input data and extra CPU time leading to extra cost.

The member stiffness matrices incorporated in the Code STDYNL are for truss, beam, plane stress and plate bending members. They may be located above the ground or within an elastic medium. For the linear elastic, linear elastoplastic, geometrically nonlinear and dynamic analyses the interpolation functions are obtained from the differential equations of equilibrium or motion for the infinitesimal elements within the members. Therefore the equations of equilibrium or motion are satisfied at any point of the members. They also include the effects of axial force, shear and rotatory inertia.

All the modules in the code STDYNL are independently developed. Any new feature can be introduced in the code STDYNL either by modifying the related module or by adding new module. The modules of STDYNL can be also incorporated in any other general purpose program.

The code STDYNL is written in FORTRAN. The BASIC version exists for static analyses.

HARDWARE COMPATIBILITIES

Besides the peripherics, the hardware requirements for the code STDYNL depend on the machine to be used to execute the code. When a main frame machine is used the additional media needed would be a disk or few magnetic tapes to store the input data of the preprocessor and the output results of the postprocessor. Additional media may be needed for large size problems to store the characteristic matrices of the large systems and to determine the generalized co-ordinates by out-of-core solution. Due to its modular structure, the code STDYNL is easily adaptable to microcomputers. Since all the modules are independently developed and the sizes of the arrays in the modules are entailed during the execution of each specific problem, for the given type of the problem a driver routine assembles only the required modules in a batch form for the most efficient use of the core capacity. Although in this manner comparatively large size problems can be handled by the microcomputers, still the slowness of the execution remains as a drawback.

The code STDYNL has been executed in RCA SPECTRA, CDC, IBM, UNIVAC, HONEYWELL main frame machines and in ZENITH microcomputers.

EXAMPLES OF APPLICATION

Various types of problems have been tested and analyzed by the code STDYNL. The stability of a parabolic dome (Fig. 2) has been investigated by using an iterative nonlinear analysis.[3] The critical value of the concentrated load P, applied at the center of the dome, has been evaluated and found to be 399.8 kips. The buckling of the dome primarily occurs because of the excessive outward

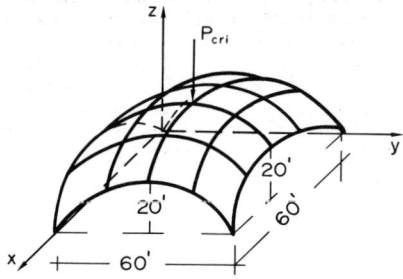

Fig. 2. Parabolic dome

deformations taking place at the crescent of the outside arch ribs. At the
buckling stage the maximum stresses are considerably lower than the allowable
stresses. The effect of geometrical changes are included in the analysis, since
deformations associated with the buckling loads are so large that they cannot be
neglected.

A hemisphere under uniformly distributed load over the horizontal plane is
considered as an example to the geometrically nonlinear analysis of elastic
shells of revolution under axisymmetric loadings. The analysis has involved
triangular and trapezoidal finite elements.[6] The analyses are performed for
hemisphere on roller or fixed at the boundaries with or without flexibility
properties. The results obtained for the radial displacements at crown is
plotted in dimensionless co-ordinates in Fig. 3.

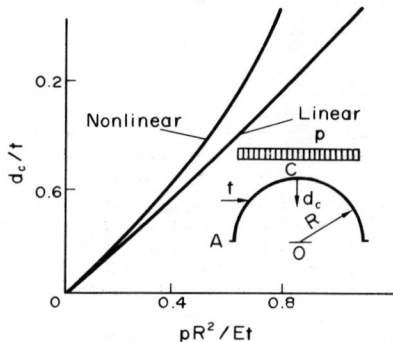

Fig. 3. Spherical dome

In the nonlinear, plastic analysis of high strength steel plane and space
frameworks the finite deformation effects, reduction of plastic moments due to
axial member forces, change in flexural stiffness caused by member axial forces
and the influence of shearing forces on the deflection are taken into account.
But the effects of strain hardening, reduction of the plastic moments due to
member shearing forces, residual stresses due to live loads and the spread of
the plastic zone are neglected.[6]

The horizontal displacements of the roof floor of a four storey, one bay high
strength steel frame is shown in Fig. 4. The numbers on the diagram show the
sequence of formation of plastic hinges.

A pipeline laying to a water depth of 85 m is considered as an example recently
developed method for the geometrically nonlinear analysis.[2,3] The pipeline rolls
over the guidance track on the barge, slides freely on 100 m length stinger and
reposes on an elastic soil at the sea floor. The lift-off angle of the pipeline
from the barge is assumed to be five degrees. The undeformed and deformed
configurations of the pipeline under its own weight and the force applied at the
barge are shown in Fig. 5. The variation of the moment with the variation of
the tension applied to the pipeline at the barge is represented in Fig. 6.
Since the pipeline slides freely on the deformed configuration, the stinger, the
variation of the moment diagram within the part of the pipeline supported by the
stinger is continuous.

The three-storey steel frame is considered to illustrate various aspects of the
dynamic responses. The data including the externally applied dynamic loads are
given in Fig. 7. The moment of inertia of the beams are multiplied by a

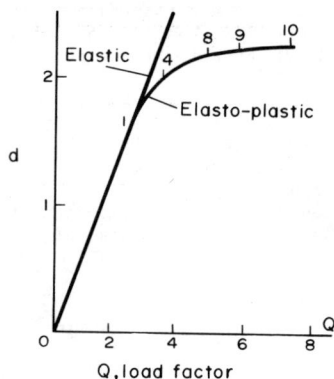

Fig. 4. d, Roof displacement

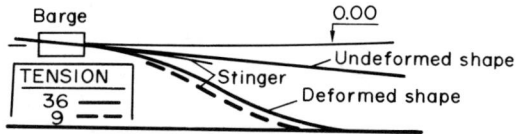

Fig. 5. Deformed configuration

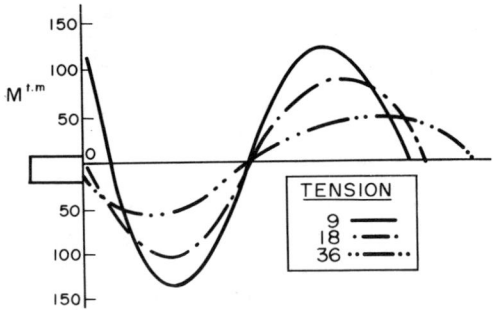

Fig. 6. Moment diagram

parameter α. The variation of the parameter α, provides the variation of the rigidity of the beams versus the rigidity of the columns. The variation of the bending moment at the base of the first floor column by the variation of the beam to column rigidities are determined in order to represent the approximation involved in the lumped mass and consistent mass matrix methods compared to the continuous mass matrix method (Fig. 8).

The effect of the member axial force on the vibration is included in the differential equations of motion written on an infinitesimal element of the constituent members of the structure. The static loads on the beams vibrating within the plane of the externally applied dynamic forces are considered as distributed on these beams, whereas those acting on transversal beams are lumped

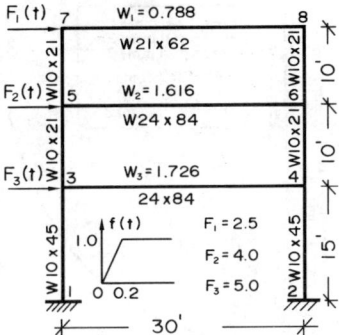

Fig. 7. Three-storey frame

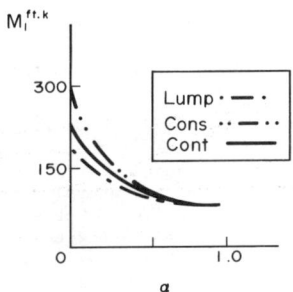

Fig. 8. Variation of base moment

at the ends of these transversal beams. Load factors m and 1 are introduced on the distributed and lumped loads, respectively. When the distributed load factor, m is zero the results tend to those obtained by the lumped mass matrix method. The variation of the first four natural circular frequencies with the variation of the static and member axial loads is shown in Fig. 9. The variation of the base moment with the increasing static loads discloses the resonance and buckling modes also (Fig. 10).

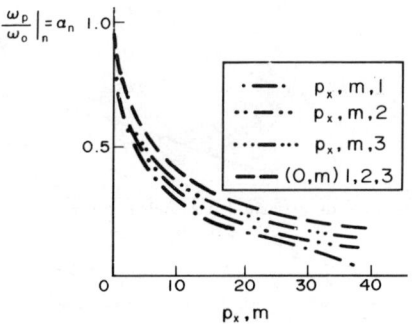

Fig. 9. Effect of member axial force

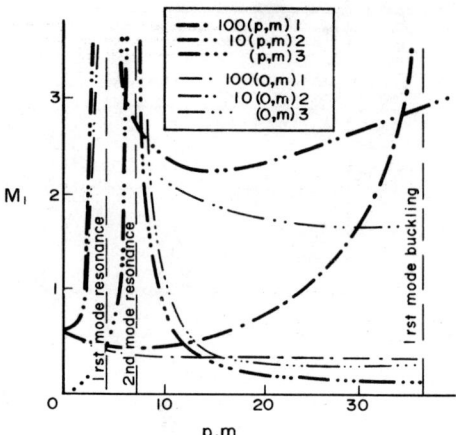

Fig. 10. Base moment

For the same three-storey steel building, the variation of the natural circular frequencies by the soil modulus depends on the boundary conditions of the bottom tip of the piles supporting the building. For frames supported by piles fixed at the bottom tip, the variations of the natural circular frequencies remain within a limited range with the variation of the soil modulus. The variation of a natural circular frequency is limited by the corresponding natural circular frequencies of three and four-storey frames with fixed bases at the ground level, whereas, the variations of the natural circular frequencies for the frames with free tip piles cover a large range with the variation of the soil modulus. Moreover, depending on the magnitude of the soil modulus, the sequence of the excitation of the modal shapes changes. Even some additional modal shapes are excited (Fig. 11).

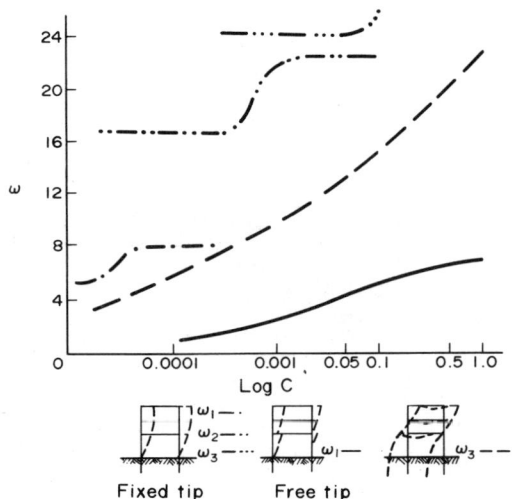

Fig. 11. Variation of natural circular frequencies

STDYNL: A Code for Structural Systems

A Sixteen-storey steel frame with and without shear walls up to sixth floor has its second floor beams pin connected to the columns. The frame has been subjected to ground motion. The data for the ground motion has been taken from San Fernando Valley earthquake, February 9, 1971. First, second and third modal shapes are plotted for various load factors (Fig. 12). Under the earthquake motion, although the shear walls up to sixth floor reduce the floor displacements at lower floors, the roof displacement with or without shear walls are very close. The effect of member axial force becomes more pronounced when the loads are getting closer to their critical values. The first buckling mode occurs as excessive horizontal displacements between the first and third floors because of the pin connections between the beams and the columns of the second floor. The second buckling mode appears on the columns between the fourth and eleventh floors. By increasing value of the load factor, the storey to storey displacements tend to zero at floors away from the buckling region of the frame. The variation of the base shear is also plotted (Fig. 13).

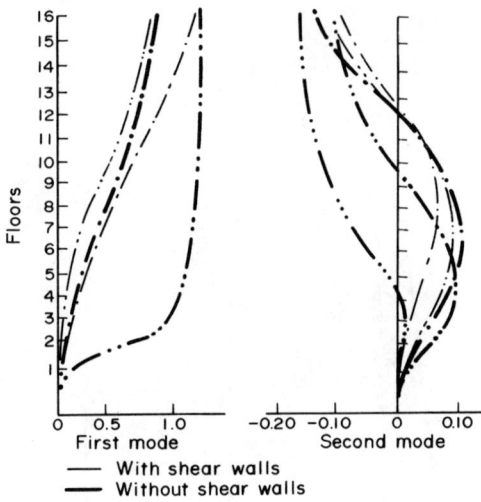

Fig. 12. Variation of floor displacements

The beams of the main and the cellar decks of an offshore platform are of size S57x18 and all other members are pipes having their diameter varying from 17 in to 42 in (Fig. 14). The frame is assumed to be subjected to wave forces. The data for the wave characteristics are collected from the information related to the Gulf of Mexico. The bottom tip of the piles are assumed to be free.

Figure 14 shows the variation of the modal shapes by the soil modulus. The variation of the natural circular frequencies corresponding to the first and second sway and the first vertical displacement are plotted versus the variation of the soil modulus (Fig. 15). The inclusion of the effect of the member axial force in the dynamic analysis reduces the magnitude of the natural circular frequencies. The variations of the natural circular frequencies with the increasing mass and static loads show that the natural circular frequencies including the effect of the member axial force reduce much faster than that without the effect of the member axial force. The magnitude of the static load which tends a natural circular frequency to zero is the buckling load corresponding to that frequency.

If the temporal part of the externally applied dynamic loads are not the same,

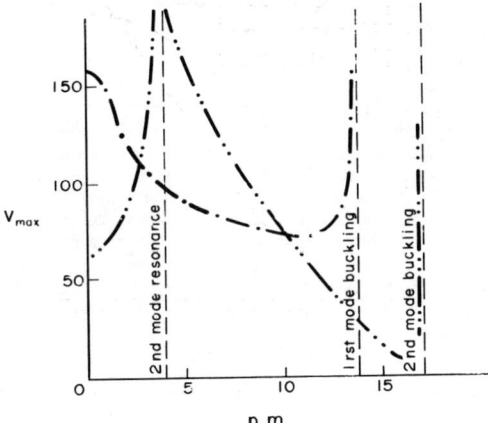

Fig. 13. Base shear

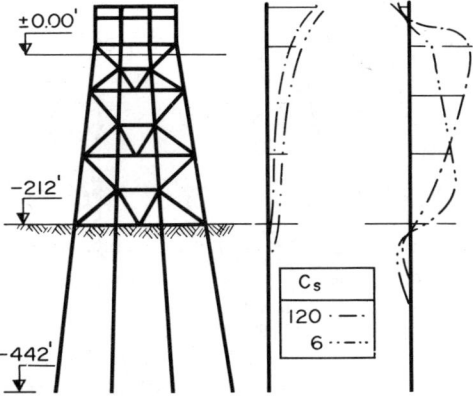

Fig. 14. Variation of modal shapes by soil modulus

the dynamic analysis is performed by numerical integration. From the generalized linear acceleration approach, the acceleration and the velocity at a time station s can be written in terms of the displacement of the time station $s-k$ as, (16),

$$\ddot{w}(s) = \frac{1}{\beta_o \Delta t^2} |w(s) + \Sigma\, b_k\, w(s-k)|$$

$$\dot{w}(s) = \frac{1}{\beta_o \Delta t} |c_o w(s) + \Sigma\, c_k\, w(s-k)|$$

where the coefficients c_k and b_k are determined from the previous c_{k-i} and b_{k-i} and β_o and γ_o are the parameters to be obtained from the integration accuracy and the stability.

The displacement at the free tip of a cantilevered elastic bar subjected to a

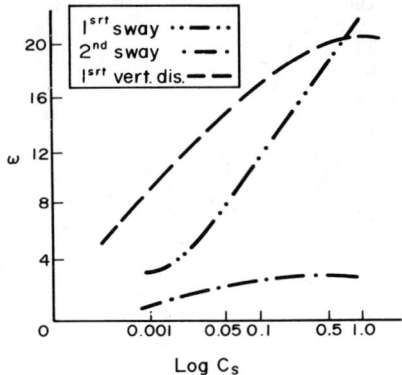

Fig. 15. Variation of frequency by soil modulus

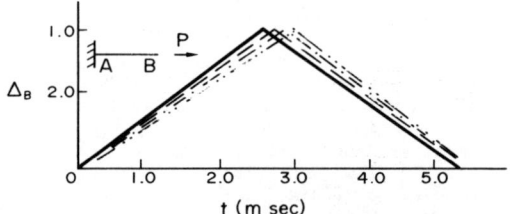

Fig. 16. Displacement at free tip

suddenly applied load at the free tip is analyzed. The numerical results match very well with the exact solution.

Selection of the proper integration time step has been always a problem in the use of the direct integration method. It appears that in this method a somewhat larger time step than the usual 1% of the natural period can be used with sufficient accuracy.

REFERENCES

1. Ovunc, B. A. (1981). Computer Code STDYNL. in: *Structural Mechanics Finite Element Computer Programs: A Decade with Finite Elements (1970-1980)*. Advanced Engineering Corporation, Sweden.
2. Ovunc, B. A. (1981). STDYNL Computer Program for Structures Handbook, *3rd Int. Seminar on Finite Element Systems*, Southampton University, Sept. 21-23, 1981. CML, pp. 434-445.
3. Tezcan, S. S. and B. A. Ovunc (1967). An iteration method for the nonlinear buckling of framed structures. In: *Space Structures*, R. M. Davies (ed.), Part IV, No. 45. Blackwell Scientific, Oxford and Edinburgh.
4. Ovunc, B. A. (1968). Non-linear plastic analysis of high-strength steel plane and space frameworks. *Proc., 8th Congr. Int. Assoc. for Bridges and Structural Engineering*, Sept. 9-14, 1968, New York, pp. 583-596.
5. Ovunc, B. A., H. Mallareddy (1970), Stress analysis of offshore pipelines, *2nd Offshore Technology Conference*. OTC. 1222, Houston, Texas, April 22-24, 1970, pp. 1727-1734.
6. Ovunc, B. A. (1971). Nonlinear analysis of elastic shells of revolution under axisymmetric loading. *I.A.S.S. Bulletin* No. 43, pp. 9-16

7. Ovunc, B. A. (1982). The geometrical non-linearity of plane frameworks. *Proc., Sino-American Symp. Bridge and Structural Engineering*, Beijing, China, Sept. 13-19, 1982, pp. 327-336.
8. Ovunc, B. A. (1982). Design offshore pipelines. *Int. J. Pipelines*, Oct. pp. 285-295.
9. Ovunc, B. A. (1974). Dynamics of frameworks by continuous mass method. *Comp. & Struct.*, *4*, 1061-1089.
10. Ovunc, B. A. (1972). Dynamic analysis of offshore platforms by frequency dependent stiffness matrix approach. *4th Offshore Technology Conference*, OTC 1696 Houston, Texas, May 1-3, 1972, pp. 11699-11708.
11. Ovunc, B. A. (1980). Effect of axial force on framework dynamics. *Comp. & Struct. 11* (5), 389-395.
12. Ovunc, B. A. (1982). Effect of soil-structure interaction on the dynamics of structures. *Proc., 3rd Int. Earthquake Microzonation Conf.*, University of Washington, Seattle Washington, June 28-July 1, 1982, pp. 821-830.
13. Ovunc, B. A. (1978). In-plane vibration of plates by continuous mass matrix method. *Comp. & Struct. 8*, June, pp. 723-731.
14. Ovunc, B. A. (1972). The dynamic analysis of space frameworks by frequency dependent stiffness matrix approach. *Publ. of the Int. Assoc. for Bridges and Structural Engineering*, Vol. *32/2*, Zurich, Switzerland, pp. 137-154.
15. Ovunc, B. A. (1985). Soil-structure interaction and effect of axial force on the dynamics of offshore structure. *Comp. & Struct.*, *21*, 4, 629-637.
16. Ovunc, B. A. (1979). Dynamic response time histories of continuous mass frameworks. *Abstracts for Research in Progress, 16th Midwestern Mechanics Conf.*, Kansas State University, Sept. 19-21, 1979, pp. 49-50.
17. Ovunc, B. A. (1982). Application of complex variable theory to the boundary element method. *Proc. 4th Int. Conf. Boundary Element Methods in Engineering*, Southampton University, Sept. 21-23, 1982, Springer, pp. 500-514.
18. Ovunc, B. A. (1983). New implementations in structural code STDYNL Handbook, *4th Int. Seminar on Finite Element Systems*, Southampton University, July 6-8, 1983. Springer, pp. 443-450.
19. Ovunc, B. A. (1984). Processors for the structure code STDYNL. *Proc. IASTED, Int. Symp. Applied Identification, Modelling and Simulation*, New Orleans, Nov. 12-14, 1984.

SURFOPT: SHAPE OPTIMAL DESIGN FOR MINIMUM STRESS CONCENTRATION BY FINITE ELEMENTS WITH THE PROGRAM SYSTEM "SURFOPT"

U. Spörl

Institute of Solid Mechanics, Karlsruhe University, Federal Republic of Germany

ABSTRACT

Optimization of the shapes of machine components is frequently concerned with minimizing stress concentration effects so as to ensure a better fatigue behaviour. The program system "SURFOPT" (Surf Optimization) optimizes load-free internal or free boundaries of plane or axisymmetric structures with linear-elastic, homogeneous, isotropic material within given variation domains. For stress analysis the FEM is used. It is possible to solve optimization problems with multiple loading cases and also axisymmetric problems with nonaxisymmetric loads. In order to obtain a minimum concentration, the load-free boundary is iteratively changed until a profile results with constant von-Mises stress distribution on maximal arc length. The type of the optimization algorithm is a "feasible direction" procedure without computation of gradients because the "feasible direction" is found by mechanical theorems.

THEORETICAL BACKGROUND

For shape optimization of a plane or an axisymmetric structure to minimize stress concentration in general, the Finite Element Method in connection with mathematical programming methods (Penalty Function Technique, sequential linear programming) are used. These procedures need the evaluation of the stress derivatives which must be done by numerical differentiation, with the risk of instability of the technique.

Therefore the program system "SURFOPT" developed by U. Spörl[1] solves the optimization problem with a "feasible direction" technique without evaluation of stress derivatives.

Initial point of the notch shape optimization is the description of the domain V of the given plane or axisymmetric body with the boundary ∂V (Fig. 1) and its kinematical boundary conditions on $\partial V_k \subset \partial V$ and its statical boundary conditions on $\partial V_s \subset \partial V$ for all loading cases.

The effective stress through which the material is stressed is the von-Mises stress σ. We want to optimize a load-free part Γ of the total boundary ∂V, with the geometrical restriction, that Γ must lie inside a fixed variational domain Γ^*. So the problem results:

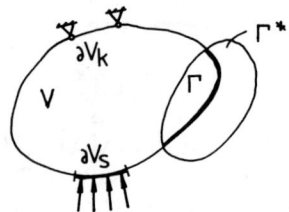

Fig. 1.

(1) $\min_{\Gamma} (\max_{V} \bar{\sigma})$

under the restriction

(2) $\Gamma \quad \Gamma^*$.

An analytical solution of this problem is not possible, therefore a discretization of the problem is necessary, and it follows from (1), (2):

(3) $\min (\max \bar{\sigma}^i(\{X\}))$
    $i=1(1)N$

(4) $|A|\{X\} \le \{b\}$.

Under the assumption that the maximal effective stress occurs on the boundary Γ, the search for the maximum in (3) can be limited to the N discrete nodes on the boundary Γ. In (3), (4), the design variables are the co-ordinates of the nodes of the finite element mesh along the boundary Γ, which form the design vector $\{X\}$. Restriction (4) results from the geometrical restriction (2).

The iterative solution of (3), (4) with the "feasible direction method" starts with an initial design vector $\{X_0\}$ and in the i-th step it follows:

(5) $\{X_i\} = \{X_{i-1}\} + \alpha_i \{S_i\}$.

It is possible to compute the feasible direction $\{S_i\}$ - which reduces the maximum of the von-Mises stress in each step i with mechanical theorems as the "fade-away-law" by Neuber[2], the "reaction law" of the notch stress theory and the Saint-Venant's principle. Therefore it is not necessary to evaluate stress derivatives.

By iterative changing of the boundary Γ with equation (5), after some iterations, an optimal shape with constant von-Mises stress distribution on maximal arc length results.

For stress analysis, the finite element method is used with triangle plane or ring elements and quadratic displacement field. An increment procedure is used for determining the displacement and stress field after each iteration step. The program system includes an automatic redefine process for the finite element mesh after each iteration step to prevent a strong distortion of the element shapes.

FIELD OF APPLICATION

"SURFOPT" optimizes 2-D problems and axisymmetric problems also with nonaxisymmetric loads.

SURFOPT: Shape Optimal Design for Minimum Stress Concentration

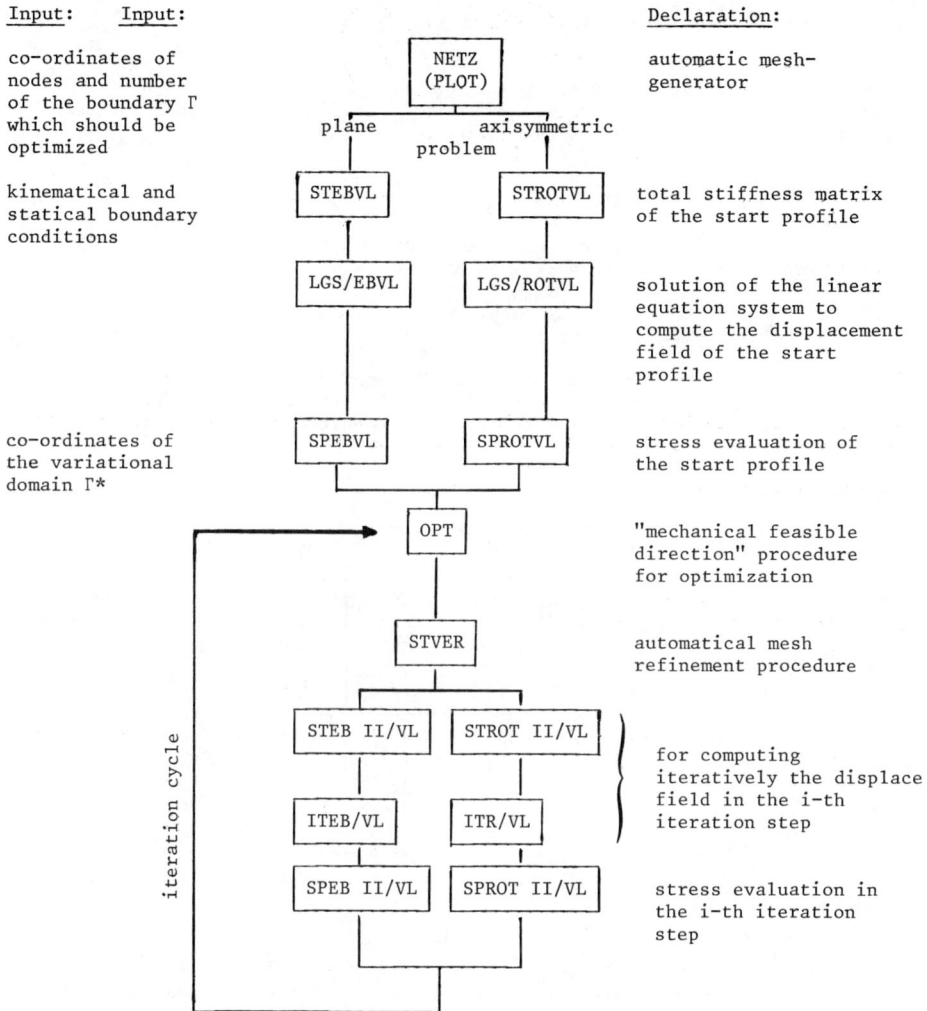

Material: linear elastic, isotropic, homogeneous.

Analysis capabilities: static structure optimization problems.

Loadings:
axisymmetric problems: tension, shear, bending, torsion
plane problems: tension, shear, bending, torsion and combinations of these.

PROGRAM DESCRIPTION

Method: Finite Element Method (Displacement method) with the optimization procedure "feasible direction".

Type of elements:
plane problems: triangle elements with 12 degrees of freedom
axisymmetric problems: ring elements with triangle cross section

Program structure:
All programs are written in FORTRAN 77. For automatic initialization of the finite element mesh, the preprocessor "NETZ" is used. The program "PLOT" can be used for drawing the mesh and stress distributions.

HARDWARE COMPATIBILITIES

The program system is developed on UNIVAC 1100 of the Karlsruhe University/ Federal Republic of Germany and is available on magnetic tape.

EXAMPLE OF APPLICATION

An example of axisymmetric shape design for minimum stress concentration is the optimal shape of shoulder fillets in a stepped bar (Fig. 2) under the load case bending. The statical and linearized boundary conditions are shown in Fig. 3.

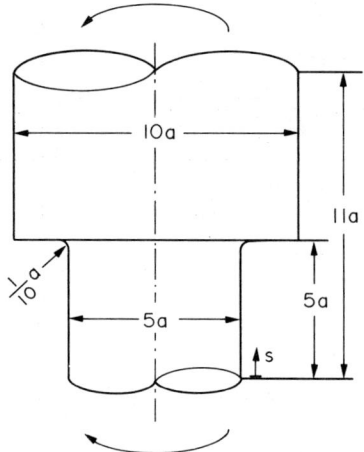

Fig. 2. Problem for optimal shape of shoulder fillets in a stepped bar under bending

A coarse finite element mesh of the start profile is shown in Fig. 4, but for the optimal shape (see Fig. 5), a more refined mesh has been used (150 ring elements, 1092 degrees of freedom).

The optimal shape of Fig. 5 and the von-Mises stress distribution of Fig. 6 shows after 12 iteration steps how the iteration cycle extends the arc length of nearly constant stress distribution in order to reduce the stress concentration until the stress concentration will disappear. The stress concentration from start profile to optimal profile can be reduced by 50%.

In Fig. 5 the influence of the variational domain Γ^* can also be seen.

SURFOPT: Shape Optimal Design for Minimum Stress Concentration 243

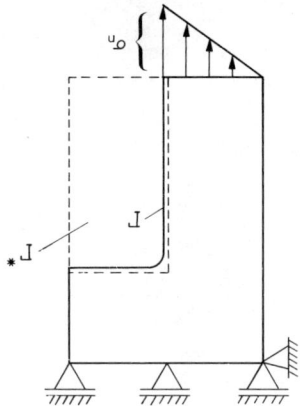

Fig. 3. Statical and kinematical boundary conditions and variational domain

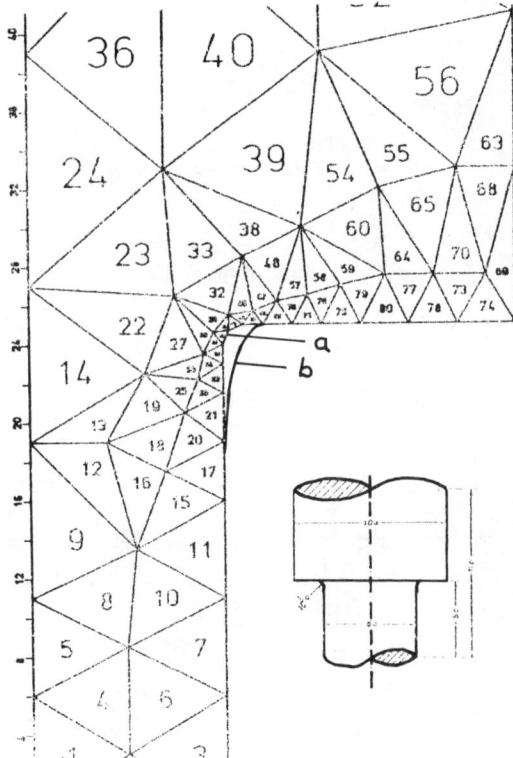

Fig. 4. Finite element mesh of the start profile a, optimal shape b under bending

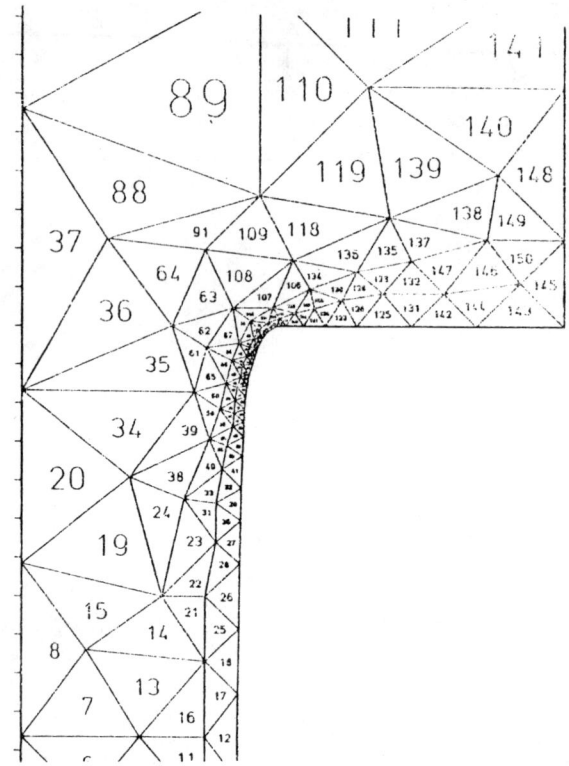

Fig. 5. Finite element mesh of the optimal shape

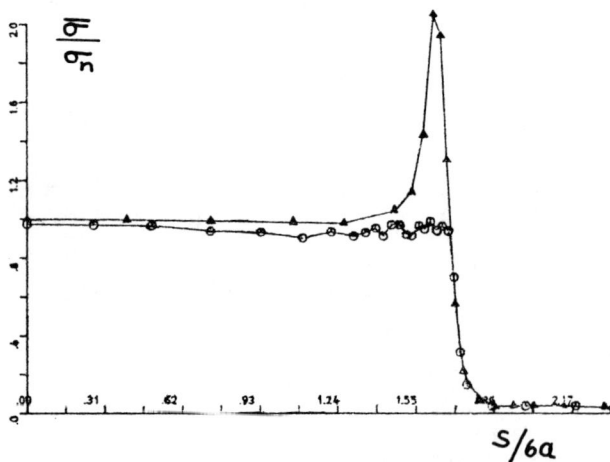

Fig. 6. Von-Mises stress distribution of the start profile Δ and the optimal profile o

SURFOPT: Shape Optimal Design for Minimum Stress Concentration

Input Data

- co-ordinates of the nodes
- statical and kinematical boundary conditions
- the co-ordinates of the variational domain Γ^*
- the number of the boundary Γ which should be optimized

Output Data

- after each iteration step, the von-Mises stress distribution in the domain V
- the new co-ordinates of the boundary Γ
- the reduction of the maximal von-Mises stress

Computation Time

180 sec CPU for one iteration step

STRUCTURE OPTIMIZATION OF STUB AXLE BOLTS IN VEHICLES TO REDUCE STRESS CONCENTRATIONS

The shape of stub axle bolts in vehicles has great influence on the resulting stress concentration under several loading cases. To ensure a better fatigue and dynamical behaviour of this component in vehicles, an optimal shape with minimum stress concentration is looked for (see Figs. 7 and 8).

As described in the theoretical part of this paper, only a statical optimization procedure was applied and for optimization of th stub axle bolt, the loading case is "bending". Figure 7 shows the finite element mesh of the start profile with two notch boundaries A (Fig. 9) and B (Fig. 10) to be optimized. The von-Mises stress distribution of the start profiles along the notch boundaries A and B is shown in Figs. 11 and 12.

The optimal profiles of notches A and B for practical manufacturing are shown in Figs. 13 and 14.

The stress concentration from start profile to optimal profile can be reduced by 22% on average.

For input and output data see Example of Application.

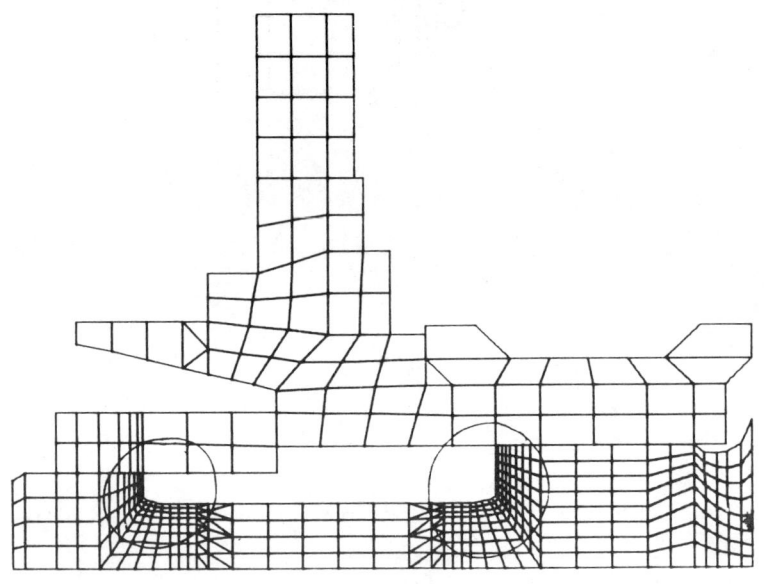

Fig. 8. Optimal profiles of two notch boundaries of a stub axle bolt under loading case "bending"

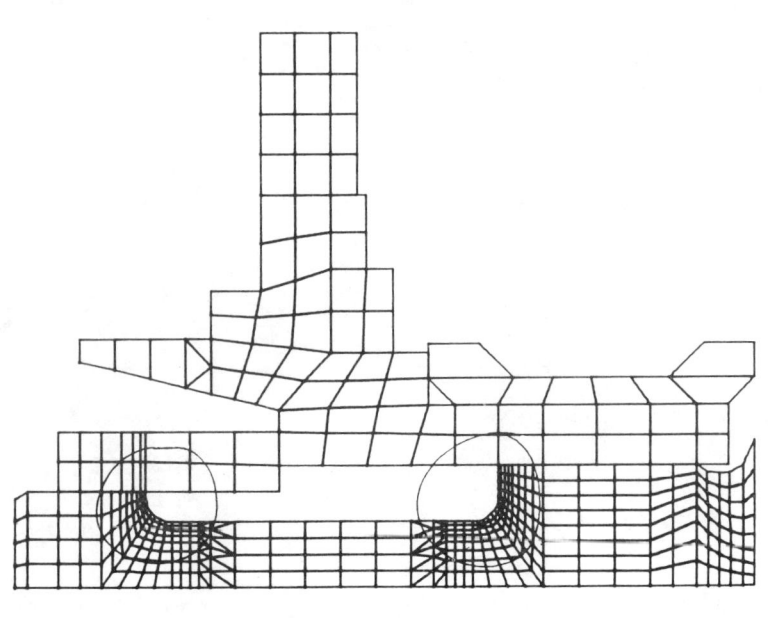

Fig. 7. Start profile of two notch boundaries for structure optimization of a suitable bolt under loading case "bending"

SURFOPT: Shape Optimal Design for Minimum Stress Concentration 247

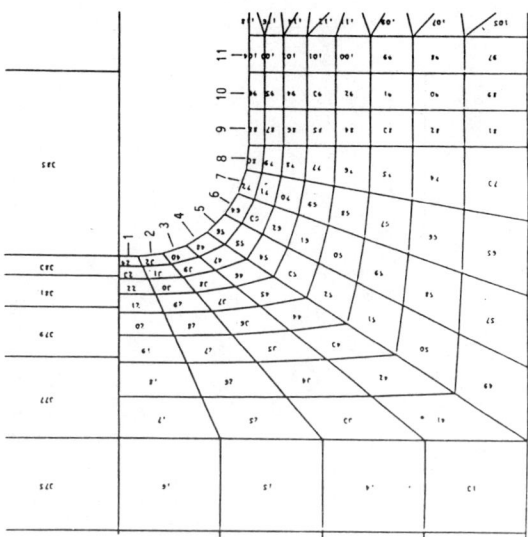

Fig. 9. FE-discretization of notch A of the start profile

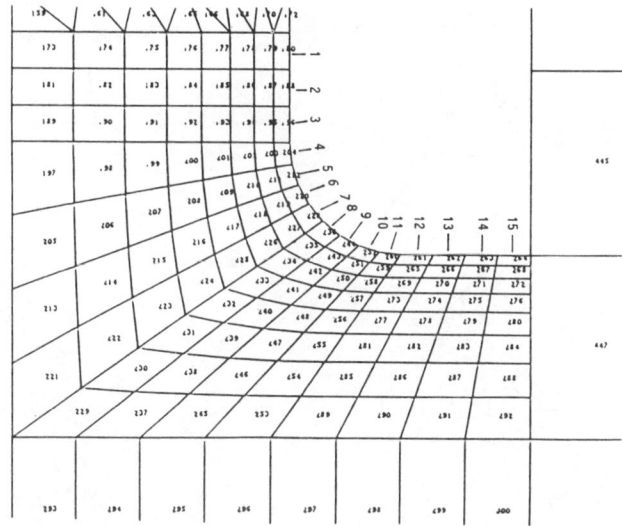

Fig. 10. FE-discretization of notch B of the start profile

248 U. Spörl

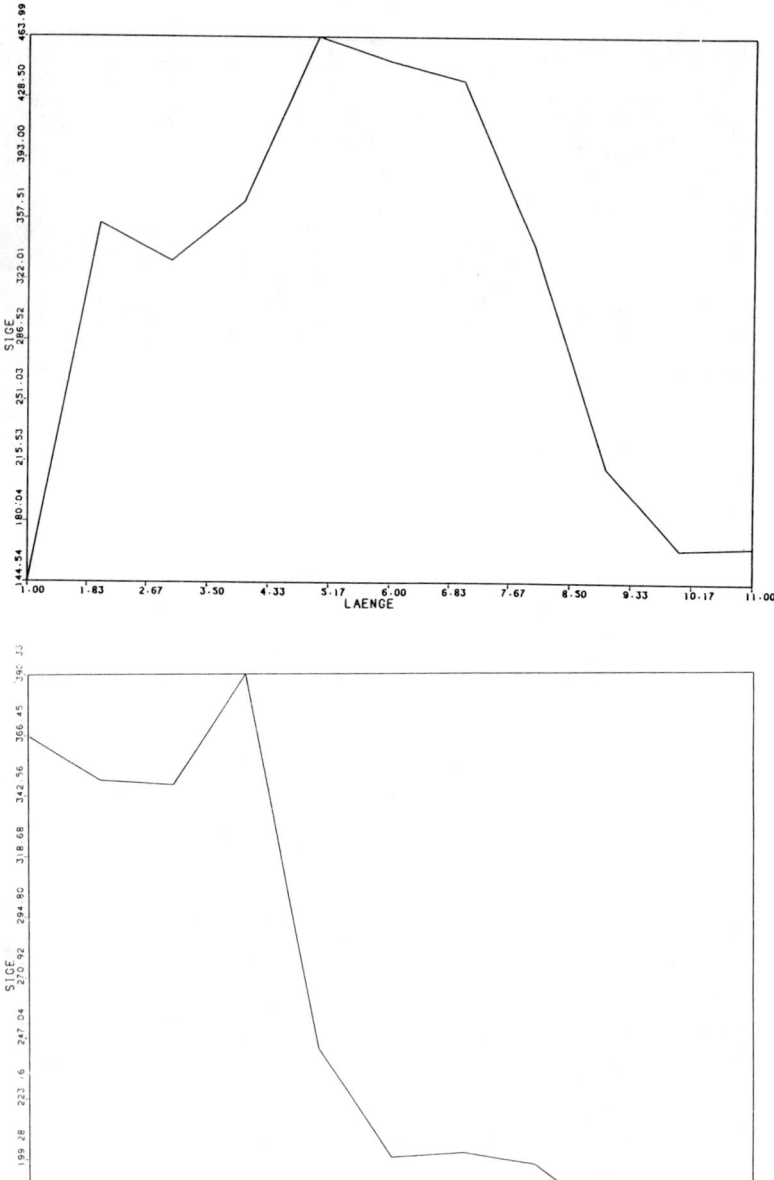

Fig. 11. Von-Mises stress distribution of start and optimal profile of notch A

SURFOPT: Shape Optimal Design for Minimum Stress Concentration 249

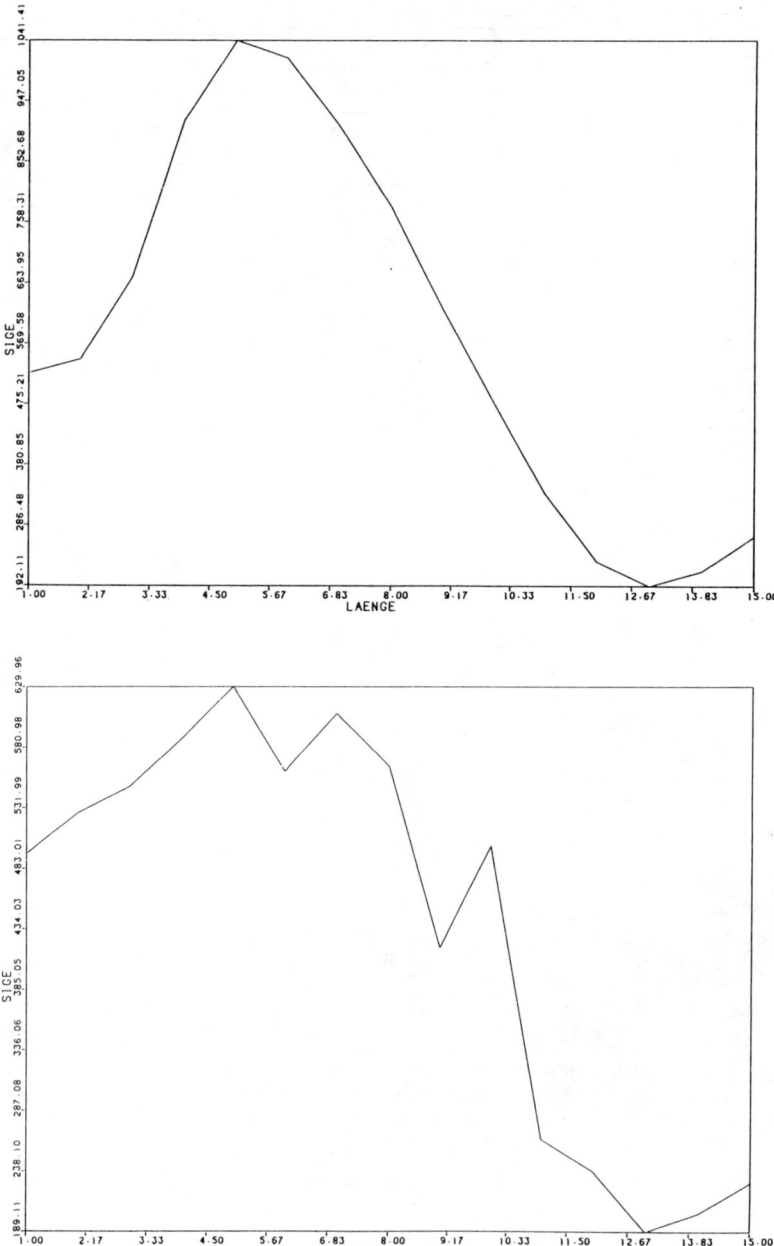

Fig. 12. Von-Mises stress distribution of start and optimal profile of notch B

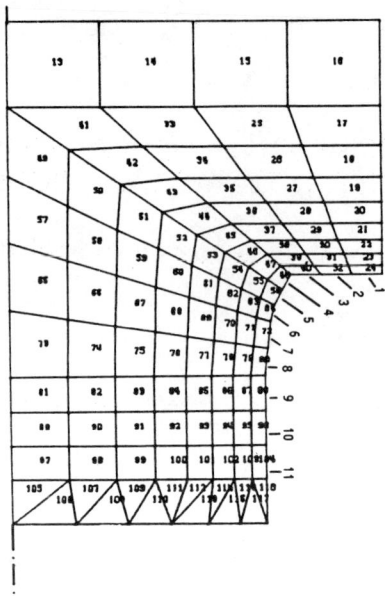

Fig. 13. FE-discretization of the optimal profile of the notch A

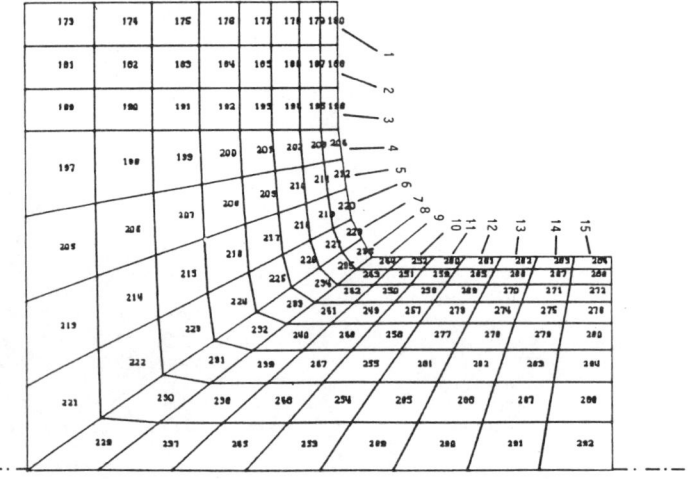

Fig. 14. FE-discretization of the optimal profile of the notch B

REFERENCES

1. Spörl, U. Spannungsoptimale Auslegung elastischer Strukturen. Diss. Karlsruhe University, Jan. 1985.
2. Neuber, H. Kerbspannungslehre. Grundlagen für genaue Festigkeitsberechnung. Springer 1958.

ZERO-4: A COMPUTER PROGRAM FOR FLUID-STRUCTURE INTERACTION PROBLEMS

E. Bon, L. Brusa, A. Cella, R. Ciacci and A. Greco

CISE S.p.A., P.O. Box 12081, I-20134 Milano, Italy

Work performed in the frame of the ELFI research programme supported by ENEL

ABSTRACT

The paper presents a description of the main features of the finite element code ZERO-4, which allows the static and dynamic analysis of 2- and 3-D solids and of axisymmetric structures with non-symmetrical loads, taking into account dynamic fluid-structure interaction effects. The structure is assumed to have an elastic behaviour and an acoustic approximation is made for the fluid. The liquid is considered as compressible and sloshing effects may be taken into account. The static analysis may be performed with thermal loads and distributed or concentrated forces on the structure. The dynamic loading may consist of distributed or concentrated forces on the structure, prescribed pressures on some part of the fluid surface, prescribed nodal displacements and seismic ground acceleration. The seismic response may be computed taking into account multiple support excitations acting both on the structure and on the fluid. The dynamic equilibrium equations are solved by means of the modal superposition method and in the case of fluid-structure interaction problems, the normal modes of the coupled system are used. One of the major problems to be considered when using the modal superposition method, is the choice of an appropriate number of modes to yield accurate results.

The modes taken into account are in general those relevant to frequencies below a cut-off value which depends on the particular excitation considered. In order to approximate the contribution of the neglected high frequency modes, the "missing modes" correction is applied. In the case of prescribed displacements, prescribed fluid pressures or loads on the structure near the constraints, a change of variable has been performed. The dynamic response is considered as the sum of a "pseudo-static solution", which represents the system response to the equivalent loads applied statically, and of a "relative solution" which is computed by the modal superposition method. This formulation greatly improves the efficiency of the modal superposition method. The numerical methods used in the ZERO-4 code are the frontal technique for the solution of linear systems and the simultaneous iteration method for the vibration characteristics computation. This method has been modified to easily treat cases in which zero frequencies exist, as may happen when portions of the fluid are completely surrounded by the structure or sloshing modes must be determined.

In order to demonstrate the potential of the code, examples of applications are presented.

THEORETICAL BACKGROUND

The ZERO-4 code is a finite element program for linear analysis of 2-, 3-D and axisymmetric structures subjected to non-axisymmetric static and dynamic loads. In the dynamic case the fluid-structure interaction effects can be taken into account by assuming that the fluid is compressible and its motion is restricted to small displacements and low velocities, so that fluid pressure is governed by the wave equation. The boundaries of the fluid region not interacting with the structure may be:

- a free surface with zero pressure;
- a surface with fixed pressure;
- a free surface in a gravity field;
- a moving surface with prescribed acceleration.

The finite element dynamic equilibrium equations of the fluid structure coupled system are:

$$\tilde{K}V(t) + \tilde{C}\dot{V}(t) + \tilde{M}\ddot{V}(t) = \tilde{F}(t); \quad V(o) = V_o; \quad \dot{V}(o) = \dot{V}_o \quad (1)$$

where

$$\tilde{K} = \begin{bmatrix} K & -H^T \\ 0 & A \end{bmatrix}; \quad \tilde{C} = \begin{bmatrix} C & 0 \\ 0 & 0 \end{bmatrix}; \quad \tilde{M} = \begin{bmatrix} M & 0 \\ H & B \end{bmatrix}; \quad V = \begin{bmatrix} \delta \\ p \end{bmatrix}; \quad \tilde{F} = \begin{bmatrix} F_1 \\ F_2 \end{bmatrix} \quad (2)$$

K,C,M are stiffness, damping and mass matrices of the structure; A and B are the volumetric and inertial matrices of the fluid; H is the fluid-structure interaction matrix, δ and p are vectors of the nodal displacements and fluid pressures; F_1 and F_2 are vectors of equivalent nodal loads on the structure and on the fluid respectively. If structure only must be considered, one has:

$$\tilde{K} = K; \quad \tilde{C} = C; \quad \tilde{M} = M; \quad V = \delta; \quad \tilde{F} = F_1$$

For axisymmetric problems the circumferential variation of the displacement and pressure fields is expressed by means of complete Fourier series of the form:

$$u(r,z,\theta,t) = \sum_{m=o}^{\infty} [u_m(r,z,t)\cos m\theta + u_m^*(r,z,t)\sin m\theta]; \quad v(r,z,\theta,t) = \sum_{m=o}^{\infty} [v_m(r,z,t)\sin m\theta - v_m^*(r,z,t)\cos m\theta]$$

$$w(r,z,\theta,t) = \sum_{m=o}^{\infty} [w_m(r,z,t)\cos m\theta + w_m^*(r,z,t)\sin m\theta]; \quad p(r,z,\theta,t) = \sum_{m=o}^{\infty} [p_m(r,z,t)\cos m\theta + p_m^*(r,z,t)\sin m\theta] \quad (3)$$

where u, v, w are the axial, circumferential and radial displacements respectively and p is the fluid pressure. If a similar expansion is assumed for the external loads, the equilibrium equations for the amplitudes of the harmonic terms are decoupled and equation (1) is relevant to each harmonic term of the Fourier expansion. The definition of static equilibrium structural equations is straightforward. Static analysis is performed by solving the equilibrium equations using frontal technique. The dynamic equations are solved by means of modal superposition method using the undamped normal modes of the system. Damping effects are taken into account by modal damping ratios. The dynamic response is obtained by time history method, and, for seismic excitation, also response spectrum method is available.

ZERO-4: A Computer Program for Fluid-Structure Interaction Problems 253

The undamped eigenvalue problem associated to motion equations (1) is:

$$\tilde{K}x = \tilde{M} x \Omega^2 \ ; \ x^T \Gamma x = I \tag{4}$$

where:

$\Gamma = K$ for structural problems,

$$\Gamma = \begin{bmatrix} K & 0 \\ 0 & B \end{bmatrix} \text{ for fluid-structure interaction problems.}$$

The first few frequencies and vibration modes are computed by means of the simultaneous iteration method.[1,2] This algorithm has been generalized to solve problems with a singular matrix without destroying its sparseness by performing pivoting operations.[2] When the loading conditions are given by prescribed nodal displacements (or velocities, or accelerations) and/or prescribed nodal fluid pressures, the motion equations (1) assume the form:

$$\tilde{K}_s V_s + \tilde{C}_s \dot{V}_s + \tilde{M}_s \ddot{V}_s = -\tilde{K}_{sc} V_c - \tilde{C}_{sc} \dot{V}_c - \tilde{M}_{sc} \ddot{V}_c = \tilde{F} \tag{5}$$

where V_c is the vector of the prescribed nodal variables; index s refers to the system degrees of freedom and matrices $\tilde{K}_{sc}, \tilde{C}_{sc}, \tilde{M}_{sc}$ take into account connections among unconstrained and constrained variables. Modal analysis can be applied to solve eq. (5), but the results are in general unsatisfactory because many modal contributions might be necessary to evaluate the dynamic response with reasonable accuracy. To overcome this difficulty a change of variable has been performed, in analogy with the procedure followed to describe structural dynamic response produced by prescribed motion of the supports.[3] The total response $v_s(t)$ is considered as the sum of two contributions:

$$v_s(t) = w(t) + v_q(t)$$

where the "pseudo-static response" $v_q(t)$ is given by:

$$v_q = -\tilde{K}^{-1} K_{sc} \tilde{V}_c(t)$$

The "relative solution" w verifies the equation:

$$\tilde{K}W + \tilde{C}\dot{W} + \tilde{M}\ddot{W} = [\tilde{C}\tilde{K}^{-1}\tilde{K}_{sc} - \tilde{C}_{sc}]\dot{V}_c + [\tilde{M}\tilde{K}^{-1}\tilde{K}_{sc} - \tilde{M}_{sc}]\ddot{V}_c$$

This equation, with proper initial conditions, is solved by means of modal superposition method.

In the case of seismic excitation in which all the support nodes are subjected to the same acceleration, the code computes modal masses which can give significant information on the accuracy of modal superposition method. The modal mass relevant to the kth mode is defined by:

$$m_k = f_k^2 \ w_k^2$$

where f_k and ω_k are the kth participation factor and frequency respectively. It can be shown that the following relation holds:

$$\sum_{k=1}^{N} m_k \simeq m_s + m_f \tag{6}$$

where N is the total number of the system degrees of freedom, m_s is the total mass of the structure and m_f is the "adjoint mass" due to the fluid. This last term is given by:

$$m_f = \rho_f \, e^T H^T A^{-1} H e$$

where ρ_f is the fluid density and e is a vector geometrically connecting accelerations at nodes and ground acceleration. A comparison between the right-hand side of eq. (6) and the sum of the modal masses relevant to the vibration modes used to perform modal analysis, may be helpful to decide if an adequate number of modes has been considered.

To improve the efficiency of modal analysis, the "missing modes correction"[4] can be computed which is aimed to approximate the contribution of the neglected modes without the need of their evaluation. This is done by assuming that the modes whose frequency is above a cut-off value α_o produce only a pseudo-static response. Therefore their global contribution may be obtained by computing the pseudo-static response of the system, from which the pseudo-static contributions of the low-frequency modes are subtracted. This technique is in general applied to seismic response computation but it can be used, on principle, for other loading conditions.

PROGRAM DESCRIPTION

The following elements are at present available in the ZERO-4 library.

Structure:

- thin conical shells in which a linear variation, with respect to the local meridional co-ordinate, is assumed for axial and circumferential displacements and a cubic variation is considered for the radial displacement;

- thick isoparametric quadrilateral and triangular linear elements;

- arbitrary elements whose geometry is undefined but elastic kinematic response can be specified by stiffness or mass coefficients. The matrix is assumed to relate two nodal points;

- 2-D isoparametric elements with 3, 4, 6, 8 nodes;

- brick isoparametric elements with 6, 8, 15, 20 nodal points.

Fluid:

- isoparametric quadrilateral and triangular linear elements;

- brick isoparametric elements with 6, 8, 15, 20 nodal points.

Axisymmetric structures may be composed of combinations of thick and thin elements. The modular build-up of the code permits ease extension of the element library.

The static loads are:

- concentrated loads;
- body forces;
- pressures;

- prescribed nodal displacements;
- thermal loads.

The dynamic loads are:

- concentrated or distributed forces on the structure;
- simple or multiple seismic excitation acting on the structure and/or on fluid external surfaces;
- prescribed nodal displacements or velocities or accelerations;
- prescribed nodal fluid pressure.

Rigid and/or elastic constraints may be considered and in the dynamic case concentrated masses may be added to the consistent mass matrix. Pre and postprocessors are available for: input automatic generation; input data checking and plotting, including element shrinking capabilities; output data elaboration and graphic presentation. Many restart options allow the intermediate results of analysis to be saved on mass storage. The user may recall any of the data sequences so obtained to perform additional analysis.

Program ZERO-4 has been coded using FORTRAN IV language.

EXAMPLE OF APPLICATION

The ZERO-4 program has been extensively used for industrial applications ordered by ENEL (Ente Nazionale Energia Elettrica), EDF (Electricité De France) and NERSA (Centrale Nucléaire Européenne a Neutrons Rapides S.A.).

In order to demonstrate the capabilities of the ZERO-4 code, two examples of applications with bearing to fluid structure interaction problems are presented.

Arch Dam with Reservoir

The fluid structure system considered is a concrete arch dam located in Northern Italy (see Figs. 1,2). The response of coupled system to the design earthquake (S_a = 1m/s^2, T < 0.8S) was computed by using the response spectrum method with the first 6 modes of the coupled system.

The finite element idealization of the dam (58 brick parabolic elements, 492 nodes, 1149 d.o.f.) is shown in Fig. 3. The reservoir was idealized by using 114 elements, 676 nodes and 548 d.o.f.

The dam frontwidth was of 126 variables and the reservoir frontwidth was of 62 variables. The maximum values of displacement, velocity, acceleration and stress are:

        displacement $\pm$ 0.002   m
        velocity $\pm$ 0.08   m/s
        acceleration $\pm$ 3.32   m/s^2
        stress $\pm$ 8.35   Kg/cm^2

Reactor Assembly of a Pool-type LMFBR

As an example of seismic analysis of axisymmetric fluid-structure coupled systems the assembly of the fast breeder nuclear reactor Super-Phenix 1 was considered. The computations were executed both for the vertical and horizontal

Fig. 1. Arch dam photo

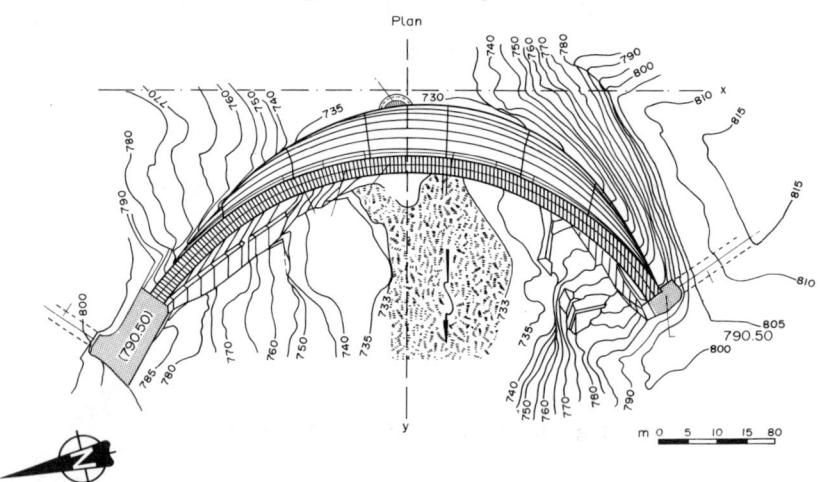

Fig. 2. Arch dam views

earthquake components (Fourier harmonic terms m = 0, m = 1, respectively). The structure was idealized with 304 shell elements while for the three separated fluid regions, 538 quadrilateral and triangular linear elements were used. Table I shows for the two cases considered, the number of degrees of freedom and the frontwidth both for the structure and the three fluid regions. The response was computed by means of the response spectrum method using the first 40 modes and the computing time on IBM 4341 was of ≃ 3 min (m = 0) and ≃ 63 min (m = 1). Figure 10 shows the fundamental modal shape for the axisymmetric case.

ZERO-4: A Computer Program for Fluid-Structure Interaction Problems 257

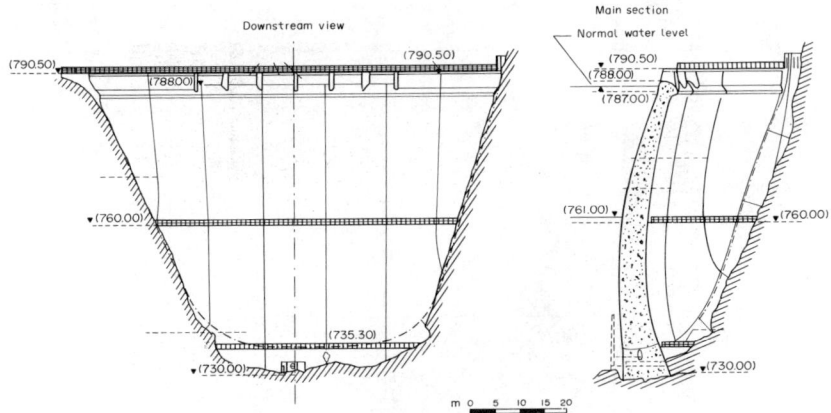

Fig. 2. Arch dam views

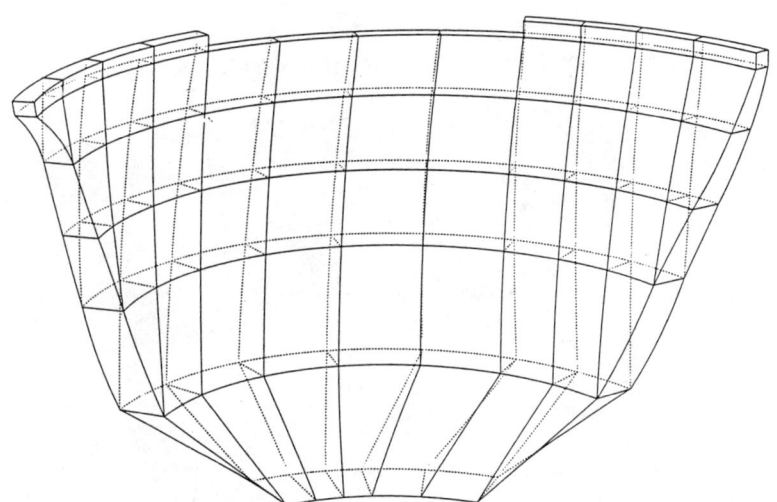

Fig. 3. Arch dam finite element mesh

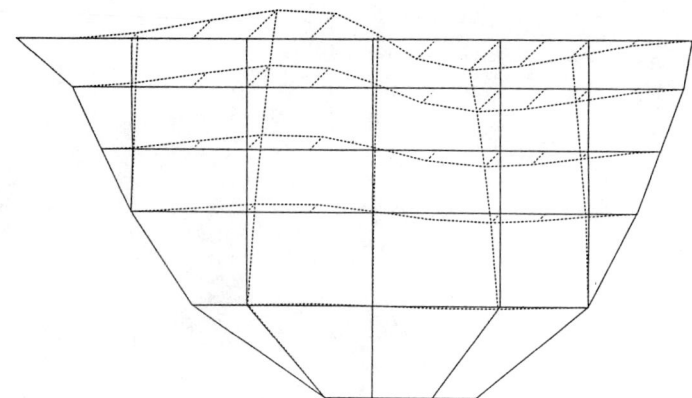

Fig. 4. I° vibration mode; frequency 4.38 Hz

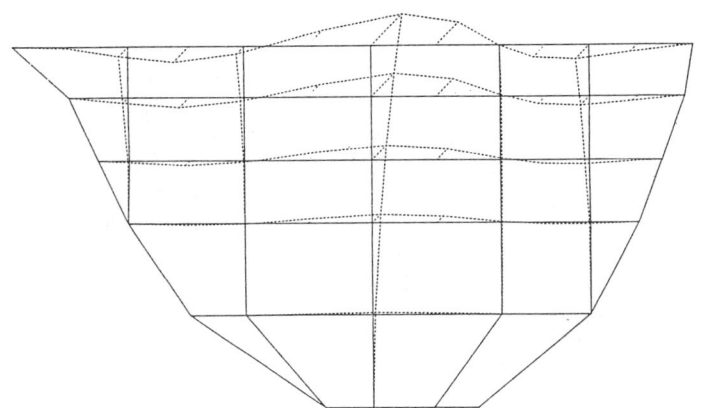

Fig. 5. II° vibration mode; frequency 5.79 Hz

TABLE 1

	n_s	n_{f1}	n_{f2}	n_{f3}	b_s	b_{s1}	b_{s2}	b_{s3}
m = 0	831	132	70	315	66	11	12	23
m = 1	1212	120	70	295	92	10	12	23

m: Fourier harmonic term
n_s: number of structural d.o.f.
s_{f1}: number of fluid d.o.f. relevant to the ith fluid region
b_s: structure bandwidth
b_{fi}: fluid bandwidth

ZERO-4: A Computer Program for Fluid-Structure Interaction Problems 259

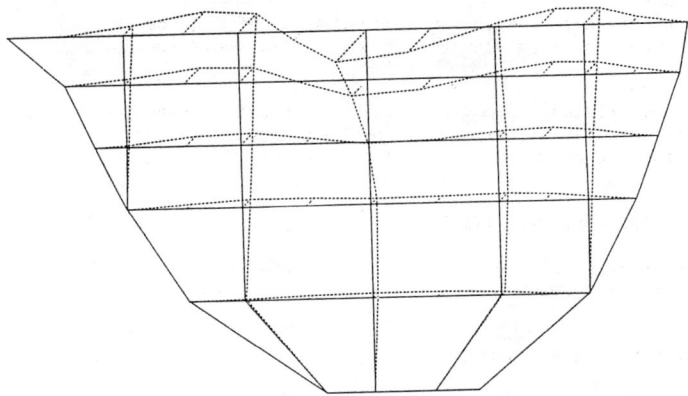

Fig. 6. III° vibration mode; frequency 7.35 Hz

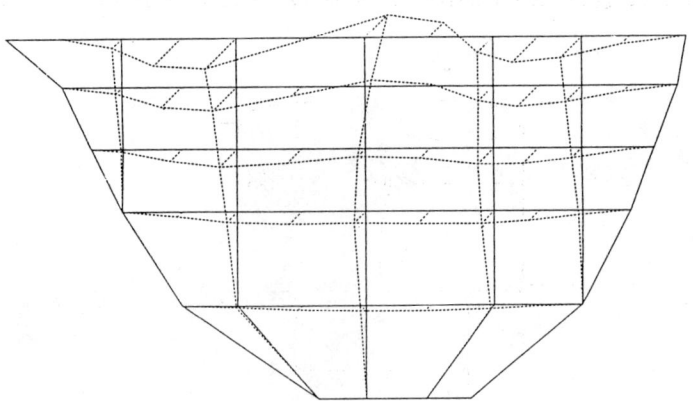

Fig. 7. IV° vibration mode; frequency 8.36 Hz

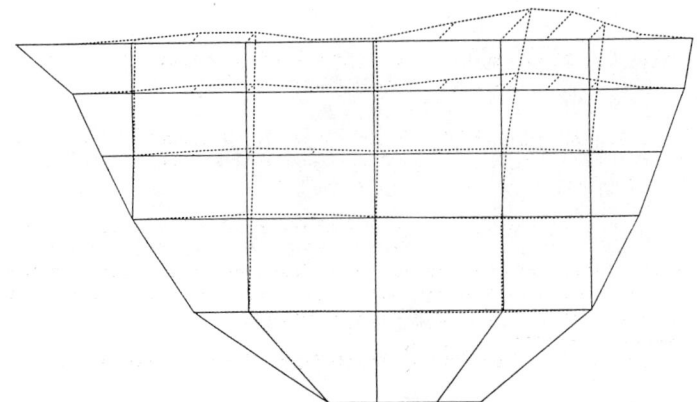

Fig. 8. V° vibration mode; frequency 9.59 Hz

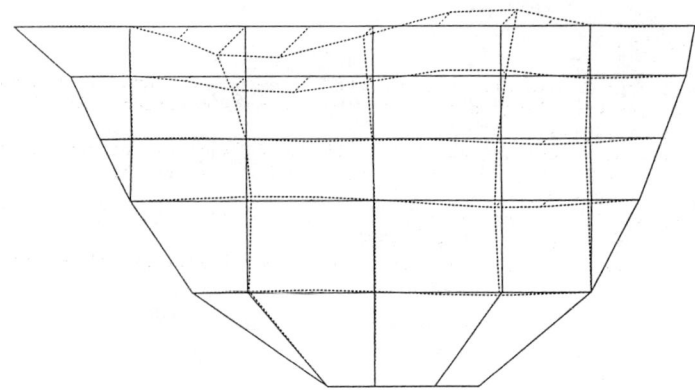

Fig. 9. VI° vibration mode; frequency 9.77 Hz

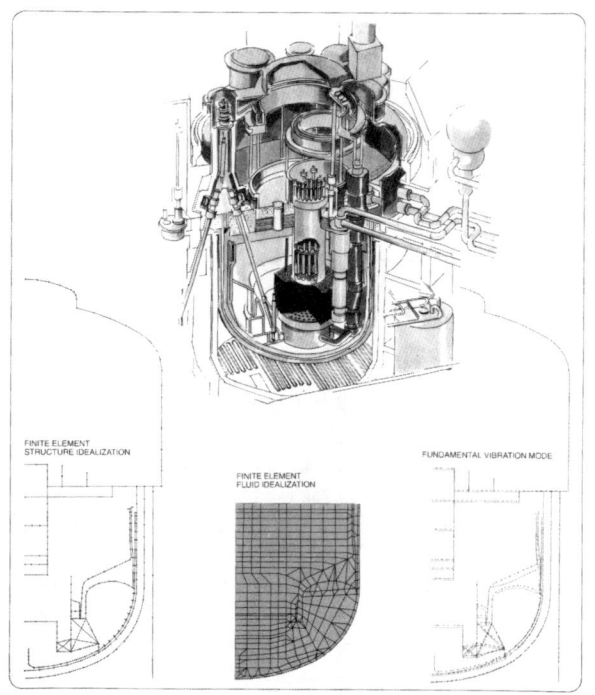

Fig. 10. Finite element idealization and fundamental vibration mode of nuclear reactor Super-phénix

REFERENCES

1. Brusa, L. and R. Ciacci. A computational method for dynamic analysis of structures with large size stiffness and mass matrices. Applications to seismic analysis. *2nd SMIRT*, K3/3.
2. Brusa, L., R. Ciacci and A. Greco. Vibration analysis of coupled fluid-structure systems: a convenient computational approach. *Nucl. Eng. Design. 70*, 1982, 101-106.
3. Gill, S. S. *The stress analysis of Pressure Vessels and Pressure Vessél components*. Pergamon Press, 1970.
4. Powell, G. H. Missing mass correction in modal analysis of piping system. *5th SMIRT*, K10/3.

CASE STUDY INDEX

The following case study index only includes the industrial examples described by the authors in their papers. Most of the programs have been used worldwide to solve a broader range of industrial problems. However, the results of such investigations are not always readily available for publication as they remain the property of the users. The present non-exhaustive study index should therefore not be considered by the reader as an indication of a program's capability, but only as a subject index.

Actuator arm, FIESTA
Aculator carriage, ANSYS
Air systems, CASTOR
Aircraft wheel leg, SAMKE
Arch, ELASTODYNAMICS (2D)
  bridge arch, AFAG, RECAFAG
  concrete, ASE
  dam, FIESTA, MODULEF, ZERO-4
Automobile body structure, ALSA

Bar, SURFOPT
Beam, S AND CM PACKAGE
Birfurcated duct, FIESTA
Bolt, ANSYS, SURFOPT, TITUS
Bracket, FIESTA
Branched structure, BOSOR 4
Bridge arch, AFAG, RCAFAG
Building, FLASH

Casks, FEMFAM
Chip/chip carrier, FEMPAC
Chopper, FEMFAM
Church, FIESTA
Coke oven, INFESA
Compressor casing, CASTOR
Concrete
  arch dam, ASE
  plate, KYOKAI
  slab, ADINA, ASE
  wall, INFESA

Connecting
  flange, CASTOR
  joint, MEF/MOSAIC
  rod, BEASY
Containment vessel, PANDA
Continuous beam, S AND CM
Cooling
  hole, FIESTA
  tower, LASSAQ
  water, AXISYMMETRIC PACKAGE
Crane, FLASH
Crank arm, CASTOR
Crankshaft, BEASY
Cryogenic cooler, BOSOR 4
Cylinders, CASTEM
  ring-stiffened, BOSOR 5
Cylindrical
  panel, PANDA
  shell, BOSOR 5, LASSAQ

Dam, FIESTA
  arch, FIESTA, MODULEF, ZERO-4
  concrete, ASE
  foundation, FIESTA
Domes, AXISYMMETRIC PACKAGE, STDYNL,
  THERMAL PACKAGE

Earthquake, PAID, TITUS
Electric engine, MODULEF
Ellipsoidal tank, BOSOR 4
Excavator, FEMPAC

Fibre reinforced plastics, LASSAQ
Floating frame, FENRIS
Floor panel, ALSA
Fluid structure, ADINA,
    AXISYMMETRIC PACKAGE, MODULEF,
    TITUS
Flywheel, ROBOT
Food processor, PDA/PATRAN
Foundation, OSTIN
Fracture mechanics, CASTEM, TITUS
Frame, AFAG, DEFOR, FENRIS, RCAFAG,
    S AND CM, STDYNL, THERMAL PACKAGE

Gear, CASTOR, UNIC GEAR
    case, FIESTA

Heat
    exchanger, ROBOT
    generator, CASTEM
Hexagonal bundle,, KYOKAI
Housing, AIT, FEMFAM
Human femur bone, FIESTA, MODULEF
Hydraulic engine, STRUGEN

Imperfect cylinder, CASTEM

Jacket, FENRIS

Landing gear, FIESTA

Mast antenna, REST
Mining excavator, NE-XX
Missile impact, CASTEM
Mixing drum, HYBRID
Motorway bridge, MICRO-STRESS, NE-XX

Notched parts, CASTOR
Nozzle, BEWAVE, CASTEM, FIESTA,
    PDA/PATRAN, TITUS
Nuclear reactor, PANDA
    housing, ZERO-4

Offshore, AQUADYN, STDYNL
    flexible arch, FLEXAN
Outlet nozzle, CASTEM

Parabolic dome, STDYNL
Pipe, ADINA, PAID
    impact, CASTEM
Pipework system, THERMAL PACKAGE
Piston, FIESTA, PDA/PATRAN
Plane frame, DEFOR, S AND CM
Plate, BEWAVE, FEMFAM, HYBRID, SAMKE
    with circular hole, NE-XX
    with variable section, ESA
Portal frame, AFAG, RCAFAG
Pressure vessel, CASTOR, MEF/MOSAIC
    head, BOSOR 5
Pylon, MICRO-STRESS

Railway wagon, FEMFAM
Reactor vessel, RAPS
    shroud, BOSOR 4

Rigid-jointed frame, S AND CM
Ring stiffener, AXISYMMETRIC PACKAGE
Ring-stiffened cylinder, BOSOR 5
Rockets, BOSOR 4, BOSOR 5, PDA/PATRAN
Rotor, MODULEF
    disk, MEF/MOSAIC

Satellite structure, SIMP
Shearer arm, PAFEC
Shell structure, CASTEM
Shock absorber, MEF/MOSAIC
Silo construction, FEMPAC
Skew grid, S AND CM
Soil structure, OSTIN
Solar arrays, SIMP
    cell, SIMP
Space frame, DEFOR, THERMAL PACKAGE
Spherical dome, STDYNL
Spray nozzle, TITUS
Stator, MODULEF
Statue of Liberty, CASTOR
Steam generator, BEWAVE, TITUS
Steel structure, ESA
Stiffened torus, CASTEM
Structural steel work, STAR 2
Submarine finder, CASTEM
Support rail, ALSA
Suspended bridge, TITUS
Syphon tank, ROBOT

Tank, ESA
Tapered disc, AXISYMMETRIC PACKAGE
Tennis racket, DAPST
Tension tower, DEFOR
Thin-walled cylinder, AXISYMMETRIC
    PACKAGE
Three dimensional frame, IBA
Torus, CASTEM
Trolley reinforcement, SIMP
Truss, S AND CM
Tube, MSRC-RB
Tubular joint, SESAM-80
Tunnel, ADINA,
    ELASTODYNAMICS (2D), OSTIN
Turbines, ANSYS, CASTOR, FLASH,
    PDA/PATRAN
Turbo alternator, FIESTA
Turbo-jet, TITUS

Valves, CASTOR, FEMFAM, FIESTA,
    PDA/PATRAN

Wall, ESA
Water
    injection platform, SESAM-80
    pipe, ADINA
Watertank, BOSOR 5, CASTOR

X-braced frame, FENRIS
X-ray tube, ANSYS

RAYMOND H. FOGLER LIBRARY
DATE DUE

BOOKS ARE SUBJECT TO
RECALL AFTER TWO WEEKS